Y0-AQM-971

THE GREAT SEESAW

By the same author

THE PEAKS OF LYELL
A CENTENARY HISTORY OF THE UNIVERSITY OF
   MELBOURNE
GOLD AND PAPER
MINES IN THE SPINIFEX
THE RUSH THAT NEVER ENDED
THE TYRANNY OF DISTANCE
ACROSS A RED WORLD
THE RISE OF BROKEN HILL
THE STEEL MASTER
TRIUMPH OF THE NOMADS
THE CAUSES OF WAR
A LAND HALF WON
THE BLAINEY VIEW
OUR SIDE OF THE COUNTRY
ALL FOR AUSTRALIA

The Great Seesaw

A New View of the Western World, 1750–2000

Geoffrey Blainey

M
MACMILLAN
PRESS

© Geoffrey Blainey 1988

All rights reserved. No reproduction, copy or transmission
of this publication may be made without written permission.

No paragraph of this publication may be reproduced, copied
or transmitted save with written permission or in accordance
with the provisions of the Copyright Act 1956 (as amended),
or under the terms of any licence permitting limited copying
issued by the Copyright Licensing Agency, 33–4 Alfred Place,
London WC1E 7DP.

Any person who does any unauthorised act in relation to
this publication may be liable to criminal prosecution and
civil claims for damages.

First published 1988

Published by
THE MACMILLAN PRESS LTD
Houndmills, Basingstoke, Hampshire RG21 2XS
and London
Companies and representatives
throughout the world

Printed in Hong Kong

British Library Cataloguing in Publication Data
Blainey, Geoffrey
The great seesaw: a new view of the western world, 1750–2000
1. History, Modern   2. Civilization,
Occidental
I. Title
909'.0981'207   D299
ISBN 0–333–46055–3

D
299
B57
1988

ROBERT MANNING
STROZIER LIBRARY

JUL 17 1989

Tallahassee, Florida

Contents

The Nature Movement and Its Quiet Influence
Flashback: A Forgotten Gold Crisis
The Slaves Diminish
Guilt and Gloom
A Luddite Revival
No Rabbit in the Economist's Hat
Economics Needs a New Home Ground

PART THREE

1 The Seesaw: A First View

In the western world a powerful seesaw is at work but is rarely noticed. The seesaw carries a wide range of beliefs and attitudes, and when the seesaw moves many of those attitudes move too. The seesaw has been tilting up and down since at least the eighteenth century, and at times it reaches an extreme angle. We recently experienced a tilt of the seesaw, so sudden that cultural and economic life temporarily seemed to lose its sense of direction.

The seesaw is an indicator of the condition of the western world, and is especially vital during a long period of relative peace between western nations. We are so accustomed to seeing our own era as anxious that we do not realise that the four decades since the Second World War have formed perhaps the most remarkable period of relative peace in the history of the European peoples. During a long peace, ideas tend to compete and clash with even more vigour and subtlety than during a major war. The seesaw helps to explain a clash of ideas and attitudes which otherwise remains a puzzle.

The Wilderness Versus the Machine

Love of Nature usually sits at one end of the seesaw and love of Technology sits at the other end. Thus the counter-culture of the late 1960s was not only sympathetic towards Nature but was also a rebellion against a civilisation that enthroned machines. In recent centuries Nature and Technology have usually been opponents but they do not have to fight. Occasionally they co-exist peacefully, but again and again they have occupied the ends of the seesaw, the one rising when the other fell. Those who admire Technology have tended to criticise Nature, and those who admire Nature have tended to criticise Technology.

Other cultural attitudes move in time with the seesaw. For example a swing towards Nature is usually accompanied by changes in attitudes to nakedness, a warm climate, clothing styles and other topics which at first sight seem unrelated.

1

Similarly an increasing respect for Nature tends to be accompanied by an increasing respect for primitive peoples, for they are seen as living close to Nature and embodying her virtues. When Nature falls from favour the primitive peoples also fall from favour. Even racism and racial stereotypes belong to the seesaw.

The arts in all their variety reflect the swing of the seesaw. It was no coincidence that such divergent institutions as jazz, the Russian ballet, Cubism and Tarzan emerged during the tilt towards Nature at the start of this century. Scholars in fields ranging from anthropology to biology are affected by the seesaw, and the audience for certain ideas is enlarged or diminished by changes in the seesaw. The movements of the seesaw influence the birth of new ideas, the way they are expressed, and the enthusiasm or apathy of scholars towards those ideas.

To my surprise I have concluded that fears of famine also fit onto the seesaw. The fears that the world will face a scarcity of food, minerals and fuels are more likely to be voiced during a certain mental climate than at a time of approaching scarcity. We should not be complacent about the future of the world's natural resources, and it is always legitimate to point to the possibility that the world's population will increase faster than the supply of food and fuel; but such anxiety has tended to arise more from a cautious mental climate than from the raw statistics of production. In essence, Technology is the sum total of mankind's current skills as a problem solver; and when our faith in those skills becomes weaker, we view more pessimistically the world's main natural resources and above all, the hope of finding substitutes for those resources.

A swing of the seesaw has strong economic effects. A loss of confidence in Technology – that powerful dynamo of modern capitalism – sends shock waves through the economic system, while an increased respect for Technology adds zest to economic activity. Although the seesaw is linked to economic life, the evidence does not indicate that economic changes are always propelling the swings in intellectual and social attitudes. Economic changes do affect the seesaw but in turn the seesaw affects economic life. The seesaw's causes and effects are complex rather than simple. Thus in the 1880s a new economic mood preceded the coming of a new cultural mood, whereas in the 1960s the cultural mood altered ahead of the economic mood. If in the late 1960s the economic forecasters had paid attention to the new cultural mood and to the swing of the see-saw as a whole, they might have predicted the serious economic downturn of the following decade.

The time will probably come when economists recognise these cultural signs. Admittedly the cultural signs are less exact and less measurable than wages, prices, levels of unemployment and other economic indicators but they are part of the same seesaw and sometimes they offer an early indication of whether the economy is likely to improve or deteriorate. This should not surprise us, for economic life does not exist in isolation. A person's economic and cultural attitudes are not usually segregated in different parts of the brain or spirit, and so a change in cultural tastes and attitudes can overflow into economic decisions. Economists might well agree with this in theory but they are only human and, like footballers, prefer to play all their games on their own home ground. They will gain in their economic understanding by occasionally playing on other, unfamiliar grounds.

The Swing of Optimism and Pessimism

The swing between Technology and Nature is in a sense a swing between optimism and pessimism. Those who believe in Tech-nology, I sometimes call the optimists. Those who believe in Nature, I sometimes call the pessimists. I know this is too simple a contrast, for many who favour a return to Nature are pessimistic towards the short-term future of their civilisation but, believing they hold the ultimate panacea, are optimistic towards the long-term future. To label the supporters of Tech-nology as optimistic and those of Nature as pessimistic is to make them wear coloured ties as emotive as such old ties as 'radical' and 'conservative'. Some intellectual circles frown on such emotive and emphatic labels, but applied with care the labels are useful; and I have not shunned them. An optimist, by my definition, respects our science-based civilisation and believes that it will continue to flourish.

Likewise there is a justifiable tendency to apply simple labels to historical periods as well as to people, and some able historians give a name to each age: thus there is an Age of the Enlighten-ment and an Era of Romanticism. These labels sometimes give the impression that virtually everybody in a particular era thought in the same way, but this is patently not so. In nations where freedom is accorded to ideas there will always be minority attitudes as well as majority viewpoints. Belatedly I learned an essential truth when I realised that in certain decades the dynamic ideas – those that gave the flavour and even the ultimate label to the decade – were held only by a vocal minority. Nonetheless those ideas forced the majority viewpoint to defend itself, and thereby dictated the intellectual and cultural agenda for that decade. Sometimes, in christening and labelling an age, we emphasise what is new rather than what is common.

Even educated people largely cling throughout their life to the ideas which they already held by the time they were twenty, and therefore the novel ideas are likely to capture only a minority of adults when they first appear. The first impact of novel ideas will be on people who are predisposed to them but were previously silent because such ideas seemed out of fashion. Again, certain new ideas, arriving at an unfavourable season, fall on fallow ground and lie asleep until they sprout a generation or more later. Certain books at first make few ripples on the intellectual pond, but long after their author is dead their ripples become splashing waves. Thus young Henry Thoreau, living in a hut in a forest near Boston, completed in 1854 an arresting book that rejoiced in Nature and scorned the electric telegraph and the latest wonders of a materialist era.[1] But his *Walden or Life in the Woods* was barely noticed amidst the applause for material progress. More than a century later it became a bestseller on a colossal scale, just when Nature rode again into favour in the western world.

Relatively small groups of people are alert to the new ideas of each era. Two centuries ago perhaps only 1 per cent of the adults in England and France were quickly influenced by fresh ideas floating in the air. Nowadays, perhaps half of the adults living in literate, democratic, western nations feel, within a decade, the effects of new oscillations in the seesaw of Nature and Technology. Many will largely ignore the new ideas but will feel their impact in some way. It is reasonable to suggest that the strong 'Back to Nature' movement of the late 1960s was, within five years, familiar to nearly all the adults in the United States of America though most did not fully accept its message.

In this book I discuss especially the English-speaking lands, for they have been crucial in most of the decades since 1750, but from time to time I also discuss France, Germany, Austria, Holland and those other western nations which seem to experience the seesaw. Understandably, the swing in ideas is more to be found in democratic societies than in tsarist and communist Russia, Hitler's Germany or in Japan in its militarist era. In dictatorships a rapid change in the intellectual mood mainly occurs when a government dictates it or consents to its occurrence.

It has taken an absurd time to gather the material used in this book, for much time was devoted to looking for evidence that did not exist or to chasing ideas which in the end were fruitless. I sensed that there was merit in probing back beyond 1750, and at times I did. My own conclusion is that a version of the seesaw existed in earlier centuries but was slower and less powerful. Later the seesaw became influential as society became more secular and as new technology became decisive. If one had a longer life and some help in research, one could conceivably ascertain, for every decade, the minor ups and downs of the seesaw and the behaviour of its riders. Instead I have concentrated on those periods when the seesaw was moving rapidly or occupying an extreme angle.

The seesaw stands at one of its most revealing positions in the period extending roughly from 1750 to 1790 when both Nature and western civilisation had powerful admirers; it illuminates the period from the 1840s to the 1870s when faith in western civilisation and specially its technology reigned supreme; it is important in the shorter period after the 1890s when faith in Nature revived powerfully, and in the recent post-war period when a strong swing towards Technology was followed by a strong swing towards Nature.

It is difficult to anticipate change in the western world if we lack a knowledge of the seesaw. The fact that at present we have trouble in understanding the world's economic system is partly because we do not realise that the seesaw is more complex and yet more revealing than the business cycle which economists have long delineated. Likewise we are mesmerised by nuclear fears in certain years rather than others partly because we do not understand the seesaw. The fact that we predict global famine in one period rather than another is partly a reflection of our inability to see how our moods rise and fall. That we had difficulty in responding sensibly to upheavals in the oil market in the 1970s shows our ignorance of the seesaw.

Riders on the Seesaw

The seesaw is more than a guide to people's attitudes to Nature on the one hand and to modern industrial society on the other. Many of our important values and attitudes are clustered at one end of the seesaw. The seesaw often carries, at opposite ends, the following riders and beliefs: .

OPTIMISTS	PESSIMISTS
Optimists believe that:	Pessimists believe that:
Man is intelligent	Man is not as clever as he thinks he is
Our industrial civilisation is admirable	Our industrial civilisation is sick
New technology is beneficial	New technology is dangerous
Reason is the highest virtue	Imagination, instinct and emotion are the highest virtues
City life is noblest	Rural life is noblest
Rural life fosters idiocy	City life corrupts and pollutes
The work ethic deserves three cheers	Leisure deserves three cheers
Paradise is full of change	Paradise is stability and simplicity
Nature must be harnessed	Nature, if left alone, is bountiful
Science will provide	Nature will provide
Specialisation is wise	The all-rounder is preferable
Competition is a virtue	Co-operation is a virtue
Modern man is the ideal	The noble savage is the ideal
The golden age lies in the present and future but not in the past	The golden age lies in the past and maybe in a far-away, utopian future

Much of this book is a history of how the western world saw itself and its future. Only in later chapters, when I have set out the pattern of oscillations, do I attempt to show the rational and irrational factors and the mental and material factors which propel the seesaw. If my description of the seesaw of ideas is accepted, then most scholars will have to scrutinise again the way in which they explain the rise and fall of many of the attitudes and ideas which, to my mind, move with the seesaw. If the seesaw is accepted, then the way we try to predict the future will also be influenced. Of course the more that we understand the seesaw, the more likely we are to modify its effects and even to drive it from existence.

Part One

Part One

2 Happy Isle

Today many thinkers in the west believe that we are an unfortunate generation. Many look ahead with fears and doubts, and some pity their misfortune to be born in this nuclear era. Our future does not seem as secure or beckoning as the future envisaged in the last century, but do we know the world's history sufficiently to be able to tell whether our era is particularly unfortunate? Are we really the first generation to fear the world's future?

Till Moons Shall Wax and Wane No More

In the three centuries stretching from 1400 to 1700, educated Europeans normally viewed the long-term future of the earth as bleak. It was widely believed that the world was nearing its end. Like man, the world was said to have a definite life span and was often likened to a person who had passed through infancy and adulthood and was now in old age. In the opinion of many scholars the world had probably existed for a mere six thousand years and could last no more than another one or two thousand years. It may be argued today that we will be even more fortunate if our world survives for another two thousand years, but at least no decision has yet been made to end our world, whereas generations of Christians thought the end of their world was inevitable, for God himself had decreed that it would end.

The hymn written in 1718 by the poet Isaac Watts, and still sung, carries a message that we no longer understand:

> Jesus shall reign where'er the sun
> Doth his successive journeys run.

When near the end of that verse Watts wrote that Jesus shall reign, 'Till moons shall wax and wane no more', he was not affirming that Jesus would reign forever. He was repeating the common belief that the day would come when the moon, stars and earth would have completed their allotted tasks.

Within the Christian tradition, strong texts pointed to an early end of the world. The Revelation of St. John the Divine

11

foretold the twilight of the human race, while the Book of Daniel's vivid prophecies of the end of empires were open to many sober interpretations. In the 1520s in Vienna a translation was made of the Jewish Talmud of Babylon; it included the Prophecy of Elias which, though not a Christian work, was believed to be close to the teaching of St. Paul. From Elias came the sobering prophecy that the world would exist for 2000 years without the law, for 2000 years within the law, and for 2000 years in the era of Christ, and then would come to an end about the year AD 2000. His prediction fitted the theory that God had taken six days to make the world, and that for each of those days the world would last for 1000 years.[1] In the religious turmoil of the sixteenth century, the words of Elias carried power. The German reformers, Luther and Melanchthon, were even inclined to think that Elias's prediction of a world ending at the close of the twentieth century was too cheerful.[2] The world would end even sooner, they said. Perhaps it would end before 1600 – the close of their own century.

Such predictions of doom or decline were common, and the decline was seen by many as inevitable. Millions of people today are worried that the world will disintegrate as soon as a nuclear war begins, but at least they can take mild consolation from the fact that four centuries ago the peril seemed deeper. People's own good intentions could not save their world. Its fate had already been decided by God. In every corner of Europe on every Sunday, priests or preachers explained the meaning of those passages of the Bible which foretold the end of the world or the second coming of Christ. That Christ would come again to raise the quick and the dead was a wonderful consolation. What did it matter, therefore, if this miserable world were re-placed by a more glorious world? In fact it did matter. The entry into heaven was not easy, and the perils of hell were emphasised every Sunday from the fiords of Norway to the forests of New England.* While it is said that today we have a new profession called futurology, Christianity was essentially futurology – a doctrine of the future.

* Two hours after writing this page I drifted into a secondhand bookshop in Boston, USA and found a pamphlet printed late in the eighteenth century. A sermon delivered at a funeral, it warned that you do not know at what instant your earthly life will be taken away. Moreover, your future life – whether in hell or heaven – will be infinitely longer than your life on earth.

The three centuries from 1400 to 1700 form too long a period to possess a uniform colour. Ideas were changing, knowledge of the world was increasing, and yet much of that period was cautious and even nervous in mood. As the English scholar, Dr E. S. de Beer, concluded: 'In 1600 the western world was backward looking. The world had been deteriorating ever since the Creation and was now hastening to its end.'[3] Many educated people of the year 1600 were more fearful of the world's future than are the worried ones today. The fact that the fears proved to be unfounded should not allow us to forget how urgent and compelling they were to people living in 1600.

Optimism: A Word is Coined

In the eighteenth century came signs of an ideological revolution. In western Europe, in the academies and in the more intellectual corners of a few royal palaces, one idea was becoming more powerful. That idea was a strong faith in man's ability to shape his future. By the use of reason and self-confidence, it was believed, man would now solve problems which traditionally God had solved or left unsolved. Significantly one word which entered the French vocabulary in the 1730s and soon crossed to England was 'optimism'.[4] Whereas the evangelicals still said that 'the end is near', the distinctive and rising voice of the eighteenth century proclaimed that human history was only beginning and that man's powers to shape the future were still largely unused. Whereas the old doctrine saw man as a pawn in the hands of god, the new doctrine saw man as king of a universe which he would increasingly change through scientific knowledge. This optimism was one cause of the era of the steam engine and the textile machine, the first stage of the industrial revolution, but it was also an effect of the increasing command of science. You may say that this argument is circular, each factor spurring on the other, but many important changes come partly through circular causation.

This revolution in thinking called itself 'The Enlightenment'. It was confident that the future simply meant progress. In Denis Diderot's *Encyclopedia* of 1751–72, 'the progress of the human mind since the Renaissance' was simply a fact to be explained, not a fact to be disputed. Man's new self-confidence, creativity

and reason were supplanting the old-time trust in miracles and
the deep respect for tradition. 'The blind admiration for anti-
quity', added the *Encyclopedia*, 'contributed to the preservation
of so many prejudices which were in turn supported even more
by some theologians'. Shame on those theologians! That was a
common message of The Enlightenment and its faith in rational
man. Voltaire, who was the dazzling star of the new creed,
believed that man was steadily and intelligently climbing a
ladder. How high he would climb was impossible to predict,
but climb he would.

It seemed that optimism was marching across the lands like
a conquering army, and by the 1760s the victory of Reason and
therefore of Progress in England seemed certain. France, the
Netherlands and Switzerland were moving towards the new age
of confidence, in Scandinavia that age had already arrived, and
on the northern plains of Europe it would surely arrive under
the patronage of the enlightened monarchs, Frederick the Second
of Prussia and Catherine of Russia. Rome certainly would not
change, but Europe could live without Rome. To the worshippers
of progress, Europe would flourish as never before when it finally
threw off the robes and rituals and ways of thinking of the
Vatican, Westminster Abbey and Notre Dame. One of the
strongest of the new beliefs was that all people had an untapped
potential which would sustain future progress, and the belief
found its way in 1776 into the United States' Declaration of
Independence in the famous words: 'We hold these truths to be
self-evident, that all men are created equal'.

Most pastors and priests lamented the new faith in progress,
and yet they could not escape it. The only dynamic religious
movement born in the eighteenth century was evangelical and
in many ways fundamentalist, but even it was flavoured by the
new optimism. John Wesley, in founding Methodism in England,
preached that men and women, by the grace of God, could
become perfect in this world. There had been Christian perfectionists in earlier generations, the Quakers amongst them, but
no sect of Christian perfectionists had ever been so numerous as
John Wesley's flock. Wesley's doctrine caught the high expectations of The Enlightenment, and in the preface to a book of
hymns in 1741 he argued that Christians could become so perfect
in this life that they would not be led into temptation.[5] Later,
he was more cautious.

The new optimism was spurred by a new view of the past. Mankind had progressed, and the landmarks of that progress were obvious. In the 1750s in France and Scotland at least six different scholars including Turgot and Adam Smith saw the past as a chain of milestones, each one an improvement on the other. They discerned, in the more advanced lands, four stages in the economic march of mankind. First came the hunters and after them came the keepers of herds and flocks such as the pastoralists depicted in the Old Testament, and third came the farmers and tillers of the soil. And finally, visible to these scholars of the 1750s, was the stage of commerce, busy commerce, with a capacity for the almost unlimited creation of wealth. Thus, just before the industrial revolution announced itself in a cloud of steam, there arose a theory into which the industrial revolution could easily be fitted.[6]

Here was a theory with profound implications, for it assumed that the way in which people earned their living had strong effects on the laws, policies, ideas and institutions of their own society. The idea that mankind had advanced by stages was also an explanation of the idea of progress, for each stage was assumed to be an advance on the previous stage. The idea was to flavour especially the thinking of the nineteenth century and the thinking in communist lands in the twentieth century. Marx was to fit his theory of history into stages, beginning with what he saw as the primitive communism of the first hunters and ending with his ultimate Utopia. The pioneers of archaeology were to hurry, like ducks to water, to the concept of successive stages; and they discerned an old stone age followed by a new stone age.

Their idea of progress was a quiet rebellion against the orthodox Christian way of seeing mankind's past and future. It was also a turning away from that other influential way of seeing human history, as taught by the study of the ancient Greek and Latin languages and the great classical civilisations. To see the past as a repeating cycle rather than a slow ascent was often the classical mode of interpreting human history. The cycle of rise and fall could be read in Plato and Thucydides, and in the glory and the ruins of ancient Athens and Rome. Scholars who knew their classics – and to know the classics was a prerequisite of scholarship – were inclined to see rise and fall rather than the exciting ascent as the lesson depicted by history.

The new four-stages theory was thus an intellectual revolution and we are still deeply influenced by its effects.

The four-stages theory insisted that the present was superior to all the pasts. The theory, by implication, applauded the future: why should our stage necessarily be the last of the stages in mankind's progress? But there are always thinking people who are not in love with the present. In the middle of the eighteenth century, especially in France, were thinkers who did not admire their own civilisation. They believed that, in the passing of the centuries, virtues and qualities had been lost, and that the losses exceeded the gains. They showed their contempt for the four-stages theory by undermining its foundation. They argued that the first stage in the history of mankind was superior to the latest. Human society, they said, had gone backwards.

A Savage on the Seesaw

The intellectual seesaw was already at work in the middle and later parts of the eighteenth century though it had not yet assumed its present importance. At one end was The Enlightenment with its faith in reason and the stages of progress and at the other end was a suspicion of European civilisation and the belief that it was now travelling the wrong way. Seated conspicuously on that early seesaw, his eyes partly turned towards the past, was a Frenchman whose ideas were helping to make the seesaw important.

Jean-Jacques Rousseau was born in 1712 and died in 1778 – just after the invention of the steam engine and just before the beginning of that other dynamo of energy, the French Revolution. When he was about thirty most of his views were typical of The Enlightenment but they turned a somersault by the time he was forty; and they were as revolutionary in their own day as were the later theories of Karl Marx and Charles Darwin just over a century later. In many ways Rousseau rebelled against what were the most modern lines of thought. He believed that people who lived in simplicity and close to nature were happier, healthier and more free and virtuous than those who lived in the cities of civilised Europe. Early man, living as a hunter and gatherer, had the special advantage of not being chained by a government's regulations and society's traditions.

Rousseau believed that in physical skills as well as in social life the primitive people were far ahead of the Europeans. He noted that at Cape Town, the Hottentots were superior to the Dutch in fishing, swimming and running.[7] They could even see with naked sight the outline of an approaching ship which the Dutch could only see through a telescope. The American Indians and the native West Indians seemed to show the same superiority in muscles and senses.

The primitive societies existing in remote parts of the world had to be preserved, but how could they remain free from the infection of so-called 'civilisation'? Rousseau had his own forthright answer: 'If I were the head of one of the nations of Nigritia, I declare that I should erect a gallow-tree on the frontier of the country and mercilessly hang the first European who would dare to enter it and the first native who would try to leave.'[8] The intruders persisted. In 1772 the French explorer Marion du Fresne was killed in New Zealand, and when his second in command, Crozet, returned to France, he told Rousseau at first hand about these primitive peoples and their skill in killing enemies.[9] Rousseau, however, was not convinced: 'Is it possible that the good Children of Nature can really be so wicked?'

Other influential people were disillusioned with Europe's scale of values and enthralled with so-called primitive societies, especially the Indians of North America. Long before Rousseau's day, several French Franciscans and Jesuits had insisted that the American Indians combined the beauty of the Greek gods with the primitive Christian virtues.[10] A few French scholars who had not visited North America vowed that in purity and goodness the American Indians were far ahead of France, which was the hub of 'civilised' Europe. Voltaire is said to have been one of the few French intellectuals of the second half of the eighteenth century who did not at one time 'succumb to the fad for primitivism'.[11] Believing in scientific progress, Voltaire saw no golden age in the past and no truth in the popular concept of the noble savage.

Outside France many intellectuals scoffed at this growing idea that people lived the ideal life when they were closest to nature. The scoffers in the 1760s included the Swiss writer, Isselin, and the professor of moral philosophy at Edinburgh, John Ferguson, and they were joined a decade later by William Robertson whose *History of America* became the respected authority on how the American Indians lived before the Europeans arrived. The debate, however, was far from won.[12] A new garden of Eden, a new race of noble savages, was ready to replace the American frontier as a prized example of Utopia.

Paradise at Tahiti

Captain Samuel Wallis, in the English ship *Dolphin*, was the first European to see the steep wooded slopes of Tahiti rising from the blue sea. Spending a month there in June 1767, Wallis saw much to praise but it was a Frenchman, Louis-Antoine Bougainville, who in the following year was to discover that the island was a paradise. He saw the very people whom Rousseau had never met but had clearly described: graceful, hospitable, happy, healthy, uninhibited, free from jealousy and suspicion, enjoying a holiday-maker's climate and leisure, and living amidst plenty. 'Farewell, wise and happy people', said Bougainville. 'Utopia', exclaimed the zoologist and physician, Commerson, who was equally reluctant to leave Tahiti.

They returned to France with a willing young Tahitian man named Aoutourou, and at Versailles in April 1769 he was presented to the King of France. Aoutourou was also inspected and interviewed by French philosophers and scientists before he began, in 1770, the long voyage home. He did not see his tropical paradise again: he died near the coast of Madagascar.[13]

Another Tahiti was glimpsed in the colder waters of the Indian Ocean in 1772 by the Frenchman, Kerguelen. From Mauritius he had ventured south towards the unknown Antarctic continent, and on the way he found the small island which still bears his name. Enthusiastically he concluded that through the fog he was seeing the coast of a new continent, the long-awaited southland. He could not imagine that such a vast land was unpopulated, and he believed that noble savages must be living there: 'We shall find, at least, natural men, living in a primitive state, without mistrust and without regret, and ignorant of the wiles of civilised men.' Like Rousseau he believed that civilisation had much to answer for![14] That was the belief which made intelligent, much-travelled men only too willing to revere a simple way of life which seemed the opposite to their own.

Another exploring expedition had by now called at Tahiti. On the very day that the glamorous Tahitian, Aoutourou, was being exhibited before the King of France, Captain Cook's ship *Endeavour* was anchored at Tahiti, and many of his men were tasting the delights of the islands. The ship's naturalist Sir Joseph Banks gave to Tahiti praise almost as high as the Frenchmen had given in the previous year. Banks called it his 'Arcadia'.

In the history of ocean exploration, many new lands have been praised lavishly for their beauty, harbours and soil, but Tahiti was unusual. It was lavishly praised partly because it seemed to show how people and their way of life could ideally be. Whereas India and Java primarily interested Europeans by offering them exotic products, Tahiti was intriguing as a society. It was a mirror in which sophisticated Europeans could see themselves. The mirror portrayed the ugly, unhappy European. This was far from the last time such a mirror would be raised.

Tahiti had a special magic in the eyes of its visitors – Wallis, Bougainville and Cook – who landed there in the successive years of 1767, '68 and '69. To the sailors who had spent months at sea, Tahiti was memorable for its beautiful women. When Bougainville was about to land, a Tahitian woman came aboard and stood by one of the hatches, just above the place where the sailors were slowly lowering the anchor: 'The young girl negligently allowed her loincloth to fall to the ground, and appeared to all eyes such as Venus showed herself to the Phrygian shepherd,' wrote Bougainville. He reported that men in his ship rushed to gain a closer view of this charming brown naked creature.[15] 'I ask', wrote Bougainville, 'how could one keep at work, in the midst of such a spectacle, four hundred Frenchmen, young sailors who for six months had not seen a woman?'

Aided by volcanic soil and moist climate, the food on Tahiti had an abundance which was scarcely believable to those visitors who knew how frugally the typical family lived in Europe. Sir Joseph Banks marvelled at a meal eaten by a high-ranking Tahitian man. His food set out on large leaves, the man ate two or three fish, three breadfruit 'each bigger than two fists', fourteen or fifteen bananas or plantains, and then a coconut-shell full of a vegetable custard with as much body in it as an English unbaked custard. Was this a special feast? Banks thought not, vowing that larger meals were often eaten.

The typical Tahitians, at least in the eyes of the newcomers, spent only the slightest effort in producing their food. Breadfruit, in several dozen varieties, was their staff of life: the name given to it in English was appropriate. A family desiring a hearty meal went to no more trouble than climbing a tree. Banks said that if a Tahitian planted ten breadfruit trees, her one hour's work would ultimately produce more food than 'we natives of less temperate climates can do', by planting in the cold of winter and reaping in the heat of summer. Nature, proclaimed Banks in 1769, has benevolently supplied them with necessities and then gone a step further by giving them superfluities – fish from the seas.[16]

When historians read these accounts of plenty they tend to overlook one simple fact which was too deficient in news value to be mentioned in the early reports from Tahiti: everyone knew it, so there was no point in saying it. The bulging baskets of food at Tahiti were remarkable because the average family in Europe, by contrast, did not possess a secure supply of food. In France in a good year the typical family probably spent half of its income on buying bread alone: a small rise in the price of grain was therefore a catastrophe. Whenever a European harvest failed, people died of starvation, just as they now die in northern Africa. France, fertile France, is said to have had sixteen general famines between 1701 and 1800.[17]

The technology of agriculture in Europe was still simple. The ploughing animals were light, the ploughs were blunt, the scythes were slow at the harvest time and the grain was not high in its yield. Heavy labour was needed to produce a small amount of grain, and then the landlords took their share from the peasant, and the king took his share from the landlords. In Tahiti, in contrast, Nature seemed to produce its food with only token effort from man. If we could see again the Tahiti of the late 1760s we might not find its abundance so romantic, but on the eve of Europe's agricultural revolution, Tahiti was impressive.

A study of the weather patterns of Tahiti helps to explain why it was so idyllic. Each of the early ships called at a favourable time of the year. Visiting Tahiti between April and the first days of August, they were thus present during these months that were dominated by the south-east trades – the winds which had actually carried them to Tahiti. As the rainfall then was only half that of the summer months, and as tropical storms were few and the humidity low, visitors gloried in the balmy climate. They would have been less enthusiastic if they arrived between December and March, when the sun was hottest and the lightest movement of the body raised a sweat.

The Tranquil Coast

Tahiti was the gem but the Pacific held other jewels. Even the Australian Aboriginals, so unfairly derided in the nineteenth century, were seen with admiration when Captain Cook's *Endeavour* discovered the eastern coast of Australia. The Aboriginals, unlike the Tahitians, did not seem to steal. To Bank's surprise 'they never once attempted to take anything in a clandestine manner'. And when Banks sailed away from Australia he noted, in a burst of philosophising, that those simple people had advanced far, possessing real contentment because their needs were few. In short they followed the alternative life style. In Europe, by contrast, the luxuries soon became necessities; and to want luxuries was, Banks argued, to experience 'real poverty'.[18]

After Captain Cook had taken his ship *Endeavour* through Torres Strait he too wrote his appraisal of those Australians whom he had seen at several points on the long coast. He argued that – compared to the Europeans – they were not skilful providers. Their houses were hovels and were 'not much bigger than an oven': their cooking fires were small and their canoes were mere *cockle shells*. Cook thought their stone tools were 'very bad if I may judge from one of their Adzes I have seen'. But while the Aboriginals might appear to be the most miserable race on earth, they were 'far more happier than we Europeans', Cook wrote. They appeared to be neither warlike nor cruel, they had no poverty, and they lived in what he called 'a Tranquility'.

> The Earth and sea of their own accord furnishe them with all things necessary for life, they covet not Magnificent Houses, Household-stuff etc, they live in a warm and fine Climate and enjoy a very wholsome Air, so that they have very little need of Clothing and this they seem to be fully sencible of, for many to whome we gave Cloth etc to, left it carlessly upon the Sea beach and in the woods as a thing they had no manner of use for.

They had some of the carefree glamour of white Australian and

Californian 'surfies' and beachcombers, these Aboriginals of the eighteenth century.[19]

It is surprising that Captain Cook, the down-to-earth sea captain, imbibed the current intellectual fashion towards tribal societies. Possibly he gained some of his sympathy from his conversations aboard his ship with Joseph Banks; and certainly some of his sympathy must have come from his own observations at the two points of the Australian coast on which he landed. More tellingly, the detective work by Professor Glyndwr Williams of London University has shown that Cook in his reading probably imbibed some of this feeling for primitivism – a feeling which predated Rousseau – from books he had read. When Cook praised the way of life of the Aboriginals, some of his phrases, even perhaps his tone of voice, came from earlier books. Williams recently pointed out that in the *Endeavour* was a copy of George Shelvocke's book of 1726, *A Voyage Around the World*.[20] Shelvocke wrote respectfully of the Indians of Southern California, concluding that 'they seem to enjoy a perfect tranquility'. One can almost hear, in that sentence, Cook's own comment on Aboriginals: 'They live in a Tranquility'. Another of Cook's comments, even to exact expressions, echoes a description of the American Indians in *The Natural and Civil History of the French Dominions in North and South America*, published less than a decade before the *Endeavour* sailed for the south seas and written by Thomas Jeffery, a map-engraver and acquaintance of Cook.

The idea that on the coasts of the warm Pacific, unaided nature produced an enviable abundance of food was to prove a strong motive for the European penetration of the Pacific. In 1788, Captain Bligh was sent from England in the ship *Bounty* to gather young breadfruit trees for transplanting to the West Indies as a new source of food, but his crew mutinied in perhaps the most celebrated of all mutinies. In the same year, a fleet of eleven ships planted the first British colony on Australian soil, initially at Botany Bay and then at the nearby Sydney harbour. The decision to found that colony would probably not have been made but for the misguided belief that the climate and soil in Australia displayed that benevolence common to 'untouched' Nature on the Pacific's shores. The settlement at Sydney paid heavily for that mistake and came close to starvation in the first years.[21] Nature was not that kind, after all.

Geography of the Noble Savage

The savage was probably more likely to be noble if he lived not only in a warm climate but also on a remote island. The warm island satisfied cold Europe's fantasies. A tropical island was also more likely than a tropical land mass to seem Utopian because it was initially healthier, being less subject to malaria and certain contagious diseases that flourished in the linked continents of Europe, Asia and Africa. An isolated island was also likely, with its sea breezes, to offer a tolerable and even idyllic climate for visiting Europeans. The people of a small, isolated tropical island were few and therefore their war canoes were unlikely to pose a military threat to a large European ship, for such a ship was a floating fort. In contrast the European settlers who went even twenty miles towards the interior of a continent or a large island soon lost much of their military advantage, for they no longer possessed their large shipboard cannon and were in now unfamiliar terrain. Above all, a small inhabited island usually carried no man-eating beasts. These were powerful reasons why the relatively primitive way of life of a small island rather than a land mass should have seemed appealing to a European.

In the eyes of many Europeans, the noble savage initially occupied a second haven: the wide spaces of North America and Australia. Those lands, by European standards, were sparsely settled, and their people enjoyed the freedom of the wide open spaces. It was this freedom to move as well as an apparent freedom from the rules, rituals and demands of western society which especially appealed to European observers. The English poet John Dryden summed up the idea[22] in three lines which, after his death in 1700, became celebrated:

> I am as free as nature first made man,
> Ere the base laws of servitude began,
> When wild in woods the noble savage ran.

To praise the noble savage was virtually to regret the European's loss of freedom and to regret those chains which the ownership of property, the daily task of earning a living, and all the orderliness of civilisation imposed on Europeans. The imagined glamour of the simple wandering life stands out in the statement issued by the Chief Justice of the colony of Tasmania in 1831, just when the native way of life was in ruins and all its nobility had been shed. Faced with the need to move all the surviving Tasmanian Aboriginals to an isolated, unfamiliar island land where they could be fed and cared for and guarded, the Chief Justice expressed the familiar European sympathy with the freedom of the savage:

> . . . that, however carefully these people might be supplied with food, they would soon begin to pine away when they found their situation one of hopeless imprisonment, within bounds so narrow as necessarily to deprive them of those habits and customs which are the charms of their savage life; he meant their known love of change of place, their periodical distant migrations, their expeditions in search of game, and that unbounded liberty of which they have hitherto been in the enjoyment.[23]

Rarely has freedom been so persuasively extolled by a judge.

Ironically the noble savage became less noble when he was too successful as a soldier. To be noble usually meant to be peaceful, and for that reason the Maoris of New Zealand, who were highly organised and skilled in warfare, were rarely enthroned as exemplars of a life lived close to nature.[24] As the noble savage was admired because he seemed to be what civilised Europeans were not, and as Europe fought long wars, peacefulness was a desirable attribute of the noble savage.

In the United States, many educated citizens tended to believe that the American Indians, at least before the coming of the Europeans, lived a life of plenty and dignity. 'In the Jeffersonian era it was axiomatic that the noble savage lived in paradise', writes one scholar after studying that era.[25] The American Indians endured hardships and discomforts, certainly, but their relation to their environment was simple and harmonious, and they were healthy and vigorous, moving gracefully and seeming to speak with a natural eloquence. Deformity was rarely seen amongst them, and this was attributed to their healthy environment and not at all to one of the crucial facts – the killing of new-born babies who were deformed. To many travellers the American Indians were potential Mr World's, perfect of figure, full of self-confidence and devoid of that self-doubt which European civilisation was said to foster. To the German philosopher, J. G. Herder, writing his remarkable survey of the world in the

1780s, the native Californians were strong, healthy, cheerful, capable of living to a great age but not frightened to die, and happy to a degree which would make Europeans envious.[26] To the settler Crévecouer, the native men from the coast were just as impressive: 'Their blankets of beaverskin fell off their shoulders, revealing their mighty chests and muscular arms'.[27] It was almost a characteristic of those who admired Nature that they tended also to admire the physique and fitness of natural man, seeing the savage as noble not only in spirit but also in body. The ideas still run in tandem, and it is no coincidence that in recent years the rise of the cult for jogging and health foods has been hand in hand with a cry to preserve the wilderness and to curb pollution.

Black Africa was rarely seen as the home of noble savages. The French, English and Dutch were not very sympathetic to black Africans, generally seeing them as lazy, immoral, and irreligious. Even when, in the eighteenth century, the scale of social virtues tilted in many minds, the Africans did not come into favour. The French had conducted their colony at Senegal, in West Africa, long before Rousseau wrote, and the several thousand Africans – mostly seamen or freed or abandoned slaves – who lived permanently in France were held in low esteem.[28]

Africa yielded no Tahiti and not even a Botany Bay to a generation of Frenchmen who would have been only too happy to find even a half paradise somewhere along the African coasts. I think Africa offered obstacles. Perhaps the strongest was that it was too familiar, and not far enough away. The fact that so many Africans had been easily enslaved by Europeans or by Africans made some Europeans doubt whether these black people, in living so close to Nature, had really sucked that love of freedom of which Nature was said to be the wet-nurse. Those who did like the simple African style of life were more often lukewarm than glowingly enthusiastic. Michel Andanson, the official French botanist in Senegal in the 1750s, expressed this quiet pleasure:

> The ease and indolence of the Negroes, reclined under the shade of their spreading foliage, the simplicity of their dress and manners, the whole revived in my mind the idea of our first parents, and I seemed to contemplate the world in its primeval state.[29]

The Europeans selected their noble savage with care. Some savages were noble; some were simply savage. Selectivity creeps into most of our attempts to create theories of human behaviour and possibly it was legitimate to select one people, ignoring many others, simply to show what human society might attain under ideal conditions. Tahiti was significant because it seemed to suggest what man everywhere was once like, and how Europe might learn the lesson and return to that happy condition.

It was even possible to find Tahiti in an English village and its simple rural life. In the year in which Captain Cook called at Tahiti, the poet Oliver Goldsmith was polishing his poem about an English Tahiti:

> Sweet Auburn! loveliest village of the plain
> Where health and plenty cheered the labouring swain,

A rich merchant – his money made probably from West Indian trade – had taken over the village and its contented way of life and enclosed it all, building mansion, park and lake. Within a few years the healthy villagers – each with a plot of ground – were driven away. Even Nature was defiled by the new owner and new way of farming, and most of the birds fled and the brook was polluted:

> No more thy glassy brook reflects the day,
> But choked with sedges, works its weedy way;

Here, alongside the slightly exaggerated cry of 'Pollution', is the familiar conflict of nature versus commerce and of the village's sense of community destroyed by individualism and capitalism. Goldsmith is sad but his poem *The Deserted Village* is also optimistic because it predicted that the new usurpers, Trade and Industry, would be overthrown by Nature:

> That trade's proud empire hastes to swift decay,
> As oceans sweep the labour'd mole away

The 'labour'd mole' was a massive stone breakwater, and in the eighteenth century many were built at the entrance to British ports in order to protect and deepen the harbour mouth or – as the very first edition of the *Encyclopaedia Britannica* expressed it – 'to defend the harbour from the impetuosity of the waves, or to prevent the passage of ships without leave'.[30] In an era of expanding commerce the harbour breakwater was as symbolic as an international airport is today. For Nature to destroy the breakwater was today's equivalent of a major airport closed permanently by rising seas.

In the last half of the eighteenth century, many English people felt a quickening sympathy for the countryside. By 1800 the mountains, which once had been derided as geological deformities, were seen with a sense of wonder, and the hills above the lake districts now swarmed with nature-lovers each summer. There also arose a new sympathy for animals. Whereas a century earlier, many Puritan leaders had looked paternally on animals, believing that mankind was the trustee of all the dumb creatures created by God, an eloquent minority in England now saw animals not as stupid but as sisters and brothers. In England between 1500 and 1800, this change in attitudes, at first slow and then quick, has been brilliantly explored by the Cambridge historian, Keith Thomas, in his book *Man and the Natural World*. While he suggested that these new sympathies 'have gained in intensity' ever since 1800, my view is rather that they tended to rise and fall with the seesaw, both before and after 1800.

A Brick-Coloured Butterfly

Rousseau was the conductor of the new orchestra of Nature but he was soon assisted by powerful trumpeters. Jacques Bernardin de Saint-Pierre was born at the French port of Le Havre on 19 January 1737. When he was twelve he made what was then an exceptional journey for a boy, travelling with an uncle to see the French colony of Martinique in the West Indies. That was the year in which Rousseau expounded his revolutionary idea on the virtues of Nature, but Rousseau did not have the opportunity to travel to those tropics in which many of his disciples gloried. If he had visited them he might not have idolised them.

When in 1768, Bernardin de Saint-Pierre sailed around the Cape of Good Hope to the French island of Mauritius in the Indian Ocean he became, for a landsman, one of the most travelled of Europeans. After working for two years as an engineer he returned to France, met Rousseau and became a disciple, lapping up Rousseau's ideas and even his literary style. In a version of that style he produced in 1773 two volumes describing his own travels to Mauritius. In 1784 he produced three volumes of universal natural history which stressed the goodness of nature towards man and the virtue attainable by those who obeyed nature's laws.

Today we cannot quite capture the excitement of Europeans who, first setting foot on a tropical land, had not been fore-warned by the sight of a picture showing the garish colours of tropical life. Saint-Pierre described the brown and white pelican of the West Indies with the 'large bag under its beak, which is of excessive length'; and he told how the bird filled its bag with fish in the morning and, its head drooping under the weight of the bill, stood as still as a marble statue. He described how in India the large white and red flamingo laid her eggs in the hillocks of mud raised just above the salt marshes: 'When several of these birds are sitting at the same time on their eggs, in the midst of a swamp, you would take them, at a distance, for the flames of a conflagration, bursting from the bosom of the waters'. Such vivid colours were, in his mind, a part of the plan of Providence. Nature had wisely bestowed on certain birds and animals striking colours which allowed them to stand in splen-dour, had given them ground where they could be either con-spicuous or camouflaged, and had given them an instinct for preservation which enabled them, in danger, to select the camo-flaged ground.[31] Such were what he called these 'wonderful accommodations' of Nature.

Once walking beside the stream which ran through the village of the Gobelins, near Paris, Saint-Pierre saw a butterfly of the colour of a brick, its wings resting against a tuft of green grass. 'On my approaching him' he wrote, 'he flew off.' After flying a short way the butterfly always settled on a patch of earth of the same colour as his wings. To Saint-Pierre, nature was all-wise. Only the wisdom of Nature could provide, close to Europe's deposits of iron, the very species of tree from which was made the charcoal that smelted the iron. Only Nature could think of providing foliage in the shape of fans, umbrellas and parasols – single leaves which in Ceylon could cover twenty people in a rainstorm. Such a message proclaiming the glory of God's creation also appealed to clergymen, and in the 1790s the minister of a Scots congregation in London, Dr Henry Hunter, began to produce an English translation of Saint-Pierre's main writings on Nature.

To spread his gospel, Saint-Pierre in 1788 completed a novel denouncing civilisation and praising Nature. That love story of 1788, *Paul et Virginie*, told of a boy and girl who grew up in the island paradise of Mauritius.[32] With powerful prose Saint-Pierre described the ripe flaming colours of the tropics and the protective umbrella of Nature and the self-centredness of civilisation, for in the end the girl dies in a shipwreck, a victim of human selfishness. His book became a runaway best-seller. In those heady days of the French revolution, hundreds of thousands of readers were willing to believe that the overthrow of the present civilisation might restore a lost and innocent world. Disillusioned with their own civilisation, they exaggerated the virtues and the promise of lands and peoples they had never seen.

They are Weak but We are Strong!

Baudin's expedition, setting out from France in two ships in 1800, tried to test once and for all, whether barefooted people living closer to Nature were physically stronger than those walking the cobblestone streets of Europe. The expedition's zoologist, M. F. Peron, had been given a new device, invented by a Frenchman, that tested the physical strength of individuals long before body building and fitness centres existed in the big cities of the unfit west. Claiming to be the first man to use his 'dynamometer' in lands far from Europe, Peron used it in Tasmania, Australia and Timor, and to make comparisons he also applied it to Englishmen and Frenchmen.[33] Here at last, he thought, was a scientific way of testing whether Rousseau and other celebrated men were sensible to 'attribute to savages all the sources of happiness and every principle of virtue'. Above all, were the savages really stronger and fitter than people in civilised Europe?

When Peron landed on the east coast of Tasmania in 1802, and saw the black Aboriginals, the undisputed children of nature, he was surprised to see that, while their shoulders were broad and their buttocks 'sizable' and their stomachs 'rounded like a balloon', their arms and legs seemed feeble. Reluctantly they agreed to use his machine. They must have wondered what in the world he was up to. Whether in those circumstances they really displayed their full muscular strength is open to deep

doubt, a doubt which Peron himself possibly shared from time
to time: 'With such a barbarous people, our experiments have
been, if not rare, at least difficult and dangerous, and most of
our interviews have terminated in aggression on their part.'
Conducting the same strength experiments in various places,
Peron gravely reported his final scores:

Englishman	71 kilograms
Frenchman	69 kilograms
Timorese	59 kilograms
Australian Aboriginal	52 kilograms
Tasmanian Aboriginal	51 kilograms

Peron concluded his essay with a denunciation of the 'dangerous
opinion' believed so widely in Europe, that savages are the
fittest and strongest of all. He himself, however, should have
been wary of the idea that strength was the only measure of
physical fitness. If this were a reasonable idea then the Olympic
Games, to be logical, should consist of nobody but weight-lifters.
He also should have paused to reconsider the validity of his
experiments when, in eastern Tasmania, three French officers
gave chase to several Aboriginal women and were outpaced by
them.[34]

There were so many different peoples, occupations and cultures in Europe on the one hand and along the Pacific shores
on the other that it was impossible to draw up simple generalisations about who was the strongest and fittest. In retrospect
the important question was not who was the fittest – the naked
savage or the well-clothed Dane? The important fact was that
so many thinkers thought this a vital question to which an
answer could be found. An answer sympathetic to the primitive
peoples was much more likely to be found between 1750 and
1800 than in perhaps any subsequent period until the late 1960s.

In the first third of the nineteenth century the cult of the
Noble Savage was to fade, being replaced in certain artistic and
intellectual circles by a cult that was remarkably similar. Peasants
were still living close to Nature in numerous regions of Europe,
and idyllic Tahiti could just as easily be the Black Forest in
Germany or an Irish bog where the turf-cutters were at work.
Tahiti could just as easily be a Swiss mountain in winter or a
Finnish marsh where people lived a simple life and were close

to Nature. The Noble Savage was no longer to be found on a Pacific island but in the cold Lake Country of England, in the glens of Scotland and wherever a life of simplicity was lived. The poet William Wordsworth saw the new Noble Savage wielding his scythe in an English field, while further north Sir Walter Scott, one of the most influential of all writers, glorified the knight on horseback practising chivalry and valour in the Middle Ages. In fact the Noble Savage was anybody in any place and time who had elemental qualities and displayed them with elegance and flair. He could as easily be a medieval bowman in France as a chieftain in new-found Tahiti. In short he could be one's own flesh and blood.

The Romantics

This way of seeing the noble savage, or a series of parallel ways of seeing him, was really a new way of seeing mankind. Called romanticism, the new vision was already visible here and there in Europe by 1750, was deepened and disseminated by Rousseau in France, and was expressed by German writers so diversely from the middle of the eighteenth century to the death of Goethe in 1832 that German literature gained a distinctive flavour: in Germany the romantic movement was to persist long after it was ebbing almost everywhere else. In the British Isles there is a bud of romanticism in Thomson's *The Seasons* as early as 1730 though it was not until the end of the century that Wordsworth and Coleridge in England and Walter Scott in Scotland expounded a romanticism in full flower. In France the romanticism of Rousseau and his followers, by emphasising the charms and virtues of nature compared to the degenerate civilisation of Versailles and the ancient regime, was one of the fuses which in 1789 began the French Revolution, though the effect of that revolution and Napoleon's rule was to trample upon romanticism and other novel ideas.

By 1800, romanticism was a glowing movement in literature and philosophy in almost every European land, even though it still had no name and even though its exponents had no clear sense that they belonged to a movement. From writers it spread to musicians, and Beethoven and Schubert, Chopin and Berlioz, and a long line of composers were romantics. A similar passion was flowing into painting, thrusting the landscape from a dutiful backdrop into the very foreground. Vividly in England, strongly in Germany and Scandinavia, but little in Spain and Portugal, the landscape was enthroned; and painters especially depicted wild scenes showing the power and even the terror embodied in Nature, though the beauty was to supplant the terror early in the nineteenth century.

The romantic movement was individualistic and differed too much from art-form to art-form and nation to be neatly described. Certainly it tended to extol nature rather than the polish of civilisation. It gloried in rural life and the ruddy cheeks of the peasants rather than the powdered cheeks of aristocrats. It praised feelings, emotions and the imagination rather than the cool intellect which was worshipped by the disciples of progress.[35] The romantics loved Coleridge's albatross soaring over the wide ocean, whereas the followers of progress preferred the mariner's painted ship and ingeniously made it sail faster with the aid of a throbbing steam engine.

The romantics believed in diversity and in the worth of different traditions and cultures, whereas the defenders of reason and progress believed that societies could be sorted according to their worth and that nearly all fell far short of present-day northern Europe. Whereas the believers in reason and progress saw merit in uniformity, the romantics tended to emphasise originality and to glory in national and racial differences, and to exult in peoples who were far away in space and time, whether a peasant in the mountains of their own land or a hunter on the plains in distant latitudes. The believers in reason and progress were ultimately to extol the scientists and natural philosophers and engineers, in short the measurers, whereas the romantics thought that writers and artists had the great insights into mankind and nature; and it was in keeping with this emphasis that Isaiah Berlin wittily defined romanticism as 'the tyranny of art over life'. There· was a sadness, a tension in many romantics, and P. van Tieghem,[36] who a century later wrote five volumes on romanticism, went so far as to argue that state of mind consisted of three basic elements: 'dissatisfaction with the contemporary world, restless anxiety in the face of life, and sadness without cause'. In their dissatisfaction with their own world, they glimpsed a cosy glow in far away places and peoples.

The Pattern of the Seesaw

The romantics and the believers in reason were both a part of secular movements, operating in a civilisation which was Christian. The believers in reason could still, if they wished, believe in Christianity; and their version of Christianity depicted a world created in all its magnificence by a God who then stepped down and ceased to interfere. They saw the world as a well-designed, miraculously tuned and adjusted machine, the wonders of which were slowly unravelled by scientific research. The romantics could also, if they were so inclined, believe in Christianity, so long as the great artist with his genius and his godlike originality was allowed to sit close to God.

These two powerful movements of the late eighteenth century – the faith in European progress and the worship of nature – were a world apart but were also close. They competed with each other but had something in common. Thus the Scottish prophet of commercial and industrial progress, Adam Smith, devised his formula for increasing the *Wealth of Nations* by over-turning the existing practice of over-regulating economic activities, just as Rousseau rebelled against the practice of over-regulating social activities. Both believed that people should cut away their chains and behave naturally and spontaneously, but Smith and Rousseau denounced different chains and pursued very different goals. Adam Smith was the high priest of commercial progress, and his followers invented machines. Rousseau was the high priest of nature, and his followers invented the idyllic South Sea Islanders.

In 1800, Nature dominated its end of the seesaw but Technology did not yet dominate that end of the seesaw symbolised by Progress. Technology was still weak: the steam engine and early textile machines chugging away noisily in a few parts of England had only just begun to change the world. But the day was coming when European civilisation would be characterised by its technology and new ways of doing, making and learning. Then Technology and Nature would be opposing forces, and the tiltings of the seesaw on which they rode would have profound effects on our life.

During the last centuries, our views about western civilisation and about primitive societies have tended to occupy the opposite ends of a seesaw. When the one rises in our esteem the other falls. When we show contempt for facets of European civilisation, we are inclined to esteem hunters living the simple life. When our European civilisation rides high in our own esteem we tend to despise the simple hunters and gatherers of faraway lands. When technology is in favour, nature tends to be out of favour: they sit at opposite ends of a seesaw. When that seesaw moves, especially to an extreme position, many aspects of human thought and behaviour seem to move with that seesaw or to be affected by its movement. Curiously, the angle of this seesaw in the late eighteenth century was an illuminating forerunner to what would happen in the late 1960s and the era of the Vietnam War and the American counter-culture.

3 The Best is Yet to Be

Slowly the seesaw of ideas moved, and by 1850 it had moved far from an admiration of the primitive life. That end of the seesaw which was crowded in 1780 was now almost deserted. Primitive peoples were no longer seen with romantic eyes, and nature was a realm to be tamed and harnessed by inventive Europeans and Yankees who were now proud of their civilisation.

Science as Conqueror

Rarely had a generation felt such pride in its achievements as earnest Europeans felt during most of the years from the 1840s to the 1870s. They were proud that they had built railways, steamships and telegraphs to conquer distance, and that they were imposing order on what they called the barbaric regions of the globe. They were proud that some nations had begun to educate nearly all their children and that the recent medical advances ensured that children would live longer. Above all, many took pride in the approaching unity of mankind – 'that great end towards which all history points', Albert the Good proclaimed. The best was yet to be, as the most respected of English poets, Robert Browning, assured his readers.

Technology and reason were increasingly hailed as conquerors. Science, it was thought, would ensure human progress. Professor J. R. Seeley, in his best-selling book of 1865, *Ecce Homo*, penned this applauded sentence: 'we live under the blessed light of science, a light yet far from its meridian and dispersing every day some noxious superstition, some cowardice of the human spirit.' That hymn to science was sung by an historian, not a scientist. Moral progress and scientific progress now were lovers who were always hand in hand: so much so that Herbert Spencer, the pioneer British sociologist, predicted in 1850 that 'the things we call evil and immorality' would disappear.

Likewise in 1850 the thing we call drudgery – the incessant toil needed to keep together body and soul – seemed to be diminishing as the energy of steam was applied to work and travel. In the fight of science against disease, extreme pain was in retreat following the invention of anaesthetics. Inventors seemed to hold the world in their hands, inspiring a faith that every material and social problem could be mastered. The optimism of the Enlightenment had so revived that it made the eighteenth century seem lukewarm.

In the growing veneration for the future, the past inevitably slipped from favour. The English historian, J. A. Froude, writing in 1870 on progress, observed that in every activity of daily life, 'in its material developments and in its spiritual convictions – we thank God that we are not like our fathers'. Charles Dickens, the novelist, showed the contemporary disdain for the past by displaying a series of dummy books ironically entitled 'The Wisdom of our Ancestors', individual books were called *Ignorance, Superstition* and *The Stake*. It was Dickens who ran the popular magazine, *Household Words*, and in the magazine's annual index issued in 1851, most of the news items ranging from Kaffir tribes to English criminals were gathered together under the heading of 'Political, Social and Sanitary Progress'. Which editor today would gather most of the year's news under the applauding heading of 'Progress'? In France there was even a religion of progress, the Positivist Church of Humanity, founded by the famous social theorist Auguste Comte, and he set out a list of saint's days commemorating those secular saints who over the ages had worked valiantly for progress. In many nations the new religion of progress was Rationalism, for reason was seen as the key to unlimited progress.

Predictions of a wonderful future, at first temperate, became overheated as inventiveness flourished. A new form of fiction, science fiction, won a wide following. In Britain in the period from 1801 to 1859, books which were set in the future had been published at the rate of only three in every decade, but in the remainder of the century they came out at an average of nearly sixty for each decade. The French author, Jules Verne, in love with the new technology, glimpsed a future that gripped hundreds of thousands of readers. His sensational book of 1864 was called *From The Earth To The Moon*, and he soon gained a larger audience with *20,000 Leagues Under the Sea* and his runaway best-seller of 1873, *Around the World in Eighty Days*. Envisaging fast global travel and even space travel, the disciplined imagination of Jules Verne influenced young inventors: Simon Lake who devised an early submarine, Santos Dumont who was a pioneer of aviation, and the Russian mathematician Konstantin Tsiolkovsky who was an exponent of rocket propulsion and the exploring of space. As the mood of the times changed, Jules Verne was to become less enraptured with 'progress' and large-scale industry and the power of big money.[1]

Meanwhile, science was seen as benevolent even in warfare. The new military inventions were widely praised because they would shorten a war. The accurate rifle and the steam gunboat which subdued the 'primitive peoples' were seen as peacemakers, for they helped to introduce a way of life which was seen as far superior, morally and materially. Even that devastating invention of the early 1860s, Richard Jordan Gatling's machine gun, was seen as an example of how new weapons could ensure progress.[2] Gatling said that he was spurred to invent his quick-firing gun by the sight, in the opening months of the American Civil War, of the enormous casualties through wounds and disease: 'It occurred to me that if I could invent a machine – a gun – that would by its rapidity of fire enable one man to do as much battle duty as a hundred, that it would to a great extent, supersede the necessity of large armies, and consequently exposure to battle and disease would be greatly diminished'. Half a century later, in the First World War, the machine gun was to be a killer on a wide scale, thus compelling millions of recruits to be enlisted and hurried to the front to fill the gaps. In the heyday of progress, however, the faith in technology was so high that a vision of the battlefields of 1914–18 was impossible.

In the middle of the century, some intellectual circles had suggested that the world's proudest era of inventiveness was coming to an end, either because there was nothing left to invent or because human ingenuity had reached its limits. Professor Oliver Wendell Holmes of Harvard, writing in 1857 his amusing and wise book, *The Autocrat of the Breakfast Table*, noted the strong belief that 'mechanical invention had exhausted itself' and that the wonderful discoveries of his youth would not be surpassed. But he lived to see such a wave of inventions that when he sat down in 1882 to write a new preface to his still popular book he listed the marvels which had come in the last quarter century. In stately sentences he referred to three of the multitude of recent inventions:

> ... we read, by the light the rocks of Pennsylvania have furnished for us, all that is most important in the morning papers of the civilized world; the lightning, so swift to run our errands,* stands shining over us, white and steady as the moonbeams, burning, but unconsumed; we talk with people in the neighbouring cities as if they were at our elbow.[3]

The Kerosene lamp, electricity and the telephone had arrived.

Darwin and his Nightmare of Elephants

Charles Darwin's theory of biological evolution, published in 1859, was a glistening mirror of the altered attitude towards nature as well as progress. Darwin could not conceive of nature as kindly: he could not conceive of it in terms of today's popular credo that mankind should live in harmony with nature. He saw nature not as a simple harmonious unity but as a deadly struggle in which some species, more suited to their environment, managed to survive while others perished.

In Darwin's view nobody had fully expressed how desperate was the struggle which continued, day and night, within nature. He rightly pointed out that we see the beauty and the triumphant life in nature more often than we see the cruelty and the death. Thus, even the slow-breeding elephant, if all its offspring lived, would multiply at such a frightening rate that within a few centuries 'the surface of the earth would not hold the progeny of one pair'. In 750 years one pair of elephants could, in perfect conditions, give rise to nearly 19 million offspring, but fortunately death checked such an increase.[4] In the first paper Darwin ever gave on natural selection, he offered this stark description of Nature: 'Nature may be compared to a surface on which rest ten thousand sharp wedges touching each other and driven inwards by incessant blows.' Significantly he resolved to describe Nature with a metaphor chosen from a steam-driven, noisy,

---

* The electric telegraph, 'swift to run our errands', had preceded the electric lamp.

workshop of the English midlands rather than from the lawns and hedges of his own secluded country house. Writing his first book, *On the Origin of Species*, he reminded readers that when they hear the sweet song of birds they often forget that the song is accompanied by the wholesale destruction of insects and living seeds, and that even the singing birds themselves, and their eggs and nestlings, become the diet of larger creatures. 'We behold the face of nature bright with gladness', he wrote.[5] We forget, he added, to see the ugliness behind that face.

Darwin did see order and pattern in nature but it was the result of long ruthless struggles rather than a divine plan. As Professor Stephen Gould of Harvard University shrewdly observed, Darwin's famous book is really a version of Adam Smith, translated into nature.[6] Darwin had been reading Adam Smith's *Wealth of Nations*, a book that was more than sixty years old when he gained one of his first insights into the mechanism of evolution. He sensed that just as the aims, and energies of millions of human beings produced some kind of order and economic progress, as if an invisible hand were at work, so a similar struggle – in Nature rather than in the economy – between hundreds of thousands of species, produced an order and pattern which for long had been seen as the invisible hand of God.

On the Origin of Species has a special place in this high noon of the belief in progress but the book itself – when read closely – is not a celebration of human progress, but an analytical examination of nature and how it works. The book is filled with a sense of wonder and also a sense of the cruelty of the remorseless processes of nature. It is possible, however, to pluck from the long book some optimistic quotations. Thus the book ends with a sentence that is almost breathless with adoration: 'from so simple a beginning, endless forms most beautiful and most wonderful have been, and are being evolved.'

Darwin barely mentioned man as one of the species in his book of 1859. He shunned the world *evolution*, for that tended to mean progress in the England of his day. He did not say that progress was inevitable, and was wary of passing such judgments. We are so accustomed to equating evolution with progress that we tend to see Darwin's theory of biological evolution, as it is commonly called, as a theory of progress. Likewise the phrase, 'survival of the fittest', invented by Herbert Spencer and readily accepted by Darwin, breathes the idea of progress. It was a sign of the times that many readers carried away so much optimism from Darwin's guarded sentences.*

Darwin himself applied his theory to man in his book, *Descent of Man*. Published twelve years after his first book, it predicted that in the deadly struggle within Nature, some sub-species of man would probably die out. He designated the Australian Aboriginals and the Negroes as doomed: likewise the gorillas would die out.[7] On the other hand Europeans, already remarkable for their achievements, could 'hope for a still higher density in the distant future'. There was far more optimism in Darwin in the 1870s than in the 1850s. He fanned the intellectual optimism of the time, but one could also suggest that the optimism of the social and natural scientists of the 1860s, borrowing from Darwin and building on him, kindled optimism in him.

For Americans the most reassuring prophet of progress was Herbert Spencer, a pioneer sociologist, who was given the proud title of the 'most powerful intellect of all time'. A prolific author, Spencer had begun life as an engineer, working for nine years on the London and Birmingham Railway in the first cut-throat railway era, before becoming a journalist in London and, ultimately, a freelance philosopher.[8] One of his beliefs, expressed in London as early as 1852, was that sheer competition, especially in an industrial society, was pushing the more intelligent and innovative men to the fore. Only the fittest would survive, and their superior mental and physical qualities would be inherited by future generations. 'The ultimate development of the ideal man is logically certain', he wrote, for he held fast to Lamarck's idea that acquired characteristics could be inherited. Spencer believed that in human society, as in nature, the weak should fall, thus making room for the strong, and that in generations to come the typical human being would be stronger, physically and mentally. The historian Richard Hofstadter has suggested

---

* Some historians see Darwin's book of 1859 as inciting optimism about man, even though man is hardly mentioned by name. For my part I doubt whether scholars reading the new book with meticulous care would have inhaled confidence. The fact that man had survived so far, and prospered at the expense of other species, would not assure him of survival in future environments in which a different set of human characteristics might be required. The long history of struggle depicted in Darwin's theory of natural selection offers some analogy to a football final. The best team does not always win: the winner is merely the best team, on the chosen gound and day.

that the United States in the years after the end of the American Civil War was 'like a vast human caricature of the Darwinian struggle for existence', and on that struggle Spencer conferred hope and respectability.[9] He was in effect the private chaplain to a hundred millionaires. Ironically his message is now called 'Social Darwinism', though he expressed it long before Darwin.

Soon a variety of scholars applied the theory of evolution to the development of man's social institutions. They argued that just as a long succession of pressures moulded man, so the same pressures led to the evolution of human institutions. From the mid-1860s onward the theory was vigorously applied to pre-history and anthropology by Lubbock, McLennan, Tylor, Morgan and others, and was applied by Maine to the development of law, and applied by many to economics and history.

Marx and the Glorious Machines

Of the original thinkers of this optimistic era, Karl Marx and Charles Darwin were the most influential in the long term. Curiously Marx is depicted so often as the historian of misery and the prophet of calamity that his ultimate optimism is easily overlooked. He envisaged that the event which he so often criticised – the industrial revolution – would finally produce a harmonious society. For him the new steam engines and mechanised mills were the key to a socialist society. In the *Communist Manifesto* of 1848 he and his friend Engels marvelled that the new commercial class had 'conjured up such gigantic means of production and exchange' that now, astonishingly, there were more goods than could be sold.[10] They insisted that such a crisis – unimaginable before the industrial revolution – would be overcome only by harnessing these mechanical inventions for the benefit of all.

The Marxian insight into the enormous potential of technology probably owed more to Engels than to Marx. Whereas Marx was the grandson of a rabbi and the son of a lawyer, Friedrich Engels was the son of a textile manufacturer in north Germany, and there he worked for his father before going in the early 1840s to manage the father's textile business in Lancashire – the 'Silicon Valley' of an era when half of Britain's exports were cotton goods made by miraculous machines.[11] While Engels argued that the industrial revolution now made life miserable for the factory workers – his book of 1844 selectively described their misery – he also knew from personal experience, even more than Marx, that machinery had the power ultimately to enrich all mankind.

Karl Marx, unlike so many revolutionaries, did not promise an immediate Utopia. Far more goods and services had to be produced by the new technology before there was abundance for every person, and then the technology had to be improved even more so that hours of work could be reduced. To introduce an instant equality for all people, however, would remove incentives and thereby prevent the leap forward which technology was now making possible. In his pamphlet of 1875, the *Critique of the Gotha Programme*, Marx was emphatic that for the time being the workers' needs would have to wait.[12] Russian communism still reflects some of Marx's priorities – in its emphasis on technology, its worship of the tractor and nuclear power house and Sputnik, as well as its shunning of equal wages.

So enamoured were Darwin and Marx with the powerful pattern embedded in their respective worlds that they virtually eliminated the concept of will-power from the mechanism which they were studying.[13] They saw the future as the inevitable outcome of fixed laws. Thus Marx believed that in the struggle between capitalists and workers, victory for the workers was inevitable. While Marx was adamant that no god guided human destinies, he had really manufactured his own god called Inevitability, and that god gave assurances that he would deliver his chosen people – the proletariat – from misery. His predictions, however, proved to be wrong. He predicted revolution in the most industrialised nations but his prediction was not realised because the increasing power of machinery and the new ways of economic organisation helped to ease the problem of poverty. In the industrial nations a fast flow of goods did reach the workers, and their standard of living did rise, and no revolution broke out. It was in the backward rural nations that the communist revolutions were to succeed – Russia in 1917, China in the late 1940s, and then Cuba and Vietnam and the Africas – and those were the very lands whose standard of living was stagnant because of backward technology. But when he wrote, he cloaked his ideas with that evolutionary optimism which flourished in the middle of the nineteenth century.

The Gothic and the Skyscraper

In the industrialised nations, people in their hundreds of thousands were abandoning the old rural way of life and moving to cities. There the hourly wages were higher than in the farmlands, the entertainments brighter, the work more freely available for their children, and the choice of jobs much wider, moreover city work, unlike rural work, was not at the mercy of the weather. Admittedly, the city sky was black with smoke on windless days, but the industrial towns of the 1860s were safer and healthier than those of the first phase of the industrial revolution. Even the architecture of the industrial cities with their tall Gothic spires proclaimed a new sense of urban confidence.

The initial revival of Gothic architecture had been part of the Romantic movement of the late eighteenth century. The Gothic was to architecture what Walter Scott's novels were to literature or what 'the picturesque' was to painting in this Romantic era. Sometimes, however, an idea which fits the mood of one era manages to maintain its popularity in a new era, and in the 1840s the Romantic movement was fast ebbing but Gothic architecture continued to flourish. Some of the reasons why the Gothic still flourished have been outlined by Kenneth Clark – the decision in the 1830s to build the new parliament at Westminster in Gothic, the patriotic idea that Gothic was an especially English style of architecture, the rise of the Oxford Movement in the Church of England in the 1830s and the belief that its ritualistic forms of worship were more effective in churches of Gothic design.[14] There is another powerful reason why the peak of the Gothic Revival coincided with the high point of faith in progress. The Gothic spire, more than any part of the city skyline except the tall factory chimney, signified a sense of triumph in both the secular and religious spheres.[15]

So the Gothic Revival entered a new phase, becoming as common as a haystack, and appearing in every English town and nearly every village in the middle decades of the nineteenth century. Significantly, in England the Gothic was to ebb in the

1880s and 1890s, just when the whole mood of optimism was challenged.

The birth of the skyscraper and the zenith of the Gothic spire are probably connected: both are symbols of high confidence. While the spire represented ancient skills and materials, the skyscraper was built with new materials – the mass-produced iron, steel and glass. The definite ancestor of the skyscraper in materials though not in height was the Crystal Palace, which was opened in London in 1851 as a temple of industrial progress and the first world fair. A similar skeleton of iron – with a cladding of masonry rather than glass – was first used for office buildings in the port of Liverpool in the early 1860s but it was in New York with its ten-storey skyscraper in the 1870s and Chicago with its soaring office blocks in the 1880s that the skyscraper became dominant.

A historian of architecture has observed that the English and the Americans made the successful experiments in commercial architecture, all the way from London's Regent Street to the skyscrapers of Chicago.[16] He offered tentative reasons, noting especially that in English and American cities the business activity was concentrated in specialised high-priced central districts and divorced from those residential apartments which were part of the office districts of say Paris or Vienna. One may suggest that a vital additional reason for the development of the skyscraper was that England and the USA had the faith that new technology could solve all problems. In England and the United States, the great industrial nations, engineers and builders expressed their special sense of power in huge railway stations, steamships which dwarfed the largest sailing ships, and sky-scrapers.[17] Quickly the infant skyscraper gained an aura 'comparable to that of churches and palaces in earlier periods'.

Modern architecture had arrived, and perhaps its main faith was in the virtues of mechanical progress, of new ways of build-ing and therefore new designs and new forms.[18] Modern architec-ture nursed the belief that human progress would come quickly and almost automatically if people devoted their energies to expanding scientific knowledge. Decades later, after the loud huzzas of this era of progress had grown hoarse, it was realised that modern architecture, for all its merits, expressed much that was hollow and misguided. It expressed what was sick as well as what was noble in the age of the machine.

The Reverend Mr Pessimist

The doubters of progress had been formidable in the first part of the nineteenth century. They believed that the frequency of war and famine made it impossible to expect progress. These fears declined, especially in the 1850s and the 1860s, and their decline was essential if faith in progress was to increase.

The belief that famine was lying just over the horizon had been unusually powerful amongst intellectuals in the early nineteenth century. The belief had been hammered and bolted into a tightly-fitting theory by an English clergyman, the Reverend Thomas Malthus, and his theory acted as a warning that progress could not be expected and was indeed impossible. Malthus argued, with a wealth of evidence culled from every continent, that even if the optimists were correct and the output of food did increase, the abundance would lead to an increase in the birth rate which before long would empty the grain warehouses, thus reducing the mass of the people again to a condition of near-hunger. His theory, stressing the impossibility of progress through new technology, held sway. As Sir Archibald Alison explained in 1840 in his massive work, *The Principles of Population*, the pessimism of Malthus had been implicitly accepted in Europe for the last forty years by 'the wisest philosophers, and the ablest statesmen, in an age boasting of the highest intellectual acquirements'.[19]

Thomas Malthus, the son of a scholarly Surrey landholder, went to Cambridge where he won prizes for declaiming in Greek and Latin. His manner of declaiming was actually his liability throughout his life, and the author Harriet Martineau recorded that he had a defect in his palate and had trouble pronouncing some of the consonants and especially the letter L; but in compensation his voice was so sonorous and he spoke so slowly that he was about the only person whom she, in her deafness, could hear clearly without her ear trumpet. Malthus had a fine mind and argued with skill, and it was an argument with his bookworm father that launched him upon a career as the most famous of prophets of doom.[20] The father was familiar with the latest French ideas that man was perfectible, and the future of the world was glorious but these ideas did not attract his son who was in holy orders and held the orthodox belief that man was sinful and that his future – without God's help – was grim. The son rebuked his optimistic father by arguing that a nation would always possess its quota of misery and ignorance. The golden age, he said, would never be attained because population had a tendency to increase more rapidly than food. His pessimistic theory of the pressures of population had many ancestors – including Adam Smith, Benjamin Franklin, Arthur Young and only twelve years earlier the Reverend Joseph Townsend – but he did not then know of these earlier writers nor of China's own living Malthus, the scholar-official Hung Liang-Chi.

The young Malthus put his argument on paper and his benign father suggested that he publish it. It came out in 1798, a smallish book called an *Essay on the Principle of Population as it Affects the Future Improvement of Society*. Concealed behind that formal title lay a barrel of gunpowder. Malthus was writing on an ideological issue as exciting to his day as was communism in our century. At a time when the French Revolution was proclaiming that a new era of reform was dawning, Malthus was replying that further progress was improbable and that mankind stood in a strait-jacket.* It is no wonder that many optimists reviled his book.

His amassing of fact upon fact, his freedom from spite, his public spiritedness and his repeating of his conclusions with hammer-like emphasis gave him the power of persuading. Moreover he used mathematics in a striking way. He suggested that in each long period the population tended to double – for instance, 2, 4, 8, and 16 – whereas food supply increased by the humbler ratio of 2, 3, 4 and 5. In our age of computers and pocket calculators we are impressed by a neat formula, and the readers of Malthus were equally impressed by what was really his attempt to decorate his theory with quantitative tinsel. Such precision was not essential to his argument, and was eliminated from the second edition of the book, but it caught the public imagination and has continued to dwell there.

Malthus somewhat changed his mind in the five years between the first and the second editions of his book but he was not sufficiently emphatic in informing his new readers of the change.[22] While he still gave warnings he hoped that education, self-

---

* It may be that Malthus, reacting against one extreme view, set out his own view in extreme form. Later he admitted such a probability: 'It is probable that, having found the bow bent too much one way, I was induced to bend it too much the other in order to make it straight'. Thus he pointed out one of the mechanisms that help explain the seesaw of ideas.[21]

restraint and an improving standard of living would lower the birth rate and prevent it from outpacing the produce of the wheat field. He even predicted that 'the virtue and happiness of mankind' would increase as a result of the industrial revolution. However, Malthus's first essay was so thumping in its impact and so suited to the emotional mood of the time that no rubbing out or rewriting could weaken it. A simple message is more likely to be remembered than a complex one, especially on the topic of life and death, and his message was simple.

Malthus became a household name, and in argument and daily conversation the listeners gleaned their views of Malthus from what others said about him. We should not be surprised at this because it happens in our own day. Much of the debate in a democratic society is spontaneous and informal, and occurs suddenly at dinner table or at work when the exact words of the writers who are under discussion are not available. This will always be so, and it is perhaps pleasing that it is so, for it denotes a society where people are free to discuss what they like when they like. The practice, however, carries the disadvantage that a man's name becomes the symbol for an over-emphatic and very portable viewpoint. Malthus became such an evocative surname – like Boycott, Lynch and other surnames which have entered the language – that his more moderate view in later editions of his book was barely noticed.

Admittedly, Malthus was writing in an era of large families and widespread poverty. He was writing when the idea of importing food from afar was usually impracticable and ultimately risky, making a nation vulnerable in time of war. He was writing before emigration was a common practice and before America was seen as a potential haven for Europeans and before the agricultural revolution was really increasing the produce of the average acre. In Malthus's day it was also unlikely that a drastic redistribution of food and wealth could solve the population problem. The politician Edmund Burke was probably shrewd in saying, only three years before Malthus wrote, that the rich and the fat were so few that 'if all their throats were cut, and distribution made of all they consume in a year, it would not give bread and cheese for one night's supper to those who labour'.

A revolutionary idea usually seizes allied notions and turns them on their head. It seems self-evident to us that over-population is a burden for a nation, but the eighteenth century had seen high merits in that very over-population which Malthus deplored. A large population was then believed to be vital to a nation's defence; it was seen as a way of increasing a nation's wealth and a sign that the nation was growing in wealth. Even an excessive population and the poverty accompanying it were seen as a spur to activity and an antidote to idleness. Malthus, in warning against the perils of over-population, was butting his head against a wall of traditional ideas.

In the forty years after Malthus first produced his *Essay*, events in Europe did not actually prove him wrong. Indeed a theory such as his could neither be proved nor disproved in such a short span of time. Several trends, however, made alert citizens see merit in his arguments. With the surge in population the fear of famine was probably higher in the period 1800 to 1840 than in the preceding forty years. Famine in the cities was especially feared because it might spark the upheavals which France experienced in 1789. Nor did the long Revolutionary and Napoleonic Wars, with armies rampaging across Europe, aid the production of food. Just when the supply of food seemed more assured for Europe's rising population, Ireland gave its own warning. The blight ruined the potato crops on which so many poor Irish families depended, and in the late 1840s the famine caused perhaps a million deaths.[23] Even such advanced economies as Germany and Belgium experienced famine in 1846–7.

Most economists supported Malthus's caution, though Marx called him a 'baboon'. Economic theory traditionally saw SCARCITY as a large signpost at every crossroads; and even if people followed the direction of the more cheerful signpost they soon came to a junction where SCARCITY again appeared on another signpost.[24] Economics was called 'the dismal science', and the first half of the nineteenth century was its most dismal period, and Malthus was its most sobering signwriter. We, of all generations, should understand the pessimism in economic theory. For centuries the main problem in economics had been one of supply – how to grow enough and to produce enough – and eventually the revolutions in agriculture, industry, and transport were largely to solve the age-old problem of supply. Then came a period, centred on the depression of the 1930s, when inadequate demand perplexed politicians and economists.

It still perplexes them and us. As an insufficient demand for goods would seem to be a more soluble problem than an insufficient supply, and as we know how tough is the demand problem, we should not be too surprised that Malthus was so persuasive with his supply argument – that the world could never supply enough food for its expanding population.

A Flood of Grain

Malthus reigned, and his gloom hovered over nearly every bread bin and marriage ceremony. His ideas were one of the sturdiest obstacles to the concept of progress, but even that obstacle showed signs of vanishing in the 1850s.[25]

How a mood can change is illustrated in the writings of William Edward Hearn, who in Ireland had resigned his chair of Greek to become the inaugural professor of history, literature and political economy at the new University of Melbourne in 1855. Through his owl-like spectacles he began to see the world and its resources in a new way. He also read in Australia the revolutionary book by Charles Darwin and extracted from it, like many others, an optimistic message. It is said that Hearn was the first to apply Darwin's theory of biological evolution to economics[26] but this is a slightly brittle claim because Darwin was as much a borrower from economic theory as was Hearne from the newer biological theory. Nonetheless, Hearn believed that man would make his way to an era of remarkable peace and plenty, and that unfettered competition within nations and free trade between nations would give to the economic world that formula – of success through struggle – which Darwin had identified in the natural world. Whereas in the heyday of the Noble Savage, European philosophers had thought it wise for mankind to limit its wants, Hearn argued that mankind's increasing wants led to inventions which improved the life of all people. *Evolution* was one of Hearn's favourite words, and he gloried in industrial civilisation and despised the simple Tahitians admired by Rousseau and respected by the earlier English economist, David Ricardo. 'Nothing', wrote Hearn, 'can have less foundation in fact than the doctrines of the virtue of the pre-social man and of the industrial advantages of an early state of society'.[27] Hearn argued with such fluency and apparent logic that many of Europe's leading economists praised him highly. Jevons called him perhaps the soundest and most original of modern economists,[28] while European apostles of progress, on receiving Hearn's message, purred like cats on a warm cushion.

Professor Hearn set out his views in a plum-coloured book called *Plutology* or the science of wealth, which was published in Melbourne in 1863 and London in 1864. He announced that the population crisis, if ever it came, would lie so far in the future that its consequences 'we may well leave to the overruling care of the Supreme Wisdom'. Not only could mankind solve the problem of overpopulation but also, he believed, such ills as poverty, crime, social disorder, economic depression, ignorance and war. So he jubilantly summed up what many saw as the trends of a glorious era.

In 1800 it was believed that the world's fertile soils had virtually all been ploughed and that only inferior grasslands – the home of sheep, cattle, geese and goats – could now be cultivated to add to Europe's food. Like the pessimists of the Club of Rome nearly two centuries later, the followers of Malthus believed that the world had nowhere to turn for new grain. The fertile land was already in use: the limits of growth had been reached. That argument, one generation after Malthus died, was turned on its head. In the slow tilting of the seesaw of optimism and pessimism the same argument sometimes moves swiftly to the opposite end.

There was now a new view of what could be grown in the lands overseas with their wide spaces and ever-improving technology. In the 1850s a Philadelphia bookseller and publisher named Henry Carey optimistically argued – with more dogmatism than the facts allowed – that the richest soils in many other lands were brought into cultivation long after the poor hillside soils, and that in North America the richest lands were still awaiting their first plough. Hearn thought that this observation was true of his corner of Australia. He thought of the forest covering the rich soil of the Dandenong Ranges, Gippsland, and Mount Warrenheip, all of which lay within a hundred miles of his university but were still uncultivated despite their 'exuberant fertility'. He even described enthusiastically the recent discovery of fertile lands in central Australia, forgetting that he must have seen, less than two years previously, the long funeral procession of the two explorers who had died of malnutrition in those so-called 'fertile lands'.[29] The tendency to float from fact towards fantasy is common at the extreme angles of the seesaw.

It was now two thirds of a century since Malthus had written the first edition of his Essay. Technology had become more dynamic, a whole world had been opened to the plough, and a long era of relative peace had fostered the international trade in grain in place of the old inefficient strategem whereby each nation tried to grow all its own food. Malthus had written during a long period of widespread war, when no nation could rely on importing food because a food-importing nation could be block-aded and forced eventually to surrender, but after Malthus's death, much of Europe's increasing supply of food was imported safely from distant lands. The decline of Malthus's influence also came from something less tangible, an economic optimism that spread like a sunrise and made even gloomy facts seem rosy.

Optimism seems to breed optimism. At the same time as Malthus ceased to be feared, there arose the hope that not only could the population grow without famine but also their quality could be improved. The birth of eugenics – the idea of improv-ing mankind by genetic policies – followed closely upon the Darwinian revolution. Francis Galton, a Cambridge graduate who had explored in south-west Africa, read Charles Darwin's famous book and was instantly converted. Galton sensed that the process of selection which his cousin Charles Darwin described in the natural world – the process by which the fit species survived – could be positively cultivated in human beings. If faster racehorses could be bred, so could more intelligent human beings.[30] In breeding – meaning deliberate selection – or in natural selection, 'a great power was at hand wherewith man could transform his nature and destiny'. By encouraging certain sections of society to increase their birthrate and by discouraging others, children of more intelligence and character could be pro-duced, leading to a nation of higher inventiveness and integrity. In his book of 1869 called *Hereditary Genius* he argued that the mere lifting of the average intelligence and capacity of a race by one small notch would lead to the nurturing of ten times as many eminent people as at present.[31] Each of these new-born children of talent would be valuable in a complex world, for 'we are in crying want for a greater fund of ability in all stations of life', Galton wrote. Eugenics now leaves a nasty taste in many mouths because Nazi Germany practised it, but eugenics initially carried an optimistic message for most Europeans, and they were flattered by Galton's argument that they had more innate talent than other races. It is a sobering lesson of modern history that some of the most optimistic periods, in their very confidence, sow the seeds of some of the most depressing episodes.

The Engines of Peace

Few trends did more to give the western world a sense of visible progress than the decline of international war. Peace was not only an achievement in itself but a vital cause of other achievements, including surer supplies of food. Above all, the decline of international war was significant because it justified the claim that moral progress was not lagging behind mechanical progress.

In the eighteenth century, war in Europe had been more normal than peace. In fact the frequency of war in Europe was one reason why the Noble Savage rose to favour: from afar he was seen as less warlike. Near the end of the century the French Revolutionary War began and with a short break this devastating chain of wars covered almost a quarter of a century. The final defeat of Napoleon in 1815 ushered in a period of relative peace between European nations. It was such a long-lasting peace, interrupted only by one of the recurring wars fought between Russia and Turkey, that people began to marvel that they had the good fortune to live in such a blessed third of a century. The peace was increasingly attributed to new technology – to the steamship, railways and telegraph which quickened contact between nations – and the new ideology of Free Trade which insisted that mutually-beneficial trade between nations was a promoter of peace.[32] More and more thinkers, especially in England, believed that wars had stemmed largely from the old system of mercantilism in which each nation treated international trade as a form of warfare, to be fought with heavy duties and penalities on imported goods and the foreign-owned ships which carried them, and that henceforth free trade would benefit all nations and remove a crucial cause of war.

Free trade was hailed as the new messenger of peace. John Stuart Mill, philosopher and economist and probably one of the most learned men in the world, was emphatic in expressing this view in 1848: 'it may be said without exaggeration, that the great extent and rapid increase in international trade, in being the principal guarantee of the peace of the world, is the great permanent security for the uninterrupted progress of the ideas, the institutions, and the character of the human race.'[33] Henry Thomas Buckle, one of the boldest historians of the era, went further and argued in 1857 that every new railway and every new steamer that joined nations together was an engine of peace. Black smoke gushing from a steamship or locomotive had become, in an era that was in love with Technology, even more a symbol of peace than the dove.

Mill and Buckle represented the era's most influential secular ideology, and it was not socialism, protectionism or rationalism but Free Trade. That ideology, like Marxism, was optimistic that human nature would be changed, and that war would be abolished. It believed it owned the formula for economic development and for the well-being of the working people, and its formula of open competition was accepted almost everywhere until the revival of protective tariffs in Germany, France, Austria, Russia, Spain and other nations in the 1870s showed that a more parochial formula was coming into favour. Free Trade, above all, saw itself as a peace movement. The big businessman is now seen by the Left as the opponent of peace and international friendship but in the 1850s the ideology of Free Trade claimed that unimpeded commerce was a 'civilising wand' and a bearer of peace. As the *North American Review* exclaimed of international commerce: 'what generous feelings, and multiplied means of human happiness, has it not every where spread!'[34] That dewy-eyed manifesto is now almost incomprehensible, for we have forgotten how widespread was the belief that expanding international commerce would bring peace to a war-torn civilisation.*

Curiously, the heyday of optimism was also a period of international war. The long peace had ended in 1848, when several short wars were fought. In 1853, Russia and Turkey went to war, and France, England and Sardinia sent troops to the Crimea to

---

* Darwin and Wallace, in their theories, emphasised the 'struggle for existence', at the very time when the human race seemed to be becoming more peaceful. I wonder whether they would have seen the theoretical struggle for existence in such a benign way if a struggle had actually involved their own country in a disastrous war. On the other hand they could afford to be olympian about the deadly struggles of animals, insects and plants.

join in the fighting. In 1859 Austria and France briefly fought: the new colour of magenta came from the name of the main battle in that war. In 1861 the Civil War began in the disunited United States and more soldiers were to die in that war than in any previous war recorded in history. Between 1864 and 1871 rising Prussia fought successive wars against Denmark, against Austria and minor German states, and against France. The momentous battle in those three wars fought by Prussia was at Sadowa on 3 July 1866, and that one-day battle absorbed over 400,000 soldiers, more than in any previous battle in recorded history.

This burst of international wars in the advanced western world rather ruffled the hope that war was slowly being eliminated. And yet in the optimistic mood of the era, excuses and reassuring explanations were found for the wars. The Crimean War of 1853–56 was explained away by the historian Buckle as occasioned not 'by a quarrel between two civilised nations, but by the encroachments of the uncivilised Russians on the still more uncivilised Turks',[35] and the war itself had been widened by the decisions of the forces of good in Paris and London to send soldiers to protect the civilised world. In the United States for a few years the American Civil War and its long death roll partly weakened confidence in mankind's future and yet in one sense it strengthened Europe's confidence because it was seen as a moral war which won a permanent victory against the evil of slavery. Moreover in the opinion of the celebrated Irish economist, Professor J. E. Cairnes,[36] that war showed how public opinion could restrain the behaviour of nations: a sentiment which was also expressed in Anthony Trollope's political novel, *Phineaus Redux*. The ideas which arise from a war are much influenced by which side is the victor. France, the loser in the war against Prussia in 1870–71, had less reason to be optimistic about the changes in the world. Generally, confidence towards the future is likely to be the property more of the winners than losers of wars.

Optimism could also be plucked from the fact that the wars between 1848 and 1871 were short wars: the exception was the American Civil War, and it surely could be called unusual because it was a crusading war. Perhaps new technology – the telegraphs which summoned troops, the railways which rushed them towards the battlefront, and the potent and accurate artillery and rifles – was inaugurating the era of the short war. Most military observers adopted that opinion. In future, they agreed, the wars would be decided in the first days or weeks – at least in those parts of the world where communications were swift. The latest technology was optimistically seen as an epoch-making creator of peace. Unfortunately, as wars were now expected to be short, military training became compulsory in nearly all European nations so that the maximum army could be ready as soon as a war began: if they arrived too late, the war might be over.[37] The emphasis on a short war was eventually to become an emphasis on early preparations for war, and by 1900 Europe began to resemble a military camp, and so the next war between major European nations was likely to be massive even if by chance it proved to be short. But in 1870 the massed armies of conscripts lay in the unforeseen future.

The years from 1848 to 1871 were marked amongst European peoples by frequent and severe wars. And yet towards the future of warfare there was a surprising degree of optimism while the wars raged. Clearly, peace does not necessarily increase the optimism towards the future nor war diminish the optimism. Events themselves influence the mood of the time, but the minds of thoughtful people contain a sieve or screen which filters the impressions coming from the real world. Thus by the 1860s the news from many battlefields was pessimistic; here were mechanised battles that dwarfed nearly all the battles of the Napoleonic Wars; and yet the optimism in certain intellectual quarters persisted despite the denial of the earlier expectations that war was on the way out.

The high optimism of that period – perhaps without parallel in modern history – casts light on the pessimism that is widespread in our period. The optimism of the mid-nineteenth century had increased more rapidly than did the evidence backing an optimistic outlook; and likewise the pessimism in the late 1960s and 1970s probably increased more rapidly than did the evidence which justified a pessimistic outlook. There is a brittle quality in these extreme moods which the western world occasionally experiences; and it may be that the extreme pessimism widely felt in our time is seen in calmer perspective if we inspect more closely the extreme optimism that reigned during the middle of the nineteenth century.

4 A Pocket Watch for Progress

The faith in progress was accompanied by a new pocket watch. It conceived of time in a different way, seeing it as a smooth line of progress from barbarism to civilisation. Moreover, time was no longer marked in centuries but in millenia. Just as the exciting future now extended countless centuries ahead, so the pitiable past lay far back in time.

The Decline of the Nòble Savage

As pride increased in European civilisation, the simpler cultures were dismissed. I recently found an obscure article written on the East Indies in 1865 by Alfred R. Wallace, who was co-discoverer with Charles Darwin of the theory of biological evolution; and in Wallace's eyes the villages in the Celebes were abject until the Dutch arrived with their cleanliness, hard work, education, law and order, and Christianity. 'Thirty years ago', wrote Wallace, 'the country was a wilderness, the people naked savages garnishing their rude houses with human heads'. The people, he said, had been constantly at war, primitive in their farming, and living in poverty on top of luxuriant soil.[1] Like all savages, he added, even their music was melancholy and monotonous, but now he was delighted to 'hear old familiar psalm tunes in these remote mountains sung with Malay words'.

Sympathy towards the Aboriginals of Australia also fell. Writers and painters began to depict them with contempt. The sixth edition of the *Encyclopaedia Britannica*, published between 1815 and 1824, announced that there were no ferocious animals in Australia and New Zealand, with one striking exception:

> Man only in Australasia is an animal of prey; and more ferocious than the lynx, the leopard, or the hyena, he devours his own species.[2]

Thus the Aboriginal was dismissed as an aggressive cannibal.

56

The Prussian explorer, Ludwig Leichhardt, the first European to cross some of the grasslands of eastern Australia, was more tolerant. He reported that Aboriginals were hospitable unless angered or contaminated by the Europeans, and were ingenious and skilled. Physically they were also fine and tall with muscles that often rippled on the back as they walked with head erect. Leichhardt had spent time in Paris and had often visited the public baths in the Seine, and he noted in a private letter of 1843 that he was 'far more pleased in seeing the naked body of the black-fellow than that of the white man.' Leichhardt did not despise 'the swarm of wayward, aimless' blacks for he believed that 'the possibilities of virtue' were open to all races, but he believed that western civilisation was definitely superior.[3]

When in April 1861 the explorer John Stuart placed the British flag in the very centre of Australia, he felt a pride in civilisation which Cook had not felt when he first landed on Australia's eastern coast nearly a century earlier. Whereas Cook had doubted whether his civilisation was really superior to that of the Aboriginals, Stuart raised the flag on a rocky hill in central Australia without any inner doubts. He noted in his diary that the flag would be 'a sign to the natives that the dawn of liberty, civilization, and Christianity is about to break upon them'.[4] How curious that liberty – which had once been seen as the indisputable advantage of the savage life – was now a novelty largely confined to European lands. A whole school of thought had been turned upside down. In writings on Australia during this period it is difficult to find a trace of the old idea that the Aboriginals traditionally lived in liberty.

The new mood was visible in a geography book written in the 1880s for children in Australian schools. The work of a scholar who later wrote a pioneering book on psychology, it sets down – admittedly with the oversimplification needed in a primer for schools – what had become the accepted opinion:

Australia, the continent in which we live, was the last to be inhabited by civilized men. It has been the home for centuries of roving tribes of dark-coloured men too little civilized to clothe themselves, or build houses, or follow trades. By day they wandered in the forest in search of roots or opossums, or they caught the fish of the rivers or the lakes; by night they stretched themselves on the ground behind their rude shelter of boughs and leaves, with smouldering fires near their feet to keep them warm. Fierce and bloodthirsty war was their greatest glory and their chief employment.[5]

It was increasingly believed that modern man, unlike the ancient savage, was peaceful and would remain so. John Ferguson McLennan, the combative Scottish sociologist and lawyer who died in 1881, put the argument emphatically; 'Lay out the map of the world, and wherever you find populations unrestrained by the strong hand of government, there you will find perpetual feud, tribe against tribe, and family against family.'[6] Likewise the world's authority on ancient law, Sir Henry Maine, saw tribal war as a frequent occurrence. The new emphasis on the warlike activities of simple societies was as much a reflection of Europe's heightened pride in itself as of new evidence of barbarism in distant lands.

The voices sympathetic to the past were now more likely to be those of artists and romantics rather than scholars. One sympathetic voice was the American novelist, Herman Melville. He had sailed in the early 1840s in a whaling ship from New Bedford on the Atlantic to the Marquesas in the Pacific; and his reading of early Pacific travellers and his imagination and experience all came together in his novel of 1846, *Typoo*. Melville had empathy with the Pacific Islanders, and suggested that they behaved like savages only because they were treated miserably by Europeans. In the daily life of the Marquesan islanders he detected a social and economic equality which he admired.[7] What could Europeans, he wondered, really offer these happy people whom they dismissed as savages:

> How often is the term 'savages' incorrectly applied! None really deserving of it were ever yet discovered by voyagers or by travellers.

Clearly, the meaning of the noun 'savage' had slipped, and it was now sliding quickly towards it present meaning of barbarous and brutal. One reason why the phrase 'noble savage' so captures our imagination today is because it seems such a contradiction, the word *noble* and the word *savage* each pointing in a different direction.

Lecturing in the United States, the young Melville was even more enthusiastic about what he had seen in 'these Edens of the South Seas'. Like Rousseau, nearly a century previously, Melville suggested that armed guards should protect these simple people from contamination by travelling Europeans. The sympathies which Melville passed on to his English and American readers were to become, in the following four decades, less common in novels and in travel books. They would not disappear – the dominant school of thought is never held un-animously – but they would be asserted less frequently.

In depicting the savage as noble in 1770 and savage in 1870, majority opinion had made a decisive mental leap, but an inkling of sympathy for the savage remained. Edward B. Tylor, a brass-founder's son who became the foremost anthropologist in England, explained that 'when we read descriptions of the hospitality, the gentleness, the bravery, the deep religious feel-ing of the North American Indians, we admit their claims to our sincere admiration.' But, he added sternly, we easily forget that 'their gentleness would pass with a flash of anger into frenzy, that their bravery was stained with cruel and treacherous malignity', and their religion was worthy of ridicule. Tylor, occupying what was now an orthodox and comfortable position on the seesaw, concluded that 'on the whole the civilised man is not only wiser and more capable than the savage, but also better and happier.'[8]

One of the few scholars who saw nobility in tribal peoples was the Russian zoologist, Nikolai Miklouho-Maclay. A brave adventurer, he landed in 1871 with a hundred pieces of luggage on the little-known northern coast of New Guinea, near the present Madang. For a year he lived amongst the agricultural villagers and, as he had half expected, he warmed to them as people and respected their morality, innocence, and way of life. He did not see them as perfect, and regretted that in parts of south-east Asia and in nearby islands they were warlike and even jubilant in their head-hunting. An odd-man-out in his generation, he read Darwin, but there is no evidence that he accepted the theory of natural selection or Darwin's careful optimism about the future of mankind. Attracted by the order and morality of tribal New Guinea, the Russian expressed some distaste for his own civilisation; and when he eventually returned to Russia he turned down his nose at the busy city streets, railways, bureaucrats and factories. Long after his death he was to be canonised by the Soviet Union and acclaimed as a devout

Darwinian and possessor of all the views deemed correct in a socialist in the mid-twentieth century, but his views in the 1870s were far removed from those of such evolutionists and apostles of progress as Marx, Morgan and Engels.[9]

Older than Adam

It had been believed until the nineteenth century that the history of the world was brief: the Old Testament said so, and even radical scientists were wary, on social rather than intellectual grounds, of contradicting such an authority. The respected *Beeton's Dictionary of Universal Information*, as late as 1861, emphasised how short was human history. For the creation of the world the date which it preferred – the result of research by Archbishop Ussher of Ireland on the Old Testament's long family tree of who begat whom – was 4004 BC. Indeed *Beeton's Dictionary* disclosed not only the year but the day and month. The world, it announced, was created on 23 October 4004 BC, which happened to be a Sunday. Adam and Eve were created on the following Friday, 28 October, and placed in the Garden of Eden which was variously said, according to *Beeton's Dictionary*, to be in China, India, Persia, Armenia or Ethiopia.[10] Another important man in *Beeton's* list of dates was Noah, who was tenth in line of descent from Adam. On Sunday 30 November 2349 BC, he entered the ark, and on Sunday 7 December it began to rain. This chronology of world history was to appear in the Church of England's *Book of Common Prayer* well into the twentieth century.

While *Beeton's Dictionary* was being consulted in many libraries, a new and contradictory version could be read in the latest books. In 1863 Professor T. H. Huxley said what his friend Darwin so far barely hinted at: that man had evolved from some related animal species 'at a remote period of time'. He did not have in mind the year 4004 BC. Man's appearance, he said, was too long ago to be assigned a date. In 1865, another friend of Darwin, John Lubbock, opened his influential book *Pre-historic Times* with the provocative sentence: 'The first appearance of man in Europe dates from a period so remote, that neither history, nor tradition, can throw any light on his origin.' The story of human origins was being extended far back into time. The past was now an enormous span of human history, waiting to be explained. Just as the duration of past time was lengthened by the new mode of thinking in the nineteenth century, so the duration of future time was also lengthened.

The passage of time, to the learned eye, was becoming smoother and more gentle in its evolution, and always leading to improvement. Gone was the old emphasis on the role of catastrophes. Sudden disasters and wondrous interventions had been a hallmark of biblical intepretations of human history – whether the parting of the Red Sea, the toppling of the walls of Jericho or the sudden onset of darkness on the afternoon of Jesus' death. The catastrophe had also been the favoured interpretation of the old guard who opposed evolution and preferred the Book of Genesis' account of the earth's history. The old guard, thinking that the earth and mankind were still young, summoned up dramatic events to explain how such profound changes in mankind had taken place in the last 6000 years. They said that the fossil relics of now-extinct species were the result of sudden catastrophes: of volcanoes, vast floods, a change in the earth's centre of gravity, or a falling comet. As late as 1812 the brilliant Frenchman, Georges Cuvier, argued that the great upheavals had been the result of global phenomena recently active but no longer in operation.[11] One of those geological upheavals had divided the yellow from the white races, and possibly another had drowned multitudes of people when the oceans had been formed. Cuvier's theory, called catastrophism, was widely held. Now it gave way to the new belief that the world was intensely old, and that geological change was mostly the incredibly slow result of causes that we can still see in operation: the erosion of rocks, the silting of rivers, the effects of wind and rain and heat and snow, slow changes in climate, and the rising and falling of the seas, all of which took place during hundreds of millions of years. Sir Charles Lyell's new *Principles of Geology*, the first volume of which was carried by Darwin when he left England on his voyage around the world, did much to convince scholars that slow evolution rather than earthquakes, colossal floods and other upheavals was the main agent in creating the mountains and oceans that we know.

Just as many scholars were now inclined to see continuity rather than dramatic breaks in the distant past, so too they envisaged the same continuity in the future. 'What we cannot do', wrote Peter Marris in 1974, 'is survive without a system of some kind for predicting the course of events.'[12] The bolder scholars saw a new continuity in place of the natural catastrophes, Armageddon, The Second Coming and other dramatic futures which were traditionally envisaged. The new secular prophets – amongst them Comte, Marx, Spencer, Darwin and Jules Verne – were like most of us when we are called upon to predict: they largely projected the recent past into the future. They forecast a continuation of progress, based especially on innovations in science, and a continuation of material and social gains. They believed that their world held not only a longer but a nobler future than had previously been predicted.

Here was a revolution in seeing the past, present, and especially the glorious future. Today many intelligent people, not confident even in the short term future, marvel at the optimism of that era. And yet the confidence in that era seemed to rest as much on the lastest science and technology as does the premonition of disaster today.

A Cheerful Lesson from Prehistory

In England Sir John Lubbock was an influential exponent of the linear view of progress. He employed his vast reading, thoughtfulness, and disciplined imagination to find out what the earliest people might have been like and to predict what people would become. Lubbock was an English banker and member of parliament – he introduced the law of 1871 inaugurating the famous Bank Holiday each August – and a sitter on countless committees as well as a spare-time scholar. He was also a close friend of the much older Sir Charles Darwin, and they lived in the Kent countryside, within walking distance of each other's house. Lubbock admired Darwin and defended him. Even before Darwin positively applied to human history the argument which in 1859 he had applied to natural history, Lubbock made the brave step of arguing that man's mind and body had improved through 'natural selection'.

In his book of 1865, *Pre-historic Times*, Lubbock assumed that those primitive societies which survived were fossilised examples of what early society everywhere must have been. He assumed that the earliest human societies were like the present wild animals and were 'always suspicious, always in danger, always on the watch'. The savage treated his wife like a dog and at times even treated himself like a dog by disfiguring and torturing himself, and taking 'a melancholy pleasure' in his own aches and pains.[13] Often suffering from hunger, extreme weather, whims and passions, and from a superstitious fear which 'embitters every pleasure', the savages were incapable of using the abundant resources around them, and so their population was small. Lubbock had not seen savages in their own environment, but he culled his evidence from other observers who visited lands where prehistoric ways of life still existed. Much of his evidence came from travellers who were confident of the merits of their civilisation and quick to judge any other by the degree to which it fell short of their own. Alas, wrote Lubbock in his remarkable book, 'the true savage is neither free nor noble'.

Lubbock peered into the future and was delighted. With increased knowledge, disease would become 'less and less frequent'. With the spread of education, crime would diminish, because most of the criminals at present in English and Welsh gaols were illiterates – 'mere savages' – and their attempts at crime had been a result more of their stupidity in not realising that they would be caught. Lubbock believed that stupidity and illiteracy were virtually the same, and he believed that education and the study of science would make people wiser, happier, and more virtuous. As for the intelligence of the human race, he believed that the human mind would be improved just as the physique of other species had been improved, thus bringing what had long seemed impossible, Utopia. He announced in the last sentence of his long story of prehistoric times that the progress of mankind would assuredly continue and that future generations would 'avoid much of that suffering to which we are subject, enjoy many blessings of which we are not yet worthy, and escape many of those temptations which we deplore, but cannot wholly resist'. He believed, like so many intelligent men of that era, that material and moral advancement would advance side by side. Proud of the long distance which mankind had climbed, Lubbock envisaged that it would continue to climb.[14]

Lubbock's view of mankind's meagre accomplishments in the distant past were partly influenced by his pride in man's present, just as his belief that mankind had once floundered in the darkness of the past now bolstered his pride in his own civilisation. It is tempting to ask which came first: his pride in the present or his contempt for prehistoric times? I suspect that first came his pride in the present, though by a narrow margin.

A Step Ladder for the World's Peoples

The evolutionists believed that mankind developed in stages and that each stage was an advance on the previous stage. In essence they applied to social and political institutions that optimistic step ladder which had first been constructed in the eighteenth century for the stages of economic development. The idea of slotting the economic history of early man into three successive ages – the stone age, bronze age, and iron age – was devised by Christian Jürgensen Thomsen when arranging exhibits for the opening of the Danish national museum in 1819, and nearly half a century later Sir John Lubbock carried the division further and used the phrase Palaeolithic to describe the Old Stone Age in which stone tools were roughly flaked, and the Neolithic or New Stone Age to designate the later period when stone tools began to resemble the work of real craftsmen.[15] The dividing of the history of mankind into successive ages or steps was accompanied by the parallel though slightly riskier idea that each technological stage tended to be accompanied by a more advanced culture. On the cultural ladder of mankind, savagery was usually the name of the first step and civilisation of the last: barbarism was often the name of an intermediate step.* This concept of the neat ascent of mankind appealed to the triumphant Victorian era, implying that it stood on the top rung of the ladder.

The most celebrated of the ladder-thinkers was the American, Lewis Henry Morgan. Alfred C. Haddon, a fine Cambridge scholar, insisted in 1910 that Morgan was 'undoubtedly the

---

* A barbarian – the word was Latin but stemmed from the Greek – was originally someone who knew no Greek and Latin or spoke them clumsily. To scholars versed in the classics, 'barbaric' and 'barbarian' therefore did not have quite the derisive meaning which they now possess. According to the discussion of these words in the two-volumed *Shorter Oxford English Dictionary*, the philosopher David Hume (1711–76) classed Cromwell as a barbarian, though he 'was not insensible to literary merit'.

greatest sociologist of the past century', but his fame has now ebbed. Morgan had moved at the age of twenty-six to Rochester in New York State where he practised as a lawyer and also studied the American Indians. In 1851, when still in his early thirties, Morgan completed what some of his learned contemporaries called the first scientific book ever written on an Indian tribe, a book that was both sympathetic to them and critical of them. In 1871 another of his books claimed to show how the human family had evolved from utter promiscuity to the superior condition of monogamy. Convinced that social progress was a fact, this gifted lawyer would have been dismayed had he seen how busy were the divorce lawyers in his own city of Rochester a century later.[16]

Evolve was his key concept – everything evolved from the simple to the complex – but he avoided such a word because it was hostile to orthodox religion. Thus his influential book of 1877 was called *Ancient Society: or Researches in the Line of Human Progress from Savagery through Barbarism to Civilization.* Morgan believed that he saw, stretching far back into the past, three stages of savagery in which the last was the invention of pottery; three stages of barbarism in which the last was the invention of the alphabet; and finally the present stage of civilisation. He thought that all societies would climb the seven rungs, though some were still resting on lower rungs, and that one day an eighth rung of the ladder would be climbed. He believed that the eighth stage would retain the advantages of the present civilisation but also restore some of the virtues of savage society, including brotherhood, liberty, and communal ownership. He had a humble pride in the human race and deemed modern civilisation to be the outcome of 'the struggles, the sufferings, the heroic exertions, and the patient toil of our barbarous, and more remotely, our savage ancestors.'

Morgan's evolutionist view of history was to give stimulus to Karl Marx but it was only after the death of both men in the early 1880s that Morgan's ideas became an important part of the socialist view of human history. It so happened that Marx in old age read Morgan's *Ancient Society* and took down notes, and Friedrich Engels later read Marx's notes before reading Morgan's book. Engels either misunderstood Morgan's lifestory or decided to alter it, for he claimed that Morgan was a gypsy who 'had spent the greater part of his life among the

Iroquois'.[17] In any case Engels was so impressed with Morgan's delineation of primitive tribal society that he made it the first stage in that sequential history of mankind – through slavery and feudalism to capitalism and communism – which is so important to Marxism. Morgan's view of primitive society as possessing no private property and no classes became a dominant view in the Soviet Union, and even Stalin incorporated it in his theories.

Marx, long before he read Morgan, had his own view about the distant past, and was convinced that materially it was to be pitied because all its activities were directed towards finding sufficient food. As the tools of the savages were meagre, their life was a constant battle against nature and its unpredictability. Nothing could have been further from Marx's thoughts than the idea that a life lived close to nature was the formula for material and social advancement, and in the *Communist Manifesto* of 1848 he and Engels made their memorable condemnation of 'the idiocy of rural life'. Marx was very much a passenger on the seesaw, for he saw the ideal society as ultimately the product of advanced technology. Nonetheless he believed that primitive society, despite its poverty, had several of the merits of communism, including liberty and a sense of equality and community.[18]

Curiously the small band of Marxists had much in common with the more intellectual of the businessmen who exulted in capitalism. Both tended to see history as a great forward march, passing through successive stages. While supporters of capitalism were inclined to believe that they were nearing their secular paradise, the communists believed that the world must pass through a revolution and yet another stage before they reached their utopia.

It could be argued that the rise of the Ignoble Savage was simply the result of new knowledge, and in part this was true. Many primitive peoples, lacking immunity to new diseases, were dying out or declining in numbers, and the new concept of the Survival of the Fittest implied that those native peoples, in not surviving, were inferior. On the other hand much of the evidence about the simple societies had been available back in 1770 but was now interpreted less sympathetically. Those explorers who now observed native peoples living their traditional life were more inclined to see them through progress-tinted spectacles, and therefore to be less sympathetic. Missionaries, now penetrating every continent, also wore their own spectacles, and quickly detected sin. Many traditional societies, already being altered by the diseases, ideas and implements of new European settlers, were low in morale, and the robe of dignity was slipping from their shoulders.

It would be unwise to generalise too confidently about European eyes. And yet there is a case for suggesting that the drastic change in European attitudes to savage societies in the hundred years between 1770 and 1870 came at least as much from what was happening to European preconceptions as from the discovery of additional primitive societies or the decay in those which had long been known.

The Fuegians: Bottom of the Ladder

Every vision, every philosophy, needs its symbol. Just as the warm beaches of Tahiti had been the symbol of the Noble Savage in the eighteenth century, now the symbol of the Ignoble Savage were the cold shores near the southern tip of South America. There the wind-battered island of Tierra del Fuego was seen as typical of the primitive society – the ultimate in misery and degradation. The small groups of Fuegian people who lived on that large, mountainous, snow-capped island not far from Cape Horn were described by Sir John Lubbock in *Pre-historic Times*, and he seemed to concur with those many travellers who regarded them as 'the lowest of mankind'.[19] Even encyclopedias now classified them as objects of pity, and the *Universal Gazetteer* of 1840 depicted them not only as low on the scale of technology but as people 'of stupidity, indifference, and inactivity'. Their way of life was also deemed pitiable, for they were said to live mainly on seal-meat, and were said to wear nothing but a sealskin which extended only from the shoulders to the middle of the back.[20]

The collapse of the image of the Fuegians tells us something about that mental process which oscillates, generation after generation.

It so happened that some of the voyagers who in 1769 found glamour on Tahiti had also landed on the large island of Tierra del Fuego in the same year. As they had enthroned the Tahitians as the happy children of Nature, surely they also must have thought kindly of the simple Fuegians who equally lived in the bosom of Nature?

Cook's *Endeavour* had anchored in a bay of Tierra del Fuego for five days in January 1769, during the voyage to Tahiti, and Joseph Banks led a party into the interior. It was so cold even in the height of summer that two of the visitors died during a sudden snowstorm. Banks also inspected a village of a dozen wigwams, each of which was half open so as to let out the fire-smoke, and he examined the villagers' bows and arrows. These half-naked Fuegians were closely observed – admittedly, without the benefit of a common language – during those long summer days of January 1769, and their life obviously was far from idyllic.

Joseph Banks and other Englishmen who sympathised with the cult of the Noble Savage could, if they wished, have excused Tierra del Fuego as an exception. They noticed that the islanders must have had previous cultural contacts with European navigators, for they used European glass for the tips of their arrows, and possessed imported beads and tatters of cloth, and therefore were possibly tainted by civilisation in a way that the Tahitians initially were not.[21] Banks also could have excused the Fuegians as untypical of nature because they had to endure the long dark winters of a latitude that lay as far from the equator as Alaska. European voyagers and scholars could easily have treated the Fuegians as an exception to their rule which upheld the merits of living close to nature, but their ideology would not permit it.

In the 1770s the ideology of the Noble Savage virtually prevented the Fuegians from being depicted as they were. An ideological veil was placed over them, as the Australian art historian, Bernard Smith, suggested in his brilliant book, *European Vision and the South Pacific 1768–1850*.[22] Two artists, Buchan and Parkinson, were in the *Endeavour* and they sketched the faces and bodies of the Fuegians. Some of their realistic sketches were taken over by artisans or artists in England and, before reaching the public, were given an elegance suggestive of a photographer arranging hired models. Parkinson had verbally described their flat faces, low foreheads smeared with red and brown paint, large mouths and small teeth, and black straight hair falling on their brows, the whole appearance being 'very uncouth and savage'. And yet I have seen one of his rough sketches, redrawn and engraved in England and showing a native man and woman wearing shapely furs that could almost have come from a fashionable furrier's shop. The woman wears a headband which curves around her head with a casual charm and the smeared paint now looks like elaborate make-up applied with a pointed pencil, and her nose, mouth and eyes have an appeal which is certainly not lost on our generation: we perhaps find 'the natural look' more attractive, from our position on the seesaw of taste.[23] A picture is often more influential than a phrase, and in the heyday of the Noble Savage various engravings – drawn artistically by London Italians and included in Hawkesworth's first account – depicted the people of Tierra del Fuego living in park-like settings, wearing flowing Grecian robes or scarves or drapes, and sitting elegantly in their dwellings like a scene from the Nativity.[24] Between the tip of South America and the artists' studios and the printeries of London, the savages had become ennobled.

Likewise, several of the key sentences written about these people had been censored or rearranged. Thus, Cook himself did not fancy the mahogany-coloured Fuegians, noting in his journal that they were 'perhaps as miserable a set of People as are this day upon Earth' – a rather sweeping speculation from one who had not yet seen most lands. Nonetheless when the travels of Cook and Banks were first published in London in 1773, they were presented by the popular pen of John Hawkesworth; and Cook's denigration of the miserable Fuegians did not appear. Instead, in his *An Account of the Voyages*, Hawkesworth quietly applied to the Fuegians an observation which Cook and Banks actually noted of the Australian Aboriginals whom they encountered in the following year.[25] Thus, Hawkesworth wrote that the severe climate and primitive huts of the Fuegians were possibly counter-balanced by what they gained in leisure, liberty and a casual approach to life. In Hawkesworth's words, the Fuegians were luckily exempt from 'the care, labour and solicitude, which arise from a perpetual and unsuccessful effort to gratify that infinite variety of desires which the refinements of artificial life have produced among us'. He was simply saying in elegant language that it was not sensible to try to keep up with the Jones's. Virtually a public relations agent for the Noble Savage, he concealed Captain Cook's view that the Fuegians were miserable.

Hawkesworth's varnish was eventually detected. Two decades after Bernard Smith had removed Hawkesworth's varnish from the Fuegians, Professor G. Williams of London went further and, repeating Smith's exposure, denounced poor old Hawkesworth for his unscholarly conduct and for writing arrant nonsense.[26] With all respect to Smith and Williams, it was not only Hawkesworth who was indirectly placing the Fuegians amongst the Noble Savages: it was Banks himself. If you read carefully Banks's own journal you find that he actually held the idyllic views loosely attributed to him by Hawkesworth. As he described the Portuguese colonists in Brazil as 'the laziest as well as the most ignorant race in the whole world', he could hardly think too adversely of the Fuegians whom he discovered, five weeks later, living without visible hunger in such a bleak terrain and climate.[27] More important, in a sentence which seems to have escaped notice, Banks offered a kindly opinion of the way of life of those half-naked people who possessed no furniture and pottery and cooking utensils and used a mere beast's bladder as a water vessel and only an open fire for cooking. Despite their primitiveness, they were 'to all appearance contented with what they had nor wishing for any thing we could give them except beads.'[28] Here indeed was contentment, if not nobility. It only required the make-up artists in England to supply the nobility for the Fuegian illustrations in the travel books.

The people of this glacier-active island were protected from undue criticism during the era of the Noble Savage, but they could no longer be protected in the light of the new busy-bee values of the age of steam when their nakedness and indolence, their lack of visible government and religion, and their low place on the ladder of technology all made them a target for contempt. Likewise, the Fuegians had been praised in 1770 because they took no thought for the morrow. They were the antipodean version of the lilies of the field who neither toiled nor spun, did not gather their harvest into barns, and certainly did not believe – to continue the words of the Gospel according to St. Matthew – that by taking thought they could add one cubit to their stature.[29] Ironically, a century later, cubits were actually taken from their stature.

It so happened that Joseph Banks had examined at least fifty Fuegians he met, and judged nearly all the men to stand from

5 ft 8 in to 5 ft 10 in in height, which was much taller than the typical Englishman of his time. Banks's shipmate Parkinson, a fine draughtsman and therefore an able measurer with the naked eye, independently noted their height and indicated that they were not small. In fact the island seems to have held races of tall people as well as short people, and in the middle of the nineteenth century both races were seen by Europeans, but the taller ones were less noticed. Captain Fitz Roy, commander of the *Beagle* in which Darwin was a voyager, noted in the 1830s that the men were 'low in stature'. As for the 'she-Fuegians' – they were not thought worthy of the name of woman – he claimed that they were only about 'four feet and some inches' in height. How the mighty had shrunk. More relevant, the perspective of European explorers and scholars had also shrunk.

A Parable of the Wild Shores

In the last chapter of *The Descent of Man**, published in 1871, Charles Darwin recalled that the first time he had seen primitive people was on a wild shore in Tierra del Fuego. They were naked: worse, they were 'absolutely naked'. Their hair was tangled, their expression was wild and startled, and they excitedly frothed at the mouth. They had no government and they had barely any arts; 'like wild animals' they lived on what they hunted; and they were merciless to members of other tribes. They even stood, in Darwin's view, on a slightly lower level of civilisation than the Australians. Darwin hoped that civilised man, having already advanced far above his barbarian ancestors, would attain 'a still higher destiny in the distant future'. In that mental picture the once-noble savage had been reduced to little more than a twitching fossil.[30]

The idea of a tilting seesaw was alien to Darwin's thought, and he could not imagine that one century later the primitive societies would return to favour and that the ragged Fuegians would be imitated in San Francisco, Amsterdam and the smart cities of civilisation. In 1970 the primitive societies were to be praised for their nakedness, pagan morality, and love of leisure – the very facets which condemned them in so many eyes in

* The book, in today's terminology, would be called *The Ascent of Man*.

1870. Infanticide, common in primitive societies and thunderingly denounced by Europe in 1870, had returned to fashion in 1970 under the new name of zero population growth. The plain needs, simple technology and collective way of life had been scorned a century ago but now were imitated by our own counter-culture. The startled look, frothing mouth and naked limbs which repelled Charles Darwin when he landed near the tip of South America now helped to attract thousands of the young to pop festivals. The rough, unprocessed grain which the savages ate was again in vogue on millions of breakfast tables: we call it muesli. The savages who were pitied because they had no mechanical means of transport were now envied for their fitness and for the long distances which they walked – they were the pioneer joggers. The forests which were despised as useless and untamed were now exultantly hailed as 'wildernesses'. Even the poisonous snakes have become our friends and seem to smile on colour television.

The primitive men who were once said to live like wild beasts are now said, admiringly, to live in elegant harmony with nature. Primitive tribes are described by many anthropologists as if they were Quakers and never warriors. A recent survey of the views of living anthropologists indicates that they do not think warfare was a major cause of death amongst hunting and gathering societies.[31] If Australian Aboriginals and other simple societies gained from this latest exaggerated tilt of the seesaw, it was a belated justice, because their ancestors a century ago had suffered through the tilting of the seesaw in the opposite direction.

Enemies of Proud Progress

The idea of inevitable progress had to skirt around powerful Victorian enemies. In educated circles, the strongest but quietest enemy lay in the classical languages, which subtly taught that there was something cyclical in human history. An education in ancient Greek and Latin spread the idea that even greater civilisations than the present had existed and that those civilisations, for all their majesty and seeming permanence, had come to an end. A study of the classics also suggested that when a civilisation or nation was too certain of its future, it was approaching grave danger.

The classics provided an early warning system in this haughty age of shining engines. They warned educated citizens that even their civilisation could ultimately collapse. In the English language perhaps the most admired of all history books available was Edward Gibbon's *Decline and Fall of the Roman Empire*. The title rang its own alarm bell. Gibbon had placed ancient Rome far ahead of his own Europe of the late eighteenth century, and without hesitation he named the years between the death of Domitian and the reign of Commodus as 'the period in the history of the world during which the condition of the human race was most happy and prosperous'. As if any further warning of the fragility of a civilisation were needed, he wrote near the end of his book of that inevitable destiny 'which spares neither man nor the proudest of his works, which buries empires and cities in a common grave'.[32]

Of England's living historians in 1850 Lord Macaulay was perhaps the most admired, and he knew the classics minutely: he listed three classical Greek poets – Homer, Aeschylus and Sophocles – but only two English poets in his list of eminent poets.[33] Today he is criticised for his pride in progress, for proclaiming that the preceding 160 years in England were 'eminently the history of physical, of moral, and of intellectual improvement',[34] but it is forgotten that he also predicted that his era would be outshone by future eras. He did not see progress as indefinite: success carried the seeds of decline. From his pen in 1840 had come the memorable sentence predicting that the Papacy, which he did not worship, might outlast the British Empire, which he did worship; and the time might arrive 'when some traveller from New Zealand shall, in the midst of a vast solitude, take his stand on a broken arch of London Bridge to sketch the ruins of St. Paul's.'[35]

The classics of ancient Greece and Rome were still widely read, though less so by the young engineers, chemists and factory managers who were multiplying. A classical education was still *the* education, and at most universities in western Europe in 1850 more time was spent by the average student in studying Greek and Latin than any other subject. Foundation stones of public buildings were often inscribed in Latin, and the language of the Catholic mass was Latin, and in Protestant England the prime minister for more than a dozen years of the imperial heyday, William Ewart Gladstone, was renowned as a scholar of ancient Greek. A knowledge of the classics – and by definition 'classics' were still the great books of ancient Greece and Rome and not of modern languages – was assumed to be common knowledge; and it was considered apt that new locomotives on England's Great Western Railway should rush along, each carrying the name of a hero in the *Iliad*.[36] In Germany, which had moved quietly to the forefront in the study of history, the topic of ancient Rome attracted Mommsen, Ranke and some of the finest historians. Just as poorer countries today search for an economic model in the advanced world, so the emerging Germany found its political model more in the ancient world and especially in imperial Rome. All places, remote in space or time, are tinted mirrors in which we view our own civilisation in flattering or despondent light, and the classical civilisations were the largest, clearest and most decorated of all such mirrors in Europe and served as a check on the worship of progress.

Just as a knowledge of the classical civilisations, their birth and death, had been a restraint on super-optimism, so too was Europe's close dependence on nature and its cycle of seasons. In the eighteenth century, most Europeans had worked on the land, their economic life had relied on nature in so many ways, ranging from the importance of the local harvests and the strength of draught animals to the streams which supplied power to mills and the wind which propelled ships at sea. And now in the age of steam mills, steam railways, steamships and steam threshing machines, nature ceased to be so important in Europe. As fewer people worked in agriculture, fluctuations in the weather ceased to be the dominant cause of economic recessions. The new trade cycle or business cycle, with its recession that came roughly every seven to eleven years, was challenging the weather as the main disturber of economic security in Europe and the United States; and the business cycle – until the crash of 1929 – was less disruptive than the age-old cycle of the weather. The belief in progress therefore came partly from a sense that unpredictable dislocations in daily life were now less frequent.

The third of the traditional opponents of a faith in progress still took its place in the pulpit each Sunday, all the way from Montreal to Glasgow to Berlin. This was simply the faith in Providence, the hope or fear that God would personally intervene in private and public life. When the bishop in Australia called for 2 November 1838 to be a day of humiliation in the hope that a terrible drought would end,[37] he was proclaiming the belief that God was still on active duty. A generation later, the Bishop of Manchester, preaching on a day in 1870 when Paris was being besieged by the Prussians, said that the bombardment was the price which Paris paid for immorality and profligacy.[38] He was simply affirming the old belief that God could wreck the hopes of mankind and that only God could foretell the future. And yet the increasing faith in progress implied that man could now foretell the future.

Declining faith in the divinity and the historical accuracy of the Bible was a vital prelude to a rising faith in the wisdom and healing powers of science. German scholars led the way in highlighting the Bible's inconsistencies and in examining the miracles. David F. Strauss's *Life of Jesus* caused a shock in Germany in the mid 1830s by casting doubt on scriptural accounts of Jesus' birth, death, resurrection and teaching.[39] Decades would pass before even whispers of his argument reached most village chapels in England or hilltop churches in Italy, but wherever new ideas were welcomed and weighed, the shock waves of Strauss and his successors were felt.

Ideas usually marry suitable wives. In the family of ideas most divorces are also predictable, but every now and then a new idea elopes with a partner whom nobody had previously thought was likely to be enticed. Occasionally, in some talented minds, Providence and Progress instead of fighting actually came together as partners. Thus some Europeans and Americans of the mid-Victorian era, like the Hebrews of the Old Testament, believed that progress was more likely in their own nation because it was specially favoured by God. On Sunday 22 June 1873, a leading Anglican theologian, Dean Stanley, preaching in Westminster Abbey to a congregation of volunteer soldiers, told them that it was in the western nations that 'by God's providence, the onward course of civilisation and religion has been appointed to march.'[40] The idea that God had his favourites among the nations became more common towards the end of the century, when nationalism increased and when Britain, Germany and France rejoiced in their vast overseas empires. The poet Kipling sang his songs of empire but, pondering on this marriage of Providence and Progress, emphasised the dangers of over-confidence by pointing to the collapse of past civilisations:

> Lo, all our pomp of yesterday
> Is one with Nineveh and Tyre!

Several powerful ideas of the nineteenth century were, in their effect, not easily distinguishable from what had gone before. In many circles the idea that man was uniquely created by God in his own image was replaced by the parallel idea that man was the unique result of the process of evolution: in both theories, Europeans possessed privileges and special responsibilities. The Christian idea that man had a special mission and that Europeans had a unique responsibility to carry the mission to the corners of the world was paralleled by the evolutionist idea that Europeans were destined to rule inferior races in far-away lands.

From about the 1840s to the 1870s the believers in inevitable progress were prone to a swaggering pride, but some exponents of progress were cautious. They retained a sense of the unpredictability of nature, a knowledge of the rise and ebb of Greek and Roman civilisations, and a lingering belief in the sudden appearance of the hand of Providence or Fate. Their view of the future therefore was more cyclical and less assured, and they were not surprised when in the 1880s and 1890s the super-confident strand in European thought began to droop.

A Seed-bed of Grand ideas

A prediction on a grand scale commands attention. If it is a long-term prediction it can command unusual power simply because, being long-term, it cannot be disproved within the shorter term of say twenty years. Such predictions accordingly are given a temporary reprieve; they cannot be shot at from the ground simply because they fly out of reach until, years later, they have to descend.

The period from the 1820s to the 1870s was astonishingly fertile in producing grand and optimistic generalisations about mankind and its future. The Frenchman, Comte, sired positivism, and his English disciple, Buckle, produced historical axioms that pointed to a glorious future for Europe, and in

South America the positivists became intellectual trail-blazers, even placing their motto of 'Order and Progress' on Brazil's new flag in 1889. The German, Hegel, wrote on how Reason developed through history, and Marx and Engels boldly described how human societies evolved through conflicts, especially in the economic sphere. Charles Darwin and A. R. Wallace studied biological evolution and the tough pressures that produced new species and extinguished old; and Lubbock, Morgan, Tylor and other students of ancient man produced theories on the stage-by-stage development of mankind from savagery to civilisation; and Strauss, Renan and other thinkers produced new theories on Christianity. Some of the grand generalisations of the eighteenth century – for example Adam Smith on the benefits of free trade – were also revamped and made comprehensive. These ideas were, in a real sense, theories of history, with also an interest in the future and a willingness – which we have largely lost – to try to predict the future.

Why did so many grand, confident generalisations appear at this time? As they flavoured the period it is vital to know the forces which gave them birth and disseminated them widely. These confident theories about man, his past and future, partly reflected the waning of the Christian church's traditional monopoly over such ideas and the increasing reluctance of certain governments to censor new ideas. The emergence of these theories also reflected the declining influence of Christianity amongst intellectuals, especially its influence on the way they saw the future. Though some of the exponents of the new theories – for instance Darwin and Morgan and Lubbock – were Christians they were not orthodox and fundamentalist in their belief. Significantly England and France, where the censorship by church and state was less stern and comprehensive, were the home of most of these confident theories.

The rise of these confident theories about man was aided by the relative peacefulness of Europe. A long war tends to lower optimism about the future of man, except perhaps in a nation which is winning the war. Significantly, no grand confident theory, to my knowledge, had been produced between 1789 and 1815, a turbulent quarter of a century which was dominated by the French Revolution, Napoleon, and the long European wars. The rise of theories – and interest in them – was aided by the increasing ease of world travel. Thus the theory of biological evolution, the theories of social development which the first prehistorians published, and even Karl Marx's theory of man's inevitable march to communism were each dependent on an increasing flow of information about other lands and civilisations. Above all, nearly all these theories were influenced by the advance of science and technology and by a world which, changing faster than ever, urgently required explanation and analysis.

To most of these theorists, the future was malleable because men and women themselves were malleable. Their outward life and their inward life could be changed. The philosopher John Stuart Mill, though too balanced to be a fervent optimist, emphasised that nobody 'whose opinion deserves a moment's notice can doubt that most of the great positive evils of the world are in themselves removable'.[41] Marx was even more confident that people could be changed. Just as capitalism seemed to foster self-seeking amongst the rich, so a new communal economic and social system would foster altruism, even changing 'human nature'. The hopes, so widely shared, that compulsory education would transform society were another sign of the optimism of this era. Whereas a century or two earlier, the accepted belief was that only Christianity could transform an individual, now the plans of man seemed capable of competing with the grace of God.

Above all, the mood of an era influences the evidence that scholars find and the way they interpret that evidence. Thus Thomas Malthus was the public symbol of the pessimism of the early part of the nineteenth century, and Darwin and Wallace were the symbols of the optimism after the middle of that century, and yet both Darwin and Wallace gained their special insight while reading Malthus or thinking about his ideas. Malthus's essay on population was about forty years old when Darwin read it and about fifty years old when Wallace read it, but its emphasis on the perpetual 'struggle for existence' was so powerful that the two scientists independently saw its significance.[42] Malthus was thinking about the struggle of only one species, the human species, whereas the two scientists were thinking about all species, and yet the three men agreed that struggle was the essence of life and that the penalty for failing was high. This same theory of struggle was vital for the message of pessimism in 1800 and for the message of optimism in 1860.

Knowing that a similar set of facts can support opposite conclusions, we see how easily an intellectual mood, in the space of a generation, could veer from fear to hope or from hope to fear.

5 Will the West Decline?

The end of the century showed in full all the signs of progress which delighted statisticians, scientists and engineers a generation earlier. Europe had extended its sway, Germany and Belgium and Italy had joined in the race to colonise the remaining tracts of Africa, and more than 60,000 white missionaries were busy in 'heathen' lands stretching from the Gobi Desert to the Transvaal of South Africa. The world was shrinking, and the longest of all railways was being built across eastern Siberia to link the North Sea and the China Sea, and the telegraph wires and underwater cables were about to be challenged by the Marconi invention which in 1901 sent the first wireless message across the wide Atlantic. In these three peaceful decades, Europeans moved about with unprecedented ease, and 21 million Europeans emigrated overseas between 1870 and 1900 while an even larger procession moved from the countryside to the cities: London and Paris were the only cities with more than a million people in 1870 but by 1900 there were fourteen such cities ranging from Buenos Aires and Chicago to Berlin and Tokyo. The inventor was even more a hero, and the Linotype machine, motor car, electric power house, pneumatic tyre, bicycle, steam-turbine, a host of new chemicals, the cinema, telephone and x-ray all proved their usefulness in these thirty years. By any measure, technology was triumphant amongst the European peoples. The scoreboard of civilisation was clear in its message but some people were not quite sure whether their civilisation was really the victor.

Rise of a Prophet

It had been difficult to imagine in 1870 that Europe might someday cease to be all-powerful. During that high noon of progress no scholar or politician to my knowledge argued that Europe's power might wane during the twentieth century. By the 1890s the cultural climate had cooled a little, and nobody illustrated the change more vividly than Charles Henry Pearson who predicted the decline of the west long before the famous

German writer, Oswald Spengler, made his prediction. Pearson was far ahead of events, but he was also in step with the emerging mood of his time.

The son of an Anglican clergyman, Pearson became in his twenties the professor of modern history at King's College, London University. Curious to see the world, he did what only a handful of Englishmen of his generation achieved: he toured both Russia and the United States and thus gained early clues to a future in which western and central Europe might not be so prominent. He began his tour of Russia in 1858 after learning the language in London, and on his return he issued an anonymous book called *Russia: By a Recent Traveller* which, to its tiny audience of 168 purchasers, offered unusual insights. The serfs in Russia were about to be emancipated by the czar, the nation seemed to stand at the crossroads, and Pearson thought it could become either another England, alert to new ideas and technology, or a mighty Pan-slav monarchy stretching from the Pacific to the Danube and 'capable of counterpoising the whole civilisation of the West'. When the Russian author, Alexander Herzen, living in exile in London, read Pearson he marvelled that he should show such a breadth of view, 'quite unknown in the world of the old civilisation'.

Ten years later Pearson visited the United States, and travelling on the new Union-Pacific railway to its temporary terminus at Cheyenne near the Rockys, he saw the vastness of the country. And yet he predicted that in some twenty years' time America would have reached the end of its frontier and, the bounty of virgin land being present no longer, would experience poverty and mass unrest. Here was a clever foretaste of the frontier theory of Frederick Jackson Turner, almost a quarter century before that theory was born. In Boston, Pearson met the literary giants – Longfellow, Emerson and Oliver Wendell Holmes – and thought their city provided perhaps the finest intellectual society in the world.[1] While proud of Europe, Pearson did not think that it was entirely the hub of the universe.

In 1871, when he was aged forty one, Pearson emigrated to Australia where he became a farmer near Port Pirie, and in turn the lecturer in history and political economy at Melbourne University, the first headmaster of the Presbyterian Ladies College in Melbourne, and from 1877 to 1892 a full-time salaried politician, including three years as Minister for Education in

Victoria.[2] He was not the hearty hand-shaking, ever-plotting politician so evident in a new democracy, but rather a frail recluse who saw the world through an eye-glass while briefly looking up from a book. Gathering evidence about the state of the world, he believed that to predict the future was no harder than to describe the present. 'If we were certain of knowing the facts of the present day in their entirety' he said, 'it would be comparatively easy to predict what was in the immediate future.'[3]

A Vision of Europe's Decay

In the early 1890s, Pearson began to write a book about the future. At a time when signs were few that Japan might rise and China might stir and Africa might become a chain of independent states, he gravely predicted that the European peoples – 'the white races' – would not always be ascendant. In stately prose he predicted that the coloured peoples would increasingly outnumber the whites, and would copy Europe's railways, irrigation schemes, medicine and sanitary engineering, for they were faster learners than was realised. 'We', wrote Pearson, 'are the blind instruments of fate for multiplying the races that are now our subjects, and will one day be our rivals'. Convinced that Europeans could not flourish in the tropics, he envisaged them retreating as rulers, once the coloured peoples had mastered the skills they were already learning. The day would come when independent nations controlled by the coloured peoples would girdle the globe, probably having gained their independence without war or revolution. The day would come, perhaps by the 1980s, when these nations would possess most of the world's commerce, most of the world's merchant warships and much influence in international diplomacy because their fleets could then be patrolling European waters. While he could not specify which would be the leading nations of what we now call the Third World, he singled out China, India and a republic in the heart of Africa.

Of China's ultimate rise he felt certain, for she had huge resources and her 400 million people had energy and tenacity. We forget that when Pearson was completing his book in 1892, the revival of China was not easily foreseen. The likelihood then was that China would be cut into slices and devoured by the main imperial powers, and in fact those powers in 1900 were to send sailors and soldiers to humiliate the Chinese in the aftermath of the Boxer Rebellion. While Pearson did not foresee China rising as quickly as Japan, he prophesied that ultimately 'the preponderance of China over any rival – even over the Unted States of America – is likely to be overwhelming'. That was a daring prophecy.

This transfer of power from Europe to Asia and Africa was more likely to come peacefully than through war. It would be a quiet infiltration, and the elite of Central America, China and the Zambesi would even marry into titled European families. They would throng the English turf, perhaps owning a horse that would win the Derby, and mingle with the haughty and smart in the Parisian salons. The quiet invasion would be aided by Europe's own internal divisions. Pearson thought it was 'sheer madness' for France and Germany to be fighting over the future of Alsace-Lorraine, or for Russia to be fighting for the keys to Constantinople when such internal disputes were 'really trifling' compared with the tremendous issue of the world's future. Was it likely that in a military crisis a weakened Europe would be saved by help from the United States and other European lands across the seas? He thought the United States was unlikely to help – a prediction which was not altogether naïve when we recall the lateness of America's entry into the two world wars.

The prospect of the decline of the European peoples, more than the likely meteoric rise of the coloured peoples, was the basis of Pearson's thinking. He believed that the dazzling era of European science was dimming. While in his opinion the Chinese, Indians and tropical peoples lacked originality, they would catch up, simply because Europe would cease to make new inventions. The increasing welfare policies of governments in European countries – he saw it especially in his own Australia – would weaken zest and originality. A sympathiser with nature, he also deplored the massing of people in big cities where their physical stamina and mental vitality could be sapped. He also predicted that as new technology ceased to stimulate commerce and industry, Europe would lose most of its overseas markets.

Whereas straight-line or linear concepts of history had been fashionable, Pearson foreshadowed a revival of cyclical interpretations of history. An admirer of the ancient civilisations, his

grasp of their history made him allergic to the opium of super-
confidence, the smoke of which he sniffed in the European air
around him. Though a civilisation might take centuries to
exhaust all its originality and creativity, the exhaustion would
come to Europe just as it came to the ancient Greeks. In his
view it was folly for a nation to imagine that 'because it is
England, or France, or the United States it is destined to
immortality.' Pearson shrewdly observed that a civilisation or
nation at the height of its power tended to explain its own
success by pointing to its 'inborn superiority', but in reality
nothing was inborn and superiority itself was fragile.[4]

Such was the message in the hand-written manuscript which
Pearson took aboard the ship when he left Melbourne in August
1892. Travelling to the heart of the largest empire the world
had seen, and carrying a warning that it was vulnerable, he
should not have expected a welcome. At least a London publisher agreed to print his book, and in 1893 it appeared in a
vivid plum-coloured cover with the lack-lustre title of *National
Life and Character: A Forecast*.

His book, to his disappointment, was discussed rather than
read. Moreover, some who read it in England must have felt
scornful that the collapse of their own far-flung empire should
even be predicted and that the instruments of its demise should
be backward races who were now living in subjection. When
Pearson read the first reviews of his book he wrote privately
that England was 'deeply permeated with the idea that it is
doubting God to believe that our temporal prosperity will ever
be clouded'. The fact that he had been away from England for
more than two decades also seemed to invalidate certain of his
predictions: what could an absentee know of England's might?[5]

One admirer of the book was Theodore Roosevelt, who was
soon to become president of the United States. Roosevelt had
recently written *The Winning of the West* with its extolling of
the frontier life and its emphasis on self-help, and so he had
something in common with Pearson. Both believed that state
paternalism could undermine the people whom it believed it
was helping. In the *Sewanee Review* of August 1894 Roosevelt
admired Pearson's deep insight but lamented his pessimism:
'with much of his forecast most of us would radically disagree'.[6]

Pearson was already dead. His book's influence slowly faded.
If the book, however, had been written a dozen years later,

after Japan had defeated Russia in war, it might have seemed more plausible. What he said was too far ahead of its time to be evaluated with a sense of proportion. Of course some of the events he predicted have so far not come to pass and some have been contradicted. And yet it is exceedingly rare for a cluster of predictions, and the reasons for those predictions, to command respect nearly a hundred years later. His forgotten book is one of the few masterpieces in that hazardous art of predicting human affairs.

A book is like a two-way radio, and depends as much on the audience as on the speaker. Pearson's audience by and large was not listening and not even tuned in. And yet his book signalled a new era. It simply could not have been written, let alone published, back in 1870 when the world lay at Europe's cosy feet.

The Yellow Peril

The feeling that Europe was being hemmed in was accompanied by a sense that east Asia would eventually compete with Europe for space. From Germany emigration was massive, but no German-speaking land could take more than a handful of migrants, and many ambitious Germans began to look east towards the Polish plains and the Ukraine. Friedrich Ratzel, a geopolitician and professor of geography at Leipzig, popularised a word which would become strident in Hitler's time, half a century hence: he called for *Lebensraum* further east, for territory in which Germans could live and multiply. It was also in the late 1890s that the German emperor, Kaiser Wilhelm, invented that phrase which would be heard even more often than *Lebensraum*. He spoke of the 'yellow peril'.[7] Germany by then was already intruding in China, and a German colony appeared on the shores of a magnificent harbour to the east of Peking. The port, Tsingtao, still has an impressive church with Gothic spire, almost as if a part of Cologne had been moved to the Yellow Sea. But the idea of a yellow peril was not a belated response to the stirrings in Japan and China: the idea long preceded the actual peril, if peril there was.

In Russia the philosopher and poet, Vladimir Solovyev, also warned of the coming power of China. Born near Moscow in 1853, he became a close friend of the novelist Dostoievsky and is said to be the original of Alyosha Karamazov in the famous novel. Possessing faith in progress for much of his life, Solovyev passed through spiritual turmoil in the early 1890s and began to turn against the west's materialism and what he saw as spiritual impoverishment. Nervous about the fate of the west, he had the claustrophobic feeling that other peoples were pressing around Europe. In 1894 his poem *Panmongolism* depicted Russia falling to the Mongolian hordes. A following book, *The Justification of the Good*, again foresaw a great clash between east and west, with Russia in the frontline. In 1900, his final book, *War, Progress, and the End of History* centred on a discussion between five Russians who met in the French Riviera. One of the five expressed Solovyev's firm verdict that 'progress – a visible and accelerated progress – is always a symptom of the end.' Today *The Great Soviet Encyclopedia* does not mention his fear of the yellow peril, preferring to note that in his last years he had 'frequent premonitions of catastrophe'.[8]

Even inhabitants of the spacious United States began to feel hemmed in. In 1893, at a conference of American historians in Chicago, Frederick Jackson Turner argued that the special characteristics of American society had been shaped by the inland frontier, by those ever-moving regions where generations of Americans had experienced 'the simplicity of primitive society.' Turner argued that Americans were a special people because, compared to Europeans, they had been shaped more by Nature and less by the cities:

> The frontier is the line of most rapid and effective Americanization. The wilderness masters the colonist. It finds him a European in dress, industries, tools, modes of travel, and thought. It takes him from the railroad car and puts him in the birch canoe. It strips off the garments of civilization and arrays him in the hunting shirt and the moccasin. It puts him in the log cabin of the Cherokee and Iroquois and runs an Indian palisade around him. Before long he has gone to planting Indian corn and plowing with a sharp stick; he shouts the war cry and takes the scalp in orthodox Indian fashion. In short, at the frontier the environment is at first too strong for the man. He must accept the conditions which it furnishes, or perish, and so he fits himself into the Indian clearings and follows the Indian trails.[9]

As the American colonists transformed the wilderness, they themselves were transformed by the experience. Eventually they emphasised individual freedom and initiative, democracy and equality, because such qualities enabled them to succeeed in an environment that was at first so difficult. Turner suggested that the finest qualities of Americans stemmed from the frontier, and for a generation his interpretation dominated the writing of American history.

Turner seemed like a Darwinian apostle of progress, who had found his true home in the humanities rather than sciences. He even explained that 'this progress from savage conditions' was an ideal topic for the evolutionist to investigate. But when he is read more closely his is the more cautious mood of the 1890s and not the earlier mood of optimism. He had the fear, common in that decade, that the European peoples had thrived through expansion, and that in the United States especially the long era of abundant land was coming to an end. 'The Western wilds, from the Alleghanies to the Pacific, constituted the richest free gift that was ever spread out before civilised man', wrote Turner in the *Atlantic Monthly* in 1903. 'Never again can such an opportunity come to the sons of men.'[10] He predicted that profound changes would come when America's internal frontier was closed, and perhaps social tension would increase when there was no longer the safety valve of abundant land for the discontented. In 1896 he predicted that America's enormous 'energies of expansion' would be diverted to the building of a fine navy and an outward-looking foreign policy, and two years later the United States did venture outwards with a war that captured Cuba and the Philippines from the Spanish.

A Life and Death Question

After 1850 the name of Malthus and his arguments were heard in Europe with less awe or reverence. Between 1850 and 1890 grain increasingly flowed across the Atlantic from the plains of the United States, and grain flowed from the plains of south Russia to the port of Odessa and so to the cities of western Europe, while in the 1870s the first frozen meat arrived from the Americas. Likewise, Australia's sheep so multiplied in number that it became the largest wool producer in the world, thus enabling large areas of Europe to grow grain for people in place of grass and other fodder for livestock. In Europe scientific farming methods used the land more effectively, and the imported fertilisers – guano from Peru and nitrates from Chile – improved the fertility of the soil, as did the sulphate of ammonia that was a by-product of the gasworks which illuminated the cities. The breeding of larger livestock and more prolific plants and the increasing preference for growing potatoes in the cold north and maize in the warm south of Europe all added to the output of food without increasing the requirement of labour and land.[11] Who knows what the Reverend Thomas Malthus would have thought of this abundance which his original iron law had decreed as unlikely?

For almost half a century the fears of a world food shortage were voiced less often in Europe, and then, almost at the end of the century, those ideas were reborn. Probably the point has not previously been made, but it can be offered with some confidence. Fears of a global scarcity of food and other raw materials tend to emerge at a certain angle of the seesaw; they tend to be felt when people are beginning to doubt the ability of science and technology to solve urgent problems.

Whereas Malthus was a clergyman with a deep sense of original sin, his successor in the 1890s could almost be called one of the new generation of clergymen: he was a scientist with a willingness to prophesy. The new Malthus, Sir William Crookes, thought a scientist was an apprentice of God, his task being to learn the mysteries of the universe which God had created. The son of a London tailor, Crookes had risen quickly to become a brilliant physicist. He investigated psychic phenomena and the idea of telepathy, for many physicists were then fascinated by the idea that silent messages could be sent from the dead to the living, and he also was the discoverer of the new element of thallium, a soft white metal. One of the early investigators of radioactivity, he was fascinated by the research of Röntgen in Germany and the Curies in France, and in 1898 he boldly announced that the energy stored 'by uranium and other heavy atoms only awaits the touch of the magic wand of Science to enable the Twentieth Century to cast into the shade the marvels of the Nineteenth.' Here in flowery words was a confident forecast of nuclear energy.[12]

Sir William Crookes made his predictions of a possible scarcity of nutritious food when he was president of the British Association for the Advancement of Science, possibly the leading science forum in the world. Speaking at Bristol to what he flatteringly described as a brilliant audience, he explained the facts of food. He did not, so far as I can see, even mention Malthus. No past authority had to be called upon by a scientist with the towering reputation of Sir William Crookes.

Carefully – to avoid creating shock – he announced that what he said would be boring. He then proceeded to shock his listeners to the marrow bone:

> My chief subject is of interest to the whole world – to every race – to every human being. It is of urgent importance today, and it is a life and death question for generations to come. I mean the question of Food supply. Many of my statements you may think are of the alarmist order; certainly they are depressing, but they are founded on stubborn facts. They show that England and all civilised nations stand in deadly peril of not having enough to eat.

The deadly peril was that the world's wheat-eaters were increasing quickly, but the output of wheat was not increasing. The wheat left in granaries, silos and flour mills at the commencement of each annual harvest was small. The world's wheat eaters now depended entirely on the harvest of the current year, and if that should fail, there would be a scarcity of bread.

For too long, argued Crookes, Europeans had expected that the United States and Russia would produce for them ever-increasing harvests simply by ploughing more acres. Everyone had become 'accustomed to look upon the vast plains of other wheat-growing countries as inexhaustible granaries'. Crookes suggested, however, that the day would come when no more of the world's land could be devoted to wheat. The United States was the world's largest wheat exporter but its own population was so increasing that within a generation it would eat all its own wheat and, trying to import more, would scramble for a 'lion's share' of the surplus produce of other countries. Russia was the other large wheat exporter – Odessa rivalled Chicago as the world's busiest wheat ports – but the peasants in Russia were multiplying. The day would come when the now-hungry

Russian peasants would eat the grain which their landlords and merchants now shipped away. While his prediction on Russia proved correct, his prediction on the United States, Canada and many other grain producers was to prove wrong.

There was a potential solution – to provide more nitrogen as fertiliser for the wheatfields and so increase the yield from each acre. Crookes did not know whether that nitrogen would be found. He did point out that England squandered nitrogen by draining its sewage into the sea, 'an unspeakable waste' of fertiliser. Moreover every gun fired by every nation in peace and war was a waste of nitrogen because its ammunition consisted of saltpetre or nitrate which could have been used as fertiliser on wheat farms. There was potentially a solution, the fixation of the nitrogen in the air and the making of artificial nitrogen. Crookes hoped that a practical process might someday be devised.[13] Ten years later an ingenious process was devised by the brilliant German, Fritz Haber, and it was to make nitrogen for munitions and fertilisers in the First World War when the blockade prevented Germany from importing raw nitrates from Chile.

Nitrates appeared to be as important to his world as petrol is to ours. Chile, then the main producer of nitrates, was equivalent to our world's Middle East, and had a dominance in producing nitrates which the Middle East has not attained in oil. In Crookes' day a procession of sailing ships carried the nitrate around Cape Horn to Europe where it was the favoured fertiliser for wheat and also vital in making explosives. But the supply of nitrate, according to Crookes' estimates, would last no more than fifty years at the present rate of mining and even fewer years if the pace of mining was increased. A world shortage of nitrates, he hinted, would be more devastating than a shortage of coal.

His warning should be seen as a landmark in the history of global predictions. Whereas in the eighteenth century the English and Chinese Malthuses had predicted a recurring shortage of food, Crookes added something new. His was probably the first well-argued warning of a global shortage of a crucial mineral. It is true that back in 1865 the English economist W. S. Jevons had argued in his book *The Coal Question* that England's material progress would be impeded seriously by 'the probable exhaustion of our coal mines'; but he was writing only of England, not of the world, and his warning was pointing a whole century ahead.[14] It is a sign of the pressures subduing those predictions which are out of step with the times – Jevons was pessimistic in an optimistic decade – that for a full year his clear and vigorous warning aroused no public interest.

In compensation, Crookes predicted that Central Africa and Brazil and other tropical lands, growing two or three crops annually on the same soil, could become large suppliers of rice, maize and tropical foods to Europe and North America. Such food would be valuable but in Crookes' opinion the tropical foods were inferior to wheat, and wheat was grown largely in the world's temperate zones. Sir William was emphatic that 'the accumulated experience of civilised mankind has set wheat apart as the fit and proper food for the development of muscle and brains.' Crookes imbibed that powerful and rising idea that European peoples were superior to others. His argument was not racist but environmental, for he argued that the European peoples had had the good fortune to be reared on the finest foods. Take away their wheaten bread and they would cease to dominate a world in which they were outnumbered. That was the crux of his warning: unless the nitrogen scarcity could be overcome, 'the great Caucasian race will cease to be foremost in the world, and will be squeezed out of existence by races to whom wheaten bread is not the staff of life.' While Malthus had no place in Crookes' address, the skeleton of Malthus is there. The old ceiling on food supplies had been lifted but population was again rising towards that new ceiling and might – in Crookes' view – press against it.

Why Malthus was Reborn

Why did such a powerful warning of scarcity make its appearance after some forty years of confidence in Europe? It should be said that a vague warning of the long-term possibility of famine is always justified, for there will always be a risk to the world's food supplies. A freak combination of events which, in successive years, drastically reduces the world's harvests must cause severe distress, whether in the nineteenth or the twenty-first century. Crookes was therefore speaking a piece of common sense that is too easily forgotten. He was also reminding his audience that the European peoples' supply of food had been multiplied in the last fifty years partly because the new world had supplied them with wheat for the first time.

It is not enough to explain Crookes' warning by pointing out the logic and evidence on his side. An equally powerful case could have been made that his conclusions were erroneous at that time. He was writing during an amazing increase in the European world's ability to feed itself and that increase in fact was far from over. A valid case for optimism could therefore have equally been made. Moreover he was making his prediction after an unusual decline in the real price of grain, and therefore it was possible that a higher price for wheat in the next decades might lead to the planting of even more wheat in many lands, thus easing any potential shortage of grain.[15]

It is reasonable to suggest that he was influenced by the increasing caution that was evident by the 1890s, a mood which made many thinkers interpret more soberly the very evidence which would have stimulated their confidence only twenty years previously. His speech was also a warning to his own nation as well as to European peoples. By 1898, international relations were less cordial, and the period of relative peace that had reigned since 1871 was now ending. From our favoured position we can see, even more clearly than Crookes might have glimpsed, that the long peace was almost over. Knowing that England grew only one quarter of the wheat she ate, he wondered what would happen if a European war broke out. It was pointless for England to own the most powerful navy that the world had seen if her homeland could be quickly starved into submission by economic sanctions or by a successful enemy attack on one vital sea lane. For an island importing most of its food, wheat was as strategic as big guns: indeed in a brief aside Crookes spoke of 'wheat as munitions of war'. Other things being equal, Malthusian fears in the 1890s were more likely to be voiced by nations that imported grain – by a patriotic Englishman or German rather than by a patriotic citizen of Russia, the United States, Austria-Hungary, France and other nations which grew most of their own food. In essence, global fears can partly be the expression of national fears. Equally, global optimism is sometimes the subtle projection of a major nation's own optimism.

Crookes' speech was like an explosion of Chilian saltpetre. His pithier sentences were telegraphed to newspapers around the world, and he followed up his speech with a book, *The*

Wheat Problem. His message, scoffed at by some, persuaded many during the following decade. Samuel Wadham, a Cambridge undergraduate, was persuaded indirectly by Crookes' predictions to study agriculture in the belief that the world would need more and more wheat.[16] Eventually, Wadham went to Australia where he was a leading agricultural scientist in 1931 which in effect was Crookes' doomsday year, his '1984'. Ironically the world then had a glut of wheat, and much of Sir Samuel Wadham's public career was devoted to finding ways of propping up farmers who could not find enough people to eat their wheat.

Soon after Crookes made his prediction, a few other scientists held up a warning finger rarely to be seen a generation earlier. In 1905, Nathaniel Southgate Shaler who had been professor of geology at Harvard for three decades, criticised the rapid depletion of the earth's resources. He warned that if the leading nations were not careful they would exhaust their best deposits of coal and iron – the main sources of industrial power – and thus leave China and north-east Asia with a virtual monopoly of those minerals, enabling them eventually to master the world.[17]

In the modern history of pessimism and optimism there is a pattern in the way in which intellectuals and businessmen express alarm or jubilation about the world's potential supply of food and minerals. Mineral resources are not exact global quantities that can easily be measured. They are mercurial, and their known tonnage increases rapidly when new technology – whether of production or transport – is applied to them, and the tonnage known to exist actually declines when the existing technology changes little, because the minerals are mined more rapidly than new reserves are discovered. When Crookes and Shaler said the world's resources were visibly limited and might become scarce in measurable time, they were forgetting that new techniques had dramatically increased the output of grain and minerals in their own lifetime and thereby created resources which did not previously exist. Even Crookes, who had considerable faith in science as a problem-solver, showed the new caution by pinning an undue urgency on the invention of a synthetic fertiliser when in fact the world's supply of grain could equally be enhanced by the direct and indirect effects of a wide variety of other major and minor inventions, whether the devising of more productive strains of wheat, the diversion of land from wool-growing to wheat-growing, the invention of artificial fibres, the provision of cheaper transport or the use of nitrogenous grasses on fallow wheatlands. Likewise, new technology can in a dozen ways increase the world's output of most minerals. Scarcity is usually the trigger for productive new ideas, for scarcity increases prices which in turn channel investment and mental energy into discovering and producing the commodities which have become scarce. Crookes the physicist and Shaler the geologist were precursors of The Club of Rome, and significantly that club was to flourish when the seesaw returned some seventy years later to the position it had held during the era of Crookes and Shaler.

6 Temple of The Wild

In the 1890s there slowly grew a reaction against the sunny cult of progress and the worship of the wonderful god of science.[1] Felt by an influential minority, the new mood forced the majority to sit up and listen. The mood affected the social sciences and the arts and their attitude to the modern and primitive, and so it slowly pushed the seesaw towards a new angle.

The Paint of Leisure

While calm reason was normally seen as the hallmark of western civilisation, the wild emotions were seen as the hallmark of primitive societies. Accordingly the height of optimism in England, its special home, had been marked by a suspicion of intense emotion: the emotions had to be battened down, like the hatches of a small ship preparing to face a storm. So much of the poetry and painting of the period from the 1840s to the 1870s, whether in England or Germany, had been sentimental and tame, the false emotions being deemed safer than the genuine emotions. By the 1890s, however, emotion and intuition were returning to favour in intellectual and artistic circles. The rational was now challenged by the mystical, and the scientific was challenged by art.[2]

France, the leader in western painting in the second half of the nineteenth century, foreshadowed the new cultural climate. Its impressionist painters led the swing away from the celebration of material civilisation to the savouring of the everyday trifle and the fleeting impression. They eventually abandoned the realism of mid-century art, which Professor Nikolaus Pevsner has argued was the artistic equivalent of those milestones in science and technology, '*The Origin of Species* and the Crystal Palace'.[3] While not an historian of art, I notice how often the French impressionists – compared to their predecessors – eschewed material and political milestones of their nation in favour of the everyday happenings and especially those of leisure: the ballet dancers, the reclining naked women, people promenading in the streets, spectators in a private box at the theatre, the young mother with sprays of flowers perched on her wide hat, and the life out of doors. Leisure was usually seen as a hallmark of a primitive society, just as mental and physical energy were seen as a hallmark of an industrial society, and so the impressionists' emphasis on leisure signified a new scale of values. Nature was also their theme, and at their first exhibition in Paris in 1874, Monet's painting – entitled 'Impression, Sunrise' – provided unintentionally the name for this new school of painters. Four years later the average price for a Monet painting was a mere seven English pounds, and there was still little sign that impressionism would be the seedbed of vital movements in painting in the twentieth century.[4]

Distant paradises now beckoned French painters. Paul Gauguin, younger than the first impressionists, used to go each summer to Brittany for its wildness and primitiveness, but in 1887 he went instead to the tropical island of Martinique in the West Indies, and four years later he went to Tahiti, for the tropics hold a special attraction whenever there is a revival of respect for the noble savage. Back in France his young friend, Vincent van Gogh, found Japanese art even more stimulating, and in his French town he could write, 'I feel I am in Japan'.[5] Van Gogh died in 1890, before the new mood became intense, but he expressed that quickening reaction against the gospel of inevitable progress and the god of material success: 'It always strikes me, and it is very peculiar, that whenever we see the image of indescribable and unutterable desolation – of loneliness, poverty, and misery, the end and extreme of things – the thought of God comes into one's mind.'[6] Man, he implied, sat proudly on the seesaw and was too short-sighted to notice that God was sitting on the humble end.

France was the spearhead of the new artistic movement in favour of the primitive, the experimental and the wild. Significantly Henri Matisse and his friends were in 1905 christened the Fauvists, which meant 'wild animals'; George Braque was briefly a Fauvist before becoming a Cubist. Likewise, Cubism was influenced by French primitive painters, especially Henri Rousseau, but also by Negro sculpture from the French colonies in west Africa. Picasso caught those African mask-like faces in the very first Cubist painting, *Les demoiselles d'Avignon*, in 1907. The primitive stared out from many of the Cubist paintings, and the novelist Marcel Proust was reminded of prehistoric cave-painters when he first saw Picasso's paintings.[7] A similar fascination with earlier and exotic cultures could be heard in the more advanced music of the era: in Richard Strauss's opera *Salome* of 1905 and in Stravinsky's *The Rite of Spring*, where, to the shock of many in the audience, a prehistoric man was sacrificed to Spring.[8] The same fascination with exotic music was seen in that Afro-American music called *jazz* which in New Orleans was beginning to attract white Americans in 1900.

In western Europe the Russian ballet with its sensuality and animal vitality became a cult almost overnight, storming Paris in 1909 and London in 1911. Is it altogether surprising that when the jungle was creeping back into favour, and when Nijinsky was leaping like an animal, Tarzan should be born? Edgar Rice Burrough's book *Tarzan of the Apes*, the story of an English child reared by beasts, was the best seller of 1914.

Hermann Hesse, the young German novelist and poet, went in 1911 to Southern Asia, hoping like Gauguin to find a paradise. In Ceylon and India he looked for a new Garden of Eden because the ancient garden in Europe was overcrowded and unrecognisable. On a rainy morning Hesse climbed the highest mountain in Ceylon and saw, looking down through rolling mists, an expanse of mountains, ravines and valleys; and in his elation he thought to himself that this was the place where, according to ancient legend, paradise existed. Then in this strangely Nordic climate and landscape, he realised that Asia's rice fields and ivory palaces, easy riches and childlike people did not quite make him feel at home. Here was nature's showplace, a lush paradise to which he did not belong:

> But we ourselves are different, we are strangers here and without citizenship. We have long since lost paradise, and the new one we hope to have and to build will not be found on the equator or on warm Eastern seas: it lies within us and in our own northlandic culture.[9]

The new unease towards Europe's civilisation was also visible in the work of the German-Swiss painter, Paul Klee. In 1902, in his early twenties, he marvelled at a visiting Japanese dancer and 'the primitive consciousness' that pervaded his troupe. In Munich two years later, watching the Chinese acrobats and their vitality, he drily noted that real Asians 'are better than English aesthetes tired of Europe'. Many of Klee's own pen and ink drawings, lithographs and paintings pivot on the puppet and marionette, for there was a remarkable revival of puppetry in central Europe at the start of this century.[10] Likewise, Igor Stravinsky was influenced by the revival of puppetry when composing his musical plays, *Renard* and *The Soldier's Wife*. It is understandable that the puppet should become intellectually fashionable at a time when so many people felt that mankind – far from being in command – was at the mercy of strings operated by forces they could not see.

Most of these cultural landmarks would have been implausible in the high noon of optimism a generation earlier. Then the human body was despised but now it was enthroned by the Russian Ballet, puppetry, Tarzan, Gauguin, the first Cubist paintings and New Orleans jazz. In some influential circles such words as 'naked', 'savage', 'jungle', and 'wilderness' were no longer despised and were creeping back to favour.

New Thinkers: The Mask Snatchers

To a new group of thinkers beginning to have their say in Europe, the word 'future' was a large question mark. Nearly all these thinkers could be called social scientists but their science did not necessarily offer a blueprint for the advancement of mankind. They included Bergson and Sorel and Durkheim of France, Croce and Pareto of Italy, such giants in psychology as the Austrian Freud and the Swiss Jung, and Max Weber and Hesse of Germany. Sigmund Freud and Vilfredo Pareto were the oldest and they were already in their twenties when the youngest, the novelist Hermann Hesse, was born in 1877.[11] These thinkers rediscovered the irrational in man and the power of the unconscious. Curious to see the real face of society, they pulled off the mask and saw a troubled face.

The historian, H. Stuart Hughes, who gathered together this group of thinkers in a fascinating book called *Consciousness and Society*, observed that many of them sharpened their teeth on Marxist thought but were eventually to react against the Marxist faith that society was developing according to a pre-ordained pattern. Nearly all, wrote Hughes, shared a sense of doom or uncertainty and could not share the faith in progress. Thus Pareto said it was no more scientific to believe in democracy or socialism – the new gods – than to believe in the old God; he thought parliamentary democracy was a façade, while Georges Sorel thought it was simply bribery on a national scale. To Emile Durkheim, suicide was one sign of the crisis in industrial civilisation. To Sorel, industrial conflict was a useful and even a healing ritual and an assertion of solidarity in a society that was now impersonal and authoritarian.[12] To the philosopher Henri Bergson, man was strongly influenced by instinct and so it was naïve to place too much faith in his reasoning powers, while for similar reasons Sorel thought compulsory education was silly. Most of the new thinkers were not Christian in the orthodox sense but were conscious of the bonding and the adhesion which society had lost through the decline of a common Christian faith.

Sigmund Freud, of all these thinkers, perhaps had the most influence on people's perceptions of their own civilisation, though his influence even in Europe was not strong until the 1920s. A citizen of the Austro-Hungarian empire, he had come from a small town less thn 20 miles from Germany and less than 80 from Russia. After studying medicine in Vienna, he became fascinated by the way in which another doctor's patient was able to recall, under hypnosis, painful memories, and to gain emotional relief from the recollection. In 1896, after more than a decade of interest in this phenomenon, Freud coined the word 'psycho-analysis' for the technique in which mentally troubled patients could recover and divulge hidden memories. He explored the processes by which people stored in their 'unconscious mind' a variety of thoughts and wishes, and how their dreams expressed these repressed thoughts. He thus began to undermine the belief that most mental processes were conscious and orderly, and that man was rational. He believed that something primeval and even savage still remained in mankind. As a penalty Freud himself was depicted as a savage by many intellectuals in Germany, England and the USA in the pre-war years. He, it was said, was the 'Viennese libertine' and sex-mad Bohemian whose wild theories were an incitement to moral licence and savagery.

Freud helped to lift that taboo – so strong in the heyday of progress – against the discussing of sex. In the new and looser morality, Freud helped to uncouple the mental links which had viewed sex and the savage as similar, and which had viewed nakedness and primitiveness as the pitiful characteristics of the savage. Once Freud saw the sexual drive as central to understanding human behaviour, especially guilt and repression, he could no longer extol Europe's civilisation with such confidence.

In sensing the weaknesses of modern civilisation, several new thinkers shared something with those who had fallen in love with Tahiti more than a century earlier. Indeed, the brilliant French educationalist Emile Durkheim echoed Captain Cook and Sir Joseph Banks in his view that a consumer society manufactured more needs that it could easily satisfy. Seeing the hustling, restless consumer society each day at Bordeaux, Durkheim placed his finger on the economic and social problem of his own time by suggesting that man's appetites were 'insatiable'. He saw discontent even in those French families who, living amongst a dozen new gadgets, had an unparalleled ability to satisfy their material needs compared to citizens of any previous civilisation. He decided that what 'is necessary for them to be content is not that they have more or less, but that they be convinced that they do not have the right to have more'.

The changing attitude to western civilisation was accompanied by a new interest in primitive societies. Whereas primitive societies had been arrogantly seen in the heyday of optimism, as a gauge of how far mankind had advanced, they were now inspected more humbly as evidence of how little mankind had advanced on certain fronts. Durkheim's book of 1912, *The Elementary Forms of Religious Life*, stressed the value of religion and myth in binding a society together and subtly offered France a lesson culled from the totemism of the Arunta Aboriginals of central Australia.

In the European lands, most educated people still believed in progress. Socialists especially hoped that their secular paradise would be created. Trusting the wisdom and unity of the working class, many influential socialists believed that if a major war should erupt, the working class would refuse to fight and thus bring the war to a halt. The other powerful secular ideology was liberalism and it was also optimistic. Its followers believed that by the free and increasing flow of knowledge, by the free flow of trade, by the granting of the vote to every adult, people would become wiser and would express their wisdom through the parliaments. Freedom, knowledge and individual responsibility would transform the world, and indeed they believed the increasing contact between nations, and the declining power of absolute monarchs, would make war virtually impossible in the civilised world. The outbreak of the First World War in August 1914 and the fervour with which it was fought was a profound shock to liberals and socialists alike.

The war was less of a surprise to Freud, Bergson and those innovative thinkers who, emerging in the previous quarter century, warned that man was emotional as well as rational and unpredictable as well as predictable. Freud showed the logic of that message in a private letter he wrote to a normally optimistic friend on 25 November 1914, in the fourth month of the war, when the roll of dead soldiers was already exceeding nearly all predictions:

> I do not doubt that mankind will survive even this war, but I know for certain that for me and my contemporaries the world will never again be a happy place. It is too hideous. And the saddest thing about it is that it is exactly the way we should have expected people to behave from our knowledge of psycho-analysis. Because of this attitude to mankind I have never been able to agree with your blithe optimism. My secret conclusion has always been: since we can only regard the highest present civilisation as burdened with an enormous hypocrisy, it follows that we are organically unfitted for it.[14]

A Diversion: The Long Cord of Pessimism

The swing away from faith in western civilisation and confidence in its future was more pronounced in continental Europe than in England, the United States and the British Empire. Even in the heyday of optimism, a strand of pessimism was vivid in Germany which, in the general to and fro of ideas, held the commanding position in the western world. Even in England many scholars acknowledged Germany's primacy, and James Anthony Froude in the early 1880s invested all his own authority as one of the masters of English history and English prose in this simple tribute to German intellectuals: 'We go to them for poetry, philosophy, criticism, theology.'[15] These German fields of excellence, encompassing the spiritual and mental rather than the material conditions of mankind, were more likely to harbour pessimism than were engineering, natural history and those rather empirical fields in which Britain led the world.

Arthur Schopenhauer was the black prince of pessimism in Germany in the first half of the nineteenth century, and his influence overlapped the mid-century optimism. Born in 1788, he was brought up by his father, a Danzig banker, to be a disciple of Voltaire and optimism but – like Malthus in a similar situation – the young Schopenhauer rebelled against his father and eventually his philosophy of optimism. There was something nervous and splenetic in Schopenhauer, and there was also a loneliness and independence. He despised the growing national pride and the new democracy, for he believed that they would foster blindness and greed – defects common in mankind. He admired geniuses and saints but found them hard to find. He admired – a frequent attitude in those who disliked their own civilisation – ways of thinking in places he had never seen, and he saw merit in Buddhism. Only in the last fifteen years of his life did his views become influential in Germany, and they were popular when he died in 1860, a year in which optimism was flying high in the English-speaking world.

Germany, more than England, continued to nurture prophets of pessimism. Nine years after Schopenhauer's death, a young officer invalided from the artillery, Eduard von Hartmann, produced his first book, the vigorously argued *Philosophy of the Unconscious*. Achieving sales that would have been impossible for such an abstract book in the English-speaking world, it reached its tenth edition in 1890. Von Hartmann in his many books argued that people should not seek happiness, which was impossible to find, but should rather pursue a moral code which would make them less unhappy than they would otherwise have been. He did not accept the belief that material progress would bring happiness and even virtue. It is noteworthy that von Hartmann's main work was fifteen years old before it was translated into English, while Schopenhauer's main work was not translated into English until the mid 1880s when he was long dead.[16]

Germany had a special capacity to nurture young intellectuals who, whenever the west proclaimed its own progress, raised their hands in disbelief at the idea that progress was really under way. Friedrich Nietzsche, who from 1869 to 1879 was professor of Greek at the University of Basle, began to criticise the faith in progress, the smugness of bourgeois values, and the sentimentalism of liberalism. How could Europeans talk of progress when in his opinion they were 'vastly inferior', to the European of the Renaissance and inferior to the ancient Greek? He wrote harshly of democracy, mediocrity, conventional culture and, not least, Christianity with its emphasis on humility and compassion. He denounced the pursuit of happiness: he denounced all ideas that were fashionable, and as pessimism had a certain fashion he denounced it too, along with the dour prophet Schopenhauer, whom he had once revered. He also hoped that through intense struggle and violence and the Darwinian law, mankind might redeem itself in the distant future. He argued that if the strength and adaptability of the human race were to depend on the survival of the fittest, why should European nations in their misguided compassion permit the weak and unfit and the imbeciles to survive?[17] In the light of Darwin's theory, a welfare state was more damaging to the human race than a long war.

Nietzsche became insane in 1889. A precursor of the new intellectual mood, he was read more and more as that mood set in. The young man who was to assassinate the Archduke Ferdinand at Sarajevo and so trigger the First World War was fond of reciting a verse by Nietzsche: 'Insatiable as flame, I burn and consume myself.' Oswald Spengler, in his book that summed up the new mood, *The Decline of the West*, named Goethe and Nietzsche as those 'to whom I owe practically everything.' And Adolf Hitler and the German novelist, Thomas Mann, though opponents, were each to find inspiration in the fiery words of Nietzsche.

Just as in Germany the black side of the tree was usually seen and analysed, so in Russia several famous novelists who were not yet popular in the west protested against intellectual optimism. Dostoevsky's *Notes from Underground* (1864) and Tolstoy's *Death of Ivan Ilyich* (1884) with their social subversiveness, were far ahead of their time. Early in our own century, hopelessness or nothingness became a frequent note in novels in the English language. Thomas Hardy had already showed it in *Tess*; and in 1902 Joseph Conrad's *Heart of Darkness*, recalling a steamboat voyage in the Belgian Congo, expressed unease towards civilisation; and a year later Henry James's *The Beast in the Jungle* was notable less because a main character in the novel was a failure than because, in the words of one modern critic, he was 'distinctively undistinguished'.[18]

The feelings of doubt about European civilisation were advancing along a wide front embracing economics, politics, culture, leisure and even manners and costumes. We have forgotten how wide was that front in 1900. The emphasis on combative, emotional and primal values probably helped to make the First World War a little more likely, simply because war as an activity was no longer so derided. The new mood also helped to make the war less of a turning point than we usually acknowledge: the turning had already been made, late in the previous century.

The Boy Scout and Niagara: New Symbols

A new respect for nature affected cities. Each western city had numerous residents who took pride in their small gardens and pot plants, their cat and dog, their stroll in the public park and the occasional outing to beach or forest, but there were now signs, not visible during the heyday of progress, of a longing for a closer touch with nature.

England again experienced the idea that in the past lay a golden rural age which should be summoned back. Raymond Williams in his fascinating book, *The Country and the City*, suggests that this longing for a lost rural happiness was most intense in three short and distinct periods: the late sixteenth and early seventeenth centuries, the late eighteenth and early nineteenth centuries, and lastly the 1890s and the first years of our century.[19] To this third period of rural nostalgia belongs the concept of the Garden City, of which Letchworth in England was the first. Its originator, Ebenezer Howard, was a clerk who, influenced by Edward Bellamy's Utopian views, decided that people in crowded cities would be happier and healthier if they could live in an isolated garden city. The nature movement also influenced interior design and architecture where Art Nouveau briefly had its vogue. Rebelling against the classical style and favouring rather the curved lines of the body or the leaf, Art Nouveau proclaimed the creed: 'Curved is the line of beauty'. The Tassel House, a terrace house designed in Brussels in 1893 by Victor Horta, pioneered this style of architecture; and photographs of its entrance hall and stairway convey the impression of a tropical garden and grotto, an effect created largely by the trunk-like columns and the vine-like brackets. This architecture has been likened to the music of Debussy and Delius.

How could the young people of the packed cities be enticed back to Nature? A German youth movement emerged about 1900, largely as a protest against the softening effect of civilisation, and each summer it sent a procession of young people to the forests with an ideology in their rucksacks. Known as the *Wandervogel*, it challenged middle-income conformity, manners, and propriety but challenged them in an almost bourgeois way. Its members preferred the hand-made crafts to those that were made in the factory; they valued a simple rural life rather than the 'great sea of urban housing'; they preferred the small group to the large; and they argued that the old courtesies and clothing thwarted communication and impaired freedom. In 1910, Hans Breuer, editing a book of German songs for the guitar,[20] set out the goals and history of this movement in words that could almost have come from the hippy 1960s: 'redeem yourself, take a hiking-staff, go outside the city and seek the human identity which you have lost, your plain, simple and natural self'.

The western world was now so webbed by contacts that a youth movement in one nation was not likely to exist in isolation. In 1905 in the United States, Daniel C. Beard began the Boy Pioneers, and in 1907 in England the Boy Scouts emerged.

The founder of the Boy Scouts, General Robert Baden-Powell, had spent some of his childhood holidays on England in camping expeditions and in forays in natural history, and when he became an army officer he acquired the arts – now associated more with guerrilla warfare – of studying minutely the landscape and watching secretly the movements of the enemy. His first book, *Reconnaissance and Scouting*, arose from his experience in the army in India, and was published in 1884 when he was barely twenty-seven. In the 1890s he served with the British army in Africa; and in the bloodless expedition against the Ashanti he first wore that cowboy hat which eventually became the headgear of the scouting movement, and in quelling an uprising by the Matabele he showed such skill as a night-scout that he earned the title of 'Impeesa', the wolf that never slept. In 1900 Baden-Powell became a national hero as the defender of the South African town of Mafeking, which had been besieged for seven months by the Boers, and that military reputation enabled him in 1907 to win support in England for his new civilian Boy Scouts. Their first camp was on an island in Poole Harbour and there, far from the great plains of the new world, they imitated explorers and frontiersmen. As a financier was needed for the scouting movement, a young newspaper magnate, Cyril Pearson, stepped in, having already shown his feeling for nature by financing the Fresh Air Fund which sent poor city children on holidays to the English countryside.

The Boy Scouts – and later the Girl Guides and Sea Scouts and that Great War invention, the Wolf Cubs – multiplied with astonishing speed in many lands. In the United States the Boy Scouts became the strongest of all youth movements. Part of their appeal was that they enthroned nature in a nation intensely conscious of what it had gained from the pioneering experience and what it had recently lost with the waning of the pioneer. The best-selling handbook called *Boy Scouts of America* insisted in 1910 that there had been a golden age, about a century ago, when every American boy lived in Nature's pocket, that the golden age could be recaptured, and that a new grasp of woodcraft and hunting would compensate the young for what they had lost in the growth of the New Yorks and Chicagos. In the eyes of Baden-Powell the white races were superior and had a special mission and responsibility for which his boy scouts must be prepared. He had faith in his civilisation but not confidence in it: his motto was 'Be Prepared'.

Most of the Protestant churches gave strong support to the new Scouts. In many lands the politicians also smiled, for Scouts were acquiring the skills and physical fitness which would be vital if a major war should come. Tense diplomatic relations in Europe, re-arming and the spread of compulsory military training were part of an atmosphere in which struggle and physical strength were lauded, for war was no longer dismissed as merely the plaything of savages.[21]

The Boy Scouts are not the perfect example of the growing respect for nature. They did not see harmony in nature and they viewed a primitive society as inferior, but they believed that civilisation would be endangered if it did not renew contact with nature and learn from the wolf's and the savage's skills of survival. Civilisation, in their eyes, would be in peril if it ignored the lessons and bushcraft of the hunters. The Boy Scouts occupied an unusual position, with a foot at both ends of the seesaw, but their concern for nature was an attitude which a mass movement could not have held a generation earlier.

North America now showed a sympathy for wilderness which was unimaginable in the days of the Californian gold rushes. In 1906 a heated environmental controversy, the first in the United States, centred on the question of saving the Niagara Falls from the demands of hydro-electric power companies and the proponents of improved navigation on the Great Lakes and St. Lawrence waterways. After a campaign led by the *Ladies Home Journal*, Congress in July 1906 protected the Falls for a crucial three years.[22] A few years later the city of San Francisco sought a site for a large reservoir and chose the narrow, high-walled valley of Hetch Hetchy in the Sierra Mountains, and the subsequent protests showed how powerful the sympathy for wilderness had become. In 1913 the debate became nation-wide, and as often was to occur in controversies on wildernesses, the enthusiasm for retaining the wilderness was more ardent amongst those who lived far from the disputed site. The contest to preserve that valley in the Sierra was lost, but hundreds of Americans had proclaimed the merits of nature as well as the competing claims of their own civilisation.[23]

John Muir, a Scot reared in Wisconsin, was the celebrated defender of the American wilderness. For him the mountains and tall trees, waterfalls and snow exceeded in beauty any architecture of man: 'no temple made with hands can compare with Yosemite', he wrote. From Yosemite the valley of Hetch Hetchy lay only twenty miles away, and in Muir's words it would equally be an act of sacrilege to convert a cathedral into a water-container as to dam Hetch Hetchy. To be in that valley in summer, standing waist deep in grasses and flowers and watching the tall pines swaying dreamily in the breeze and a waterfall flowing like a silver scarf down the granite cliff, was to know that 'no holier temple has ever been consecrated by the heart of man.'[24]

Meanwhile in bookshops and libraries, the public showed a new fascination with the primitive and the wild. Popular writers who are now remembered mainly as apologists for British rule in Africa and India were in fact divided in their attitudes; and Rider Haggard often displayed sympathy for black Africans, and Rudyard Kipling saw magic in the road to Mandalay. In America in 1903, Jack London produced his galloping best seller about a domesticated dog that had run wild, *The Call of the*

Wild, and it caught the imagination more than did his opposite
story of a wolf which became a family dog. Jack London himself
sat comfortably on the new angle of the seesaw, for he saw the
Innuit Indians who hunted in cold Alaska as superior in material
well-being to the average worker in an English factory.[25]

The denunciation of city life became a theme of some of the
best American writers, and Upton Sinclair in 1905 called the
novel that he set around the meatworks of Chicago, *The Jungle*.
Sinclair was a socialist and a believer in ultimate progress, and
in many ways he despised Nature. His regret, unlike many of
his contemporaries, was that man was still too close to Nature,
and he described Chicago as a wilderness in which human
beings fought 'like wolves in a pit'. In this period many others
who hated cities tended to seek a haven in socialism or in
Nature.

In the lending libraries another kind of book had a vogue
such as it has not experienced since. This was the Utopia, a
secular book describing an imaginary land, sometimes halcyon
or sometimes frightening. It was not a practical blueprint of
social reform but an indirect criticism of the existing way of life
and of the direction in which it could be heading. Whether W. H.
Hudson's *A Crystal Age* (1887) or William Morris's *News from
Nowhere* (1891), such books were rather an assessment of modern
civilisation and where it might or should be heading. In Britain
the Utopian novel, uncommon in the 1870s, reached a peak in
the period between 1890 and 1909, after which the decline was
rapid.[26] It would be rash to generalise too much about such a
diverse branch of fiction but there is evidence that the Utopian
books of the 1860s were more optimistic and more in love with
technology while the typical Utopian books of the 1890s were
more apprehensive of the future.

The Flesh of Fashion

Those people receptive to new ideas were not necessarily most
receptive to new fashions in clothes, and yet the new fashions in
clothes and ideas late in the nineteenth century had more in
common with each other than one might expect. Clothes are dis-
posable and perishable, and so their owners can quickly respond
to the latest ideas in fashion. Moreover, as fashions in clothing

reflect, directly or indirectly, prevailing attitudes to nakedness, they are also a mirror of changing viewpoints towards primitive peoples – the savage so often being associated in European minds with the lustful and the naked.

The heyday of progress had been marked by diligence in publicly concealing the female body, so that prudery and progress walked hand in hand – in gloved hand. The prevailing fashion concealed much of the female form, and in the 1850s and 1860s women's clothes resembled more a tent than a garment when the crinoline, a fashion from France, became popular. A large round cage of whalebone and cord, the crinoline helped to carry the weight of the three or four petticoats and heavy dress of velvet or plush. It also concealed the hip, thighs and legs so effectively that the wearer from the waist down was like a walking wigwam. Then the crinoline fell from fashion, and the shape of the female body could almost be guessed until the half-cage or bustle briefly reappeared in high fashion in the late 1880s.

In those very years, curiously, came a drastic change in the attitude to woman's bare flesh. A little flesh, just a sliver of it, was exposed in the new sleeveless evening gown in 1886. As a woman normally wore black gloves that covered the forearm, only four or five inches of her upper arm and shoulders were exposed by the new sleeveless gown, but that was enough naked flesh to constitute a revolution. More daring fashions were to appear. Hitherto the hips and buttocks were concealed by corsets but in 1907 a French fashion house designed new costumes and displayed them on young mannequins who not only pranced about in bare feet but were said to be 'in their skin', for they wore no corset. The women's bathing dresses moved in the same free and easy direction, and those women dwelling on the heights of fashion now revealed a little flesh, mostly below the knees, when they waded into the shallow sea.

The last two decades of the nineteenth century are a turning point in women's fashions: indeed, in the opinion of some historians there is no change of similar importance in the sixty years before and the sixty years afterwards. A more relaxed attitude towards nakedness is a vital part of this turning point, and the attitude dovetails with a new intellectual sympathy towards the sensual and the emotional.

These turning points in female fashions were accompanied by changes in men's dress. By the 1890s the tweeds, rough in

feel and decidedly plebeian by traditional standards, were becoming the country wear for gentlemen and for style-conscious
Bohemians. Most tweeds were not woven by machines in British
textile factories but woven by hand in Scotland, thus signalling
a swing in glamour from the factory towards the rural cottage.
Likewise, in formal dress, the white tie and black tails of formal
evening wear were challenged in New York in 1886 at a fashionable country club called Tuxedo Park where a dandy appeared
in a novel dinner jacket and black tie. Nowadays we think of
the tuxedo as formal wear but it was informality itself when it
crossed the Atlantic to England. Changes in evening fashion
are rare, and it is remarkable that on opposite sides of the
Atlantic two revolutionary styles – the sleeveless evening dress
and the tuxedo – should appear at the same time.

One other female fashion offers a message. By the 1870s the
formal bonnets and hats were heavily trimmed with fruits,
flowers, leaves, birds and the brightest paraphernalia of nature.
The fad increased, and the fashionable wore dresses that carried
birds on the shoulder and butterflies and moths wired to the front,
while their hats were decorated with birds and insects. Some
hats were so decorated with doves' wings they foreshowed the
aerodrome. In 1895 it was estimated that 20 or 30 million dead
birds were imported annually into the British Isles to satisfy the
demands of the hat makers. 'Never before', wrote the Cunning-
tons in their *Handbook of English Costume in the Nineteenth
Century*, 'had a woman of fashion so closely resembled a per-
ambulating Zoological Garden.' I hesitate to suggest too confidently why the female hat was converted into an aviary or a
bird mortuary but the evidence suggests that the change partly
mirrored the revival of romanticism and a quickening interest
in nature. And yet nature was so caged and captive that these
hats were also a symbol of man's and woman's domineering
attitude towards nature.[27]

The Return of the Native

As the discontent with civilisation became wider, alternative
ways of life could no longer be dismissed. The savage might not
be noble but he was often able, and his society was now seen as
more complex and more logical in its rules and rituals than had

previously been thought. A few scholars even wondered whether primitive society might not offer a cure for some of the sores and wounds they believed they now detected in European civilisation. Whereas primitive societies had once been despised, now they were sometimes seen as repositories of wisdom and were examined more in their own terms than by the yardsticks of Paris and Manchester. Here was an upset in the tournament of ideas.

When Lubbock, Tylor and the evolutionists had examined what they understood to be the implements and economic life of simple societies they understandably disparaged them. Such societies were weak in equipment and hardware; their spears were pitiful compared to the machine gun; their canoes were puny alongside the steamships; and their huts were abject compared to the cathedrals. In fact the primitive societies depended much more on skills – many of them impressive – than on hardware but this truth was rarely appreciated. Only the hardware could be placed effectively on display in the European museums: moreover, only the hardware and not the vanished skills were found in archaeological excavations. Above all, mechanical ingenuity was the hallmark of the optimistic middle years of the nineteenth century. People living in the cities of the era of steam knew that inventions were changing daily life more quickly than ever before, and in their pride they judged a primitive society by that mechanical criterion in which they themselves so excelled.[28] How could the Fuegians or the nomads of inland Africa and Australia, owning not even a wheel, survive such a comparison?

By the 1890s many Europeans, now more accustomed to mechanical and material progress, were less inclined to despise the primitive economic order. Moreover, conscious of some of the social weaknesses of their own cities, they were more willing to see merits in the social organisation of primitive societies. Some of the anthropologists emerging from the 1890s onwards found the social structure of primitive societies more complex than the economic life. Once the social relationships, the myriad of obligations, and detailed marriage patterns of a few African and Australian tribes were examined, they could not easily be dismissed as uncomplicated and simple.

Sir James Frazer's *The Golden Bough* was a monument to this more sympathetic era. Thirteen volumes, carrying the subtitle of 'A Study in Magic and Religion', they seemed initially to provide a simple step-ladder view of man's history. In explaining how early man thought about the world, Sir James Frazer saw three clear steps or stages: the magical, the religious, and the scientific. He speculated that eventually there might come a fourth stage, a 'totally different way of looking at the phenomena – of registering the shadows on the screen – of which we in this generation can form no idea.'

Frazer travelled in his eighty two years no further than from Glasgow to Greece but he became a post office for myths and stories from all over the world. He arranged them and interpreted them, often with an unusual willingness to see primitive people as capable of subtle reasoning. Differing from the extreme Darwinians of several decades previously, he saw mankind's first stage as admirable rather than abject. In his opening volume in 1890 he proclaimed that 'most of the fundamental truths of our civilisation we owe to our savage forefathers.' While Frazer applauded order and reason, his sympathy for the primitive imagination was passed on to his readers; and Kipling, D. H. Lawrence, A. E. Housman, Ezra Pound and T. S. Eliot were amongst the creative writers who, as it were, plucked fruit from *The Golden Bough*. The talented New York man of letters, Lionel Trilling, even argued that this was perhaps the book of the nineteenth century which had most influence on literature.[29] It set the compass for a new epoch of writing which, no longer expecting man's journey to be one of progress and rationality, turned more to the unconscious, the mysterious, the intuitive, the ecstatic, the unpredictable, and to the view that women and men were not necessarily the mistresses and masters of their fate. The long human journey, as so many of the influential new writings were to imply, was more an experiencing and a wandering than a triumphant pilgrimage.

A Cat Among Pigeons

The study of ancient peoples was attracting scholars from diverse fields. While Frazer was a classical scholar who turned to social anthropology, Franz Boas, the commanding figure in the new American anthropology, was originally a physicist and mathematician. After studying physics in his native Germany, Boas turned to geography. Initially intrigued by the influence of environment on man, he ended on the opposite side as one who believed that man's mental and cultural processes largely conditioned his environment. He thus escaped from the determinism, the idea of inevitability, which was often part of the thinking of the disciples of Spencer, Huxley, Darwin, Lubbock, and Engels and other scholars living in the high noon of progress.

Boas was in his mid twenties when he first saw what few continental European scholars had seen, a so-called primitive society. It was in 1883, and he observed with surprise that the Eskimos on Baffin Island adapted skilfully to their bleak environment whereas he had assumed that they would be its captives. He admired much in their life and in some ways compared them favourably to civilised Europeans. He was already on the path towards the idea that every society had its merits and weaknesses, depending on one's point of view, and that it was difficult to arrange them neatly on the ladder of progress. Emigrating from Germany to the United States in 1887, he began to formulate his view that culture was more influential than climate, resources and terrain in shaping a people and their ways of thinking. For long he was little known in England and France but he was influential in America through his writings and through those talented students whom he taught during his forty years at Columbia University. Thus the young Margaret Mead went to Samoa mainly to test his bold theory that it was culture – and not physiology – which determined the sexual and social attitudes of adolescent girls.[30]

Professor Boas challenged a central idea of the cult of progress: the certainty that primitive peoples had a precarious standard of living compared to the modern citizen of Toronto and Copenhagen. Studying the Kwakiutl, the American Indians who lived on Vancouver Island, he noted that while they did not tend gardens they seemed to live well, capturing large sea mammals and trapping the migratory salmon. Boas marvelled at their huge fish feasts known as potlatches, and the generosity with which fish were given to friends and neighbours and even enemies. For forty five years, in a shelf full of writings, Boas described the Indians and the high standard of living they won from a kindly Nature. In the words of Professor Marvin Harris, 'Boas's account of the potlatch has probably been the most influential ethnographic description ever published.'[31] Like the

parable of Christ and the fishes in the New Testament, it was
to young anthropologists a compelling sermon about the good
fortune of those tribes living close to Nature. The wheel of anthropology had turned far since the day of Lubbock and Tylor.

After Boas died, scholars would look again at the potlatch.
They would critically note that he had not been studying a
truly primitive society but rather a society dislocated for nearly
a century by the Europeans, by the decline of the Indian population, and by the resultant surplus of salmon. Even when Boas
had first witnessed the potlatch, the local Indians were living in
a seasonal abundance that probably contrasted with the scarcities
of their ancestors. Anthropologists in the 1960s were to interpret
the potlatch not as a sign of normal abundance but as an attempt
to cope with seasonal surpluses of fish which had become a
veritable glut in the European abnormal times.

In a field of investigation where the surviving evidence was
sparse, somersaults could easily occur in interpreting the flimsy
evidence. The question – how did a primitive people actually
live? – was not easily answered. The first outsiders inevitably
saw the simple way of life through their own telescopic lens.
Nor could they know whether they were looking at a primitive
society in a normal or abnormal year. Often they set eyes on a
primitive society just after its population had been tragically
cut back by new diseases and by the other dislocations that
came with the conquering newcomers.

Boas was a cat prowling amongst the elderly pigeons of the
previous generation. The fact that in science he had been reared
as a pigeon made him all the more skilled in pouncing. He denied
that one society was necessarily superior to another, and that
modern societies were innately superior to primitive ones. His
idea of a primitive prosperity quietly challenged the belief that
modern science alone could provide bread and meat for every
dinner table. He also began, just before the First World War, to
question the increasing emphasis on race. At that time many
Darwinians and a host of people who hardly knew the name of
Darwin believed that Europeans were a superior race and that
their superiority was the outcome of a long conditioning by
particular environments. They believed that their own racial
superiority, the product of countless ages, could not be overtaken
in the space of centuries, if ever it could be overtaken. They
saw race and culture and language, whether of Germany and

France, as interlocked facets of the same process of conditioning. Against these ideas, Boas rebelled. He insisted that all races were equal. It was simply that their cultures were different, and culture was man-made and ultimately changeable.

Boas's creed came in part from his own Jewish background and an instinctive desire to fight the increasing anti-semitism in Europe by insisting that 'race' – whatever that meant – hardly mattered. His viewpoint also came from the combative nature of intellectual life with its legitimate tendency to correct and surpass those who had come before. Of his intellectual mentors in Germany he owed much to Theodor Waitz, who at the University of Marburg in 1859 produced an influential book *Concerning the Unity of Mankind* and Rudolf Virchow, the leading German anthropologist who at Munich in 1877 rebelled against Darwin.[32] In the vocabulary of these scholars progress was spelled without a capital P. Strange to say, there are few alert biographies of intellectuals, especially of their mental and emotional processes, and we can only guess at the mix of forces stirring the mind of Franz Boas.

I know of no Boas in the earlier noonday of progress, except perhaps Maclay the Russian, and he was hardly influential in his lifetime. But in the reaction during the 1890s, the Boas viewpoint became more frequent in anthropology. Those who believed in the progress of mankind were now jostled by the relativists and other doubters. One extreme position was tending to provoke another, and American anthropology, as one historian observed was trapped on 'the treadmill of oscillation between extremes of polar theoretical distinctions.'[33]

Australia: One End of the Seesaw

While attitudes to primitive peoples changed in every European land the speed of change differed from country to country. In Australia, the ladder theory of mankind persisted, with little opposition, into the twentieth century. The British settlers in Australia were proud, as so many new peoples are, of how quickly they had transformed the land. In contrast, the black Aboriginals of Australia seemed to be dying out; and were thus unfit according to the iron rule of the 'survival of the fittest'. In Australia in 1900 the seesaw of Nature and civilisation showed little sign of that tilt already perceptible in western Europe and North America.

As the land which illustrated the far end of the seesaw, Australia replaced Tierra del Fuego, for the mahogany-coloured people of the far tip of South America were seen as too sullied by civilisation to serve any longer as a human laboratory. The next favourite, Tasmania, could no longer be called upon because the last of the Aboriginal Tasmanians was dead and the part-Aboriginals who survived, no longer followed even a semblance of their old way of life.* The erasing of those regions from the list gave to Australia a new importance because, in the words of Malinowski, it was 'the best-known and the most extensive country inhabited by a very primitive race'. Far from the settled coastal districts of Australia were regions, some in the desert and some on the tropical coasts, where the Aboriginal's way of life was relatively untouched.

The two path-finding anthropologists in Australia at the turn of the century were Baldwin Spencer, professor of biology at the University of Melbourne, and F. J. Gillen who had begun to learn one of the Aboriginal languages while supervising the telegraph line that crossed the dry centre of the continent. They were probably the first to organise expeditions specifically to study the Aboriginals, and they lived close to tribes who were still leading their traditional life. Spencer had an early movie camera and, producing one of the first ethnographic films, to be made in the field, he screened his scenes of 'savage life' to an audience of 2,000 in the Melbourne town hall on 7 July 1902.[34] His own mental equipment, however, is now seen, whether rightly or wrongly, as more antiquated than his ancient camera. To his credit he felt an urgent need, for science's sake, to collect all he could about the lives and beliefs of the Aboriginals before they vanished from the earth, but the thought that they had much to teach the people of Melbourne did not enter his head. In his eyes – he was a follower of Darwin – the Aboriginals sat in the infant classroom in the school of mankind, and that room was about to be closed, having served its purpose in the evolutionary scheme.

* The last full Aboriginal in Tasmania, the woman Trucanini, died in 1876. Two others, it is said, lived on Kangaroo Island, off the coast of South Australia, until 1888.

Baldwin Spencer admired the Aboriginals' powers of observation, their willingness to share, and their sense of fun, but after some twenty years of intermittently observing them, he concluded that they were driven by superstition and were mentally 'about the level of a child who has little control over his feelings and is liable to give way to violent fits of temper.'[35] Nonetheless he was one of the first to see merits in the x-ray art of the Arnhem-landers on the far northern coast of Australia and he relished the imaginative quality of their paintings which depicted the backbone, heart, alimentary canal and general anatomy of fish and animals in colours of black and brown, white and red. He gave his praise to primitive art about the same time as Picasso and a few other Europeans were admiring and half-imitating West African art.

The information gathered in Australia was increasingly filtered and reinterpreted by scholars in Europe. It permeated Sir James Frazer's *The Golden Bough*, and it fired the young Polish physicist, Bronislaw Malinowski, who was later to revolutionise anthropology. Whereas the old Aboriginal societies had been used during the high noon of progress as simple signposts showing how far civilised man had travelled in his triumph, now on occasions they were signposts with a different message. Not long before the First World War, two famous European scholars – Durkheim and Freud – saw the Aboriginals as providing insights or guidance for a civilised Europe which now had symptoms of sickness. That the Europe of compulsory education, big cities, fast trains, a sense of civic order and many other tangible virtues should be seeking social insight from the wandering, illiterate, far-away Aboriginals was a sign of a faltering confidence in western civilisation.[36]

The Two Faces of Progress

Imagine somebody who was born in 1814, who became interested in ideas and fashions when a mere teenager, knew the ideas her grandparents held long before she was born, watched intensely all the successive changes in mood in the western world in the nineteenth century, and was still alive at the start of 1914. Such a centenarian would have concluded that the intellectual mood of the world was capable of changing even more rapidly than material conditions changed, and that in certain circles an extreme hope or gloom towards the future arrived more rapidly than the visible messages of the real world – wars, famines, peace, epidemics – would logically allow. At certain times, hopes rose and hopes fell in a way not easily explained.

Many of the crucial changes were two-headed, pointing equally to a glorious or dangerous future. Thus, the web of railways could increase contact between nations and seemingly promote peace, but the same railways, when a war commenced, could rush troops and munitions to the battlefront in such numbers that a day's casualties were prodigious. Compulsory education could teach children to show goodwill to a rival nation, but it also taught children to withdraw their goodwill. The opening of new grainlands across the world, and the invention of steamships, could lead Europe from the door of starvation but they also enabled the feeding of huge armies and the maintaining of them in the field long after a scarcity of food would, in other conditions, have ended the war. Those wonderful factories that made steam engines for locomotives and ships also made machine guns and heavy artillery. Democracy gave self-esteem to people but it also conferred on the mass of people the responsibility for making decisions in areas where they so far had scant experience. Thus during the First World War, public opinion in the western democracies was probably even more influential than the will-power of soldiers in forcing the fighting to continue at a time when peace was becoming feasible.

Every advantage has its corresponding disadvantage and every liability has its asset. The new instruments – whether machines or organisations – were capable of uplifting as well as downgrading people. They were capable of bringing virtue or evil, peace or war. Professor John Passmore wrote wisely in his book *The Perfectibility of Man*: 'It is one thing to say that the mechanisms for perfecting men are now at our disposal; it is quite another thing to say that they will in fact be used in order to perfect men.'[37] Progress is two faced: so is decline and degeneration.

Early in this century many who analysed the state of the world felt bewildered by the sheer speed of change. In the dilemma they tended to be emphatic, either reaffirming their faith in progress or raising serious doubts about the direction the world was taking. Of the lofty English names of the high noon of progress, Darwin died in 1882 but Wallace and Spencer lived into our century and could give their verdict on the changing world. Wallace kept faith, marvelling at the achievements of his lifetime, and in a book called *The Wonderful Century* he listed the thirty-nine fundamental advances in the history of mankind and noted that all but fifteen of them came in the nineteenth century.[35] But Herbert Spencer was no longer so definite about the progress of civilisation and he expressed his views with more humility than in the past. Now that European nations occupied the far ends of the earth, their treatment of the weak was often offensive, and Spencer lamented that whereas bow-and-arrow tribes merely took a life for a life, the 'so-called civilised' nations were now taking many lives for a life. 'To my thinking the nations which call themselves civilised are no better than white savages', wrote Spencer in 1896.[39]

An intriguing epitaph on the era was pronounced in the final narrative volume of the long *Cambridge Modern History*, published in 1910. Surveying Europe's world since the end of the Franco-Prussian War in 1871, it concluded that the four decades had witnessed remarkable material progress in most nations but not noticeable moral progress. Nor was the atmosphere as exuberant as it had been at the start of 'The Latest Age':

> The age has been prosaic and unromantic; the enthusiasm for the mechanical and scientific triumphs of the early Victorian period has somewhat faded; the belief in constitutional government and universal education as a remedy for all political and social evils has been shaken; the blots on our economic and moral order have been relentlessly drawn to light: self-complacency is no longer fashionable; it is more popular to decry than to praise the world in which we live.[40]

One fact shouts out for our attention. The 'latest age' was emphatically an age of achievement and yet was not viewed as such. In many ways it achieved as much as the previous forty years, and perhaps more so than any block of forty years going back century after century, but perhaps some of its spokesmen were disappointed simply because they had not achieved as much in the forty years as they had originally hoped. It is fair to suggest that the return to nature, and the more cautious hopes placed in science, and in European civilisation, reflected in part the disappointment of the optimists, just as the previous optimism had arisen partly because earlier expectations of

Europe's future, proving too cautious, had been ultimately disowned.

In essence this minority mood, so vigorous at the turn of the century, was wary of technology and European civilisation, sympathetic towards nature, and intrigued by the primitive and its connotations of the savage and the naked, the magical and the emotional. The mood carried the intuition that the limits of the earth had been reached and that mankind would soon be hemmed in. Though not as influential as it was to become in the 1960s, it disputed strenuously the idea of endless progress.

7 Cold and White: The Role of Climate and Race

We understand more about the seesaw if we see that it carried, as hidden passengers, notions of racial as well as cultural superiority. Thus, those intellectuals who marvelled at the achievements of Europe were inclined to claim that Europeans were innately more energetic and resourceful than other races. Some went further and argued that a powerful reason for the superiority of Europeans was an invigorating climate. From that climate stemmed energy, ingenuity and organising ability; and since the climate was unlikely to be changed, the inventiveness and energy of the inhabitants were unlikely to sag. Here in this simple theory was a wonderful assurance of continual progress. Not surprisingly the zenith of this theory was that heyday of faith in progress in the nineteenth century.

Climate: A Secret of Greatness

The wide-ranging French scholar, Charles Montesquieu, set the fashion for attributing a strong influence to climate. In 1748 he argued that a difference in climates could explain why one nation's outlook and institutions differed from another's.[1] Almost a century later, climate was emphasised even more by the English historian Sir Archibald Alison who produced two large volumes – 1000 pages in all – on *The Principles of Population, and Their Connection with Human Happiness*. He saw the cold northern climate as the source of energy and valour throughout human history. In his eyes, ancient history was marked by 'the eternal struggle between the energy of the north and the riches of the south', and he saw the triumphs of earlier civilisations as the fruits of emigrant races rolling down from the north. He deplored modern Italy and Spain because of their 'state of degeneracy and languor', and said that they could be regenerated only by a new race from the north. The Mahometans seemed to be an exception to this rule, but they had come from those harsh deserts which were as bracing as the poor soil and harsh climate of northern Europe. Alison insisted that the 'tide of conquest has in every age rolled from the north to the south; from the regions of poverty to those of wealth; from the seats of hardihood and courage to those of effeminacy and corruption'.[2] A view not unlike Alison's was spread in Germany by Gustav Klemm in ten volumes in the years 1843–52. In Europe, wrote Klemm, the active races originated in the north and the passive in the south.

The climatic theory flourished in the 1850s. Henry Thomas Buckle, one of the boldest historians of that era, explained that whereas the early civilisations – Egypt and China – arose from the rich soils and warm climate and the bounty of nature, the later and superior civilisations of western Europe sprang from the energy generated by a cold climate. Buckle thought England and Germany had the ideal climates but in contrast Norway and Sweden were too cold for year-round work and Spain and Portugal too hot. He observed that those four countries are 'all remarkable for a certain instability and fickleness of character'.[3] Likewise, Francis Galton, the famous geneticist, predicted in 1887 that the British living in the unnatural heat of India would be saved from racial degeneration only by new technology: they would be able 'to sustain their constitutional vigour' for many generations only by freely using artificial ice and by refrigerated air. Alfred Marshall, writing in 1890 the most influential economics book of his generation, emphasised the role of climate. He thought that the 'lands of frost and snow' were the real cradles of energy and that a warm climate and luxury were the enemies of civilisation; and therefore Britain could lose India if her officials living there were sapped of vitality, the secret of Britain's power.[4] Not all agreed with him; and Herbert Spencer, the celebrated sociologist, curtly dismissed a cold bracing climate as one of the historical keys to national greatness.

Historians continued to see merit in the idea that Europe's climate was vital in making it successful. One of England's best known scholars, H. A. L. Fisher, produced in 1936 a massive *History of Europe* which was so esteemed that in the next ten years it was reprinted eleven times and was even reprinted in the Second World War during a famine of printing paper. Fisher believed that the patterns seen in history were largely imaginary:

One intellectual excitement has, however, been denied me. Men wiser and more learned than I have discerned in history a plot, a rhythm, a predetermined pattern. These harmonies are concealed from me.

And yet he did see one pattern – the role of climate. Unlike his fellow historians who placed emphasis on the coldness of northern Europe, Fisher thought a temperate climate helped to make Europe so prosperous and such a shaper of the world. It was the changeability as well as the lack of extremes of heat and cold which provided 'the most favourable physiological stimulus to activity and enterprise'. In depicting climatic effects, he included the refreshing influence of the sea whose long arms – the Baltic and Mediterranean – plunged far into the landmass of Europe. Fisher excluded the vast Russian interior from his enthusiasm, and insisted that 'the cold, dark winters of the Russian plain are inimical to the spirit of activity, vigilance, and criticism.' His broad interpretation of the influence of climate – suspect as it might seem today – won wide support.[5]

The Danger of the Midday Sun

The white topi became a symbol of the British belief that a white man was essentially a child of a bracingly cold climate and so was lethargic and fragile in the tropics. It so happened that in India the pith of the leguminous swamp plant, the sola, was ideal for making a white hat, and increasing numbers of British soldiers and officials wore it. Initially called sola topi (topi was the Hindi word for hat) the phrase probably entered the English language in the 1820s, when the white topi or pith helmet was about to become the everyday sign of British authority in India as well as a protection against the insidious rays of the sun.[6] According to the book *Health in Hot Countries*, published in 1904, no substance was as effective as the pith of the Indian rush 'in intercepting the peculiar vibrations which cause sunstroke' in Asia and Africa. While the hat protected the head, only common sense could protect the hands, and that common sense was eagerly imparted to travellers in the tropics, as the English writer Peter Fleming recalled:

On a morning in December, 1931, I stook on the deck of a steamer watching the scurry on the dockside as she was warped into her berth at Rangoon. The deck was covered, but the

midday sun (which at that season in Burma is not particularly
fierce) struck down on the rail in front of me. On this rail rested
my hands . . . I felt a tap on the shoulder and, turning, was
gently admonished by an elderly fellow-passenger. I was, he
explained, needlessly exposing myself to danger.[7]

Faith in the white pith helmet remained high, and the enter-
tainer Noel Coward indirectly honoured it with his verse of
1936; 'Mad dogs and Englishmen go out in the midday sun'.
Fortunately the Englishman had his white topi to protect him
from the effects of his madness which, the song proclaimed, the
Chinese and Hindus avoided.

Then almost overnight the white topi was questioned. The
Japanese invaded south-east Asia, and in the green vegetation
of the tropics the white gleaming helmet served as a target.
Attracting a fiercer enemy than the sun, the Japanese sniper, it
was replaced by a camouflaged hat or steel helmet. When the
war was over, those Englishmen who walked hatless beneath
the hot sun no longer seemed to suffer from the peculiar vibrations that were once said to cause sunstroke.

The theory that a cold climate or at least a cold winter made
for national greatness was reassuring to the British, Germans,
Scandinavians, Russians, Austro-Hungarians and also to every
big city in North America, except perhaps San Francisco, which
a century ago could hardly be called a big city, and of course
New Orleans and the cities of the deep south. As Britain, Germany and the United States were the main industrial nations,
and as France and Germany and Russia and Austro-Hungary
were believed to have the strongest armies of the world, and as
Britain ruled the seas, there was never a time in modern history
when a cold climate seemed, in theory, to produce such decisive
results. The theory, nonetheless, ran into difficulties if its theorists looked back to the earlier might of Spain and Portugal and
other warm lands, or to the greatness of ancient Greece and
Rome and the earlier Middle Eastern civilisations. In the nineteenth century, as now, many theorists thought the present was
unique and so, unwisely, they saw no point in studying the
past.

In warm parts of the new world in which Europeans had
settled, the climate theory was not consoling. New settlers in
South Africa, sub-tropical America and the warmer parts of

Australia were often warned that a warm climate promoted sloth and that only with effort could they overcome the inertia. Cricket matches between Australia and England were looked upon as a test of whether a warm climate had weakened young men whose ancestors had come from the British Isles; and when in 1873–74 the Australians defeated the visiting English cricket team, *The Sydney Morning Herald* was jubilant, exclaiming that the British blood obviously 'has not yet been thinned by the heat of Australian summers'.[8] The fact that the team fresh from England might not yet have been acclimatised to the heat and so have played poorly was an alternative explanation of their defeat, but to Australian nationalists that was not a palatable explanation.

In the mind of many intellectuals, Europe's pride and sense of mission rested not only on its technology and culture but also on its geography. These ideas went hand in hand. To show disdain for the heat was not only to disapprove of the culture of tropical peoples but to justify Europe's guardianship over them. The climatic theory at the peak of its influence subtly extolled the power of man over nature, for the dynamic nations were those which rose above the difficulties of their environment. The theory also dethroned nature because the tropics, with their luxuriant vegetation and two or three crops a year, were the very showplace of nature and yet there mankind seemed the most lethargic.

How sharply the seesaw had tilted in the century since the Noble Savage! Then those Europeans who had extolled Nature and the simple life saw no virtues in a chilling climate. Captain Cook envied the Australian Aboriginals partly because they lived in a warm and fine climate and breathed a wholesome and unpolluted air. Joseph Banks similarly admired the balmy climate of Tahiti. A love of Nature and of a warm climate seemed to go hand in hand, just as love of European civilisation and a bracing climate went hand in hand.

Since the Second World War the western world seems to have drastically altered its main attitude to climate. Few observers now regard – or dare to say so in public – a warm climate as leading to laziness and cultural degeneracy. We no longer see the tropics as so hazardous to live in, and indeed Australia, North America and Europe have recently experienced an internal migration of people from their colder to their warmer regions.

The latest text books on economics no longer have a chapter attributing the economic miracles of Germany, Japan and South Korea to a bracing climate.

It is easy to put forward convincing material reasons why our fear of hot climates has declined in the last one hundred years. Tropical medicine has improved the health of people in the tropics. We no longer do much hard manual work, and so a hot climate is less punishing. Likewise, air-conditioning and the refrigerator have eased daily life in the hot towns and provided a portable climate which can be carried anywhere in the world. Another important cause of the somersault in our attitude to climate is mental. Those who lauded the stimulating cold climate a century ago were really implying that their energetic and triumphant civilisation was imperishable, for the source of its greatness could not be removed. European intellectuals are no longer supremely confident of the merits of their own civilisation, and so they see no necessary relationship between a cold climate and national well-being.

Nakedness on the Seesaw

Attitudes to nakedness, as we have seen in an earlier chapter, also change. Nakedness tends to be in favour when nature and primitive societies are admired, and it was especially in favour at the turn of the century and, again, from the 1960s. In contrast during the mid-Victorian era, educated Europeans frowned, publicly at least, on the naked. Mid-Victorian prudery reflected not only religious views but also reflected a disdain for the savage. As the savage was out of favour, and as the savage in the popular imagination was naked, then nakedness was also out of favour. Nakedness was seen as the mark of people who not only had no morality but appeared to lack the simple skills and energy necessary for the making of clothes. Moreover the savage skin was black or brown, and that made the white skin of a northern European seem all the more precious and to be shaded at all costs from the sun.

Our attitudes to climate, nature and nakedness are partly mirrors of our confidence or lack of confidence in our own technological civilisation. Even cleanliness has a place on the seesaw. Thus in the heyday of their pride, western Europeans tended to despise not only the 'savages' but all other peoples of Asia and Africa as unclean, but they could hardly have made such comment a century earlier when they themselves were not so keen on washing. Indeed in 1770 those coast-inhabiting savages who were seen by European travellers as idyllic tended to be seen as clean: they could frequently wash themselves in the warm sea that lapped their villages. Traditionally, parts of Asia placed a higher value on cleanliness, and it was from colonial India that the British are said to have 'learned habits of personal cleanliness.'[9] It is reasonable to suggest that if in 1770 the Tahitians had been derided as filthy, the concept of the noble savage might have arisen less easily. The noble savage is, in part, an aesthetic concept.

Leaping forward a hundred years to the 1860s and 1870s, we find that cleanliness was more valued amongst European peoples. Soap was now used widely in the United States and was one of the first items to be heavily advertised.[10] Soap had already appeared in English and American slang, and to 'soap up' or 'soft-soap' was to flatter: it was about 1860 that Samuel Wilberforce, Bishop of Oxford, was christened Soapy Sam, a reference to his unctuous manner.[11] To be clean was becoming one of the accepted western virtues, and cleanliness and tidiness and personal order were naturally equated with law and order, in which the west saw itself as superior to other civilisations.

We can glimpse what travellers think of their own land by seeing what they criticise when they travel abroad. The uncleanliness of distant lands perturbed many European globe-trotters. Captain F. Burnaby, riding a horse across Asia Minor in 1877, frequently used the words 'dirty' and 'muddy' when describing the Anatolians and Kurds; and David Carnegie reported similarly on Australian Aboriginals he met in Western Australia in 1898; and Robert Jack, a geologist travelling overland from Shanghai to Burma, depicted the Chinese of the far interior as energetic but unclean in his book of 1904.[12] I have the strong impression that Europeans travelling in a strange land were now more conscious than ever before that cleanliness was a hallmark of their own civilisation. The English naval officer, J. G. Goodenough, was clearly in the new mainstream when he implied in 1875 that islanders in the New Hebrides lacked the glamour once seen in the Tahitians: 'Nothing can be much lower than these people; their houses are but 5 ft 6 in under the ridge pole and filthy.' He regretted that their faces were filthily smeared and that their desire for clothes did not extend beyond a coloured handkerchief.[13]

A variety of factors ranging from the price of soap to the skill of engineers who brought water to every big city, enabled Europeans to become cleaner. But a sense of superiority over backward lands also played a part in this new emphasis on cleanliness. Significantly, when a century later the seesaw stood at the opposite extreme, the young American followers of the counter-culture were to oppose what they saw as their own civilisation's hygienic tidiness by wearing tattered jeans, walking in bare feet, and priding themselves on their wild and unwashed hair.

Colour and Race

In this high peak of confidence, Europeans increasingly believed not only that they were superior in culture but also in race.* Biology – the soaring science and the celebrant of progress – had an obsession for classifying and categorising all living species including mankind. Darwin exemplified this new interest in race when he marvelled at the achievements of the Europeans but regretted that lesser peoples such as Negroes and Australian Aboriginals, being unable to cope in the terrible competition for survival, would soon vanish from the earth. Biology was believed to provide a new certainty to speculations about peoples and races. It provided an inevitability in its predictions of the human future. In an era where science was now reverenced as a new religion, the conclusions of Darwinian biology carried weight and were even credited with that most rare of abilities – the ability to predict. The emphasis on race was seen as simply a branch of the new cult of biology.

While pride in western civilisation was riding high, the proud tended to see their own kinsmen or race as possessing innate qualities that persisted from generation to generation. Likewise, in an earlier phase of optimism, some supporters of reason had

* The word 'race' is loose and has many meanings. The main meaning of the word – if there is a main meaning – has also changed drastically over the years. Some scholars argued that there is no such thing as 'race'; but if many people believe such a phenomenon exists it has to be taken into account, simply because their view of 'race' influences events.

seen innate virtues in European peoples and regretted that primitive peoples in the hot lands were incapable of acquiring those virtues. The famous Voltaire dismissed Negroes and Jews with a sweep of his hand and a pinch of half-baked evidence. The Enlightenment, quick to classify peoples and arrange them on a permanent ladder, tended to admire the ancient Greeks and Romans not only for their achievements but also for their racial qualities and especially their looks.[14] In contrast those who were disillusioned by their own civilisation could hardly see themselves as innately or racially superior. Worshipping the Noble Savage, they did so in the belief that he could be emulated, for all races were malleable.

Between the 1840s and the 1870s, assertions that certain races were innately superior to others were widely made in over-confident Europe. One of those assertions was to become basic to racial theories. That was the long *Essay on the Inequalities of the Human Races*, written by the French diplomat Joseph Arthur de Gobineau and published without fanfare in 1853 and not well known for perhaps another twenty years. He argued that one branch of mankind, the Aryan race, had provided all that was worthwhile in the Greek, Roman and later civilisations.[15] Much in Gobineau's argument was guesswork, much of his recounting of human history was fragile, but in Germany especially he found more and more followers.

Pride in race, especially in an Aryan race, was high in Europe in the second half of the nineteenth century. It would be surprising if it were not high, given Europe's advances during that half century. In that period of racial pride lived many of the finest thinkers of which the human race has record, and therefore we should in fairness be careful to place them in the context of their time, remembering that they had actually discovered certain of the insights by which we now harshly judge them.

The Cult of the Anglo-Saxons

Not all the white-skinned peoples were regarded as equally superior – some were less superior than others. In Germany, the British Isles, and the United States, numbers of thoughtful people began to insist that they were special people, being descendants of the settlers of the forests of north-western Europe.

They argued that they loved freedom and respected democracy because their Anglo-Saxon ancestors had been inculcated with those virtues during their hazardous life long ago in the forests of north-western Europe. The forest supposedly had the quality of encouraging independence just as certain tropical islands had given rise to a leisurely and idyllic way of life. For many Romantics in the early nineteenth century, the cold ocean or the dense forests of north-western Europe made people what they were, and even the Protestant religion was seen as the special product of environments specially favourable to the growth of liberty.[16] It did not matter that the theory was probably based more on wishful thinking than on historical fact. Some of today's most respected and scholarly theories may meet the same fate.

Again and again thoughtful writers, trying to explain the success of the Anglo-Saxon peoples as explorers, colonisers and conquerors, pointed to what they saw an innate qualities. 'Race' was the word they frequently used, and sometimes they used it too tightly (as in phrenology, that skull-measuring science of the 1820s) and sometimes too loosely, endowing it with as many meanings as people use today. Thus Commodore Perry, the American who in the 1850s virtually ended two centuries of Japanese isolation, envisaged a noble global mission for the Anglo-Saxon 'race' and especially the Americans.[17] He predicted that they would emigrate more and more to the west 'until they shall have brought within their mighty embrace multitudes of the islands of the great Pacific and placed the Saxon race upon the eastern shores of Asia'. Sir Charles Dilke, an extreme democrat by the standards of English politics, toured the United States, New Zealand, Australia and India as a young man in 1866 and 1867 and was fascinated by the success of the English-speaking peoples, attributing it primarily to their racial qualities. The long book he wrote about his travels is not arrogant but expresses an awesome pride in what he called 'the grandeur of our race' and the prospect that it might 'overspread' the earth.[18] He retained that pride a quarter of a century later, though by then he saw the Russians as challengers.

One of those who detected remarkable qualities in the people of the English-speaking lands and the 'Saxon heartland' of north western Europe was Cecil Rhodes, the young South African politician and mining millionaire. When his bequest in 1902 set up the Rhodes Scholarships to finance a host of young men who wished to study at Oxford University, they were specifically awarded only to residents of the British Empire, the United States and Germany.

In many intellectual circles in the United States, by the end of the century, the faith in Anglo-Saxon or Nordic superiority was deep. Sociologists and historians and politicians proclaimed it. A progressive senator announced that his people had a mission to carry civilisation to China and other lands of chaos and darkness: 'God has not been preparing the English-Speaking and Teutonic People for one thousand years for nothing. He has made us the master organisers to establish system where chaos reigns'.[19] In the mixture of reasons behind the Australian government's decision in 1901 to accept no immigrants from Asian lands, and the United States' decision in 1917 to prohibit illiterate immigrants and therefore most people from poorer lands, there lay not only the legitimate desire to preserve a culture and a standard of living but the less legitimate prejudice that certain European peoples had innately superior qualities.

The so-called Saxon world by 1850 had valid reasons why it should be delighted at its own achievements, and for the next half-century there were additional reasons why pride but not arrogance should grow. England, the United States and Germany continued to lead the world in most fields of science, in many of the arts and in the standard of well-being of their average citizen. By the end of 1870 there could be no dispute that Germany had the world's most powerful army and England the most powerful navy. While many citizens of these nations preened themselves, they could not yet see the dangers into which their new technology and pride would lead them. They were conscious only of the remarkable progress in recent years. Just as the ancient Jews, in their gloomiest years in exile, moulded a religion to explain their predicament and to give them heart for the future, so these European peoples in their unprecedented triumph also came to see themselves as a chosen people.

In emphasising blood and race or the special effects of the climate and forests as the basis of the supremacy, these nations were offering potentially dangerous interpretations of success. Such thinking precluded the possibility that the nations would decline. Moreover, it ignored the crucial fact that most of the previous civilisations of the Middle East and Europe had been the product of warm climates and had ruled or ignored the backward peoples from the chilly north west. A learned man writing the history of the world might well have asked himself why, until recent centuries, the north-west Europeans had achieved little compared to the peoples of the Mediterranean and the Middle East. Was it the same chill climate and the same enclosing forests, he might ask, which for long had impeded rather than stimulated the English and Germans?

It is easy to deride the super-confidence and sense of superiority within the English-speaking world late in the nineteenth century. The derision now comes from the typewriters of young sociologists, political scientists and historians who, in their sweeping condemnations, sometimes show that overbearing sense of superiority which they had initially set out to denounce. Admittedly, to criticise many of the spokesmen of the English-speaking world in the nineteenth century is appropriate. But to accuse whole nations of racism and to accuse a whole era of arrogance can be sweepingly unfair, especially if the accusers do not even try to explain why these people of the past held particular viewpoints.* We learn from history only if we try to be open minded. Otherwise we are likely to repeat many of the past's mistakes and especially those mistakes which we indignantly insist must never be repeated.

It is sometimes argued that Europeans who saw themselves as belonging to a superior race were really trying to justify or rationalise their increasing dominance over coloured peoples. It is true that the emphasis on superiority was often strong when the pursuit of new colonies was intense, but in some decades colonial expansion was not accompanied by a sense of racial superiority. In the first heyday of the Noble Savage, Britain and France were acquiring colonies, and in 1788 the British planted their first settlement on Australian shores in the belief that the Aboriginals, while different, were not inferior as human beings. Indeed the original plan was that Australia should be a multiracial colony with the men overwhelmingly from the British

---

* Some who sweepingly denounce the racial bias of a bygone era and everyone in that era are actually displaying the prejudice they profess to denounce. Similarly some who denounce their own nation as racist seem to be haters of their own people and culture and, in revenge, befriend people of other cultures. We are not yet accustomed to these new forms of racial prejudice, and in our puzzlement we even applaud them.

Isles and the women from New Caledonia and those South Pacific islands which Captain Cook had, significantly, named the Friendly Islands.[20] Likewise, in the second half of the nineteenth century some thinkers who adhered to racial theories and therefore should have theoretically supported the idea of imperial expansion actually opposed expansion. Gobineau himself did not wish France to expand her empire: that would increase the danger of the French marrying into 'lesser' peoples, thus propagating the racial mixture to which he attributed the fall of the Greek and Roman civilisations.[21]

Europe's confidence during the period from the 1840s to the 1870s was reflected in the unfortunate disdain for primitive people's but later the seesaw moved. The new thinkers of the 1890s, in assailing their own civilisation, increasingly saw merits in those primitive societies and peoples who had previously been disdained, and not least in their painting and music. Moreover those key thinkers who were losing faith in the west and its technology mostly believed that Europeans did not possess innate qualities which would be handed on from generation to generation. Professor C. H. Pearson, Sir William Crookes and other sober prophets of the 1890s could not, by definition, see an innate superiority in Europeans, because they were now fathoming the possibility that Europe's power would decline. Thus Pearson argued that the noontide of Europeans' inventiveness had probably ebbed, and that even in daily work their energy was lagging compared to the Chinese. In Pearson's eyes the Europeans still had special virtues, including a capacity to show mercy during warfare, but he believed that their mercy would ultimately impair their military supremacy. Likewise, Sir William Crookes, in predicting that Europeans would be weakened by a scarcity of high-quality grain, argued that they depended less on their inherited brain cells than on special food, and were therefore at the mercy of international factors beyond their control. While Pearson, Crookes and other prophets of the 1890s were in a minority, they showed how the extreme confidence of the previous generation could be logically turned on its head.

A few readers who in recent years have rediscovered Pearson's lost book, tell me that, contrary to my view, he places emphasis on racial factors by designating 'higher' and 'lower' races. And yet it is only fair to him to explain that he used the word *race*,

as most use it today, in a loose way and that he saw no characteristics and virtues as inborn. It is clear from *National Life and
Character* that the higher races in Pearson's eye are simply
those 'which are held to have attained the highest forms of
civilisation' – meaning law and order, institutions of self government, the Christian faith, and a respect for the Greek and Roman
classics and those 'letters and arts and charm of social manners
which we have inherited from the best times of the past'. In
short he used race in the sense in which we use culture.[22] Pearson
believed that the Chinese or Africans could adopt, if they wished,
the present characteristics of European civilisation. Challenging
the Darwinist idea that 'inferior' races would die out, he predicted that instead they would adapt and survive, and thus he
emphasised that they were not innately inferior. It was he who
made the memorable prophesy that Africa and Asia would be
welcomed as allies in Europe's quarrels, while their citizens would
'throng the English turf, or the salons of Paris' and marry into
European families.[23] When in 1893 these words were published,
it was unbelievable to most Europeans that the day would come
when a Muslim from the Middle East would own the fastest
horses of the English turf and an Italian woman would be
married to the prime minister of an independent India, but that
day has come.

Towards the very end of the nineteenth century, as Pearson
and Crookes and other forecasters revealed, there was a weakening of that confidence in the destiny of the European peoples
and their civilisation. Confidence was widespread but here and
there it was cracked. In art and the theatre and literature the
crack was deep by the 1890s and early 1900s.

A Surge of Anti-Semitism

An extreme faith in one's own civilisation tends to be marked
by notions of racial superiority; and when the faith declines,
there is a decline in the sense of innate superiority over other
peoples. If this is so, then is anti-semitism partly explained by
the seesaw?

During the heyday of faith in progress, anti-semitism in Europe
was not strident. By some measurements it was low, and in
England for eight of the twelve years between 1868 and 1880

the elected prime minister was Benjamin Disraeli, of Jewish origin. Similarly in Germany in the middle of the nineteenth century, anti-semitism was probably in decline, and several racial theories of that era actually placed the Jews in a high position. Thus the famous German jurist, Johann Bluntschli, argued that though the Aryans were the noblest race, being the creators of science and intellectual liberty, the second noblest were the Semites, the creators of advanced religion. These two races, in his view, had once been one. Those who were proud of modern European civilisation and especially its science could hardly see the Jews as lying outside that civilisation to which they had recently contributed so much. Moreover those Europeans who derided nature and the peoples living close to nature could hardly place the Jews, a people primarily of the cities and towns, amongst those living close to nature.

Anti-semitism grew from the 1870s, especially from 1873, the year of the financial crash in Vienna and Berlin where much blame was attached to Jewish financiers. Likewise in France in 1892 a financial crash associated with the canal promoter, de Lesseps, aroused an anti-semitism that became virulent two years later when a French army officer of Jewish descent, Alfred Dreyfus, was convicted of espionage. In Russia, attacks against the Jews, especially in 1882 and 1903, not only spurred their emigration to the United States but also to Germany where tensions were soon felt.[24] These pressures helped to give birth in 1897 to the Zionist movement and its resolve to find a safe land for the Jews.

Prejudice against Jews was more likely to be high when European civilisation felt insecure. Whereas prejudice against primitive peoples across the seas was likely to be highest when Europe was supremely confident, the prejudice against the Jews was likely to increase rapidly when Europe was lacking in confidence. Then the Jews tended to be seen as the enemies within. As they were so prominent in finance they were the scapegoat – and sometimes the appropriate target of criticism – during financial crashes and depressions. As they retained their own religion and as they tended to live in the same suburbs, and as most – but far from all – were identifiable by appearance, they were likely to be singled out in times of extreme uncertainty within a western nation. As many talented Jews became successful in medicine, journalism, banking and those other city professions open to them, and as many became rich as manufacturers and financiers, they easily became a symbol of the modern in Germany.[25] They were thus more likely to be attacked by the traditionalists, the romantics and the Christian conservatives who looked back to the past than by those who were proud of the present and its technology. In Germany many of the articulate writings against the Jews from the 1870s onwards are really attacks on modern civilisation and on the Jewish role in facets of that civilisation, not least the big and anonymous industrial cities.[26]

Feelings directed towards the Jews were unlike those directed towards the people of Tierra del Fuego or the upper Zambesi. The perceived fault of those peoples was that they were too backward but the fault of the Jewish people was often that they were too advanced. To be successful can be more menacing. As the Jews were seen as a threat, the threat was more likely to be viewed seriously when a European nation felt itself to be threatened in a wider sense. Thus the Dreyfus affair arose when France, having been humiliated by Germany in the war of 1870–71, was successfully rebuilding her military strength; and her charge against Captain Dreyfus – a charge later dismissed – was that he disclosed military secrets to the hated enemy. Likewise the humiliation of Germany at the end of the First World War gave rise to a search for scapegoats. Hitler was such a searcher, and his success in blaming the Jews for Germany's military defeat owed much to the fact that large numbers of Germans were eager to find a scapegoat outside their own ranks. Whether Germans were especially inclined to search for a scapegoat is not clear. In recent centuries England, the United States, Canada, Australia and New Zealand have not suffered a humiliating defeat in warfare nor have they been subjected to a harsh peace treaty; but if they had been so humiliated, they too might have hunted for a scapegoat.

Of the arguments and assumptions expressed against Jews in Europe after 1870, the strongest was nationalism. As nationalism increased, the Jews were especially singled out even though most Jews in western Europe probably tried to accommodate themselves to the demands of their own particular nation. 'But nationalism, no less than Jehovah, is a jealous God', wrote the historian Conor Cruise O'Brien.[27] He added that the Jews were not only an international people but were seen in Europe as the only international people, and therefore their loyalty – even when they contributed all that their nation demanded – was not fully accepted.

Collectively, the Jews occupied a special position on the seesaw. They were to remain in that position and be especially vulnerable during episodes of political and economic adversity and during times of intense nationalism in Europe. Not until after the Second World War were Jews widely recognised as standing not outside the walls but in the very heart of western civilisation.*

Nationalism – A Heavyweight on the Seesaw

Whenever the western world becomes intensely divided by nationalism, the seesaw of ideas is affected. Nationalism, being emotionally a heavyweight, almost takes over the seesaw, occupying both ends so that the seesaw ceases to be quite the same. When intellectuals fall under the influence of nationalism they usually have difficulty in retaining either a strong faith in western progress or a strong faith in nature, for their faith is now centred in their own nation. It is possible, however, for nationalists to have intense faith in the narrow technology that will protect their own nation and also an intense faith in nature as embodied in their own national soil and landscape. In essence, at certain times of national crisis, both technology and nature can be appealed to simultaneously so that they almost cease to be opposite ends of the seesaw.

---

* In the four decades between 1945 and 1985 the Jews' new standing in the west was to be aided by a powerful mix of ingredients, including the decline of nationalism amongst European peoples, the absence of a major financial crash in the western world, the decline of Christianity and its equivocal attitude to the Jewish religion and people, the memory of the Holocaust, and the increasing influence of Jews in the media and in intellectual life, especially in the English-speaking world. On the other hand the creation of the state of Israel made the Jewish position more fragile in the eyes of the Arab world, and Israel's close links with the United States made the Jewish position fragile in the communist world. In terms of the seesaw, Jews were now envisaged less often as a tight group gathered at one end, and more often as a loose group which, as in the past, provided many of the brilliant minds who expressed viewpoints at either end of the seesaw.

The swing of the seesaw towards technology between the 1840s and the 1870s and the swing back towards nature at the close of the century both took place in a period that was relatively peaceful and was not stirred by strident nationalism. But nationalism was increasing, and as international diplomacy broke down and as re-armament was emphasised, the seesaw ceased to function in the familiar way. The evidence suggests that the swing towards nature visible in the 1890s and the first few years of the 1900s was unable to sustain itself in the five or ten years before the First World War, partly because the roaring wind of nationalism was increasingly heard. In the tensions between European alliances, nations turned to the latest technology – machine guns and heavy artillery and the dreadnought battleship – and vigorously re-armed in order to increase their own security. This renewed faith in technology was both supported and opposed in intellectual circles, the support being stronger amongst scientists and engineers than in the humanities. So long as the belief was widespread that all future wars would be short and therefore not too devastating, it was easy for many intellectuals to see merit as well as security in the latest form of armament because, reportedly, they would shorten the war.

There was a stark contrast between the swing towards nature around 1900 and the intense swing towards nature which was to occur around 1970. The earlier swing of the seesaw was halted by growing international tensions which ultimately led to a renewed faith in technology, but the swing of the seesaw around 1970 was not halted because the international tensions – whether in Vietnam, the Middle East or elsewhere – did not promote a widespread faith in military technology. In the decades separating the world of the machine gun from the nuclear world, armaments were no longer seen so widely as a solver of problems.

8 The Great War and Other Half-Shocks

On the eve of the First World War, most of the staunch enemies of mankind were in retreat, at least in Europe. In most regions not one year of severe famine had occurred in the last sixty years. For most Europeans the standard of living was much higher than in the day of their grandmothers. Similarly their health had gained from the curbing of pneumonia, diphtheria, enteric fever, syphilis and even tuberculosis.

The typical family was intensely conscious of material progress as the driving force of the age but the sense of progress was felt less keenly by intellectuals. The seesaw of ideas had tilted perceptibly in the 1890s and much of that tilting remained. There was now a growing view that material progress was two-faced, smiling at one moment and glum the next. The new emphasis on the emotions, on the mysterious and magical, the primitive and the wild, on leisure, the arts and nature itself, represented a search for what had been lost in the materialist striving and achieving. Likewise the revival of Malthus's message, the sense that European peoples had nowhere to expand, the predictions that the era of marvellous inventiveness was over, and the beginning of prophesies that Europe might not always rule the world – such fears and premonitions were signs of an ebbing confidence in some influential minds.

Why the London Clerk did not Brain his Mother

In this complex mood, where popular faith in progress stood alongside an intellectual disquiet, there was a common buttress of optimism. International wars had become shorter, thus suggesting that the material gains of recent decades had been supplemented by a moral gain. Moreover, long periods of peace, though interspersed by wars, gave the century from 1815 to 1914 a shining halo. Thus, the end of the Napoleonic Wars ushered in a period of European peace and the end of the Franco–Prussian War in 1871 ushered in a peace of thirty years that was broken by only three short wars – a war between Russia and Turkey in 1877, between Serbia and Bulgaria in 1885 and between Greece and Turkey in 1897 – and each of those wars was concluded before the serious readers of newspapers could even grasp the geography of the area that was fought over. Meanwhile the main European powers continued to fight small wars at the edge of their expanding empires in Asia, Africa and the Americas, but they were seen more as peace-keeping ventures among barbarians. It is true that in the prelude to the First World War, the overseas wars involving Europe became more frequent but all were short. In 1898 Spain and the United States fought, in 1899 the Boer War began, and in 1900 many nations sent troops to China to quell the Boxer rebellion. Four years later Japan and Russia began a war which, to the astonishment of most European observers, was won by Japan. In 1911 the Italians fought the Turks, and in 1912–13 the two Balkans Wars produced a long death roll in Turkey, Greece, Bulgaria, Rumania, Serbia and Montenegro. The First World War in 1914 therefore did not erupt from a blue sky. Nonetheless, of all the measurable activities in Europe, war did not seem to be an exception to the 'law of progress'.

Various peaceful portents were fluttering in the wind in the last years of the nineteenth century. International languages – Esperanto and Volapuk – were invented in eastern Europe in the hope of curbing misunderstandings, for the old national languages were seen as dangerous repositories of pride and partisanship. Many nations actually came together at The Hague in 1899 to find ways of regulating war, if war should occur, and to regulate the declaring of war. A host of ideas for promoting international contact and peace were devised.[1] The revival of the Olympic Games in 1896 was one idea, and the Nobel Peace Prizes a few years later were another. That Alfred Nobel, the maker of high explosives, should bequeath this fortune to promote science and peace seemed to be an omen that more and more swords would be turned into ploughshares.

High hopes persisted even after the high peak of optimism had been passed. George Peabody Gooch, one of the ablest young historians in England, was of that generation which believed that man was good and that the world would assuredly become a happier place. The nations were coming together, and he showed the new amity by marrying a German woman.

When the Boer War began he was alarmed at England's aggression and later called that summer of 1899 'one of the most harrowing memories of my life'. His optimism revived, and in 1913 he concluded his book, *History of Our Time*, with a rousing declaration: 'We can now look forward with something like confidence to the time when war between civilised nations will be considered as antiquated as the duel.'[2] Whether his was a majority viewpoint amongst intellectuals is unclear, but it was widespread.

The First World War was to be shattering, partly because a war of that magnitude had been generally thought to be impossible. An English journalist, Norman Angell, in a famous book of 1910, *The Great Illusion*, implied that a major war was unlikely – or would soon be ended – because under modern conditions there could be no victor. He argued that in heavily-armed Europe, war would not pay an aggressor. He took comfort from his observation that human nature was changing. He thought it was absurd to suggest that 'the feelings of the paleolithic man who ate the bodies of his enemies and of his own children are the same as those of a Herbert Spencer, or even of the modern Londoner who catches his train to town in the morning'. If human nature had not changed, argued Angell, we might as well expect the London clerk, when he reached his home in the evening, 'to brain his mother and serve her up for dinner'.[3]

Big-selling books are often banners, and the meaning ultimately attached to them comes less from those who have read them than from those who have not. Angell's book eventually attracted the judges of the Nobel Peace Prize. Rather than being a force for peace, his book probably made war in 1914 a little more likely. In short, he persuaded many leaders of opinion that a major war would not come, and so they were less prepared to cope when it came.

War as a Shock

The magnitude of the First World War was a shock to believers in peaceful progress. At its end the German dead numbered 1,800,000, the Russian numbered 1,700,000, and in Russia the civil war was about to multiply their dead. The French dead were 1,400,000 and the Austrian-Hungarian Empire's dead were 1,200,000. The death roll of these continental nations dwarfed, in their death roll, that of the British Empire, in whose ranks 1,000,000 died. In all, the military deaths numbered about 8,500,000, far more than in any war hitherto known in history. How many Europeans died as a result of war-induced sickness is impossible to know, but hunger and malnutrition and typhus and cholera were massive killers in eastern Europe. Professor Gilbert Murray estimated that a total of about 25,000,000 died either directly or indirectly as a result of the war.[4] To the dead must be added 21,000,000 wounded, many of them incapacitated for the remainder of their days. As a host of the most talented and fittest young men of Europe were killed in the war, Darwin's theory of natural selection – hitherto interpreted as the ruthless ally of progress – could now be seen as equally the enemy of progress, for it killed the fittest. Without the war those minor soldiers, Hitler and Mussolini, might not have come to power.

The war also proved to be a shock because it was long. Many economists in step with Angell had thought that the dislocation of international trade and the shortage of food would quickly end the war, while others thought that a burst of dizzy inflation would halt it. Many socialists thought the war would be soon ended by a general strike or by working men refusing the command to fight.[5]

Most of Europe's civilian and military leaders thought the war would be short because the typical war in Europe in the last seventy years had been short. Modern weapons and swift means of communication gave rise to the view that a war of long duration was impossible.[6] Today we hold the same view about a nuclear war involving the major powers. Perhaps we are equally wrong, for a war involving nuclear weapons at some stage does not necessarily have to be a short war, and to believe that it must be short is to repeat a new version of the fallacious dogma of 1914.

The shock was magnified in the eyes of many intellectuals because Germany was singled out as the main instigator of the war: that same Germany which had led the world in the physical sciences, in the composition and practice of music, and in some branches of the social sciences. A civilisation cannot easily take pride in itself if its most glittering ornament is blackened. The war also shocked by showing the destructive side of science and technology. The high explosives which in peacetime had blasted tunnels for new railways were now blowing up thousands of men on the battlefront. The precision engineering which made the sewing machine and so eased the evenings of millions of housewives was now mass-producing the machine gun and killing the husbands of the women who stayed home to sew. The Chilean nitrates which had fertilised the harvests for an expanding population were now turned into nitro-glycerine, thereby reducing the population by blowing young men to bits. The barbed wire which had transformed life on the treeless plains of the new world by providing cheap fences for cattle and sheep was now mass-produced to build an entanglement extending along hundreds of miles of the European battlefronts, trapping the advancing soldiers and rendering them an easy target. The chlorine gas used in the great textile factories in bleaching cotton and linen in order to clothe cheaply half the world was now used in gas warfare on French battlefields. The new petrol engine which drove the motor car and the city bus also made possible the submarine, a vessel that had been unworkable in the age of steam, and in the Atlantic and North Sea and Irish Channel the German diesel submarines destroyed a tonnage of deep-sea ships such as the whole world probably did not possess when the industrial revolution was beginning. In 1917, the most successful year for the German U-boats, a total of more than 2,400 Allied and neutral ships were sunk at sea.

That millions of soldiers could be killed, that such huge armies could face each other all the way from the cold Baltic to the cliffs of Gallipoli, was itself a sign of that powerful productive machine which had grown up in the western world. Napoleon's era had called for a large proportion of the population to be constantly employed in growing food, and so relatively few men could be released for military service. Then the average warring nation could annually afford to spend about 13 per cent of its national product on fighting the war: the other 87 per cent was needed largely to keep body and soul together. In contrast in the last two years of the First World War, Europe was spending about 50 per cent of its national product on the war.[7] Science and ingenuity had made the European economy infinitely more productive, but a lot of that product could now go into destruction.

The First World War shook the scaffolding of progress because it was deadly and unexpectedly long: it showed that technology could be two-faced. The war delivered one other insidious attack on the idea of progress by raising a moral question which the believers in progress had taken for granted: had the morality of Europeans improved during the long era of 'progress'? It was understandable back in 1800 to believe that the average European – if liberated from the drudgery of heavy daily work, if liberated from ignorance by a compulsory period in school, and liberated from fear of famine – would prove to be more public-spirited and compassionate. Now, after a century of swift social change, it was not easy to answer with clear confidence the question of whether moral progress had occurred. While it was easy to measure how many people could read and write, what they ate each day and how many hours they worked, there was no way of measuring whether they were more humane and more peace-loving. The war, however, offered a rough and ready answer, and Walter Gropius voiced it when he returned from the German front late in 1918. 'This is more than just a lost war', he wrote. 'A world has come to an end.' For many priests and clergymen, however, it was the same old world which the nineteenth century had happened to misunderstand. They believed that man was sinful and that the hopeful ideologies of the nineteenth century had now been proved to be paper-thin.

Some intellectual circles were, at most, only half-shocked by the events of the First World War. Cautious towards technology, sceptical of progress, and conscious of the recent tilt of the seesaw, they could only be half-shocked by the long and terrible war. Sigmund Freud, who saw the irrational in mankind long before the war, was not surprised as he watched his countrymen march away from wartime Vienna to suffer terrible casualties. Wilfred Trotter, an English surgeon and sociologist, had also warned that civilisation was far from stable, that the animal instincts in man were far more powerful than people had been prepared to admit. In 1909 he wrote the powerful warning that 'it needs but little imagination to see how great are the probabilities that after all man will prove but one more of Nature's failures, ignominiously to be swept from her worktable.' The war showed that his ideas had much sense and in 1915 he turned them into a book, *Instincts of the Herd in Peace and War.* It was a best seller, for such a learned book. It emphasised the neglected side of Darwin: how easy it was for mankind 'to sink to the irresponsible destructiveness of the monkey'.[8] Many other intellectuals who sat on the cautious end of the seesaw had also been prepared mentally for the war.

The Wings of Victory

The First World War bestrides our century, not only because it was so lethal but also because it is believed to have initiated a chain of other tragic events – the world depression, Hitler's Germany, the Second World War and nuclear weapons. But these other events were not the inevitable effects of the First World War and even people of the gloomiest disposition could hardly have predicted them in 1918. At the end of that war, the confidence in mankind, while bruised, was far from battered. In literature and painting were strong signs of disillusionment or doubt, but perhaps no more signs than in 1910. On the other hand a feeling of quiet satisfaction was held by tens of millions of Europeans: they had the deep satisfaction of victory, and moreover they saw victory as permanent. President Wilson of the United States was one leader who proclaimed that it was not a war against an enemy so much as 'a war against wars'.[9] Victory in a war fought ostensibly to end all wars was a wonderful source of content and moral satisfaction.

Nor did the war seem a catastrophe to those who believed in socialism, because war paved the way for revolutions in Russia, enabling the Bolsheviks to seize power with surprising ease in November 1917. While beyond Russia's borders, the creation of the world's first socialist state dismayed millions of people, it also delighted millions. A new order seemed about to dawn, and Lenin and Trotsky predicted that similar revolutions would transform Europe.

Further west the liberals who, in the words of Britain's foreign minister of 1914, had seen the lights go out all over Europe now saw them go on again. Independent nations were exultantly created from the wreckage of the defeated German, Russian and Austro-Hungarian empires, and there was rejoicing amongst the Poles, Czechs, Latvians, Estonians and others who were able to create their own nation. Likewise, high hopes were placed on the new League of Nations as the adjudicator of disputes, and its members even agreed that they should not go to war until a dispute had been examined by an arbitrator.

Many intellectuals sustained their optimism by assigning blame for the First World War to the armaments race, an event which they hoped would never be repeated. They were correct in arguing that big manufacturers such as Vickers-Armstrong in England, Krupp in Germany, Schneider-Creusot in France and Skoda in Austria-Hungary had sold their armaments with vigour in the decade or two before 1914 and that an armaments race had probably increased tension between the major European powers. But much of their blame on the pre-war armaments race had a slender basis in fact. Looking at the expenditure of the major nations on armaments in the period, I have come to the conclusion that the armaments race was more an illusion resulting from inflation and innovation than from the massive diversions of funds. Britain was said to be a sprinter in the armaments race just before the First World War, but what was forgotten was that Britain's spending on defence was not keeping pace with its spending on other public activities. Britain spent 60 per cent of its budget on defence in 1860 and only 44 per cent in 1913. The question of arms races is complex, but if we survey the prelude to the First World War it is very easy to exaggerate the dangers of re-arming.[10]

As the arms race was increasingly blamed for the war itself, disarmament was correspondingly praised. Such a formula intuitively pleased those liberals in England, Germany, and other nations who saw capitalism as promoting the sale of armaments and an arms race as leading to war. The formula appealed to that small minority which was nervous of new technology, and it appealed to those believers in the goodness of man who saw the First World War as the result of unprecedented causes which could be removed, never to appear again. Voters also saw merit in the process of disarmament because it would cut the heavy defence bill and thereby ease taxes. The idea that a disarmament campaign will simply lead to peace is, as a general rule, as deceptive as the opposite idea that a rearmament race will lead to war, for many other factors also determine whether war or peace will come. Nonetheless, for a variety of reasons – some of them credible and some of them gullible – disarmament became the vogue in many intellectual circles.

The liberal democracies, which largely won the war, gave themselves another cause for confidence about the future. Optimistic towards human nature, they argued that rational discussion could solve conflict, that democracies fostered rational discussion, and that one of the main causes of the war in 1914 was that Germany an Austria-Hungary, not being real democracies, were inclined to solve disagreement by arms rather than by discussion. The victorious allies specifically blamed Germany for the war and that blame was written into the treaty that ended the war. The faith in rational discussion was later apparent in the activities of the English prime minister, Neville Chamberlain, who flew to Germany to make concessions to Hitler in September 1938 and returned with the message, 'I believe it is peace for our time.' That phrase was understood to signify thirty or forty years of peace, but the peace lasted for one year.

The weight of evidence suggests that, contrary to the view of most historians, the First World War – once it was over – was not felt as a long-lasting shock to confidence, especially by most people in the English-speaking world. At times, attitudes are capable of moving towards optimism or pessimism without a prior push from the real world of events, and attitudes are capable of withstanding a buffeting from an event as powerful as the First World War. Undoubtedly the four years of war did display the terrors of technology, but a large measure of optimism persisted because of the intellectual alibis used to explain the war and because of the outcome of the war: the rise in Russia of the first socialist state, the military victory for the English-speaking world, the belief that it had been a war to end wars, and the general victory of the democracies. Moreover the war, to many, could not be too disillusioning, because since the 1890s a diminished faith in progress had already been expressed in the arts, philosophy, political prophecy and even in certain of the social and biological sciences. The terrible war diminished the belief in *inevitable* progress, a belief already pricked, but it probably did little to weaken the belief in the likelihood of progress, except perhaps in the defeated German-speaking lands.

The Seesaw is Stuck!

If this book were trying to describe every tiny tilt of the seesaw, the period of twenty one years between the end of the First World War and the outbreak of the Second World War would deserve a book to itself. That period, while unstable, did not represent a definite swing away from faith in technology or progress. The nations which had won the war did not despise technology, for it helped them to victory. After the war, there was also a deep hope that new inventions would transform everyday life; and in the 1920s and 1930s millions of lives gained from the radio, talking cinema, cheap camera, mass-produced car and motor cycle, the vacuum cleaner, household refrigerator, electric stove and improvements in medical diagnosis and cure. Possibly the strongest influence on the mood of people was the movie, and it flashed a carefree and optimistic view of life onto the screens of thousands of cinemas. The United States dominated the world's film industry in the 1920s and most film-goers in Europe were captivated by the America they saw. In the words of film critic, Stanley Kauffmann, they marvelled at 'the reach of the horizon, the bustle and immensity of the cities, the spirit – true or not – of infinite possibility.'[11]

After the revolution the Soviet Union virtually abandoned its seat on the seesaw of western civilisation. The flexible seesaw of ideas and attitudes is largely the creation of a relatively free world where ideas can strenuously compete with each other. The Soviet Union now represented a frozen replica of the seesaw which had existed in the heyday of optimism in the nineteenth century, but the Soviet Union continued to influence the seesaw which operated in the western world, and the Soviet view of the future affected foreign nations and minority groups inside nations.

In the new Soviet Union in the 1920s faith in technology was virtually a religion. The miracles of science were ready, it was believed, to abolish hunger and drudgery at the flick of the switch. Electricity, tractors, new fertilisers and new breeds of plants were expected to transform Soviet living standards. It was no wonder that Lenin, the head of state, had to write a warning to a high bureaucrat in 1921: 'There is too much talk of electrification'. No nation in modern times and probably in any era had given such emphasis as the Soviet Union to the scientist and machine-maker. Science was the new god, and amongst its strange high priests were the geneticist T. D. Lysenko and the agricultural scientist V. R. Williams, the son of an American railway builder, while Stalin himself had eccentric views on where to drill for oil and how to grow the Australian eucalypt in the chill air of the Moscow region.[12] Later, in a variety of disciplines ranging from linguistics to oceanography, the holders of unofficial theories were either killed or sent to prisons. Hitler's Germany, ascending almost as far as Stalin's Russia in worshipping science, paid a similar price for injecting too much politics into scientific research, and lost those services of brilliant Jewish physicists who in America were to play a vital role in developing the first nuclear weapons.

The Soviet Union believed that the world could be hammered into shape with a precision not seen before in the history of mankind. Science, technology, and Marx's theory of politics and history would be the strong hammers. Optimistically the Soviet Union in 1928 unveiled its initial Five Year Plan, which inspired four-year, five-year and six-year plans in countries as different as Poland, Turkey, Mexico and even Hitler's Germany, the fiercest opponent of the Soviet Union.[13] These plans assumed that progress was certain if new technology were applied skilfully.

Processions of visitors reached Russia, eager to believe. Given the special privileges open to tourists in highly regulated societies, most went home with praise. It was not simply that they shut their eyes at appropriate times or were hoodwinked: they saw valid evidence for thinking that the Soviet experiment might succeed. Measured by most of the expectations of 1917 it did not succeed until some forty years later, by which time the definition of success in the western world had become much higher, but at first there was legitimate ground for hope. Tom Wright, an Australian trade unionist who toured Russia in 1927, reported that as the social revolution gained speed it reduced drunkeness, illiteracy, prostitution, theft and a cluster of old social evils.[14] For every five Tom Wrights there was at least one Bertrand Russell. Visiting Russia in 1920 with a delegation from the British Labour Party, Russell shuddered at the misery and the air of suppression. 'With every day that I spent in Russia my horror increased', he wrote, 'until I lost all power of balanced judgment.'[15]

Lost Eldorados

While Marxists saw their golden age in the future, the western world was more inclined to see its golden age in the recent past. The 1920s often showed nostalgia for the pre-war way of life and for that old full moon of peace and prosperity which many politicians hoped to retrieve from the halcyon evenings of say 1910 and 1900. The pre-war decades were especially remembered for stable prices such as the western world has not seen since, and accordingly many leaders of the 1920s insisted that price stability rather than full employment should be the first goal, though they hoped that stable prices would also lead to high levels of employment. In 1925 the nostalgic decision by Britain, still a financial giant, to reinstate the gold standard in the hope of stabilising the price level is now widely believed to have had the opposite effect and to have been a cause of the world depression.

An influential book which showed the economic glories of the past to a vast audience in eleven languages – ranging from Rumanian to Chinese – was *The Economic Consequences of The Peace*. Its young author, John Maynard Keynes, warned that the favourable balance between population and the supply of food had been disrupted by the war, and that Europe could no longer rely on the unusual conditions that had enabled both its population and prosperity to increase in the preceding century.[16] While he argued that until the eve of the war there had existed an 'economic Eldorado', others saw the world before 1900 as a political Eldorado which solved problems through conferences rather than a show of arms, and they hoped that the new League of Nations by the lake at Geneva would provide an almost continuous conference at which problems would one by one be solved.

The domestic politics of many nations were perfumed with nostalgia. The landslide victory of the Republican, Warren Harding, in the presidential election of 1920 was seen as an expression of nostalgia for an America that had almost passed away. The accession to power of conservatives in England, France and Germany and the rise of European dictators can partly be seen as a desire to return to what was remembered too fondly as the stability of earlier eras. By 1926, dictators or autocrats ruled Hungary, Italy, Spain, Poland, Portugal and

Lithuania as well as the Soviet Union. In Italy, Mussolini saw himself as reviving the glory of ancient Rome, and the word 'fascism' actually came from the Latin 'fasces' which denoted the insignia of authority in ancient Rome – a bundle of rods with an axe projecting. Likewise the Nazi emblem, the swastika, had been a symbol of the Teutonic Knights during the medieval crusades, and was chosen by Hitler because of its history.

In the years between the wars, the increasing popularity of detective stories was another hallmark of nostalgia. The country house and its comfortable, leisurely way of life were common settings for detective stories. Professor Ernest Mandel recently argued in his history of the crime story, *Delightful Murder,* that this wonderful period of crime fiction was largely the fruit of nostalgia, the longing to leave a disturbed era and find a lost golden age. In expressing confidence in Europe's previous peacetime, citizens were not expressing a distaste for technology, because the prosperity and high hopes of that previous peacetime had largely come from bursts of inventiveness.

There was a faltering continuation of that fascination with nature which was noticeable in the quarter century before the First World War. At the end of the 1920s America witnessed a brief vogue for a paradise where people lived close to nature; and Margaret Mead's Samoa became a South Seas Hollywood where the adolescents were free from sexual taboos. Enthusiasm for nature was to decrease in the 1930s when so many people had no work; to provide work was then the highest priority, and if nature stood in the way of a new gold mine or highway it was blasted aside. A quickening interest in nature is usually part of the revolt against technology, but there was no pronounced revolt against technology between the end of the First World War and the start of the Second World War; this suggests that the seesaw had moved only a fraction during the two decades.

The fear of famine, revived in the late 1890s by Sir William Crookes, lingered in the 1920s. To John Maynard Keynes, the young economist, overpopulation could have been the main cause of the Russian revolution. In 1923 E. M. East of Harvard University quickened the debate by arguing that at the present rate of increase the population of the world would double every sixty years, and by the 1990s the years of poor global harvests would lead to widespread famine, even in Europe, and that in turn would spur wars of conquest. 'It is not a pretty picture', he concluded. In 1928 another American professor, E. A. Ross, made his own warning in a book pointedly titled *Standing Room Only?*[17] In a world conscious of the danger of war, famine was seen – without much supporting evidence – as the likely provoker of wars, and in this tradition an Australian scholar-official in 1942 argued that if Asia's millions lacked food, 'a modern Genghis Khan will sooner or later rise in justifiable wrath to sweep selfish barriers aside'.[18] A shelf of new literature already challenged the pessimists, and by the 1930s it was winning. As a result of the loss of young men in the First World War and the later poverty, the marriage and birth rates declined, and the new crisis eagerly discussed in the late 1930s in books by Reddaway, Spengler and other economists was that of under-population.[19]

The depression of the early 1930s was a perverse commentary on how far the world had advanced materially. About one in every four members of the workforce had no work but the desolation was not as deep as it had been in the 'depressions' of the eighteenth century. The proportion of Europe's population suffering from malnutrition had probably been much larger in the worst years of the more serious famines of the eighteenth century than in the one economic depression of the 1930s. That depression was a calamity and shock, but amidst all the unemployment, technology was not denounced as a destroyer of jobs with the indignation voiced today. Nor was technology seen widely as a polluter.

Economic theory reflected the continuing faith in technology. Many economists began to wonder whether the vexing economic problem was not the supply of goods but an inadequate demand for them. Engineers and farmers had been so successful in solving the ancient problem of scarcity that perhaps the new problem – a responsibility of economists and politicians – was how to distribute and use the abundance of food and goods. Leftist economists had long argued that the core problem was not supply but demand, and in the 1930s, J. M. Keynes and other economists whose politics leaned more to centre than left, loosely accepted this radical interpretation, thus showing how wide was the confidence in technology during the worst depression the world had known.

The depression of the 1930s, traumatic and divisive for intellectual circles in Europe and the United States, provoked a powerful swing to the right and a powerful swing to the left, laying waste much of the old middle ground. The history of ideas in Germany, Sweden, Italy, Spain, England, the United States, New Zealand, Argentina and a dozen other countries in the 1930s was bitterly flavoured by the powerful appeal of fascism and communism and social democracy, though that intellectual turmoil largely lies outside the theme of this book. The differences between communism and fascism and liberalism were wide, but seen in terms of the seesaw their respective adherents had more in common than they cared to imagine. Clustering together at the technology end of the seesaw, they believed in progress and they believed that technology was an indispensable instrument of progress. While Nazism had sympathies towards nature they were the nationalist sympathies felt for the landscape and soil of the fatherland – towards a tiny tract of the earth's surface – rather than for all nature. A century from now, many historians might see communism, social democracy, fascism and liberalism as possessing far more in common than we are prepared to concede, just as two sides in a civil war or two sides in a warring family are eventually seen long after the quarrel as really sharing many of the same values and loyalties.

In the 1920s, '30s, '40s and '50s such a heresy was unimaginable, so distinctive did each ideology appear to be and claim to be. Since most of the intellectual debate in those decades centred on the question of Left versus Right and Liberty versus Authority, it was almost impossible to conceive of rebellion and radicalism as disporting themselves outside the ropes of that well known boxing-ring of ideas. That was why the late 1960s were to be puzzling and even inexplicable to those who had learned, during decades of intense ideological conflict, to see the left–right issue as perpetual and all-important. They could not conceive that technology versus nature, in a less spectacular way, would form such a corrosive issue for the western world. Intellectuals who were attuned to the discordant drum beat of left–right–left were quite unprepared for the new intellectual clash and at first could make little sense of it.

Three Atomic Bombs

Science and technology had come a long way in the previous
two centuries, and by 1945 they were the torch outshining
Christianity in much of the western world. Even the enemies of
science were increasingly speaking the language of science, and
were imitating science by their constant measuring, their
emphasis on specialists rather than generalists, and their faith
that objectivity was easily attainable. Science seemed unassail-
able at the beginning of 1945, and who indeed would wish to
prevent such a powerful instrument from protecting nations
against their enemies? There was one flaw in that hope. What
if, in harnessing science to stave off their enemies, they created
a scientific monster?

The atomic bomb, though a monster, arose from a series of
quiet scientific triumphs. Several of the early triumphs were in
England where J. J. Thompson discovered the electron and
Ernest Rutherford, his former student, conceived a new model
of the atom and James Chadwick discovered the neutron.
Other insights came from the work of physicists on the continent of Europe, especially Mendellev the Russian, Planck the
German, Bohr the Dane and Fermi the Italian. The final
triumph came in the Second World War when Americans and
exiled Europeans worked together in Chicago and Los Alamos
to produce three atom bombs.[20] The first was tested in New
Mexico on 16 July 1945. The second was dropped on the
Japanese city of Hiroshima on 6 August, and 71,000 people
died immediately and thousands more died as a result of delayed
effects. The third was dropped on Nagasaki on 9 August and
killed even more people. These atomic bombs helped to
terminate the war against Japan, thereby saving indirectly
more lives than had been lost in Hiroshima and Nagasaki. A
balance sheet of that first year of the nuclear age, however,
must have many debits and credits, each of a magnitude which
we cannot yet grasp, let alone calculate.

Such weapons seem to have been a tragic end to one of the
most triumphant roads that scientists had ever travelled. That
lucid expositor of the history of science, Jacob Bronowski, knew
that creative science and the creative arts overlapped and that
the best in science as in the arts represented new insights and
visions, and he argued that physics was the finest collective

work of art of all time. 'The human imagination working communally', he proclaimed in his celebrated television series, 'has produced no monuments to equal it, not the pyramids, not the *Iliad*, not the ballads, not the cathedrals.'[21]

It is possible to agree and yet disagree with his idea. One lesson of history is that every gain has its potential loss. The highest human achievements carry the danger of pride, and pride can lead blindly to disaster, just as failure can fortify the determination and so lead slowly towards triumph. Alternating or competing moods of confidence and doubt are almost central to the human condition. Just as biology, the scientific triumph of the nineteenth century, could support alternative messages of optimism and pessimism about mankind's future, so the notable scientific triumph of the twentieth century, the leap in physics, could arouse pride on the one hand and despair on the other. What Bronowski called the collective triumph of the human imagination introduced a new factor into future-gazing and prophecy. Science, having undermined the hell of the theologians, had created another hell.

Part Two

9 The Beckoning Moon

The two world wars and the world depression did not sap the confidence of serious-minded people in the west's technology. But events in 1945 and 1946 were more alarming. The victory against Germany and Japan was dulled quickly by the impact of atomic weapons and, even more, by the Soviet Union's occupation of eastern Europe and by the start of the Cold War.

Visions of 1984

Between the two world wars, communism had remained a fashionable alternative amongst intellectuals in the capitalist west, but its harsh attitude to political and civil liberties was now more visible. It occupied a vast area of Europe and might spread west, either by military action or by social upheavals within democratic nations. There had been a serious recession for a few years after the First World War and so a serious postwar recession was expected again; and if serious unemployment were accompanied by the continuation of the wartime scarcities of food and fuel, the chance of communism snatching power in some western European nations would be high. The Marshall Plan and massive American economic aid were still a dream. Few could envisage in 1945 the speed with which prosperity would come to the bomb-damaged cities of Europe. Nor could alert people in 1945 share the hope, felt at the end of the previous world war, that a further world war was unlikely. In 1945 another major war was high on the agenda of possible events.

George Orwell thought that it was 'not easy to believe in the survival of civilisation'; and his celebrated book, *Animal Farm*, published during the Cold War, implied that human liberty was endangered everywhere. When, just before his death in 1949, Orwell published *Nineteen Eighty-Four*, he again caught the extreme pessimism of so many of those who, a decade earlier had cheerfully seen Marx as a guide to Utopia. Orwell's book was a perceptive warning, made when millions of people were at the mental and emotional crossroads.[1] It is still read widely but if his warning had become true his book would be little read now, Big Brother having pulped all available copies.

Other strands of crisis thinking, born in the 1930s, were made more persuasive by the war and the post-war fears. Existentialism, a philosophy designed to help people face a meaningless and chilling world, ran strongly in French intellectual circles.[2] Similarly, Crisis Christianity, propounded by Karl Barth in German and Swiss universities, insisted that man deceived himself by his faith in reason and progress. This outstanding theologian of the Protestant world was joined by the most famous historian of the English-speaking world who expressed the same sense of crisis and even of approaching catastrophe. Arnold J. Toynbee had read Spengler's *Decline of the West* soon after it was published, and it quickened his interest in why civilisations rose and fell. Beginning an impressive programme of research, Toynbee published three volumes of his *Study of History* in 1933 and another three in 1939. Curiously the war did not deepen his pessimism – it was already intense – and when in 1946 he was commencing the final volumes he felt a tinge of hope. Although each of the past civilisations had wilted, he believed our own could escape decline if we sought God's help 'in a humble spirit and with a contrite heart'.[3] In the United States, a global power for the first time, many citizens were tantalised by Toynbee's diagnosis of political and moral power, and a massive audience read his views in the magazines *Time* and *Life*, finding some consolation in his tenth and final volume, complete in 1954.[4] Like a global judge summing up a long trial in his own international court, Toynbee promised not to send mankind to the executioner if it promised to reform its ways.

Anxiety mixed with guarded hope was typical of the west in the late 1940s. Military weapons made their long shadow everywhere, but there was no point in denouncing technology and turning to nature for solace. Soldiers and civilians during the war had had enough of living in tents, dugouts and ships, close to nature: they had had enough of the ice, heat, mud, winds, and tough sea voyages. In Germany, Russia, England, France and the most crippled nations the people living in cities had been pushed closer to icy nature, partly because many of the aids of technology had been destroyed. Memories of the war and of the world depression made people even more sympathetic to technology and the city comforts which it promised, and even more wary of nature and the vagaries of climate.

The Surge of Hope

The low expectations so common after the war were not fulfilled. Slowly hopes began to rise, despite the continuation of the Cold War and the outbreak of the Korean War, despite the Soviet's acquisition of the atomic bomb and America's invention of the hydrogen bomb. New technology now conveyed glamour even more than gloom. Only new technology could maintain the west's military ascendancy against the Soviet Union, and also lift the standard of living of people who for too long had suffered poverty in the ports and factory cities all the way from Naples to New Orleans. Quickly there emerged a new period of optimism, for which there was no parallel in the twentieth century.

A remarkable assault on disease, quietly gathering momentum during the war, now reached the hospitals. Wonder drugs, appearing many years after the German dyestuffs factory of I. G. Farben, made the first step towards the sulphonamides, eventually reduced the mortality of some infections from as high as 50 per cent to as low as 5 per cent. Antibiotics appeared, including penicillin which was first made in big quantities in 1943. Soon a range of antibiotics could attack syphilis, tuberculosis and typhoid, while DDT attacked the breeding ground of the carriers of typhus and malaria, cutting back the incidence of malaria in Italy from 400,000 cases to a mere 5 in the decade ending in 1955. Dysentery, sleeping sickness and other diseases transmitted by insects also succumbed to new insecticides. Vaccines weakened the striking power of influenza and of polio. Tuberculosis, a killer on a huge scale as late as 1900, was tamed by a new vaccine and a new drug of 1944 – streptomycin. Most of these cures and preventives belonged to the years between 1930 and 1950 and, ironically, were spurred by the scarcities and needs of the armed forces in the Second World War.[5] Here was the swiftest medical revolution so far known to man. Much as it prolonged human life and eased suffering, it could not be hailed simply as a cause of optimism because it rapidly increased the world's population in the first two postwar decades, but even that problem was at first submerged in the rising optimism.

The quarter century running from 1945 to 1970 had several of the hallmarks of a second but less painful industrial revolution.

The computer arose, the electronics industry blossomed, and assembly lines were automated to a degree which was unimaginable in the 1930s. Agriculture in many lands was made astonishingly productive, and one man and a machine could harvest an area which in his grandfather's era called for a small regiment of farm labourers and many draught horses or oxen. New commodities or new versions of old commodities changed everyday life. The contraceptive pill shook morals and manners; the cheap television set and the transistor radio and hi-fi changed leisure and communications; and a hundred ancient monuments were torn down with hardly a sigh or protest to make way for freeways and skyscrapers.

The word 'revolution' was invoked to encapsulate the speed and magnitude of the changes: there was a medical revolution, a green revolution, a media revolution, a transport revolution and an electronics revolution. It was easy to count the number of revolutions, for the cheap pocket calculator had arrived. The remarkable fact was that all these new inventions at first were cheered with a voice as loud as that cheering the inventions a century earlier.

The Race to the Moon

Man could even jump over the moon, though the final success came from many practice jumps. On 4 October 1957, in the first bold jump, the Soviet Union launched Sputnik I, a machine no heavier than a strong footballer. A marvel, it was sought at night in the skies by a thousand million eyes as it circled the globe. On 3 November 1957, Sputnik II was sent into orbit with a Russian dog. These early achievements of the Soviet Union spurred the United States to galvanise her science and technology, and under President Eisenhower, she poured money into high schools in a long-term plan to attract students and produce scientists. Gimmicks were required, and as the dissecting of a frog would make biology more interesting for a lukewarm student, a fortune in federal money bought frogs for school laboratories, and about 100 million federal frogs had been dissected by young Americans by the time the first spaceman landed on the moon.[6] The moon-landing almost marked the noonday of science as a major God. After 1969, science ceased to soar highly in the public imagination.

A glow had surrounded the word SCIENCE in most years of this first quarter century after the war. Jonathan Benthall, director of the Royal Anthropological Institute in England, observed that the years from the late 1950s to the mid 1960s marked a heyday of hope in technology.[7] Science was hailed as society's problem-solver, and for a time its mistakes and its power to destroy were almost forgotten.

Much of the rising optimism, as the years passed, came from the fact that the worst fears of the late 1940s had not been realised. Another world depression had not come; a major war between communism and capitalism erupted in Korea but did not spread far; nuclear weapons multiplied but were not used; and the fear of revolution in the west was dispelled by prosperity. Those legitimate fears of 1945 had proved so far to be an illusion and twenty years after the war there was far more serenity than could reasonably have been expected at the end of the war.

The Economics of the Prodigal Son

The woe of the pre-war world had been 'the trade cycle' or, as it was called in the United States, 'the business cycle'. This was the tendency for economic life to walk the drunken pathway between boom and depression, a pathway so hazardous that John Maynard Keynes in 1936 erected a warning sign: 'It is certain that the world will not much longer tolerate the un-employment which, apart from brief intervals of excitement, is associated – and, in my opinion, inevitably associated – with present-day capitalistic individualism'.[8] In a brilliant diagnosis Keynes argued that the difficulty was not in producing and supplying goods but in so arranging a national economy that people had the money to buy them. The poor and the politicians, even if they did not quite understand his doctrine, saw its advantages because Keynes said that in lean times a government should spend vigorously rather than balance its budget. Such advice sounds sweet to the typical politician, for his instinct is to throw a lifebelt to every voter in distress. It is fair to say that Keynes delighted most people when he said that it was more blessed to spend than to save. In the short term that policy boosted economic activity, but in the long term it usually led to inflation. It was Brendan Bracken, an astute member of the

English cabinet, who in the 1950s confided that Keynes would go down in history as the man who made inflation respectable.[9]

To my mind the views which John Maynard Keynes brilliantly expressed in his *General Theory* attempted not only a revolution in economic thought but also a moral revolution. Overnight he carried economics from the Old to the New Testament. The Old Testament is laced with warnings that wrong-doing, whether economic or moral, leads to disaster and punishment but The New Testament can offer a different lesson. It presents a new economic theory in telling the story of the Prodigal Son who wastes his money in high living in a distant land, returns home and, instead of being humiliated, is welcomed by his father with the words: 'bring hither the fatted calf, and kill it; and let us eat and be merry.' Hitherto, in classical economics a depression had been viewed as punishment for the prodigality of the preceding boom, but Keynes gave the Prodigal Son a respectable, not a shameful place, in the new economics. Keynes, in saying there was to be no deliberate punishment, became in the study of economics what Dr Spock would become in child-care. Whereas the old remedy for a depression was to save and tighten the belt, Keynes's new remedy was to spend and loosen the belt. By playing down the dangers of inflation, Keynes helped give confidence to economic activity but, as the Austrian and Chicago schools of economists warned, inflation would remain a danger.

Another economist who helped prescribe the *Conditions of Economic Progress* for the post-war world was Colin Clark. In his book of that name, written when he was the economic adviser to the Queensland government, he made the statistical steps necessary to back Keynes's theory: he was the virtual inventor of the vital concept of the Gross National Product. A revolution in how we see events often depends on an advance in measuring as well as an advance in deciding what should be measured. Clark, unusual amongst economists, suggested in 1940 that the world could escape from the thick fog of recent decades.[10] He would have received a Nobel Prize for economics had he lived in a major nation.

Economics became a glamorous occupation. Economists proliferated, like engineers in the nineteenth century. The White House employed its first economic adviser in 1939, but just over one third of a century later more than 4,000 economists worked for the federal government, and they mostly agreed that they knew the answers. Not since the golden age of theology had one of the social sciences lived in such esteem. Economics was praised because it had helped to bring material progress and prosperity to a generation which had known the hardship of the 1930s and the austerity of the war years.

The birth of the 1960s proclaimed the new sense of mastery, especially in economic life. Rarely has a new decade been entered with such confidence. Old people could recall that in the 1950s the Cold War was still chilling, that in 1940 the Second World War had begun, that in 1930 the world depression was becoming serious, and that in 1920 it was feared that the Russian revolution would spread. In the light of this pattern of fears, the start of the 1960s was unusual in its smugness, so much so that the London *Economist* felt a need to warn England at 'the gates of the new decade' to beware of over-confidence.[11]

The sense of triumph was intense on the west side of the Atlantic. Eric Goldman wrote that the USA in the late 1950s was so prosperous that it was positively fat. Another historian, Jim F. Heath, described America as confident it could lead the world 'to new plateaus of achievement'.[12] Amongst the goals which America sought early in the 1960s were victory against poverty and racism at home, the outpacing of Russia in the space race, and the guarantee of some freedom to people in the new nations. Professor Stephen E. Ambrose, looking back, justifiably wrote: 'It was a breathtaking program, which we know now was far beyond reach. The problem is, why did so many believe in it? This brings us back to optimism – never in the nation's history have so many felt that so much could be done so quickly.'[13]

A series of catch phrases summed up these years. Mr Harold Macmillan, as prime minister of England, told his people that they had 'never had it so good'. Germany was described by the new phrase 'the economic miracle', while for Australia the editor Donald Horne invented the phrase 'The Lucky Country' though he emphasised that the luck might not last. For the western world, J. K. Galbraith coined the phrase 'The Affluent Society'.[14] Such was the cheerful glow of the time that phrases like 'Affluent Society' and 'Lucky Country', though devised to criticise as much as to praise, soon became in the public's hands a new international coinage of self-congratulation.

In the social sciences there was a sense of mastery. The problem of poverty in the western world had been largely solved, and the solution had come from capitalism and not from a revolutionary formula. A new era seemed to be dawning. Daniel Bell, the sociologist, was one of the first to diagnose thoughtfully the coming era, and he called it the post-industrial society while Herman Kahn called it the post-economic society. Peter Drucker called it 'the knowledge society', for knowledge was growing so swiftly as to create *The Age of Discontinuity*: that was the title of his book of 1971. Not since the heyday of the idea of progress in the nineteenth century had there been, among social scientists, such a widespread belief that the future would be reassuring and, above all, manageable.[15]

Unveiling The Great Society

The mood in the western world is strongly influenced by the mood in the leading nation of the era. If that nation is super-confident, other nations can imbibe that mood even if they do not share all the reasons for being confident. In the period from 1945 to 1970 the United States was the inspirer of confidence. Even stronger than Britain had been at the height of her power, the United States was the most powerful economy in the world and her average citizen had the highest standard of living. She led in new technology, her nuclear arsenal was devastating and her conventional forces were impressive. Russia's Sputnik of 1957 created a shock primarily because observers had taken it for granted that the United States automatically led in the expensive fields of inventiveness.

The United States seemed to have the world at its toes. President Kennedy promised a world shaped in a younger, fresher image. The word *charisma* accompanied him, even to Dallas. The magic wand passed to his successor, Lyndon B. Johnson, who, in his commencement address at the University of Michigan in 1964, unveiled his plan for 'The Great Society'.[16] The address today reads like that of a master magician, surveying the last 150 years and gesturing towards the future:

> For a century we labored to settle and to subdue the continent.
> For half a century we called upon unbounded invention and

untiring industry to create an order of plenty for all of our people.

The goal of the next half a century, he announced, was even more ambitious. By adding mental and spiritual riches to material riches, Americans could build The Great Society.

The international economy was now impeccably behaved, and it is surprising to look back on the stability of the prices of foodstuffs, minerals and other basic commodities. In 1966 the prices were almost stationary, the rise being 0.1 per cent: a rise of one unit in a thousand is hardly worth recording. The years 1967 and 1968 were notable because in the midst of the inflationary effects of the Vietnam War the world index of the prices of commodities actually fell. While the prices of food and industrial raw materials were falling slightly, there was some increase in manufactured goods and services and therefore a small rise in the consumer price index. The stability of that index was to end in 1969 when inflation reached 8 per cent, followed by 6 per cent in 1970, but the following year recorded a mere 1 per cent inflation.

The politicians in power were aided by these stable prices, while manufacturers, farmers, mine-owners, investors, bankers and trade union leaders could also feel more assurance in making their decisions because of the relative stability of prices. For wage-earners the years from 1955 to 1969 had the wonderful boon of rising wages along with fairly stable prices. This Era of the Beckoning Moon also had cheap energy, and the oil gushing from the wells of the Middle East, Indonesia, Nigeria, Mexico and California was so cheap that machines could afford to waste it. This was surely an industrial era when in the language of The Bible, the world's cup runneth over. Indeed the economist, Barbara Ward, argued in retrospect that the cheap oil and grain were vital for the good times of the 1960s.[17]

A long economic boom went hand in hand with faith in new inventions, each aiding the other. For Europe, North America and all the capitalist democracies, the daily life of the average wage-earner was transformed. The miserable levels of unemployment of the 1920s and 1930s were not repeated. Economic growth was rapid, and in the ten years from 1945 to 1955 the nations of Western Europe expanded their industrial production at a faster rate than that achieved after the First World War. Whereas that earlier expansion had been halted by the world depression, the economic growth in the jet age went on and on, so that Holland, Germany, France and Italy redoubled their industrial production between 1955 and 1968.[18] The iron ore, coal, oil, copper, alumina, timber, and all the raw materials needed for this expansion were produced with ease, making the earth seem inexhaustible.

Fast air travel was the hallmark of this era as much as fast rail travel had been of Queen Victoria's and Bismarck's era. It was expected that everyone would fly, and fly everywhere. During the first decade of the jet aircraft from 1958 to 1968, the costs of travelling each mile were cut with such ease that governments and airline companies began to forecast that their passengers would increase at 15 per cent a year. The new wide-bodied aircraft would carry tourists at cheap fares, 'burning fuel at ten cents a gallon and not a penny more', noted a Boeing executive. The giant 747 plane, far too big to be profitable, was a brainchild of the exuberant mid 1960s, but exuberance was almost universal during the long post-war boom.[19]

That brilliant economic and social observer, Professor Kenneth Boulding, asked himself what mark an examiner would give to the world for its economic performance in recent years. Using the American system of marking in which F is a clear failure, he awarded an F to the 1920s and 1930s. 'In contrast, the 1950s and 1960s deserve at least a C+, and perhaps even a B.' He justified a higher mark for the post-war years by pointing to the increasing wealth of the advanced countries, the improvement in most of the poor countries, the absence of a second world depression and of a third world war, and the converting of most of the old colonies into independent nations.[20] He pointed to a world transformed.

Great Leaps Forward, and Sideways

Now that the secret of economic growth had been learnt from Keynes, even the poorest of nations could be lifted from poverty. Nothing illustrated so clearly the optimism of the post-war era than the idea that new nations in Africa and Asia, just struggling to gain self rule, could quickly improve their standard of living.

Send them a plane-load of experts, and they would begin the climb towards prosperity.

Back in the 1920s the idea of abolishing poverty and starvation in India, China, and the Africas had seemed Utopian. It was widely believed that poverty was their eternal lot, and that without the recent efforts of England, France and other imperial powers, they would have been even more backward. Trusteeship was a favourite word: the people of Europe were guardians for races which were permanently under-age and could not care properly for themselves. The native peoples were said to be idle; the hot sun was said to deter them from hard work; and some of their customs were hostile to saving, investing, and economic progress. Such judgments seem condescending, and in part they were, but they also recognised the wide gulf then existing in achievement and in effort between say western Europe and central Africa. In the colonial era the tropical peoples had seemed incapable of bridging the gap, and even seemed to lack the desire to do so.

The Chinese and the Japanese were exempted from these pessimistic observations but only half-exempted. They might compete through sheer hard work and self sacrifice, but they were said to lack the ingenuity to be real competitors. Japan was seen as primarily an imitator, not an innovator. These were common views in North America and Europe in the period 1919–39.

In 1949 the long war in China was ended and the communists won control, and many westerners believed that a new form of government would work wonders there, even though the task was forbidding. The peasant's equipment was simple and there were few railways to carry relief foods to famished areas, especially those in the far interior. 'The least failure of harvests, the occurrence of a severe flood, was bound to inflict vast misery', wrote Professor C. P. FitzGerald of the China of 1900, and it was still true.[21] Despite the peristence of traditional problems, the optimism within China remained surprisingly high.

In 1958, Chairman Mao called for A Great Leap Forward and coined a slogan that was almost too long to be painted on a banner: 'Catch up and surpass Britain in the output of major industrial goods within 15 years.' Britain at that time was dynamic, and Mao's ambitious goal became clear when he predicted that three years would be sufficient for China to surpass Britain. Soon there were said to be 600,000 small blast furnaces operating in China, baby backyard furnaces producing molten iron by the bucket full. It was all rather hair-brained.[22] That leap forward proved to be the leap of the lame, and yet optimism persisted. China's exploding of its first nuclear device in 1964 showed how far she had come in several branches of science.

India was a source of despair and optimism. While its huge population was vulnerable to famine India was also a source of optimism because, during the British rule, new railways and irrigation projects had reduced the impact of famine; and indeed one historian argued that between 1880 and 1943 'death from starvation' was virtually eliminated in India, and another called it 'the conquest of famine'.[23] Probably this praise was too extreme, for in the 1901 famine perhaps one million Indians died in British-governed territories and another three million died in the native states. Starvation became less common, and the loss of at least two million lives in the Bengal famine of 1943 was a shock partly because of the preceding decades of improvement. In fact the harvest in that hungry year was close to normal, but the distribution of grain was impeded by wartime dislocation, weak British administration, price controls, and by Indians who hoarded the scarce grain. All in all the long British campaign against famine in India was successful enough to encourage the idea that a war against want would eventually succeed everywhere.

By the mid 1950s many European economists began to have a vision of a billion coloured people wearing a clean white shirt every morning and eating a steaming bowl of food two or three times a day. The new nations were eager to improve literacy and health and over-eager to westernise. The belief that the third world could be developed with relative ease was supported by a variety of arguments and intuitions. As its peoples increasingly governed themselves, they could make policies to suit their own needs. Fear of communism prompted some western nations to invest heavily in these poor lands, though much of the aid was futile. Above all, the new knowledge of economics was believed to provide a sharp weapon for reducing poverty. Multiplying knowledge was an energetic contributor to the sense of mastery now so widespread in Harvard and The Hague, Paris and London. 'We know' was almost the motto by 1960.

The Return of the Ladder with the Easy Steps

An idea which had once been the vogue in anthropology, biology and religion, and was still powerful in left-wing economics, now reappeared in right-wing economics. This was the evolutionists' idea that all nations must pass through certain stages of development, that each stage was the logical step to the next, and that each stage was an improvement on the last. The ladder theory of progress served indirectly as a cheer squad for nations of the third world. If they patiently imitated the formula they too would climb to Europe's prosperous heights.

The American economist and historian, Walt W. Rostow, was the celebrated economic evolutionist of the 1950s. Rostow was professor of economic history at the Massachusetts Institute of Technology and later the special assistant to President Johnson, serving him as a prominent hawk during the Vietnam War, but his real fame was established in 1952 when he produced a guidebook to economic development called *The Process of Economic Growth*. In some ways a do-it-yourself book for backward countries, it stressed the role of new technology and analysed how successful countries had reached prosperity. Rostow suggested from a study of history that there was a simple flight-path along which each nation could travel towards abundance. They simply had to pass through five stages: traditional society, the preparation for take-off, the take-off, the drive to maturity, and finally maturity. There was a neatness about his stages, and the metaphor of 'take-off' suited the new age of rockets and jet engines, thus endowing his formula with authority as well as simplicity.

Missions of economists and delegations of bureaucrats landed at airports in India, the Philippines, East Africa and central America and breathed a confidence that if their advice were taken, economic development would be rapid. Capital would pour in, agriculture would be modernised, big industries would arise in the cities, railways would be built and beggars would vanish. In the incoming luggage and the outgoing reports of these travelling advisers was a new language. Poor countries were no longer poor but were 'developing' or 'under-developed'. Curiously, while there were under-developed countries in the world, nobody said there were over-developed countries, and yet an equally persuasive case could have been made for the

existence of the 'overs' as the 'unders'. Thus the valuable
Everyman's Dictionary of Economics described 'Under-developed
Countries' as extremely poor but did not leave them at that.
Their key attribute was that they were 'literally countries capable
of economic development'.[24] The definition showed the
period's in-built optimism. It was equivalent to defining poverty
as primarily a condition which could be cured, and yet poverty
by definition must be poverty, irrespective of whether it is
curable.

In the 1960s, a wordy optimism was in the air. The General
Assembly of the United Nations christened the 1960s the
'Development Decade' and set a minimum target of economic
growth of 5 per cent a year. In Washington in 1959 the future
president, John F. Kennedy, had actually informed the US senate
that plucky India had virtually reached the take-off stage. In
Delhi the director of the Institute of Economic Growth, Professor
V. K. R. V. Rao, reported in 1965 that India's economic achievements in some ways had been 'truly massive' and that by 1970
the economy might well reach the take-off stage. Even in Ceylon
where population grew by almost half between 1948 and 1962,
and the unemployment rate was a forbidding 11 per cent, hope
was still alive in the officials who planned to exceed the USA's
rate of economic growth and to create a job for everyone in the
space of a couple of years.[25] Every new nation was to try to be
another Japan, for it was becoming the economic marvel.

Japan had been in a sad plight in 1946. Food was so scarce
that the typical worker in a city was allowed only 1600 calories
a day, and raw materials and equipment were so paltry that
industrial production was only about one sixth of the pre-war
level. Slowly and then quickly Japan recovered. In the twenty
years after the war it doubled its rural output while reducing its
army of farm labourers by millions. The building of ships was a
special success, for in 1955 Japan built less than half of the
tonnage of British shipyards but ten years later it was building
four times the British tonnage and was about to complete the
largest tanker the world had seen, a vessel that dwarfed the
Queen Mary and *Queen Elizabeth* and *France* and the huge ocean
liners. The gargantuan Japanese tanker was a showpiece of a
nation that by the mid 1960s led the world in shipbuilding, was
second in synthetic fibres and the production of cars and buses,
and third in steel and sulphuric acid. Japan specialised in the

small as well as the big, breaking into the electronics market with miniature transistor radios and the 8 inch television screen. Japan's economic achievements ran far ahead of the informed world's appreciation of them.[26] Japan did not boast of success: it just succeeded. The time will come when historians probably see Japan's growth in the 1950s and 1960s as a vital cause of the optimism of those decades but the truth is that at the time much of the western world ignored Japan. The Second World War and its memories of Japanese militarism were still vivid and deterred westerners from singling out Japan as a guiding light for poor nations to follow.

Brilliant economists – Albert Hirschman, Ragnar Nurkse, Hans Singer, Paul Rosenstein-Rodan and others – offered their own competing theories of how to enrich the poor lands. The task at first was not seen as herculean, but there were disagreements on how to achieve it. The disagreements increased as the results lagged. In 1968 the Swedish economist, Gunnar Myrdal, celebrated his seventieth birthday with a long book, *Asian Drama*, which challenged the main line of thinking that there would be an early and happy ending to the struggle against poverty. The discussion he aroused showed that the seesaw of ideas was moving again.

The profession of economics, glamorous since the war, was later to be egg-spattered a little, but to most economists the prestige of economics in the 1950s and 1960s needed no explanation: in their eyes its prestige was merited by the advanced state of economic theory while its later inadequacies came from factors largely beyond economists' control. To offer a contrary explanation for the prestige of economics is, I know, to run the risk of committing heresy against a proud and capable profession but an alternative view can be offered. There are some periods in which economic progress comes rather easily, and the economic theory of the day, whether Keynes's or Marshall's or demand-side or supply-side, may well be only one contributor to that progress. Moreover the capitalist economy is more likely to flourish when western civilisation is confident and likely to be weaker when that civilisation is gloomy. Overall the cultural environment is more relevant to prosperity than we imagine.

It would be foolish to think that the real world of climate and harvest, new products and new ways of making old products, of changing birth-rates, of peace and war, does not affect economic

events, moods and theories. At the same time most of those
events of the real world – and above all the way in which we
interpret those events – are also influenced by the wide cultural
mood, by the way people think and by the attitudes they hold
at one time rather than another. Ideas and attitudes can virtually
have a momentum and dynamism of their own. They can assert
themselves, they can change pace and direction even when all
the economic evidence suggests that they are tightly harnessed
and controlled by the economic world.

To say that the economic conditions and mood of a year
affects the songs that are sung is to say the obvious. It is also
true that the songs sung, the books written, the pictures painted
and the films made do affect the economic conditions, both now
and a little later. Such an hypothesis is more likely to appeal
to a pop singer than to an economist. And yet it is fair to say
that in the late 1960s, on the eve of the main turning point in
post-war economic life, the portents of change were more visible
in the music charts of the Top Forty than in the latest securities
chart from Wall Street.

10 The King is Dying: The Swing against technology

When we despair of a way of life, wrote the Spanish philosopher José Ortega Y. Gasset, our instinctive remedy is to turn our existing values upside down. 'If wealth does not give happiness, poverty will; if learning does not solve everything, then true wisdom will lie in ignorance.' Whatever is fashionable can suddenly become unfashionable. The late 1960s witnessed such a reversal of values, and it still shapes our times.

Scientific advance, widely worshipped as a key to a better world in 1960, was no longer trusted in certain influential circles in 1970. Some critics began to denounce technology as producing an era of extravagance in which people consumed what they did not need. Some critics thundered that industrial growth was evil because it was the tool of the rich rather than the poor and of rich nations rather than all nations. Some lamented that technology, in temporarily overcoming disease and famine, was producing a surplus of population which would ultimately bring back famine and disease. In the opinion of Robin Clarke, technology's crime was its ruthless anonymity and lack of soul: 'Ours is a society dedicated to replacing people by machines, one in which the last forms of social communion are fast disappearing.'[1] Even leisure in its new abundance was a target for thoughtful critics of technology; the whale-sized stadiums of spectator sport vexed Lewis Mumford, television vexed Jacques Ellul, automobiles vexed René Dubos, and the cult of hot dog and coca-cola was distasteful to Theodore Roszak.[2] The most pervasive critics said that technology had become the enemy of Nature, endangering it with wars, pesticides, the pollution of ocean and atmosphere and other acts of folly.

The admired post-war prosperity was an essential prerequisite for the swing in values and attitudes. The quarter century running from 1945 to 1970 was the great success story of recorded economic history. Based on the busy application of new technology and a respect for material success and a galloping confidence, it saw the old economic ills of poverty and unemployment as curable, even in the third world. But there came a time

175

when material success was almost taken for granted by some. The prosperity was such that it could even finance the new opponents of material success. All those followers of the ways of nature, essentially people of leisure, were heavily subsidised by the material prosperity against which they rebelled. But if economic times had been harsh, and if technology had been simpler and less productive, most of the young people who went to Woodstock and to the rallies against the Vietnam War and the crusades in favour of nature would instead have been working hard for a living. Just as the prosperity financed the protests, so the prosperity and the triumph of technology also provided the ammunition for its new enemies. The world's soaring consumption of food and minerals became the warning bell for those scholars who saw ahead a period of exhaustion and famine, while the pollution that came from the new machines and new products nourished the fear that this stampede of production, consumption and waste would eventually imperil nature and even mankind.

The Swing from Technology to Nature

There had been numerous warnings against rampant technology in the early post-war years but few had listened to them. Aldo Leopold, an American forester who had long campaigned on behalf of wilderness, wrote a distinctive book insisting that the rights of nature should be respected, just as the rights of slaves had been belatedly respected.[3] His *Sand County Almanac*, published after his death, met mainly deaf ears in 1949 when the public motto was still 'everlasting economic growth'. In 1954, Jacques Ellul, a French theologian and philosopher, proclaimed in his book *The Technological Society* that the machines were producing more of everything but that quantity was bowing to quality in daily life. His book was not deemed relevant enough to be translated into English until, ten years later, it was extolled by Thomas Merton, monk and mystic, as one of the most important of the era.[4]

Warnings of the hidden dangers of technology were now reaching millions of homes. One of the first popular warnings was Rachel Carson's *Silent Spring*, an exposure of how DDT and other new chemicals were harming America on land and shore. Published in 1962, her book was a little ahead of its time, but it helped to bring the time a little closer. Even the cigarette was now seen as a pollutant, and in the United States at Christmas 1963, the Surgeon General delivered his report on the dangers of smoking cigarettes. Although pollution as a general issue aroused no concern in Gallup polls, individual episodes of pollution were arousing alarm and would coalesce in the late 1960s as the seesaw continued to swing towards nature.

Modern man was now being seen as the enemy of nature on every front. He was fouling his own nest with his chemicals, sprays, factory fumes, oil spills, nuclear tests, spray-cans, and his centrally-heated civilisation. In the advanced lands the farmers were guilty of new practices which were astonishingly wasteful of fertilisers and fuel and said to be astonishingly destructive of soil. Barry Commoner set out the case dramatically, calling the present system of production 'self-destructive' and the path of civilisation 'suicidal'.[6]

Allegations against technology that seemed eccentric in 1960 were now respectable. Thus the carbon dioxide which entered the atmosphere from the burning of oil, coal and wood was said to be turning the planet into a hothouse in which artificially high temperatures would inflict disaster on some regions. This idea was not new, having surfaced during an earlier and short-lived tilt of the seesaw. In 1896 the professor of physics at Stockholm University, S. A. Arrhenius had published an article on *The Influence of Carbonic Acid in the Air upon the Temperature of the Ground'*, and three years later President Chamberlain of the University of Wisconsin offered a similar warning. Both scholars came from regions of ice and snow where a change in temperature and an increase in dryness would harm the harvests. Their theories, however, won few converts. 'For reasons that are hard to understand', wrote two research scientists at Princeton, 'this startling hypothesis attracted relatively little attention until the 1960s.'[7]

'For reasons that are hard to understand'? I wonder! A gap of some seventy years between the enunciating of a theory and its next step up the slippery ladder towards acceptability is not rare, particularly in those fields of knowledge sensitive to the angle of the seesaw. With the revival of the climatic fears in the 1960s, the two Princeton scientists estimated what would happen if the amount of carbon dioxide in the atmosphere was increased rapidly in the following decades. If it doubled, the earth's temperature would rise about 3° C, and it would be even hotter in the northern hemisphere. The scientists suggested that if the world continued to burn fossil fuels on an increasing scale, the dryer climate would eventually harm the vital grain-producing areas of North America and the Soviet Union, reducing the world's supply of food. In compensation, dry areas of the world would be moister and China, Australia and California would gain overall, and most of Africa would gain. The fear that excessive amounts of carbon dioxide would alter the climate gave rise to anxiety that the ice near the poles might slowly melt, thus raising the level of the oceans and drowning coastal cities. The research was backed by statistics straight from the computer and that gave urgency to the warnings. In the late 1960s in Europe and the United States, much of the research on the earth, climate, oceans and outer space was reassuring, but side by side was a thickening cluster of more pessimistic research, for a nuclear war as well as carbon dioxide could wreck what was seen increasingly as the benign balance of nature.

In explaining the fear, an intense fear, in the late 1960s that nature was being permanently damaged by technology and that natural resources were in danger of exhaustion, many critics emphasised that the world itself was shrinking rapidly through new means of communication at the very time when its population was bulging. Without doubt this sense of a shrinking world was strong in the late 1960s, for television pictures were sent by satellite across the world, and man was about to land on the moon, and mass international travel had arrived. But it is relevant to ask why this sense of a shrinking world should have been a cause for pessimism rather than optimism? The taming of distance and the swift global flow of knowledge are as capable of promoting optimism as pessimism. Indeed, the world had also been shrinking in the late 1950s – the time of the first Sputnik and the time when the aircraft was superseding the passenger ship on long-distance routes – and yet the sense of a shrinking world was not then seen with gloom.

Significantly, the same fear of a shrinking world had appeared in the period 1890 to 1905, alongside those aggressive slogans of over-population, The Yellow Peril and Lebensraum. The 1890s had much in common with the late 1960s, and in each era the feeling of shrinking space and diminishing resources is illuminated by an understanding of how the seesaw works.

Crusaders

Campaigns to save wildernesses, beaches, cities, the sea and the air now implied, or suggested, that the whole world would be endangered unless the process of economic development was halted and even reversed. In the United States, 1969 and 1970 were years of dramatic campaigns. In California an oil rig spilled oil on the sea like a vast vomit, leading to an outcry for reform, and a campaign halted plans for a jet airport in the Everglades National Park in Florida. Attempts to lay an oil pipeline across the wilds of Alaska were thwarted under the new National Environment Act. The Congress, facing the question of whether to continue to finance the development of supersonic air transport, refused further aid for a project which would have been applauded a decade earlier. In the United States, perhaps 1971 marked the peak of the concern about the environment but in many countries the peak of concern lay years ahead.

The quickening interest in nature spurred new organisations. The Friends of the Earth were born in 1969. Campaigns were launched to aid endangered creatures, 'Save the Whale' being one triumph. In Washington in 1972 the Committee on Population Growth and The American Future reported to President Nixon that no 'substantial benefit would result from continued growth of the nation's population' and that a stable population would help to preserve wildernesses and natural resources. At Stockholm in the same year the United Nations held a conference on the human environment, a theme which would have been unappealing one decade previously. The Club of Rome issued its report of gloom in the same year.[8]

In the cities thousands of young professionals began to alter their way of life, and in their leisure hours they imitated the simplicity of nature. The bicycle was revived, even before the petrol crisis of 1973 induced more people to press the foot down on a pedal rather than an accelerator. Joggers appeared on footpaths and parklands, and in 1974 those naked sprinters called 'streakers' made their brief dashes in public places. In the mid 1970s, in American cities and then in cities as far apart as Sydney and London, the mass-participation marathon or 'fun run' became the vogue. Health foods and diet charts were multiplied. The smoking of cigarettes became less fashionable, partly because of the new fear of lung cancer but perhaps also because the cigarette was seen as yet another pollutant and yet another artifact of a scurrying, tension-filled society.

It was in this atmosphere that Ivan Illich, a scholar and priest, called scientific medicine 'one of the most rapidly spreading epidemics of our time', and spoke well of witch doctors and of the noble savage as healers. People should shun doctors and their 'sick making' ways, and heal themselves or, if necessary, learn to live with pain. His book, *Medical Nemesis*, was a vivid example of that somersault in which Nature was seen with new respect. It is fair to suggest that the operating theatre with its robed and masked people, its isolation from the world, its sterile air, artificial oxygen, sense of high purpose and appearance of tension had become – on television screens – another version of the cabin of a spaceship. To attack medicine, especially the medicine of the cavernous hospitals and secluded research institutes, was to attack technology itself and its ally, the cult of the new.

Small is Beautiful, Big is a Menace

In the reaction against technology, many enthusiasts did not go the whole way. They saw nature and technology as vital and searched for a way in which the two could live side by side. One seeker of a truce, E. F. Schumacher, believed that 'there is overwhelming evidence that the great self-balancing system of Nature is becoming increasingly unbalanced' and he pointed to Lake Erie and many other polluted places. The existing attitudes, so wasteful and polluting, also limited the scope for creativity and enjoyment in one of the most vital of all daily activities, work. He called for smaller factories, workshops and farms on the grounds that the smaller unit was more personal and responsible and less likely to harm the environment. 'There is wisdom in smallness', he wrote in 1970. Schumacher's name became associated with the slogan, 'Small is Beautiful', for he was the theoretical defender of the folk of the counter-culture who busied themselves in such economic enterprises as hand-weaving, organic crop-growing and the keeping of free-range hens and woolly goats.[9] His slogan summed up a crucial facet of the swing of the seesaw, for it was moving from a worship of industrial growth to the seeking of emotional and aesthetic satisfaction. The jet turbine and nuclear reactor were making way for the flower.

Vietnam and the Noble Peasant

The distaste for technology was intensified by the war in Vietnam which was seen by some as a struggle between destructive technology and innocent nature. Brutal machines were fighting the people of nature – so one wave of propaganda implied – and to the surprise of many the simple people were winning. The fact that many Vietnamese peasants used the latest Russian weapons was not so often noticed by young American opponents of their nation's involvement.

Vietnam was seen as the battleground for moral combats, the rich versus the poor, the materialist west versus the spiritualist east, as well as Technology versus Nature. In that struggle, both nature and people were violated each day: the craters could be seen right across Vietnamese landscapes, and simple villages were wrecked and trees flattened and irrigation systems ruined and animals killed. A distorted picture of the war, it was plausible enough to be widely accepted. It touched the poetic sentiment as well as compassion, and it subtly glorified a new version of the Noble Savage – the Vietnamese peasants who were acclaimed as morally superior because they were uncorrupted by the materialist, industrialised west.

Michael J. Arlen, writing on television for *The New Yorker*, called Vietnam 'the living-room war'. Perhaps six in every ten Americans received most of their news about the war on television, often seeing an event filmed less than thirty hours previously. Arlen observed that television, with its preference for scenes rather than words and for action rather than inaction, gave 'an excessively simple, emotional, and military-oriented view of what is, at best, a mighty unsimple situation.'[10] It was like looking at a war through a keyhole. Most of the war was out of sight and much that was in sight was disconnected and almost scatter-brained. Such a war seen in such a way could easily be portrayed as a cruel assault by the technological west against nature's simple homeland in the east, especially in the minds of viewers who were emotionally predisposed to such an interpretation.

The influence of the Vietnam war came partly from the way in which it cut American society down the middle. The nation was drawn and quartered by the war, and young opposed young, old opposed old, and young and old were opposed. If the Vietnam War had actually endangered the security of the United States it would have knitted the nation together; but because the war was not such a threat, millions of Americans could afford the luxury of opposing it. Their opposition was not simply to war itself but was extended to the very culture and values of which the war was believed to be the product. They opposed America's emphasis on technology, especially in warfare. They opposed American materialism and individualism, in contrast to what they saw as the frugality and the sense of community of the Vietnamese. They opposed their own nation of cities which fought a nation of peasants. And so by these mental somersaults they came to oppose or question mainstream American values as well as the bombing, napalm and other products of America's military technology.

Rarely in the last two and a half centuries has a major nation been so divided by a war. It is true that French opinion was divided by the long war in Algeria from 1830 to 1848; it is true that France again was divided by her defeat in the Franco–Prussian War of 1870–71; it is true that England was divided by the Boer War of 1899–1902 and Russia too was divided, as much as a police state can be divided, by her unsuccessful wars against Japan in 1905 and against Germany in 1917. Opinion in France was also divided when she tried, after the Second World War, to use force to cling to her old colonies in Algeria and Indo-China. But of these wartime nations only Russia in 1917 could be compared in visible divisiveness with America during the war in Vietnam. The division along the middle of American society had a profound effect in diverting many of those who opposed the war into also opposing many of the mainstream values of American leaders who justified the war.

It would be a mistake to see the war simply as an independent event which added to the distaste for technology, heightened a new respect for nature and therefore largely set in motion the great seesaw. Just as the war affected the seesaw, so the seesaw affected the war. The seesaw is an aggregate of influences; it is the mood and opinion of a particular time, and that mood is so pervasive that it can affect the conduct of a war and the interpreting of a war. In a different intellectual mood, there would have been less guilt at America's use of her military technology, there would have been less sympathy for the Vietnamese simply as peasants and members of a different culture, and less toleration towards those Americans who wished to sabotage the war effort.

The Strange Oscillations of Nuclear Fears

Surprisingly in the western world the fear of nuclear weapons was not a dominant fear during the Vietnam War. Since nuclear weapons were the most frightening symbol of technology, we would expect a rising fear of technology to be expressed most pungently through hostility to nuclear weapons. In the late 1960s the opposite happened. The nuclear fears declined in the very years that the fear of technology in general seemed to be rising. I have not seen this contradiction pointed out, and it is an obstinate piece in the jigsaw.

The campaign by private citizens against nuclear weapons, especially in the United States, was weak in the late 1940s. Later the radioactive particles which entered the atmosphere after nuclear tests began to arouse concern, because no corner of the world could escape contamination. In 1953 the word *fall-out* was first used, and in 1954 the effects of nuclear fall-out could be seen on Japanese fishermen. In 1955, radioactive rain fell on Chicago. Within a few years the popular fear of nuclear war had become a subject for movie-makers, and *On The Beach* and *Dr. Strangelove* were seen by tens of millions on cinema and television screens.

Many Americans began to oppose nuclear weapons after 1957, when the launching of the Sputnik suggested that Russia might outpace the United States in sophisticated weapons. Americans who previously had held little fear of nuclear weapons because they believed that the United States was the master of nuclear warfare now changed their mind. A nuclear disaster ceased to be something which America might inflict on its enemy. It was now conceivable that a nuclear missile might hit New York, and the fear was multiplied during the Cuban crisis of October 1962, when Russian missiles were detected opposite the coast of Florida. For a few days Russia and America seemed to be close to what the Russian leader, Khrushchev, called 'the abyss of a nuclear war'. The tension eventually promoted useful discussions, and in July 1963, President Kennedy and Mr Khrushchev signed a treaty in which both nations agreed to make no further nuclear tests in the atmosphere. A nuclear war was not banned; underground tests of nuclear arms were not banned; nor did France and China agree to forgo their own testing of nuclear arms in the atmosphere.

The solving of the Cuban crisis and the agreement on nuclear tests between the world's two great powers ushered in a less nervous era. Fear of nuclear war seemed to recede, and only 16 per cent of Americans saw nuclear war as their major fear in 1965. Almost unbelievably, nuclear war even slipped from the pollsters' list of the main fears of the American people for a decade or so. Not until the mid 1970s did nuclear fears rapidly revive.

It is not easy to explain the decline of nuclear fears, especially at a time when technology as a whole aroused more fears than perhaps at any previous time in the twentieth century. It is true that by the late 1960s, nuclear power was being used for peaceful purposes, and more nuclear power stations were being planned by industrial nations, but that was not necessarily a source of reassurance because these power stations could generate their own brand of fear. It is true that the propaganda from pro-nuclear scientists, soldiers and politicians was becoming more effective, and the new missiles were even given cuddly names like Hound-Dog or patriotic names like Minuteman or names which, like Poseidon, were culled from the ancient classics. But why was the counter-propaganda against nuclear weapons so weak? It is probable that talented leadership, so vital for any crusade, was diverted from the anti-nuclear cause to the more urgent and specific movement against the Vietnam War. The crusade against that specific war drowned the vaguer anti-nuclear movement. The fact that America did not use nuclear weapons in its long war in Vietnam (1964–1975) tended to quieten the anti-nuclear campaigners.

In the study of international relations the novel and vexed question of how national leaders would act during a nuclear crisis had settled down. Many scholars agreed that major nuclear nations would be wary of using a weapon that could be used against themselves. In essence the nuclear weapon now resem-

bled one of the most ancient of weapons – the returning boomerang – and it was widely believed that, as it might return to
decapitate its thrower, nobody was likely to throw it. Such
factors may help explain why the fear of nuclear war was waning
during the years 1963 to 1975 but they are not quite adequate.
These same factors still operated in some form or other in the
early 1980s when nuclear fears again became widespread.

The Soviet-American ban on nuclear tests in the atmosphere
was a soothing step forward in 1963, but nuclear testing continued underground, and the United States conducted more
tests in the following five years than in the preceding five years.
The arms race went on, with Russia developing a tentative
defence system of antiballistic missiles, and the United States
building its own defences against Russia's nuclear missiles. In
1972 the SALT 1 Treaty was signed, and the two big powers
agreed to limit any increase in nuclear missiles for the next five
years, but they stepped light-footedly around that treaty by
making each missile more deadly.

It is possible to argue that the Soviet-American arms agree-
ments, especially of 1963 and 1972, were vital causes of the
public's lessened fears of nuclear war, but an effective case
could be argued that in those same years the reasons for concern
in the world were not diminishing. Again and again, in examining changes of moods in the last two centuries, one is forced to
conclude that there is not always a simple relationship between
changes in the real world and changes in attitude. Fears, hopes
and perceptions sometimes lag behind the events of the real
world and sometimes they run ahead of events.

The rise and fall of expectations helps to explain the changed
fears towards nuclear war. From 1945 onwards the fear of nuclear
war was a justified cause for alarm. In the 1950s the fear was
accentuated by the discovery that nuclear fall-out crippled or
killed those outside the area which was damaged. The fear of a
nuclear war reached its peak, especially in the United States,
during the Cuban missile crisis of October 1962, but the fear
could not be maintained permanently at that level. No fear can
be sustained year after year if it is unrealised. The boy who too
often cried 'wolf' was no longer listened to. As expectations of
an early nuclear war had not been fulfilled, and as Vietnam did
not become a nuclear war, the fears ebbed, slipping beyond the
point where realistically they should have halted. Expectations

of nuclear war were low by the mid 1970s, and the dangers arising from nuclear energy in peacetime were also lower. These low expectations of disaster were thus ready to be jolted by the emergence of events which showed that nuclear dangers were too real to be ignored. The coming of age of young people who had not lived through the earlier stage of fear also provided a new audience. Having not really experienced the fear, common in the 1950s, that a quarter of the world might be shattered by a nuclear war, the young had been nurtured in the confidence that the world had a future. They were more easily shocked when nuclear fears were spectacularly revived in the late 1970s by a consciousness of Russia's growing nuclear strength and by America's competing plan to install new missiles in Europe and also to produce a neutron bomb that would destroy people rather than buildings.[11] By the early 1980s the fear of nuclear technology was very high at a time when the fear of technology overall seemed to be declining a little.

The Gods Reshuffled

Most of those immersed in the nature movement saw mankind as the main potential victim of technology but many came to believe that nature itself – the ocean, wilderness and tamed land, the soils and rocks and minerals, and every living creature – was as precious as mankind and no less vulnerable. Increasingly nature became an altar to which worshippers came.

As technology was more distrusted, the face of nature took on a new image and even attracted a halo. Nature was now benevolent rather than harsh, an impression heightened by the new producers of programmes for colour television. Nature represented those wonderful forces, creativity and renewal. Nature embodied a miraculous and delicate mechanism of checks and balances which, if heeded, could prevent famine befalling the world's expanding population. Meanwhile the polluted rivers, beaches, cities, forests, clouds, and the radio-active rains increasingly created a feeling of guilt, of collective more than individual guilt towards nature. Guilt over the recent history of western nations became widely felt in the late 1960s, and was expressed in a new sympathy towards coloured peoples as well as towards nature. Vincent Buckley, poet and professor of

English, observing in 1971 the concern of poets with the topic of pollution, concluded that a new 'movement of religious awareness' was abroad.[12] Nature was sacred because it was life itself.

While technology was viewed as the callous commander of the present and the future, nature was depicted lovingly as king of the past. Nature belonged to that childhood world of innocence which Garrett Hardin, professor of biology in the University of California, recalled in 1968:

> It did not much matter how a lonely American frontiersman disposed of his waste. 'Flowing water purifies itself every ten miles', my grandfather used to say, and the myth was near enough to the truth when he was a boy, for there were not too many people. But as population became denser, the natural chemical and biological recycling processes became overloaded.[13]

In the writings of many other scientists nature was increasingly seen as Garden of Eden, suddenly despoiled by man.

It was heartening now to see a great writer who had tried to extol nature a century earlier, when the seesaw was at an unsympathetic angle, now receiving his due acclaim. In 1849 Henry Thoreau had published the first book on his wanderings amongst nature, *A Week on the Concord and Merrimack Rivers*, but the intellectual mood was hostile and after four years not quite 300 copies of his book had been sold or given away. Thoreau loved the untrod wilderness and saw liberty in the wild wide rivers: 'River towns are winged towns'.[14] He disliked fences, railways and telegraphs, and – echoing the eighteenth century admirers of Tahiti – he said that those who were happy with little were possessors of the most wealth. Thoreau admired 'the so-called savages', for they knew more than other Americans about nature, that greatest of all teachers, though in his view they were not capable of profound thought.

After his death in 1862, Thoreau had two revivals of influence. One revival was during that next swing of the seesaw, in the 1890s, when his book *Walden* inspired wilderness writers in America, while his essay in support of *Civil Disobedience* (he spent a night in gaol for refusing to pay a tax in support of his country's war against Mexico), inspired a young Indian reformer named Ghandi. The atmosphere of the 1960s was even more favourable for Thoreau's message; and his love of nature, his contempt for surplus possessions, and his hostility to a war-waging government delivered him ready-made as a hero for the counter-culture. More Americans must have read his books in the 1960s than in all the previous decades added together, and they now read him as if he had had their needs in mind. Thus they saw the Mexican War as 'Thoreau's Vietnam', according to the foreword of one new edition, and they saw him as the living foe of The Establishment: 'he distrusts authority, tradition, the state, organised religion, formalism of any kind.'[15] Thoreau would have been even more relevant had he taken drugs and heard the over-amplified sound of rock music, but at least he had sounded an early alarm against what one of his modern admirers called 'our industrial–technological civilisation'.

With the rising worship of nature, the old gods one by one seemed to retreat. Socialism and capitalism, in the eyes of many or most intellectuals in the west, had failed. Socialism had come to power with the promise that it could give the average family a higher standard of living, but in Europe it clearly was not as efficient as capitalism. Eastern Europe was no match for western Europe in its standard of living, nor could it guarantee individual liberty. Likewise capitalism, though performing more impressively than ever before as a producer of goods, was, by 1970, the target for a variety of criticisms. It was said, in the Vietnam years, to be more likely than communism to cause war, it was said to be exploiting the third world, and the technology which it used on the large scale was seen as the major agent of pollution. As these arguments could have been used against capitalism in the previous decade, their increasing use was a sign of a change in the intellectual mood and less a response to changes in capitalism itself.

In essence the western world had worshipped five main gods in the space of the last two centuries. Of these Christianity was the oldest. Three others – Capitalist Individualism or Liberalism, Science or Technology, and Democratic Socialism – were largely creatures of the nineteenth century and its fascination with progress. These three younger gods saw technology as the mainspring or the essential guarantor of progress. A loss of faith in technology was therefore a major blow to each of the secular gods that had arisen in the nineteenth century; it was even a minor blow to Christianity. Compared to most Asian religions,

Christianity had tended to be sympathetic to technology and indifferent to nature. A Persian professor of philosophy, Seyyed Hossein Nasr, has argued persuasively that the Christian tradition, unlike other religions, saw nature as a force or sphere to be conquered or harnessed.[16] Even St. Francis of Assisi did not succeed in establishing nature as a major spiritual concern of the medieval church.

In the mid 1960s the reaction against technology was in effect a reaction against Christianity. The way was thus open for Nature, that fifth god which had been a vitalising creed during the Romantic era early in the nineteenth century, to become vital again. Nature could be invoked both by those who opposed technology on rational grounds and by those who detested it on emotional grounds. In the intensifying swing against Technology, Nature became a secular and even a spiritual god.

Postscript: The Intellectuals' Enemy

The distrust of technology was increased by a long-term factor: it was seen in intellectual circles as allied too closely to capitalism. Technology was falling from favour partly because capitalism was less in favour, while the falling prestige of capitalism came partly from the suspicion directed towards its partner, technology.

In the western world for much of the nineteenth century there had been an alliance between capitalists and intellectuals, for most intellectuals came from the families of capitalism and were largely financed by the profits of commerce. Who else could finance them in a period when the government gave them virtually no subsidies and when the universities were small and few? Once the ideology of free trade came into favour, most businessmen became general advocates of the free flow of ideas as well as commodities. Compared to the landed interests, businessmen in 1850 were radicals, eager to hear new ideas and to support that freedom which suited intellectuals as well as businessmen. Intellectuals for their part were also happy to support new technology, because the steam printing press, the telegraph, and the printing paper made from wood pulp were amongst the many inventions aiding the spread of knowledge and the rising role of intellectuals. Of course capitalism was distasteful to many intellectuals, but when in 1913 the English Fabians called for the nationalisation of mines and railways they were a tiny minority swimming against the English intellectual stream.[17] The possibility that one day a large proportion of intellectuals in the humanities and social sciences would be hostile to capitalism and also to technology seemed remote. And yet the remote became the reality. In 1969 Professor John Passmore suggested that the 'twentieth-century radical' is normally hostile to big business and often suspicious of little business.[18] A decade later, Professor Robert Nisbet, writing his excellent *History of the Idea of Progress*, approved of Passmore's observation and even took the liberty, maybe unconsciously, of slightly misquoting it by saying with some truth that intellectuals in the twentieth century, had a 'characteristic repugnance for things economic', especially if capitalist things.[19]

It is not easy to explain convincingly this strong intellectual hostility to capitalism, especially when the alternative was bleak. One source of hostility lay in capitalism itself and its inability to solve unemployment between the 1880s and the 1930s, and another in its inequitable apportioning of rewards. Intellectuals' hostility to capitalism came also from the initial attractiveness of socialism, especially the hopes pinned on the Soviet Union between 1917 and the late 1940s. Amongst scientists there was less suspicion towards capitalism, for it strongly supported technical change and the application of ideas fresh from the laboratories.

The rift between intellectuals and capitalism came, at times, from envy. Successful capitalists made far more money and seemed to hold more power than intellectuals held. The fact that money now seemed to possess more prestige than that other form of currency – ideas – was vexing to many intellectuals. There can be little doubt that in the last hundred years the prestige of business – previously low compared to the prestige of intellectuals and landed interests – had risen in the eyes of the general public.

Many intellectuals felt a moral superiority towards business, seeing it as tainted by the profit motive, but such moral superiority was not widespread a century ago. Then the income of most intellectuals did not come from governments, universities and other public institutions but rather from business, whether that of families or patrons. Darwin and Wallace, Spencer and

Marx received no income or protection from universities or the state but depended largely on money that came directly or indirectly from commerce. Later the rise of an intellectual industry, with its own secure base in universities and other public institutions, enabled scholars to become independent of business. Thus, as America involved itself deeply in the war in Vietnam, and as many intellectuals criticised that involvement, they extended their attack to big business and the military technology which it manufactured. That target was summarised in the ubiquitous phrase of that era, 'the military industrial complex'.

One of the key facts of modern history, this slowly changing relationship between big business and intellectuals was also affected by the great seesaw. In the two decades from 1945 to 1965, the rift between intellectuals and capitalism was partly repaired in economics, political science, history, sociology, educational theory, and allied disciplines. Capitalism was seen by fewer scholars as an ogre. By the 1970s, however, the seesaw had again tilted, and capitalism and technology were increasingly seen as the source of most social ills.

11 Rise of the Counter-Culture

Prosperity and plain sailing on the economic ocean boosted the challenge to existing values in the late 1960s. Money and material comfort were now taken for granted, a well-paid job was seen as a bore rather than as a privilege, and a roof over one's head and a free ride along the road were seen as a right. To travel lightly, with few possessions, was as much a delight in the late 1960s as it had been a burden to the young unemployed in the days of the world depression. The counter-culture was like the American war-effort in Vietnam: both activities were heavily subsidised by an economic machine of stupendous productivity. Without the earlier triumph of technology, the wide-ranging attack on technology and on the civilisation it supported and shaped would have been impossible.

Sergeant Pepper's Lonely Hearts Club

The prominence of the young in the new mood of the late 1960s was foreshadowed by the Teddy Boys, Elvis Presley and especially the Beatniks. Noisy in the United States and in Britain in the late 1950s, the Beatniks favoured free sex, drugs, a dash of eastern religion and black neck-high sweaters and blue jeans. A well known Beatnik was the American novelist, Jack Kerouac, who named one of his books *On The Road*. The title is significant: to be on the road was to be ambivalent towards private property and the money-seeking world. A favourite word of this cult was 'cool', which was the antithesis of the friction-hot, hurrying cities of America.

Fashions and face were also an early mirror of the new mood. That revolutionary assertion of the glamour of the young, the mini skirt, was the rage in 1966. Moreover youngish women were discarding the bland, hard face that they had affected in the strained decades from the 1930s to the 1950s, and now cultivated 'the natural look'. From 1964 their hair became shoulder-long and often wild, the make-up was translucent or sparse, lipstick was pale or was sparingly used, and there was a liking for Indian cosmetics such as henna. It was a time to be natural, though the natural quietly called for careful arranging. The English model of the mid 1960s, Jean Shrimpton, with her vulnerable and rather sweet face, was called 'gypsyish' by that discerning student of fashions, Angela Carter, and it is significant that the gypsies had been Europe's traditional children of nature.[1] The new facial fashion appeared just ahead of the new and parallel fondness for nature and primitive peoples.

The swift rise to fame of the four singers, The Beatles, in the first half of the 1960s showed the youthful support for ideas not widely cheered a decade earlier. Confident and casual, The Beatles disowned much of their own past and music's past; they had what James Morris called in the *Saturday Evening Post* an 'absolute aloofness to old prejudices and preconceptions'.[2] They came with the era of the cheap transistor radio, cheaper records and unprecedented prosperity, and catered for a teenage population which had been enlarged by the post-war baby boom. Between 1964 and 1966 eleven of their records topped the charts in the United States where sales of their recordings probably exceeded 100 million dollars. In England their influence was stronger. Though they came from Liverpool, London even more was their captive; and they helped to make it the 'swingingest city' in Europe.

The Beatles of the mid 1960s were not yet a clear portent of the counter-culture. Their most popular record, *I Want to Hold your Hand*, hardly seems revolutionary, and yet their songs announced that there were far more important things than national prestige, that music was a more penetrating weapon than the long-distance missile, and that authority should not command obedience. They were half rebels. Their popularity also portrayed a new unity amongst people of the same age in many places, and that unity was to become a powerful political and social weapon in the late 1960s.[3]

As The Beatles became famous their ceilings stretched upwards, and India floated into some of their songs. George Harrison even went to India for six weeks and studied a musical instrument, the sitar, under a famous musician, Ravi Shankar. Its exotic sound dominated the celebrated song, *Baby You're a Rich Man* which satirised the jet age and the 'beautiful people'. To another Beatle, Paul McCartney, the Indian music conveyed a vision, and merely to play it was to meditate. 'You can play it forever', he said. The Beatles dabbled in psychedelic drugs and browsed amongst the theologies and mysticism of the Orient. In some of the interviews we see a belief that in India all things were possible to those who believed; and the law of gravity could be repealed, the Ganges could flow upstream, and India's wisest men could conquer death. Thus, Paul McCartney earnestly told the British writer Alan Aldridge about an Indian mystic who had died in 1953:

> Medical reports in Los Angeles three or four months after he died were saying, 'This is incredible; this man hasn't decomposed yet.' He was sitting there glowing because he did this sort of transcendental bit, transcended his body by planes of consciousness.[4]

The real immortality of this Indian mystic, named Panmahansa Yoganada, was to arise not from his death but from the placing of his photograph on the coloured cover of The Beatles' long-playing album entitled *Sergeant Pepper's Lonely Hearts Club Band*.

The fascination with the Orient was visible on American streets when the followers of the Krishna appeared in 1966, their chanting and their dress as puzzling as the Salvation Army had once been. The Krishna is said to have first lived on earth some 5,000 years ago but his followers did not demand an exclusive monopoly at the expense of later prophets, and they saw truth in The Bible and The Koran as well as in the old Vedic literature of India. Emphasising simplicity and a puritan life, and promising ecstasy to the individual and peace to the world, they said: 'Chant these words, and your life will become sublime'. The Hare Krishna was heard right across the United States by the end of the 1960s.

From that same Vedic tradition came the cult called Transcendental Meditation. Its founder, Maharishi Mahesh Yogi, was tuned into the twentieth century, having studied physics at Allahabad University in India. He first visited the west in 1959 and proclaimed that through meditation people could reach new heights of intelligence and self-awareness. The Beatles, Shirley Maclaine, Mia Farrow and other stars gave him publicity; and by 1972 he was said to possess a quarter of a million followers, mostly students, in the United States. Those who tired of him could turn to Zen or the Divine Light Mission or other eastern or half-eastern sects or prophets.[5]

Liberation of the Teenager and Young Adult

The exact way in which the seesaw swung, and the passengers and attitudes it carried, was influenced by the new liberty of teenagers and young adults. Since the end of the Second World War the bargaining position of those between the ages of say seventeen and twenty six had been enhanced by the widespread prosperity and the scarcity of labour. Many of the young could now afford, if they wished, to leave home before they married; they had less need for the subsidy which the family for centuries had traditionally provided to those who did not earn adult wages. Another sign of the new prosperity was the increasing proportion of the young who entered tertiary education. Without them, the counter-culture of the late 1960s would have been weaker.

University students became a large and distinctive group with those essential ingredients for direct action – plentiful leisure, a certain idealism, and the absence of external authority and influence. As many students gathered in the one place they could easily be organised. As jobs were plentiful, students could work in long vacations and so make themselves, financially and ideologically, free of their parents. Students also possessed, in the event of conflict with the authorities, a strategic advantage which even a trade union did not usually possess, for the university in most free nations was assumed to be a sanctuary, a modern version of the medieval cathedral, into which the police and army did not intrude except in an emergency. That temporary immunity from the arm of the law gave students, if conflict arose, a startling initial advantage.*

---

* Strong bargaining position and relative immunity from arrest are vital when trade unions and other special groups try to win campaigns. At one time the most successful trade union in Australia, now a citadel of trade unions, was an unlikely union at first sight: the union of sheep shearers. But in the 1880s its members worked in large, isolated shearing sheds far from those capital cities where the police and militia were concentrated, and therefore the organisers of the shearers could use threats and a limited amount of force to gain higher pay and improved working conditions.

Here then were a powerful set of new liberating forces. In 1964 the birth-control pill became another potential form of release from the authority of parents and those social rules and pressures they imposed.

The Rise of the New Left

Campaigns and crusades are always rising and falling. Whether they wield influence depends as much on the climate in which they mature as on the message they deliver. In the late 1950s a medley of new movements was attracting the young but it would have been a bold forecaster who said which would survive and which would fade away.

The new left was born in 1956, soon after Mr Khrushchev's exposure of the internal atrocities committed by Stalin, and soon after the Soviet invasion of Hungary. Unlike the old left it did not see the hope of the world in the Soviet's form of communism nor did it see the working class as the dynamic, progressive class without which no revolution could come. In the United States the new left gained a foot in the gate of some campuses, forming itself at the University of Michigan into a group called Students for a Democratic Society, and arranging a national convention in 1962. One of its first targets was academic bureaucracy, and at the University of California at Berkeley in 1964 it was prominent in a student revolt that so aroused the public's imagination and nerves that, in the subsequent backlash, it helped the Republican, Ronald Reagan, win election as governor of California. Radical students became more active in the black rights movement, at first in the southern states and then the northern cities. The student political movement was already strenuous before the Vietnam War gave it a further boost.[6]

The widening of the war in Vietnam early in 1965 increased the scope and incentive for student radicalism in the United States. The drafting of the young to fight in Vietnam multiplied the radicals, even though students still studying were exempted from the draft. Before long many of the black leaders withdrew their support from the war, partly because the ratio of black casualties in Vietnam to the total black American population was almost double that of the white ratio but more because the war seemed another instance of that ideology, might is right, of which they had long been the victims in America. White radical students followed the same line of thinking. America's military campaign in Vietnam and its traditional treatment of the blacks at home seemed part-and-parcel of the same corrupt, hypocritical, power-obsessed behaviour, in the eyes of large numbers of students, many of whom were not otherwise radical. Such a wide indictment of Washington automatically embraced those who supported the government and mainstream American values. The universities thus became an obvious target, not only because many of their staff engaged in military research or went to Washington as policy advisers but also because universities could easily be disrupted by students. Disruption reached its peak in 1968. The anti-war movement by then was far wider than a student movement but students organised the most newsworthy and emotional protests against the war.

The ideology of the new left did not come primarily from the students. Perhaps its brightest source of ideas was Herbert Marcuse, who had belonged to the critical branch of Marxism known as the Frankfurt school. He regretted that the Soviet Union and the United States were travelling along the same track of advanced technology. Still believing in revolution he did not envisage the working class leading it and could not even glimpse the destination of the revolution. He thought that in the revolutionary turmoil, a guiding light would appear: after trial by ordeal, the light would be seen, dazzlingly bright. This message had the potential to attract radical students who were weak in theory but adept in organising.

Marcuse was still an orthodox Marxist in that he placed hope in technology. While the machines had conquered drudgery they had fallen amongst thieves, namely the capitalists, who controlled mass communications and soaked the proletariat in sensuality and pornography, making them unfit to lead a new revolution in the west. Marcuse was almost seventy when his hopes of a new Freudian–Marxist Utopia suddenly reached an enthusiastic audience. As the Manuels' fine history of Utopias describes it: 'By one of those quirks of world spirit, in 1967 and 1968 he became the philosopher of a widespread student rebellion and the seer whose foretellings were read as the imminent future.'[7]

A Competing Culture

The increasing prosperity and liberty of young people and their consciousness of themselves as a special group did not necessarily lead to radical ideas. It led more to independence than radicalism. Some of the effects of that independence were radical because youth had so much money to spend, but most young people of the 1960s were conformist in most of their actions and attitudes. They were especially sympathetic to technology and wanted a station-wagon or a car, a stereo, a tape recorder, a transistor, cheap records and maybe an electric guitar, and they also preferred products that were packaged wastefully and advertised lavishly.

Even at the height of the Vietnam War most of the young Americans did not join the protests nor were they disillusioned with their nation and civilisation. But a large minority of the young, mostly those of above-average education and coming from homes with above-average income, did become disillusioned with facets of their civilisation and especially its all-pervasive technology. At one extreme were the political protesters who campaigned against political policies such as war, urban poverty and the fate of the black minority, and at the other extreme were those who rebelled against the American way of life. Both the political and cultural protesters were closer together in 1965, when they were often the same people, than in 1968 when the student of the Left was often far apart in sympathies and priorities from the ragged, pot-smoking hippy of the counter-culture.

The counter-culture was political more by implication than direct action. The counter-culture favoured feeling rather than reason and co-operation rather than competition though even in co-operation it tended to be more effective in spirit than in fact. It favoured the simple rather than the complex, equality rather than status – its clothes showed this preference – the spontaneous rather than the planned in sex and morals, and tawdriness rather than tidiness in manners and clothing. 'Make love, not war' was one of its catchcries. Eschewing technology and courting nature, it belonged very much to the new swing of the seesaw. While it rebelled against technology it depended heavily on the large subsidy which society at large through its technology, was willing to give it. The counter-culture was heavily subsidised, eating far more of the nation's grain than it grew, milled, baked or bought.

While the drop-out and lay-about gathered around the counter-culture, many members were dynamic, exploratory and visionary. They believed the world was in a crisis, human and ecological, and that solutions had to be found. 'In the commune, in the thirst for eastern religious experience, in the search for new vision – these are the hunting grounds of a new society', wrote Robin Clarke. 'What is to be found there none can say, but it certainly seems a happier place to search than in the wilderness of a failed experiment in urban-industrial living.'[8] Some spoke of a new liberated, loosely-organised matrilineal family which would produce the wonder child. 'Such families already exist', wrote the Beat poet, Gary Snyder.[9] He claimed that their children were different in personality and outlook 'from anybody in the history of Western culture since the destruction of Knossos.' Even after the counter-culture had been a recognised movement for a decade, some of its high hopes remained. In Australia the historian Ian Turner believed it was capable of vieing with the Renaissance and Reformation in reshaping priorities and goals.

The aims of the counter-culture were such that its followers had to be together as much as possible. While members of most dynamic and revolutionary political or religious movements had to come together only for such special occasions as a rally, meeting or Sunday service, the hippies of 'flower power' had to form their own communities and communes. Their new way of life could not be part-time. In the late 1960s their assemblies and haunts became famous; they included parts of the Haight Ashbury district of San Francisco, sections of many suburbs in the east coast, and the fringe of big university towns; they overflowed into the countryside, establishing communities in states such as New Mexico where the laws against drugs were not strict.

There was a remarkable contrast between the boy scouts, who were the main youth culture in the earlier back-to-nature phase, and those of their grandsons who were hippies. While the early boy scouts and the modern hippy respected nature because it held special virtues which city civilisation had lost or was in danger of losing, the boy scouts wished to rejuvenate their own civilisation rather than repudiate it. A sharper difference was that the boy scouts had a respect for planning and organisation which they embodied in their motto 'Be Prepared', whereas the hippies shunned planning and placed a childlike trust in spontaneous happenings. The hippy belief that planning was pointless and even self-defeating was reflected in their increasing liking for drugs and for astrology and for that emphatically unplanned event called 'the happening'.

Hallucinations

Drugs were a craze during the counter-culture, and in the late 1960s their usage by young people increased dramatically in the United States and, with a time lag, in Holland, West Germany, Denmark, Australia and all prosperous western nations. Marijhuana was the cheapest drug and the most popular. From US universities with high prestige it spread with the swiftness of the common cold to the high schools where its reported usage even in the conservative state of Utah was higher in 1969 than it had been amongst university graduate students in Los Angeles four years previously. A massive advertising campaign was not needed to push this commodity: thousands tried it in order to proclaim to themselves or others that they were rebelling against American laws and values. The other popular drug was LSD or 'acid', an artificial drug which was made on a large scale in California from 1965 and disseminated by Berkeley and San Francisco Bohemians and half-intellectuals. The source of the glaze on the faces of hundreds at the Great Human Be-In at the Golden Gate Park in January 1967, 'acid' was also the source of an enormous amount of satisfaction, stupefaction and tragedy amongst teenagers and young adults. Heroin, curiously, had little place in the counter-culture, being more the favoured drug of the black ghetto in New York.[10]

In more articulate circles of the counter-culture, the taking of drugs was in part a revolt against technology. It was a revolt in the direct sense which Helen H. Nowlis explained in her book *Drugs on the College Campus*: the young were retreating from a machine-dominated world which prolonged adolescence and wrapped adult life in uncertainty. The war in Vietnam provided much of that uncertainty, and at a White House reception the black singer Eartha Kitt stunned Mrs Lyndon B. Johnson when she insisted that young people were taking marijhuana because they were disgusted with the war waged in Vietnam.[11]

The revolt against technology had another influence on drug-taking. During the seesaw's swing away from technology, it became easy to rationalise the taking of drugs. While technology required a regular, predictable way of working and living, drugs promised excitement and unpredictability – in short 'the happening'. Whereas technology emphasised reason, the drugs emphasised the emotions. Indeed one of the best-known periods of drug-taking was the romantic period of the early nineteenth century when opium was favoured in English literary circles. Whereas technology emphasised the role of the creative, striving elite and the value of competition, drug-takers claimed that through drugs they entered a genuine community and found tranquillity and inner harmony: just as harmony was now diagnosed as the special and precious quality of nature, so harmony was greeted as the special, mystical attribute of those who consumed drugs together. By that line of argument, marijhuana was virtually a lazy city substitute for the primeval forest, and twice as scented. In the minds of other addicts, drugs had the exciting savour of more primitive lands, for some drugs came from Asia while most of the marijhuana in the USA came from Mexico, whence the word itself was derived.

It could be argued that the use of drugs would have swiftly increased, irrespective of the swing of the seesaw, but that argument is dubious. The consuming of illegal drugs was partly an act of rebellion against the materialism of capitalist society, especially its war in Vietnam. Drugs were strongly defended by some intellectuals, and indeed the philosopher Professor John Passmore made the shrewd comment that Marx, had he been alive, might have announced that 'LSD is the religion of the intellectuals'.[12] In the new angle of the seesaw, LSD, the hallucination and mental escapism briefly held a respectability that would have astonished anybody who followed intellectual discourse twenty years previously. To praise trances, mystical communion and other drug-induced forms of wackiness was an indirect way of reacting against technology and its all-seeing protector, Science.

When Aldous Huxley had argued in his book of 1954, *The Doors of Perception*, that drugs increased human perceptions, he half-opened a door which, in the day of the counter-culture, was to be flung wide open. It was now said that intuition could challenge logic and that a dream could come closer to the truth than could a social scientist with all his hygienic methods of collecting and processing data. Now the arts, as fountains of creativity and understanding, were said to be more than a match for science when vital issues of mankind had to be faced. A reaction against the extreme claims made on behalf of science and the scientific method was long overdue. It was all the more extreme because it was overdue.

Art found a special throne in the counter-culture, and Lionel Trilling, the American critic, was perturbed by the pronouncement that art always tells the truth. Art's revelations could be as false as those of science, he argued in 1966.[13] Art can 'generate falsehood and habituate us to it', he wrote. At that time the claims on behalf of the arts and intuition were like a soft sunshower but in the late 1960s they became a rainstorm. A new dogma was drowning the old. The English poet, Robert Graves, showed how fierce was the duel between the old dogma of technology and the new dogma of the arts when in 1971 he wrote: 'Technology is now warring openly against the crafts, and science covertly against poetry'.[14] He accused international financiers of capturing technology for their own greedy ends. Much of the hostility to technology now rested on a distaste for capitalism, for in the western world the trio of technology, capitalism and culture had become almost inseparable.

Woodstock and other Happenings

Folk music as much as science was increasingly seen as the purveyor of truth. The Beatles in their cheerful, cynical way had led the first assault on the fortress of science, making it easier for a young leftist folk singer with a Huck Finn corduroy cap to present a serious message. Bob Dylan had sung his first hit in 1963 and began to compose more of his own songs. Waging a campaign against mainstream western values, he was more a patient besieger and underminer than a leader of frontal assaults. From his songs and guitar – and even more from the later San Francisco style of music – floated out the vague message that a new world would somehow emerge as the young found themselves and discovered new goals. The guitar had become the missionary. To Bob Dylan the museum and art gallery and library were cultural cemeteries and the new music was 'the only thing that's in tune with what's happening.'[15]

In 1969 the popular book *The Age of Rock* (subtitled significantly as 'Sounds of the American Cultural Revolution') insisted that singers such as Bob Dylan were singing to a generation 'alienated from technological, manipulative society'. They sang to a generation disgusted with the bombing of 'innocent hamlets' in Vietnam:

> Rock music was born of a revolt against the sham of Western culture: it was direct and gutsy and spoke to the senses. As such it was profoundly subversive. It still is.[16]

Much of the subversion in the songs came from the stress on drugs. Bob Dylan's famous song of 1964, *Mr Tambourine Man*, obliquely celebrated the peddling of drugs. Slang terms for drugs or hallucinations appeared in dozens of hit songs, not least in the titles. The words of The Beatles' song, *Lucy in the Sky with Diamonds*, made sense when they were interpreted as describing a trip on LSD, and indeed the posters advertising the song highlighted the first letter of each noun in the song's title, namely, L, S, and D. The Beatles' hit, *Yellow Submarine*, was understood by millions to refer to the 'yellow jacket', a barbiturate shaped like a submarine and capable of submerging those who took it. Rain was a frequent and evocative title for hit songs, and The Rolling Stones' song called *Coloured Rain* signified the drug Methedrine. *High* was often in the title of popular songs, as was the name Jane, meaning the marijhuana that sent her 'high'. Many hit songs offered the ambiguous messages of an attack on society but the abandoning of society by a retreat into drugs. One critic noted with irony that the 'radical protest movement has adopted *Street Fighting Man* as an anthem and yet the song points towards apathy'. The arrows fired by the counter-culture often flew in opposite directions.

The happening, the half-spontaneous festival, was the glory of the counter-culture, for it seemed to show how the spirit of the spontaneous could wrap itself around a huge assemblage and perform a miracle with the aid of guitars, amplifiers and a glow of goodwill. Such happenings were depicted as the coming together of the tribes or even 'the nation', for Californian hippies initially saw themselves as returning to some of the practices, rituals and values of the American Indian along with drugs and a dash of religion from India proper. As the poet Gary Snyder wrote in 1968, in celebration of the exciting new cult:

> The celebrated human Be-In in San Francisco, January of 1967, was called 'A Gathering of the Tribes'. The two posters: one based on a photograph of a Shaivite sadhu with his long matted hair, ashes and beard; the other based on an old etching of a Plains Indian approaching a powwow on his horse – the carbine that had been cradled in his left arm replaced by a guitar. The Indians, and the Indian. The tribes were Berkeley, North Beach, Big Sur, Marin County, Los Angeles, and the host, Haight–Ashbury. Outriders were present from New York, London and Amsterdam.[17]

The most miraculous of the happenings was 'Woodstock' in New York State in the summer of 1969 when more than 300,000 young people came together for a rock festival which for four days drowned the air with music and, in the opinion of many, with ecstasy. Though the planning of the festival was lean, and its agenda seemed to arise rather than be imposed, these were seen as gains, for goodwill and 'good vibes' and spontaneity and a miraculous sense of 'togetherness' knitted the gathering together in such a way that Woodstock was recalled for years afterwards as a paradise.[18] The rock festival, the open-air happening, became common throughout the western world at the end of the 1960s and early 1970s. Just as it was capable of turning into a wonderful occasion, into the new field of the cloth of gold, the absence of planning meant that occasionally it would be a field of mud, sewage, quarrels, brawls, ear-blasting music, mind-blasting drugs and disillusionment. The chaotic rock concert staged by the Rolling Stones at Altamont in California in 1969 marked the end of the big happening in the USA – four deaths 'happened' – but in other nations the musical stars and hippies and promoters were just beginning to stage their happenings.[19]

Woodstock was a nuclear-age version of the eighteenth-century idea that people living naturally, in harmony with nature, could attain a happiness that was impossible in the tightly organised, structured, money-seeking city. But the Woodstock of 1969 could rarely succeed in imitating Tahiti, for that island in 1768 was a structured society, not a happening. The coconuts might have just happened to fall from the palm trees onto the balmy beaches but somebody had planted those palms and tended them when young. The refusal to organise, the enthusiasm for the impulsive and individualist act, was the source of the disasters as well as the triumphs of the counter-culture.

Why Nature was Kind in the West

The eagerness to set up rural communes, and the tendency to sanctify nature as the very opposite of competitive Wall Street, portrayed a vision of nature which would have surprised Charles Darwin. He had emphasised the ruthless competitiveness of nature but the new counter-culture tended to depict nature as the pivot of tenderness and love. 'In harmony with nature' was a credo of this new era, and it implied that inside nature all was concord and kindness, and that the eagle and the lamb slept side by side.

The revival of sympathy for nature was possible only because of two little noticed facts. Firstly, nature in the western world, as we shall see, did differ from nature in Asia and Africa, at least in recent centuries. It was easier to find harmony – if one was intent on seeking harmony – in nature in Europe than in most of Africa and Asia. Secondly, it was easier for a city dweller than a rural dweller to see an inner harmony in nature, and in Europe most people now lived in cities. The cities now were so large and so cut off from nature that most city children did not see the ruthless competition for survival by the myriads of plants and animals in the countryside. They did not think of the slaughtering of the livestock on which their own dinner depended. If they did go to the countryside and see wheat and cattle, they did not realise that those species were heavily protected from natural competitors by selective breeding, fences, pesticides, chemical dips, and a wide variety of recent technological aids designed to protect the favoured crop or livestock.

Charles Darwin a century earlier had had to remind himself that behind the sweet singing of the birds – 'the face of nature bright with gladness' – was a brutal struggle for life.[20] It was much more difficult in the urbanised society of the 1960s and even in the regulated and tamed countryside, to see such a struggle for survival. It was even more difficult to see a brutal

struggle when coloured television programmes began to roman-
ticise nature and appeal to the new mood of the counter-culture.

In the west, nature's harshness and arbitrariness had silently
been tamed in other ways. A hippy could see a kindness within
nature which a peasant in Cambodia might not see, for the
simple reason that technology had made Californian farmlands
productive and 'kind' in ways scarcely noticed by most hippies.
Nature, at least in recent centuries, also gave the appearance of
being kinder towards the European lands of the temperate zone
than to Asia, Africa and the tropical lands.

It was not that Europe had been free from disasters inflicted
by nature. Thus Finland probably experienced the worst famine
in modern Europe, losing one in every three or four of its people
in 1696–97, and in Ireland in the 1840s the starvation was
acute.[21] Russia continued to experience famine and two popular
travel books published in 1892 were mainly tales of recent
Russian hunger: Hodgett's *In the Track of the Russian Famine*
and Steveni's *Through Famine-Stricken Russia*.[22] Soviet Russia
was to lose five or six million people in the famine of 1932 and
1933 but the losses came as much from the Kremlin as from the
sky.

Earthquakes also struck European cities, and Naples is said
to have lost 93,000 people in the earthquake of 1693, and Lisbon
is said to have lost 60,000 citizens in the earthquake and tidal
wave of 1755, but these earthquakes inflicted meagre casualties
compared to Indian and Chinese earthquakes. In 1557 an earthquake in north China is said to have killed 830,000 people – or
nine times the Naples death roll – and near Calcutta and the
mouth of the Hooghly River in 1737 an earthquake and hurri-
cane killed some 300,000 people. Floods also were more devastating in eastern Asia than in Europe, for the rivers rising in the
snowy mountains of central Asia were enormous as they ap-
proached the coast, and when they brimmed their banks they
flooded some of the most intensely settled districts in the world.
In China the Yellow River, appropriately, was called China's
Sorrow or the Scourge of the Sons of Han or 'The Ungovernable'.
Drought too was devastating in Asia, and one famine in north
China in 1877–78 is said to have killed nine and a half million,
and at the same time a famine in India killed five million.[23]
The economic historian Professor Eric Jones, in explaining why
Europe was the first to achieve an industrial revolution, gives

some weight to the fact that natural disasters were fewer and less deadly in Europe than in Asia.[24]

If it is true that western Europe had fewer natural disasters and fewer of those disasters called famines, Europe also was more capable of lessening the impact of those disasters that did occur. Europe had cheap sea transport, for its coast had many headlands and gulfs and three large indentations – the Baltic, the Mediterranean and the Black Sea. Most districts of Europe were within easy reach of an ocean-going vessel or a river boat, and it was possible for ships to carry foods cheaply from a region of surplus to a region of famine. The railways increased the ability of Europe to send food from one region to another in the event of famine. In essence, the tropical and warm lands were not only more prone to natural disasters arising from climatic extremes, but were also less capable of coping with disasters. This was especially true of the mighty agricultural regions strung along the Nile, Mekong, Yellow and a dozen other fertile valleys. When floods devastated those valleys and caused famine, the source of emergency supplies lay along the same river, but farmlands near the river usually had no surplus, being victims of the same flood. There were, alas, no railways to carry food overland from other river valleys.

Europe, North America and most of those other temperate lands to which millions of Europeans emigrated in the nineteenth century provided the special message that nature could be tamed. The intense cold of winter could be eased by the firewood, coal, wool and other raw materials provided by nature. Even diseases of the temperate zone were more tameable than those of the tropics. Moreover these regions of old or new European settlements had no widespread famines which could be attributed to natural disasters rather than war. Nature was seen to smile, but it was not fully observed that at least half of the smile came from the skill of man. The apparent kindness of nature in the homelands of western civilisation was one of the reasons why nature was available for worship in the late 1960s, when the old gods were believed to have failed.

The seesaw contained its own mechanism that tended to produce periodic movements towards nature, but the size of the swing or the particular emphasis expressed in that new swing depended on external conditions. And the increasing role of cloistered city life and the increasing taming of nature in Europe,

North America, Australia and other lands of the European peoples enabled young adults of the cities to see nature in a benign way which would have been less plausible one or two centuries ago.

Prophets from the Asylums

Strange prophets found a widening audience in the English-speaking world and their message on science and nature was translated into many other languages. One cannot be sure how typical they were of this period, nor can they even be categorised with safety. The exact border between the rational and the irrational is faint, and many of the major advances in science seem irrational to scholarly critics when they first appear. Moreover it is often difficult to know whether some mass-selling books belong to the anti-technology cause, or are celebrating the wonders of technology in an eccentric way.

Better known than Lévi-Strauss and Marcuse in American bars and beaches in the 1960s was the late Edgar Cayce. An uneducated rural prophet, born in Kentucky, he made countless predictions of doom, many of which were based on earthquakes, wars, and rising seas. He was said to have predicted the coming of the two world wars and the 1930s depression. One of his themes was the triumph of Nature over human achievement and technology, and that fitted the new mood of the 1960s. Entering a trance he had predicted the flooding, far into the future, of cities in Japan and Scandinavia and the flooding by the seas of New York and San Francisco. Cayce confided that he himself in an earlier incarnation had lived in the 'lost city of Atlantis'. Conveniently it was near the Bahamas and so was not far from his old Kentucky home. In 1967 a book describing his predictions – Jess Stearn's *The Sleeping Prophet* – became a best seller in the United States.[25]

The mysterious Bermuda Triangle was born about 1964. The idea that there was an expanse of the Atlantic Ocean with occult powers was propounded by a freelance writer, Vincent Gaddis, who argued that in the Bermuda Triangle an unusual number of ships and aircraft had mysteriously vanished. The idea was spread by word of mouth and by newspaper articles and comics, and even generated two books in 1974.[26] The idea of a haunted stretch of sky and ocean depends heavily on the omission of crucial evidence, and it would seem that a higher proportion of ships and aircraft are not lost there than in dozens of other similar-sized areas of ocean.

Many people read with wonder about the Bermuda Triangle or the chariots of the gods coming from outer space and reserved their judgment, but Gallup polls found that large numbers of people believed the pseudo-scientific stories which circulated. In Great Britain in 1978 one quarter of the people questioned believed in the existence of flying saucers. Of the Canadians who had read or heard of flying saucers or other 'unidentified flying objects', 57 per cent believed they were real, while in Uruguay more than half of the people believed in the existence of flying saucers.[27] It is understandable that in an era of moon probes, ordinary people should try to encompass this new world, and in one sense their fascination with the multiple possibilities of outer space is a tribute to their mental flexibility, their open mind, as well as their credulity.

I know no statistics which indicate that various kinds of credulity are increasing, or for that matter, decreasing, in societies which have experienced at least a century of compulsory education. In popular culture, however, magic did seem to be making inroads into science. The faith in chariots of the gods, Bermuda triangles, lost Atlantis's and flying saucers became so widespread that by the end of the 1970s a typical bookshop in an American city possibly held more books on pseudo-science than on science. According to Professor Paul Kurtz, a philosopher at the State University of New York, a 'dispassionate observer of the current scene can only be astonished by the widespread growth of bizarre beliefs in recent years'.[28]

Was fear of the future propelling people towards fantasy or were these simply signs that fairy stories and folk tales were being updated and that the magic carpet had been superseded by flying saucers? Or was the Bermuda Triangle simply a modern offshore Tahiti? Just as Tahiti in the eighteenth century seemed to tell proud Europeans that they had not advanced far in human happiness and social relations, so the Bermuda Triangle, by exemplifying Nature's mysterious powers over the latest machinery, seemed to say that man was not yet the master in that field in which, in our times, he had taken the most pride: technology.

A Chronology of a Cultural Uprising

From the mid 1960s onwards came a cluster of cultural uprisings of a kind and intensity that had not previously been seen in western civilisation, except during the French, Russian and other revolutions. The United States was the home of most of these uprisings; late teenagers and those in their twenties were the age group which provided most of the followers and many of the leaders for these new movements; and their ideas quickly spread to other nations where censorship of new ideas and manners was not normally imposed. This uprising was a reaction against the dominant American values but it was also against the American government and its war in Vietnam: it would have been less vigorous if there had been no war. It was a protest on so many fronts and expressing itself in so many facets of life that we can only see its essential unity if we set out the relevant events.

A short chronology of the years 1964 to 1972 shows the ferment and how it fed itself:

1964	Fierce controversy and clashes over Black Rights.
	Free Speech Movement at University of California (Berkeley).
	Bob Dylan's *Mr Tambourine Man*, a song celebrating drugs.
	The beginning of shoulder-long hair.
1965	America sends combat troops to Vietnam and begins heavy bombing of North Vietnam.
	The Beatles become famous.
	Beginning of boom in underground radical press.
1966	The Hare Krishna movement penetrates US cities.
	In China the cultural revolution begins, creating intense interest amongst western radicals.
	Soaring demand for LSD and hallucinogenic drugs.
1967	The start of the boom in Transcendental Meditation is aided by The Beatles.

The commune movement begins, along with runaway migration to the hippy San Francisco suburb of Haight Ashbury where marijhuana and LSD are the vogue.

In Detroit 43 killed in Black riots.

1968   The Black Power movement, founded in California, launches its *Black Panther*.

North Vietnam's Tet Offensive begins on 31 January.

The My Lai massacre in Vietnam.

Assassination of Martin Luther King, Jr., in Memphis (4 April).

Student revolt in Paris.

Students for Democratic Society active in disruptions, especially at Columbia University (NY) and the Chicago Democratic Convention.

1969   Founding of the Gay Liberation Front for homosexuals.

The Woodstock (NY) rock-music 'happening', a huge open-air festival attracting some 350,000 people in four days.

The sponsoring of the Club of Rome, which three years later was to produce its doomsday report on world economic development.

The Weathermen, a Nihilist faction of the SDS, believing that chaos will lead to a new brotherhood, sets up bomb explosions to help the chaos.

Young pilgrims flock to Glastonbury, UK.

America begins heavy bombing of Cambodia to 'shorten' Vietnam War.

Festival of Light, a counter to the counter-culture, begins quietly in London.

New Society lists the authors of the four serious gospels of the movement against reason as Lorenz, McLuhan, Laing and Lévi-Strauss.

1970   Women's Liberation, flourishing in the late 1960s, spreads through two influential books of 1970: Germaine Greer's *The Female Eunuch* and Kate Millett's *Sexual Politics*.

Friends of the Earth, newborn and vigorous.
First homosexual demonstration in London.
Alvin Toffler's *Future Shock* warns of 'massive adaptational breakdown' because of overwhelming pace of change.

1971   In Vietnam, 20,000 American soldiers treated for serious drug abuse, but only 5000 treated in hospital for combat wounds.
Publication of the *Pentagon Papers*, exposing the USA's conduct of war.

1972   Club of Rome publishes book of economic and ecological doom, *The Limits of Growth*.
The Friends of the Earth issue a campaign manual to save the whale.
The musical, *Jesus Christ Superstar*.
Americans cease heavy bombing of North Vietnam, and negotiate for peace which was signed on 23 January 1973.

By now the many-sided cultural movement was running out of steam but it was not running out of influence and indeed it was increasingly affecting the world's economic life.*

* Part of this chapter represents a detour from the book's main theme, the frontline of competing ideas, but the detour seems necessary. The counter-culture and all its fellow travellers represented a surprising turnabout: its views were so widely held amongst the young, and the 'young' will be here for decades to come; and the sheer popularity of some of the ideas associated with the counter-culture affected strongly the seesaw of ideas and the economic pessimism in the 1970s and even 1980s.

12 The Return of The Noble Savage

When the seesaw moves it carries a similar group of passengers at each end. Occasionally, during the swing of the seesaw, one passenger seems to stand out from the others. In the late 1960s that passenger was black. There arose a new veneration for the noble savage, and the concept of the savage was so widened that much of Africa, Asia as well as the favoured Pacific islands shared in the new veneration. As the Europeans and Americans who idolised a simple way of life were essentially showing a distaste for their own civilisation, there was little limit to the variety of remote societies for which they could feel sympathy – so long as crucial facets of those societies were the polar opposite of their own.

Anthropology Comes of Age

The Noble Savage had always retained well-wishers. A few anthropologists, missionaries and eccentrics continued to believe that the primitive societies were not inferior to western urbanised societies, but there were obstacles against such a belief in the years 1914 to 1945. Britain, France, Holland, Belgium, Portugal, Spain and Italy – the imperial powers – saw the native peoples in their colonies as infants requiring European guardians. Communism in Russia tended to denounce racial prejudice but conceived of the noble savage as a quaint historical relic who stood on the bottom step of the historical ladder. Fascism saw that bottom step as very low indeed. Likewise the intellectual discipline called eugenics, which was thriving in the 1920s, did not smile on primitive peoples and implied that they were primitive largely because of their genetic background.

In the confident cities of the western world in the 1920s there was at least one trojan horse. Its name was behaviourism, and in the United States it was strong in education, philosophy, sociology and psychology. In social anthropology it also had

213

exponents who shunned any type of ladder theory that arranged societies and cultures in an hierarchy of worth. A. L. Kroeber for example pointed out that many native languages were complex; and given the importance of language as a measure of mental power and sophistication, it would be foolish to denigrate a people whose technology was simple but whose language was impressive.[1] Franz Boas preached a similar message, being sceptical of the west's pride. He dismissed the common idea that the mental capacity of a white woman from Chicago was any larger than that of a black woman from Charleston. He insisted that any American who walked through the big museums of Europe would soon see that Africans had their own worthwhile arts and industries and 'cultural achievements of no mean order'.[2] All races, he believed, had great potential and only culture made them different. All peoples had untapped capacities, and what was tapped depended largely on how each national culture programmed its members from infancy.

Boas gained a wider audience through the books of two of his students, Margaret Mead and Ruth Benedict. Margaret Mead's first field research, undertaken at Boas's suggestion in 1925–26, seemed to be a triumphant endorsement of his view. In *Coming of Age in Samoa*, she argued – using evidence which is now disputed – that social life there was more harmonious than in the USA, and in the book's preface Boas explained that the lucky Samoans had no 'adolescent crisis'.[3] Boas and his students helped to pave the road for the revival in North America of the cult of the Noble Savage in our time.

Significantly, between the wars, Africa was not the sympathetic topic of many American books on anthropology. Racial tensions were perhaps too much part of Americans' consciousness to allow them easily to see Africa, the home of the ancestors of their own blacks, as also a home of the Noble Savage. Indeed in no recent century has the huge continent of Africa been able to compete with tiny Pacific islands in providing a Garden of Eden for Europe's imagination.

British anthropologists were the main students of tribal Africa in the two decades between the world wars, for Britain ruled much of Africa and gave its scholars access to African cultures. The dominant British school of thought in anthropology was now structural and functional, and such scholars as Radcliffe-

Brown, Evans-Pritchard and Malinowski were more interested in the question of how a society actually functions than in that optimistic question of how earlier societies climbed up the ladder towards civilisation. For them Africa was an ideal studying ground, with its wide variety of tribes, exotic rituals and beliefs, and sophisticated kinship networks that so far seemed little altered by Europe. Thus Evans-Pritchard, detecting a logical structure underlying the witchcraft of the Azande in central Africa, was impressed with 'the powers of hard reasoning' to be found in a primitive society.[4]

Outside Africa, such islands as the Andamans in the Indian Ocean and the Trobriands to the east of New Guinea had been studied brilliantly in this new intellectual mode in the period 1900–18. These sympathetic studies, unlike those conducted by the European-proud anthropologists of the previous generation, examined the life of a tribe in its own terms and, seeing it as a whole, found it more explicable. Bronislaw Malinowski set the new standards for field work, using the native language to make his enquiries, and in 1922 his book *Argonauts of the Western Pacific* made it very difficult for readers to dismiss 'primitive' Melanesian society as lacking in logic or impoverished in culture.

Anthropology was becoming a western voice speaking on behalf of primitive societies and trying to explain them to the world, but its voice could not yet be heard clearly because universities were proud of the intellectual fabric of western civilisation and wondered about the worth of anthropologists who put forward messages to the contrary. Intellectual life is spiced with politics, no matter how neutrally most scholars try to tiptoe. Every intellectual field, especially the humanities and social sciences, has political messages. Historians for example are often nationalist and condone their nation's history, though since the 1960s large numbers of young historians have increasingly become as hostile to their own nation's and civilisation's past as their predecessors were loyal. Other fields of research can also take political sides, either applauding the values of their civilisation or doubting them. On the eve of the Second World War, social anthropology had linked itself strongly to the side of primitive societies, either as a supporter or a sympathetic explainer. Anthropologists' influence was to widen dramatically in the post-war moods so favourable for their message.

Descent from the High Pulpit

Europe's moral position suffered after the Second World War. It had been bolstered by wartime patriotism, propaganda and the sheer will to survive against powerful enemies. But after 1945 it was no longer easy to emphasise that European civilisation owned special virtues, when twice it had been the battlefield on a scale unknown in human history. It was not easy to plead that Europe was more civilised than say Japan when in the six years between 1939 and 1945 Hitler killed millions of Jews and waged a crusade against Gypsies and Slavs, when Russians committed serious atrocities against the Germans and Poles and other peoples, and when Britain and her allies so bombed Hamburg and Dresden that the casualties of civilians in the one day rivalled those of the deadliest one-day battles in the world's history before 1900. The First World War had been a blot on European civilisation, but the Second World War was more so, often becoming an all-out war which treated women and children, the old, sick, lame and insane with the contempt typical of the religious wars of three centuries ago. The experience of two world wars impeded the ability of sensitive Europeans to mount their high pulpits and preach, as they had been accustomed for centuries to preach the virtues of their civilisation to the peoples of darkest Africa and Asia. After 1945, some European intellectuals could easily see their society as an example of moral decay just as a similar sense of decay had spurred philosophers in the eighteenth century to discern exemplary virtues in Tahiti and other remote lands.

In Europe this growing consciousness of moral decline was to be felt much more in 1965 than in 1945. In the early post-war years, Danish and English citizens, for example, had seen no reason to accept blame for the atrocities of Fascist and Stalinist forces. As the English saw themselves as English and the Danes as Danes rather than as common citizens of Europe, why should they accept any blame for what Nazis did to them? But later a European economic community would emerge, and it would also become tentatively a moral and cultural community for whom the war could not always be blamed on an outsider. Many Europeans would begin to wear a waistcoat of guilt beneath the coat of pride.

The Empires Dissolve

The Second World War helped to promote a begrudging respect for those societies previously seen as standing on the lower rungs of the ladder. By weakening the imperial powers of western Europe, the war helped to puncture the myth that they could maintain their grip on colonies in the faraway world. England, the greatest of colonial powers, was humiliated by the Japanese in Burma, Hong Kong, Singapore and many Asian territories in the space of a few months. Moreover, England had to purchase India's loyalty during the war by promising her early independence, and the liberation of India in 1947 was a blow to Europe's long-proclaimed superiority over tropical peoples. France, Holland and several other colonial powers refused to accept the evidence that their imperial days were numbered, and after the Second World War they fought to retain such colonies as Algeria Indo-China, and Indonesia. These colonial wars proved to be surprisingly expensive in life and money.

Between 1945 and 1965, Europe's empires shrank as India, Pakistan, Malaysia, Burma, Indonesia, Tanzania, Nigeria and dozens of new lands gained independence. Their liberation was accelerated by the fact that the United States and the Soviet Union, the two strongest military powers to emerge from the Second World War, showed ideological opposition to the old empires and often lent a loud voice, money and sometimes arms to groups in the colonies that sought independence.

The quiet turbulence which England's prime minister, Harold Macmillan, called simply 'the winds of change' was at first greeted with optimism by a range of western people.[5] Many intellectuals gave to the new rulers in Asia and Africa the benefit of the doubt. Why shouldn't they be given the benefit? Europe, with its two major wars and its economic depression, had hardly made a complete success of itself in the last fifty years. But at times too much leniency was shown to the third world perhaps because there was a little too much guilt in the first world. Thus in the spring of 1966 the playwright Arthur Miller, interviewed at his farm in Connecticut, spoke more sympathetically of Africa than Europe. He argued that western cities, where people cease to accept their social responsibility and where tender feelings are quarantined and daily violence disturbs city streets, were no different in spirit from a concentration camp. 'I have always felt that concentration camps', he said, 'though they're a phenomenon of totalitarian states, are also the logical conclusion of contemporary life'. He thought that concentration camps could not emerge from Africa 'where people had no connection with the basic development of Western civilization'.[6] Miller spoke before Idi Amin's Uganda and the Central African Republic were to spring into the news, and before Africa showed that it was capable of producing its own miniature black Hitlers.

In the United States the rising temperature of the issue of black rights reflected and furthered the swing of the seesaw. For long the American blacks had been held back by the prevailing white view that they did not display – except in professional sport – the work ethic and the materialist drive, but once the quest for possessions and the 'rat race' began to fall in white esteem the blacks were not so easily disparaged. The rise of new nations in Africa, and the arrival of their delegations at the United Nations' headquarters in New York, increased the bargaining position of the black citizens in America, providing them with vocal allies and making their claims for civil rights seem unexceptional. Furthermore, how could the United States persuasively proclaim that it was fighting to preserve the freedom of South Vietnam when it was not giving adequate freedom to a people who had long lived in the United States and had actually been liberated, just a century ago, by a civil war which had some of the hallmarks of the new war in Vietnam?

Never had there been such racial disturbances in American cities as during the years 1964 to 1967. More than a hundred major riots occurred, mostly in northern cities, and in Detroit alone 43 people died as a result of the rioting in July 1967. A few black leaders encouraged violence, H. Rap Brown simply noting that 'violence was as American as cherry pie' and that there should be more of it. The assassination of the moderate black leader Dr Martin Luther King, Jr. on 4 April 1968 was one misplaced footnote for his argument.[7]

Turning History on its Head

Doubts about American civilisation aided respect for unwesternised nations, and as the counter-culture made headway it praised the more primitive societies. These remote peoples had few possessions and that gave them prestige in the new anti-materialist mood of western nations. Possessing small populations which were mostly static or declining, they gained prestige as exemplars of zero population growth. Living close to nature, they were icons for a new era which was more conscious of the rampages of western civilisation and the price paid by nature for the gospel of economic growth.

A surprising happening of the 1960s was the re-enthroning of the noble savage. In the middle of the eighteenth century Adam Smith, Condorcet, Robertson and other French and Scottish observers had postulated the simple ladder theory of economic development whereby the stage of hunting and gathering gave way to herd-keeping, then to farming and fourthly to the commercial stage, each being an advance on the previous stage. In the 1960s the four stage theory was challenged. At the very time when mainstream economists were exulting in the unparalleled economic progress of the western world, a few scholars studying the economics of 'primitive societies' were moving towards the seditious conclusion that many of the acclaimed achievements of the era of the washing machine and the jet aircraft were illusory. In short a civilisation that seemed so successful in devising machines that saved time and increased leisure was not yet receiving as much leisure as enjoyed by societies which possessed few tools beyond the bow and the digging stick. Thus in the late 1950s E. R. Service and Marvin Harris argued that the hunter and gatherer had leisure in plenty. In 1960 appeared part of the long-awaited report of the Australian–American Scientific Expedition to Arnhem Land, an ambitious survey which showed that only five or six hours a day were spent in gathering food by those Australian Aboriginals still following a traditional way of life, and therefore that a large amount of leisure was available to them. Likewise, in the early 1960s from the Kalahari Desert came evidence disputing the traditional idea that primitive peoples spent all day in their struggle for existence.

This new way of thinking defied the orthodox concept of progress whereby economists assumed that, over time, mankind had gained in standard of living and security. By 1968 some anthropologists and prehistorians believed that those small tribes of hunters and gatherers had lived so well and enjoyed such ample leisure that they were probably 'the original affluent society'.[8] Rarely in the history of human assessment have those who are last become quickly the first. In prehistory and anthropology the research was ready, in advance, to support that wide wave of thinking which challenged the superiority of the present.

The new hypothesis turned history upside down. Just as the so-called simple societies were now honoured for their economic performance, so too were they proclaimed as less warlike than modern societies. A survey in the early 1970s revealed that most American anthropologists, unlike their predecessors, thought warfare was only a minor cause of death in 'savage' societies.[9] Similarly the primitive societies' arts and religion, their complex and rich social life and their skills in foreign languages were recognised more than ever before. Even the old idea that many primitive peoples were cannibals was to be challenged in 1979 from that home of challenges, New York.[10] This revolution in prehistory of course had vigorous opponents but the revolutionists penetrated far into enemy territory.

Primitive societies had already gained indirectly from another spearhead of research which pricked the pride of western civilisation. In 1963 the Austrian zoologist and anthropologist, Konrad Lorenz, in his influential book *On Aggression*, argued that the human race was like the animals in its general instinct for aggression. In essence he was reminding readers of that side of Darwin's message which was often ignored, that man was an animal. Whereas Darwin's message to the human race was essentially, 'Look how far we have come!' the message of Lorenz a century later was 'Look how far we haven't!' Lorenz also argued that civilisation was a form of domestication and that the domestication of species, including man, could lead to moral and maybe genetic deterioration. That was an indirect warning – widely publicised in the 1960s – to those who idolised modern societies at the expense of the primitive. A similar warning came from the Frenchman, Levi-Strauss, whose four volumes on *Mythologiques*, based on the fables of early American peoples, stressed what was common to all cultures, whether of the nuclear era or the age of poisoned spear and boomerang.

The halo now placed on simpler societies came occasionally from the new archaeology. The invention of the technique of radio-carbon dating in 1947 enabled the chronology of recent mankind to be driven far back into time. Thus the original inhabitants of Australia who were thought to have arrived only a few thousand years ago were assigned to 23,000 years ago by the finding of the remains of an ancient cremation ceremony on the shores of a lake in 1968 and the use of radio-carbon dating on those remains. Soon the date of the first Aboriginal occupation of Australia was pushed back to 40,000 years ago. Such a discovery of longevity, if it had been made in the era of Lubbock and Darwin, might have provoked the disparaging comment: 'The Aboriginals lived there so long but produced so little.' At the new angle of the intellectual seesaw, however, no such comment was made, for the goal of rapid material progress was being challenged by the new goal of living in ecological equilibrium. Accordingly, the longer the Aboriginals had inhabited Australia the more praiseworthy was their apparent protection of the natural environment. In October 1971, presumably with the aid of the latest anthropological opinion, the Prime Minister of Australia, William McMahon, read to his Parliament a formal statement praising the Aboriginals as careful custodians of a continent: 'For tens of thousands of years they have inhabited this continent, living in harmony with it and its creatures.'[11] The conservation crusade in many western nations gained from the unease or disillusionment with the present civilisation and the consoling belief that in the distant past lay a golden age in which men lived in harmony with nature and cared for all living creatures: a happy garden in which the hunters carried no spears, every stream was clear and no apple was sprayed with insecticide. The same intellectual mood enthroned babies and infancy, and the new-born baby was virtually proclaimed as civilised by the child-care manuals of the Spock era.

As all surviving tribes now were somewhat tainted by western civilisation, their original Garden of Eden had to be resurrected from the meagre historical records. In 1860 in Nebraska Territory the anthropologist, Lewis Henry Morgan, had interviewed a French-Canadian trader named Martin who for long had worked amongst American Indians; and Trader Martin gave him a careful account of the Indian peoples before the coming of white soldiers and missionaries. He said that the American Indian women were very beautiful – especially the 'Sheyennes, Crows and Sioux women' – and were never maltreated by their husbands, who were proud, manly, honest, warm-hearted, loyal and neighbourly. 'He thinks the old Indian before the advent of the white', concluded Morgan, 'must have been the happiest man on earth'. A century later, in 1974, a leading American anthropologist, Ashley Montagu, after resurrecting Morgan's old interview with Trader Martin, felt obliged to comment that Martin's assertions that the untouched Indian was the happiest man on earth 'are almost certainly true'.[12] With all respect to Montagu, his was a naïve verdict. He had little means of knowing whether the American Indian then was happier than hundreds of other peoples in thousands of other centuries. His assertion showed how intellectual extremism becomes plausible when the seesaw rests at one of its sharpest angles.

Fresh intellectual tides usually face contrary currents and undertows. While the latest research in Australia, Canada and other European-settled lands depicted the original inhabitants as happily living in harmony with nature, another viewpoint disputed the existence of that harmony. In Australia the same radio-carbon dating which pushed back Aboriginal history also suggested that unique species of animals – for instance the big diprotodont and the largest species of kangaroos – had been extinguished in the last 20,000 years and that the early Aboriginals were probably their destroyers. In essence, the Aboriginals were not always the kindly caretakers of nature, and in some regions they had altered the vegetation through their constant use of fire, turning scrubland into grassland.[13] Similarly, Edward O. Wilson of Harvard, wary of the idea that simple African tribes were gentle, pointed out that even 'the gentle Kung Bushmen until recently had a murder rate comparable to that of Detroit and Houston'.[14] Nonetheless in the cut and thrust of learned debate in the 1970s the savage usually remained noble, with the dispute centred more on the degree of his nobility. Here, through another tilting of the seesaw, was one of the more remarkable changes in the history of thought.

Is Climate Still a Weathercock?

Many European economists, historians and philosophers had once stressed the importance of certain climates and had rejoiced with the eminent British historian H. A. L. Fisher in belonging to 'that section of the human race which, being favoured by the temperate climate of Europe, has so prospered'.[15] As the cold was believed to be a vital source of their energy, they did not long for a life on a tropical beach. In 1900 the typical European, North American and Australian who could afford a holiday preferred cool hills and forests for their rest in summer, and those preferring the sea went there not to lie in the midday sun but to take in the summer sea-breezes. A self-respecting woman strolled along the sands in her long dress, long gloves and wide-brimmed hat, with a parasol to provide additional protection from the rays of the sun. This preference for the cool climate was weakened, especially in the post-war era. Alongside the increasing sympathy for the noble savage was a liking for warm climate. Those who now worshipped nature tended to love a hot climate and craved for the beachcomber's life on the sandy beaches of Hawaii, Queensland, California and Bali. Favouring the minimum of clothing and footwear their attitude to climate was reminiscent of the Europeans who, two centuries earlier, had loved the noble savage.

Those who still admired western civilisation rarely clung, at least publicly, to the view that it depended on a cold climate. A powerful combination of ideas – the belief in hard work and new technology and the need to subjugate nature – still sat together at the same end of the seesaw, but the belief in the virtues of a cold climate was no longer by their side. Air-conditioning, refrigerators and insulated houses enabled Europeans and North Americans who had to work in the tropics to carry their own preferred climate with them: the cold or changeable climate which they believed was so favourable for work was now portable. If they themselves had to work in the tropics, they could use machines to do most of the manual work and could apply new medical technology to fend off tropical diseases which once were deadly. In short, technology had partly kidnapped the climate, removing it from the realm controlled by nature. In addition, thanks to new technologïes, most people in an industrial nation now had far more leisure, and thanks to incredibly cheap energy and transport they could afford to spend as much as possible of that leisure in a warm climate. Many preferred to live permanently in a warm climate, and in the 1960s and 1970s Americans migrated towards their own Sunbelt of the warm south and west, Australians began to move away from the colder south-east corner of their continent, and northern Europeans moved to retirement resorts along the Mediterranean.

The growing preference for a warm climate is one of the fascinating changes of recent decades, and also one of the least explained, perhaps because the topic is entangled with racial issues which are not easily discussed unless discussion conforms · to the prevailing intellectual taboos. The rise of the new tropical nations between 1945 and 1970 almost placed the old climatic argument out of bounds. I do not know whether most intellectuals in the west ceased to believe in the virtues of a cold climate for European peoples, but many ceased to utter such a belief, partly for fear of upsetting citizens of, and apologists for, the third world. To imply that a hot climate impeded economic growth could be construed as telling Nigeria, Pakistan and Ecuador that their hope of rising quickly out of poverty was slim. To tell them that they had less hope of quick economic or intellectual achievement was also to risk pushing them into the arms of the Soviet Union which was only too willing to explain how it possessed, in socialism, a certain recipe for economic growth in hot or chilly climates. Some westerners on the other hand now denied that a hot climate was the enemy of economic growth. Others believed ardently that climate and nature were friends of the emerging tropical nations. Such nations, they believed, had been generously endowed by nature, but their fruits were being exploited by the capitalist west.

It was probably because the old climatic theory and the old racial prejudice marched neatly in step that most versions of the climatic theory were abandoned so emphatically by intellectuals in Europe and North America. Indeed, Stephen Graubard, editor of the magazine of the American Academy of Arts and Sciences, pointed out in 1985 that to assert the importance of geography, of which climate was a crucial component, was 'to contradict the conventional wisdom'.[16] In the view of a geographer at Berkeley, 'it is a rare geographer who, even today, will not bridle a bit if charged with a tendency to environmental determinism.'[17] To emphasise the powerful role of geography was perhaps to absolve mankind from responsibility at a time when contemporary society was expected to feel especially guilty or ashamed. Perhaps to emphasise geography was also to emphasise the harshness and the sheer power of nature at a time when, in intellectual circles, nature was more often seen as kind and gentle.

While attitudes to primitive societies and to race belong to the seesaw and move with the seesaw, perhaps the attitudes to climate are tied less tightly to the seesaw. The increasing post-war preference for a warm climate may well be a permanent change, being largely the outcome of new technology, especially cheap and fast transport, and abundant leisure. On the other hand the mental oscillations associated with the seesaw could well be an important part of this new climatic preference. If so, the rapid growth of the sunbelt states in the USA and Australia and the warmer holiday coast of southern Europe might not be such permanent trends as they now seem.

13 Voyage to the 'Ocean of Misery'

The world was smaller by 1970. Few events in its long history had so cut it down to size as the first photos taken from outer space. The world, it seemed, could never again be huge and mysterious. Whereas a fear in ancient times was that people might fall off the edge of the world and disappear, a common fear now was that it was impossible to disappear or hide in a fast-shrinking world.

The Sense of a Shrinking Globe

The race to the moon had been spurred by the desire for scientific gains and the hope – perhaps unconscious – that the moon would be a new America, but it was clear that the moon would not be a New World in our time. The shrinking world which in the time of Charles Darwin proclaimed man's ever-increasing command of new resources, was seen now as the cause of insoluble problems. By the early 1970s, influential circles thought that the limits of expansion had been reached and that few new resources of worth would be discovered. It was almost as if, to the whole world, there had returned that feeling of encirclement which came briefly to the European lands in the 1890s and was designated by Frederick Jackson Turner as 'the end of the frontier' and by Kaiser Wilhelm II as 'the yellow peril'.

The world is not only a resource bowl but also a sump and sewer, a problem deepened by the quick increase in the world's population in the 1950s and 1960s. In the nineteenth century Europe had more easily disposed of its waste products: the steam and soot and carbon dioxide went into the air, the smelter slag and coal slag onto vast dark dumps, the sewerage into the rivers or market gardens and later into treatment plants, the domestic garbage – for it contained few bottles and no plastic – to the pigs and other animals, and the horse manure to the gardens as fertiliser. The waste could harm health and disfigure some landscapes, and each region paid the penalty in smog, sooty buildings, cholera and typhoid for those problems which it did not solve. A century ago the only pollution which was exported to other regions was the sewage drained into the inland rivers, and except on the Rhine and a few large international rivers that problem was rarely exported to a neighbouring nation.

The export of pollution was now less manageable. The sinking of a huge oil tanker of an innocent coast devastated the beaches and marine life whereas the sinking of a collier – and they crossed the seas in their hundreds a century ago – caused no devastation except to the poor crew and the ship's owner. The effects of nuclear tests and accidents went far beyond the land where the test was made, and perhaps affects everyone on earth. The clouds of sulphur dioxide given off by the burning of coal and crude oil were turned into sulphuric acid, and an acid rain fell on countries far from the chimneys which spewed the wastes. The same burning of fossil fuels, by releasing carbon dioxide into the atmosphere, was said to be forming a blanket which blocked the escape of heat and increased the earth's temperature, thus giving rise to a fear that masses of polar ice might melt, and the level of the world's oceans might rise. Such momentous global changes were little feared fifty years ago.

The global consciousness began to foster pessimism more than optimism. The faith in science and technology as gods all-wise began to ebb, and fears about the adequacy of the world's supply of food and minerals began to flourish. Whereas the depression of the early 1930s had stemmed from a seeming glut of food, fuel and metals, the new economic crisis of the early 1970s arose from a fear of a global scarcity. That global fear can be explained partly by the economic effects of a soaring population but also by cultural changes – by the shift in mood discernible in new paperbacks and the songs heard on transistor radios, the new reverence given to clear streams and wildernesses, and by the new suspicion of commercial tinsel and the latest gadget. We will not understand the slump that caught much of the western world by surprise unless, having learned what we can from demographers and economists, we enquire elsewhere. We have to look beyond the visible hands of the Economic Clock.

The Doomsters

The soaring population of the world was the first trigger of the unease. In 1951 the United Nations showed guarded optimism towards the world's population, for the first world-wide census suggested that the likely increase would not necessarily out-number the rising production of food. In the 1950s the continued rapid increase in the world's population aroused the widest discussion and some unease but no scholarly book predicting doom gained a wide hearing.[1] Indeed some predictions about the world's ability to feed itself were re-assuring. The celebrated economist, Colin Clark, writing in 1960, rejected the belief that the world did not have enough fertile land to feed a multiplying population. He argued that very little land was needed to feed a large city, so long as that land was fertile and was sensibly cul-tivated: 'Today the best agriculturalists in Europe – the Dutch – produce a very good and varied diet on the equivalent of two thirds of an acre of land per person.' If everywhere the farmers cultivated the patches of fertile land as successfully as the Dutch, the world could feed – and feed satisfyingly – 28 billion people, or about ten times its present population. Even the 28 billion could be multiplied, maybe up to 100 billion, if the Japanese farming methods and eating habits were adopted everywhere. Clark was not predicting what would happen. He was rather firing statistics at those pessimists who, without calculations, were insisting that the world would soon run into famine.[2]

By the late 1960s the attitude to the population problem was changing in many intellectual circles. Warnings of over-popula-tion increased and received more publicity. One bestseller was Paul Ehrlich's *The Population Bomb*: the Reverend Thomas Malthus had returned, disguised as a professor of biology at Stanford University, to issue warnings of doom and to offer salvation through Zero Population Growth. Speculating on Britain of the year 2000, he pointed to the likely prospect of famine, nuclear war, plague and pollution. He said in 1969 that if he was a gambler he would bet even money that 'England will not exist in the year 2000'. If by chance Britain did survive disaster, the odds were strong that the quality of life of its citizens would be decidedly poorer.[3]

A United Nations' commission, reporting at the same time, pointed more towards Ehrlich's pessimism than to the earlier hope. The elderly Canadian politician, Lester Pearson, was chairman of the investigation, and his statistics emphasised that earlier expectations about rising population had been too optimistic. In 1950, at a time of moderate optimism towards the peopling of the world, the world's population had been expected to double in the next 85 years, but it now seemed likely to double in less than half of that time. The pressures on food in the 1970s and 1980s, warned Pearson, would therefore be far more dramatic.[4] A balanced, not sensational report, it argued that hopes of feeding the poor nations were diminishing.

At international conferences this pessimistic message was often heard in 1969. In September at Stockholm, Harrison Brown, the president of the International Council for Scientific Unions, gave headline warnings. Economists and agricultural scientists were out of touch, he said. Food supplies, especially in the poorer nations, would become precarious. Brown went on to suggest that the world was on the verge of famine and 'a new stone age'. His likely scenario depicted a widening gap between the rich, well-fed nations and the mass of 'poor, hungry, and permanently miserable people' in the third world. But even the rich nations, being heavily armed, might collapse: 'Sooner or later a nuclear war will take place and technological civilisation will crumble. The poor will then inherit the earth and will live miserably ever after'. That was the future which he painted in black colours.[5]

How far were the revival of Malthus's fears the effect of perceptible events in demography and how much did the fears arise from political motives? Politics usually has some role in prediction, and many doomsters really wanted to change the world, and many of the complacent wished to preserve the present basis of wealth and power. Certainly the increase in the population of the world in the two decades 1950 to 1970 had been alarmingly rapid. On the other hand the increase in the supply of food was even more rapid. Grain is the world's main food, and the production of grain for each person in the world increased by 14 per cent in the 1950s. In the following decade the production of grain, for each person in the world, increased by 8 per cent. Thus in the space of two decades the enormous increase in the world's population had been accompanied by an even larger increase in the annual production of grain.[6] In that period the grain theoretically available for each person increased by about one quarter, a substantial increase. The performance was so impressive that it encouraged over-confidence. To prick that complacency was not the least merit of the warning uttered in the late 1960s by Ehrlich, Harrison Brown, and Pearson.

The increase in the world's harvest of wheat, rye, rice and most other grains was not necessarily a foretaste of what might happen in the 1970s and 1980s. Caution could be legitimately argued. For example the production of food was increasing in the richer nations but the poorer nations of Asia, Africa and Latin America were, in aggregate, becoming less capable of feeding themselves. Whereas before the Second World War they were overall exporters of food they now were net importers of food. By 1970 they imported in aggregate some 44 million tons of grain, and their imports by 1980 were to exceed 100 million tons.[7] But that was not enough, for hunger and malnutrition were still widespread.

Was the switch from exporting food to importing food a clear sign of failure? Western Europe, in the late nineteenth century, had to import an increasing part of its food, and indeed one mark of its success was that it could afford to import food from afar. To see food-importing as simply a sign of failure is perhaps to see the world through the eyes of peasants. But to import food for which you can barely pay is another matter and that was true of many nations in the Third World.

Much of the increase in the world's supplies of food in the quarter century between 1945 and 1970 came from the rich nations. Much came from great plains and prairies which had been first ploughed and sown in the nineteenth century. The largest exporters of grain were those lands pioneered by western Europeans in the nineteenth century – the United States, Canada, Argentina and Australia – and in the 1960s they loaded most of the grain ships that went to the poor lands which could not feed themselves. Of the exporters of grain, the United States was dominant. She was the key to feeding the hungry because she alone held grain surpluses of sufficient magnitude to feed, at short notice, several hundred million people in nations where harvests failed or were inadequate.

In the world as a whole the years 1950–70 were unusually favourable for grain. Even the inadequate growth in grain output between 1959 and 1964 was not enough to alter the total picture of rising output. In the 1960s harvests were improved by the new seed varieties of the 'green revolution', by massive doses of fertiliser, and by the spraying of chemicals against pests. Moreover, the United States government, partly for the purpose of satisfying her own farmers, purchased grain and built up reserves which proved vital in relieving famine in India and other nations. Washington also deliberately paid American farmers to retain cropland in fallow – such was the fear of producing too much grain.[8]

The Seasons Were Silly

One piece of evidence was often ignored in the 1960s – the climate. Economists, demographers and agriculturalists in the western world – indeed almost everyone except farmers – tended to take the climate for granted. They ceased to see it as a vital variable which occasionally went beserk, killing or starving millions. An English environmental scientist, John R. Tarrant of the University of East Anglia, after carefully weighing the evidence, drew this almost breath-taking conclusion: 'By the early 1970s the weather was no longer considered a significant factor in grain production'. And then, almost taken aback by the accusation, he guarded himself by adding that at least this was the assumption of the powerful US Department of Agriculture. It is fair to say that, in the 1960s, there was a playing down of the erratic role of climate. This was the Achilles' heel of the optimists.

The evidence does suggest that in the 1960s the weather for crops was relatively favourable in the grain lands of the Soviet Union and the United States. The grain lands east and west of the River Volga are especially subject to the whims of climate; and those whims were unkind in the 1930s but kind in the decade ending in 1972. Curiously the United States showed a similar contrast, the 1930s being marked by such meagre rains that they were called 'the dust bowl era'. Summer rain is vital for corn, and in the cornbelt the rain was below average in every summer of the 1930s except one. In contrast, in the 1960s the summer rain was above average in every year except one, and even in that year the rain was average. Here was an astonishing contrast, but most observers of American agriculture forgot that the climate in their cornbelt could again become unfavourable for harvests. Americans and Russians, taking the weather for granted, were not prepared for a deterioration in the weather of their grain lands.[9]

In the grain belts of the temperate zone of the northern hemisphere an unreal confidence was increased not only by the run of good seasons but also because more of the economists and the food planners were living in cities and lacked rural experience. In Chicago and Moscow in 1900, when the economic well-being of everyone still depended on the harvests and so much of the nations' workforce still worked with the soil, every bureaucrat and city businessman had known from personal experience that the yield of harvest could not be safely counted until the grain lay in the granaries. In contrast, by the year 1970, some of the learned discussion on global food issues suffered because the cities and their politicians and media were increasingly divorced from farms.

The post-war world as a whole had increased its supplies of grain faster than its population, but that remarkable achievement depended far more on the farms of the prosperous west than on the peasant patches of Asia, Africa and central America. Between the mid 1950s and the late 1960s the farmlands of the industrialised countries had experienced another agricultural revolution and their yield of cereals for each hectare had risen by about 67 per cent. In contrast the yield for each hectare in the third world had increased by a mere 23 per cent, which was not as fast as the increase of its population.[10] It is ironical that there was increasing unease towards western technology at the very time when it was triumphing in the production of grain. Likewise there was a rising respect for the peasant way of life at the very time when that struggling way of existence was showing its deficiencies.

'Ocean of Misery'

Despite the impressive food-growing achievements since the Second World War, there was no certainty that they could continue in the 1970s. Too many imponderables were at work: politics, social attitudes, the climate, the costs of fertiliser and transport, plant diseases, and the profitability of farming compared to other economic pursuits. Even if all these factors were favourable, would the supply of food keep pace with the population? The evidence of the late 1960s did point more to a guarded optimism than to the likelihood of famine. Interestingly the doomsday forecasts arose not when the agricultural statistics supported a Malthusian case but when the evidence pointed in the opposite direction. One is forced to conclude that the pessimists – and the massive audiences which listened to them – were influenced more by the mood of the time than by the evidence from farms and grain silos.

The public fear of famine came partly from distinguished scientists, many of whom spoke in a slightly shrill voice, for the mood of the time had penetrated the citadels of scholarship. Geog Borgstrom was a perceptive scholar of fisheries and agriculture, the recipient of many honours and the head of Swedish food institutes before moving in 1956 to the United States where he became professor of food science and human nutrition at Michigan State University. He wrote books on Japanese fishing and on the principles of food science, and also examined the crucial question of whether the earth would be able to feed its multiplying population. In 1969 appeared his wide-ranging book called simply *Too Many*. The 'too many' were the world's peoples, and the subtitle to his book was *A Study of the Earth's Biological Limitations*.[11] Scanning the earth and ocean for evidence of what could be grown, his book denounced the super-optimists and the complacent. He rightly ridiculed the predictions made by notable scientists that by the year 2000, both disease and famine would be eliminated. Instead, laying out his alarming evidence, he claimed that almost four fifths of the human race lived in abject poverty. Then two pages later he stated that about half of the human race lived in poverty.[12] The two statements don't match. And what are we to make of his conclusion that the people of eastern and southern Europe, Japan, and the Soviet Union in the late 1960s 'keep up a running battle to hold their chins over the waterline in a mounting ocean of misery'?[13] In fact the standard of living in Japan and Italy and Greece was rising rapidly, and even the Soviet Union was proud that meat was now on nearly every dinner table.

Professor Borgstrom held that view which tends to become the first commandment whenever the seesaw dips towards pessimism – the idea that the world's main period of inventiveness is over, and that new inventions cannot be expected. Thus, noting how much land at one time was devoted to growing feed for the horses, and how the tractor has enabled that same land to grow food for 250 million human beings, he warns his readers that this is a one-time gain: 'the next generation has no such trick up its sleeve'. In fact in a technological society each generation holds unexpected tricks up its sleeve.

Many of Borgstrom's statements are over-inflated balloons. He is entitled to question the massive spending on the race to the moon, but the way he expressed that criticism raises an eyebrow: 'And, as the climax of absurdity, we are deserting the globe for celestial adventures of highly questionable value to man's future.' Deserting the globe?[14] The phrase, with all respect, is fantasy. He also predicted famine or near-famine for 1984: 'The fact is that the world in all likelihood, and this on the basis of most available evidence, is on the verge of the biggest famine in history'. The logic of the sentence is shaky. If all available evidence pointed in that direction then he would be entitled to use the phrase 'in all likelihood', but if you look at his sentence again you will notice that he admits that not *all* the evidence does point in that direction. And of course he employs the opening words – 'the fact is' – which disguise the point that he is actually speculating rather than dealing with fact. These are the kinds of loaded sentences which slip past readers, both the wary and the unwary.

Borgstrom explained that most of the white nations were so gluttonous for soil, forests, energy, water, and minerals that their wastefulness could not continue for many decades. Our present extravagant way of life was an historical freak, he said. Here much of what he wrote was beyond dispute, but even readers with little knowledge of Professor Borgstrom's special field would – if they read his words carefully – blink at some of his affirmations. His predictions are a little all-knowing. His statistics seem to carry grave authority but are fragile. Thus he defined the coming famine as 'the biggest famine in history' not by counting the proportion of the world's people who would be hungry but the total number of the hungry and malnourished; he thus forgot that according to the same definition the world was now enjoying the 'biggest banquet in history', for more people were well fed than ever before.[15]

To read Borgstrom's arguments is to feel again the powerful emotions of the late 1960s. Here was a humane and learned man, writing on his own topic with urgency, and seemingly building a strong scaffolding out of tight statistics. And yet rickety logic, skewed arguments, misused language, and contradictory statistics were sufficiently common to render his conclusions more extreme than his evidence allowed. Moreover, by the time he wrote, the rate of growth of the world's population had already passed its peak and was no longer so menacing.[16]

The Club of Rome

In 1972 appeared a smallish book which virtually exploded in the minds of many who read it. Written by a team of four – Meadows and Meadows, Randers and Behrens – it was called *The Limits to Growth*. It said that the world could not continue to grow in prosperity, decade after decade. There was not enough arable land, not enough oil and mineral deposits, and not enough potential to make the industrial equipment to sustain the dizzy growth of the previous quarter century. If population continued to grow, and if more resources were exploited and more pollution was vomited out by cities and more forests were cleared by the ever-extending farmers, suddenly would arrive a day of reckoning. Catastrophe would come in the second half of the twenty first century – maybe in 80 or 100 years' time – unless a halt were called. The book gained in credibility because it used a computer to predict what would happen as the world's population multiplied. Just as Malthus's numerical formula seemed to give him authority, this book gained stature from its use of the new computer at a time when computers were assumed by many to be infallible. As the four authors were indicting a whole civilisation and its wastefulness and rapacity, their message was powerful.

The promoters of the gloomy book belonged to The Club of Rome, and hundreds of thousands of people would have been happy to join the club if it had offered them the rights of membership. Nature conservationists rejoiced in the book, the new mystics cheered its denunciation of materialism, and those who were hostile to commercialism were pleased to come across a powerful tract that seemed to weld together new science and old morality. Sales of *The Limits to Growth* soared. One benign critic pointed out that the book was about to be reprinted for the twelfth time when an error of astonishing magnitude was noticed and corrected. An erroneous table of statistics in the book had denounced the United States as an industrial glutton for burning far more coal than it produced when in fact it produced far more coal that it could burn and was really the world's main exporter of coal.[17] By then a host of other critics had begun to dismantle the book. Economists were especially critical of its detail and assumptions. They rightly pointed out the risks and even the folly of projecting the trends of recent years – the world's mounting consumption of everything from food to copper – unblinkingly into the distant future. And yet it should be said that in the preceding optimism, some economists had made the same kind of automatic projection and convinced themselves that economic growth would never end.

The Club of Rome made its forecast at exactly the right time. Although the club was looking decades ahead, events in scattered parts of the world rapidly seemed to create an early example of the crisis the book had forecast.

The Strange Harvest of 1972

The first startling event in the economic chaos of the early 1970s took place in Russia, where the recent harvests had been abundant. Under Nikita Khrushchev the farms had moved further into the marginal grain areas of Siberia and Kazakhstan, and years of favourable climate in the 1960s seemed to confirm the hope that these areas would provide much grain. The success of Russia's ambitious Five Year Plan for expanding agriculture in 1971–75 depended on those years of kind climate continuing. In the first weeks of 1972, however, the dry cold weather damaged many of the crops already sown in western Russia. The snow on the ground was unusually thin, and did not protect crops from the frost. The soil froze deeper than usual, and vast areas of seed were destroyed. The loss might have been remedied with the very heavy sowing in the Spring of 1972 but those crops suffered from dry summer weather, especially in European Russia. The cereal output of the Soviet was thus only 90 per cent of that harvested in the previous year. Moreover, the Soviet's stocks of grain were small, by American standards.[18]

Grain was urgently needed in Russia and eastern Europe not only for bread. In the previous ten years the diet of the typical

Soviet citizen had improved because of the greater supplies of meat; but in the long winter the multiplying livestock required cereals to remain alive, and those cereals could come only from bountiful harvests. A solution was to kill more livestock and thus divert to the baking of bread that grain which previously would have been used, less efficiently, in the fattening of animals. The solution, however, would endanger the improvement in the people's diet which was one of the achievements of the previous decade. The attractive answer was to import grain from the United States. Even that solution required an assessing of world politics. Should the Soviet Union, even temporarily, become so dependent for food on its strongest opponent? To trade food-stuffs on a large scale is really to strengthen diplomatic relations, and both the United States and the Soviet Union were willing to take that step. So began the massive grain shipments from North America to Russia, shipments far larger than those made briefly in the mid 1960s. Unlike India, which was the main importer of grain in the mid 1960s, the Soviet Union in 1972 could afford to pay, and was made to pay, thus inflating the world prices of grain. In the following year, Russia was again a big buyer of American wheat.

China, meanwhile, reaped a fine wheat harvest in 1972 but a poorer harvest of other cereals. The journal *Foreign Agriculture* noted that rice and other crops in China had suffered because of the 'worst drought in several decades combined with water-logging, frost, windstorm, hail and insect damage'. On 7 December 1972 the Communist Party journal, *Red Flag*, called on every Chinese to 'save a mouthful of grain each day'. As heavy imports were also needed, China joined in the anxious scamper on the world's wheat market.[19]

Increasing commercial contacts between communist and capitalist nations were therefore one cause of the surge of grain prices. If Russia and China had remained in relative economic isolation, and had quietly coped with their own methods of rationing food, and had not given publicity to their own shortage of grain by their overseas purchases, there would have been much less talk of a world food crisis in the early 1970s. The crisis was in part a reflection of a shrinking world.

The world's harvest of all grains in 1972 was somewhat below expectations. Not only did Russia and China have shortages, but in India the monsoon rains were inadequate, in Australia a drought cut the wheat harvest by one quarter, and the wheat yields in Canada were lower. The United States, knowing that the price of exported grain was not very favourable when the sowing season commenced, had planted a reduced acreage, and a wet winter retarded the crop in many states. These deficiencies in some lands were outweighed by the excellent harvest in other lands, and western Europe probably had the greatest harvest in its history. All in all, the climatic conditions for agriculture in the world in 1972 were a little below those of the previous decade, but then again the main wheat areas had enjoyed an abnormally favourable climate in the previous decade. Measured against the average climatic conditions of the twentieth century, 1972 was probably close to normal.[20] But observers had come to expect more than a normal climate, and therefore the world's slight shortfall in grains caused far more excitable bidding than if the shortfall had been expected.

The astonishing thing about the harvests of 1972 and the period of profound unease which they generated was that by historical standards they were good harvests. In the history of the world's agriculture, the corn harvest of 1972 was the second highest on record, while the wheat harvest, in spite of the Russian failure, was the third highest on record. It is strange that such harvests should have initiated deep unease. Publicity, however, was given less to the sheer magnitude of the harvests than to the shortfalls in certain countries, especially Russia. In fact there was an overall decline of less than 1 per cent in the world's total agricultural output compared to the excellent year of 1971, but the harvests were especially low compared to the optimistic targets set by international officials, governments, and grain merchants. Admittedly, 1972 was unusual in that four of the key crops – wheat, corn, rice and barley – each recorded a lower output than in the previous year. And yet in aggregate, the world's production of all food in 1972 – the year seen as a disaster – formed one of the three best harvests in the world's history.

The grain shortage was obviously not the result of one or two dramatic events but of a salad of events. One of these events took place off the coast of Peru, and at first sight it seemed to have no relation to the harvests on land. Peru had recently become the world's major fishing nation, and in a normal year it caught about one fifth of the world's catch. The main fish off the coast of Peru and Chile was the anchovy, and it fed on the plankton which flourished in the Humboldt Current that ran along the Pacific Coast,* but for reasons not fully known a change in the temperature of the sea current diminished the plankton and the anchovies too. In 1972 the anchovy catch off Peru was disappointing. In 1973 it failed again. It so happened that in a normal year most of the anchovies were converted to a fish-meal which was high in protein, and indeed more productive of protein than one of the world's major sources of beef, the South American grasslands. Since the fish-meal was exported as food for fattening the livestock in Europe and North America and Japan, the decline of Peru's fishing quickly accentuated the global shortage of cereal products.[21] Soy beans were now in stronger demand as an alternative to fish-meal and their price soared, increasing two and a half times between 1970 and 1973.[22] As the soy beans competed with other crops for the same fertile lands, the soy bean boom pushed up the prices of other farming commodities, especially Brazilian coffee.[23]

If we assemble the factors which contributed to the scarcity of cereals in the world in 1972, the list is long: poor weather in several major farming nations, the willingness of communist nations to import large amounts of grain, the fast growth of population in the third world, the failure of the anchovy fisheries in Peru, the widespread prosperity which enabled people to spend more money on food, and the slightly diminished acreage sown in the United States which was the main producer of export grain. All these factors, in creating a relatively small deficiency in grain, pushed up the price of grain. Furthermore the fears for the future made many nations hoard grain, and that pushed up the price again.

To offer these explanations of the rising grain prices is not necessarily to offer a complete explanation. The fact that 1972

---

* The cormorants which fed on the live anchovies were said to be the source of the huge guano deposits on the Peruvian coast. These guano or nitrate deposits had long supplied Europe with fertiliser, and the imagined decline of these deposits was one reason for Crookes' famous prophecy of 1898, outlining the danger of a global scarcity of wheat. Three quarters of a century later, some scientists were beginning to argue that El Nino, the coastal current which in normal conditions was a massive source of nutrient for anchovies, was a crucial indicator of abnormal weather conditions in distant parts of the world.

was still one of the largest harvests in the history of the world
does not make it easy to explain why the price of grain rocketed.
It can explain a rise in grain prices: it cannot easily explain a
leap. Moreover, 1972 was a year of relatively mild inflation in
most western nations, and so the expectations of general inflation
did not make buyers bid up the price of grain, thinking that
they should buy before the price soared; in the United States in
1972 the rate of inflation was a mere 3.3 per cent, a decline on
that of the previous four years.

Grain does not always leap in price when a harvest is deficient.
Twice in the 1960s – in 1961 and 1965 – the world's production
of grain had actually fallen but the price did not soar then
partly because the shortage of new grain was largely met by the
huge reserves stored in the United States. Indeed in 1965, after
the failure of the monsoonal rains had impaired India's harvest,
American wheat arrived in an armada of 600 ships, and those
ships and cargoes were massively subsidised. By the early 1970s
the world's grain reserves were lower, and the United States –
yielding to budget pressures – deliberately carried lower grain
reserves in its silos, and it could not easily spare emergency
supplies for other lands. Each new harvest was therefore vital.
In the United States the harvest of 1973 was excellent but 1974
was not. Across the globe in 1974 the harvests were larger than
those of two years ago but they fell below those of 1973. Thus
in the space of three years two of the world's harvests, being below
expectations, compounded the sense of a shortage of grain. In a
short span the wheat prices were to increase threefold. I doubt
whether in the previous two centuries, the price of the west's
basic foodstuff had increased more dramatically.

Were the gloomier forecasters correct, and were the events of
the early 1970s one sign of their accuracy? A decade later the
grain supplies of the world were far larger than the influential
doomsters had foretold. Grain production for each person in
the world was continuing to rise, especially in poorer nations,
and the world markets in 1986 actually had a glut of grain.
There were huge pockets of hunger, especially in southern Asia,
but the proportion of the world's population suffering from malnutrition was lower than at any time since the Second World
War. Nearly fifteen years after loud, learned warnings of a population explosion, the food supplies in the world had improved,
not deteriorated.

While we know that the doomsters were mistaken in their predictions that a global famine might grip the 1980s, some evidence was on their side in 1972 and 1973. For some years they had been forecasting famine, and here were the first signs, appearing even earlier than they had predicted. Moreover, they believed that the world's resources were too small for the soaring population, and as the population had increased by an alarming 46 per cent in the quarter century 1946–70, they expected minerals and energy as well as agriculture to feel the pressure of a population that consumed more and more of everything. They predicted a shortage of oil, iron ore, copper, coal, fertilisers and ultimately a shortage of every raw material.

By 1973 that sweeping prophecy seemed to be enjoying an early fulfilment. Many major commodities were showing the indications of shortage – their prices were soaring. The price of a bushel of wheat and rice doubled between 1971 and July 1973 – it would soon treble. The price of cocoa on the world's markets had more than trebled, and the price of zinc and animal hides had almost trebled. In the same period, commodities as diverse as wool, sugar, peanuts and rubber, coming from very different rural regions of the world, had each doubled. A variety of commodities – ranging from copper to beef – had increased in price by about 50 per cent.[24] Other commodities such as tobacco and newsprint had increased by little in price, but the raw materials which came from the rocks and soil and were becoming scarce – or were believed to be scarce – were numerous enough to enable the doomsters to say, 'We told you so.'

Today, in the public memory, the economic crisis of the early 1970s was dominated by petroleum. In July 1973, when the fear of a shortage of grain was foremost, petroleum was not a matter of grave concern, for since 1971 its export price had increased by a mere one third. Three months later, petroleum copied wheat and rice. Its price soared, arousing intense anxiety in a world which depended on cheap petroleum not only for transport but for the making of those fertilisers on which agriculture increasingly relied. Here was a clear vista of the ocean of misery.

14 Oil Crisis: A Turning Point

The 'energy' crisis of 1973 was unique. If we look back over the world's history we can find earlier energy crises but they were milder or arose slowly.

Wood was for long the world's main fuel, and in some lands the supply of wood ran low; but such shortages came slowly and gave their own warning. Moreover there was a solution: farmers could plant more trees, so long as they could divert land from the growing of food. Oil, in contrast, could not be planted. In England, not long before the industrial revolution, there was a shrinkage of the forests which produced the wood which made the charcoal which smelted the iron in the furnaces. So numerous were the charcoal-burners that in some parts of England whole forests vanished.[1] The ultimate solution, found by Abraham Darby, was to use coal instead of wood to produce the special fuel required, and so the more efficient coke began to replace charcoal in the smelting of iron from the 1750s.

The Contrasting Eras of Coal and Oil

Coal became the dominant fuel of the industrial revolution, and by 1900 it was the basis of the industrial world. It was the fuel for factories and mills and for the steamships and steam trains which were the fastest forms of transport, and it provided gas for heating and cooking, coke for the steel works, and raw materials for dyestuffs and chemicals. Never before had an advanced society relied so intimately on the one mineral, and yet no international crisis had centred on coal supplies. If an OPEC or cartel of the coal mines had arisen and if it had imposed an embargo in say 1920, international commerce would have been more prepared for the oil crises of our day.

Why, then, was there no comparable coal crisis? Coal deposits were more common than oil, and every industrial country had its own coal mines. The voracious consumers of coal were also large producers of coal: Britain, America, Germany, France

242

and Belgium, the main industrial nations, were miners of coal, and the international trade in coal involved only a tiny fraction of the world's output of coal. Nature had dispersed her deposits of coal in so many lands that there was little scope for a coal monopoly or cartel which might hold to ransom the importers of this basic raw material. In 1900 virtually no nation gained most of its export income from the sale of coal, and so no nation had a glittering incentive to try to raise the price of coal unduly. Furthermore, if the price of coal did become too high on the international market, a variety of new coal deposits would have become producers in the following three years. The long-term supply of coal in the heyday of steam was certainly more elastic than is the supply of oil today. Indeed, in 1872 and 1873, years of hectic industrial boom, a famine of coal in England forced up its price though not with the speed of the oil spiral in 1973. Promptly new coal deposits were explored in England, and in the space of two years, 1,400 collieries were opened, helping to halve the price of coal in the space of a decade.[2]

These were the main reasons why in the history of coal there had not been the equivalent of the oil inflation of 1973. The events of 1973 were unprecedented, and that was partly why they took the world by surprise. And surprise or shock were vital causes of the dislocation which followed.

The world depended even more on oil in the 1970s than, half a century earlier, it had depended on coal. Nearly all the major nations now imported all or part of their oil from foreign lands across the seas. They were therefore, potentially, at the mercy of the oil exporters, should certain conditions arise. A coal embargo in the era of steam would have been a clumsy weapon and almost unusable. An oil embargo in the era of the motor engine was a more lethal weapon, partly because cars and aircraft had no alternative to petroleum.

The amazing boom in the western world since 1945 had relied much on abundant and cheap supplies of oil. Oil was cheaper than any previous fuel; it could be shipped cheaply to remote lands; and its by-products included cheap fertilisers which helped to increase the world's supply of bread and rice. Being a commodity which would ultimately become scarce, oil was probably too cheap. It was so cheap that in many parts of the world less wood was cut and less coal was mined, and fewer hydro-electric plants and fewer nuclear power-houses were built, than would otherwise have been. The designing of the largest ships in the history of the sea enabled oil to be carried cheaply to the remotest lands, and by the 1970s more than half the tonnage of the international commerce on the oceans consisted of oil.[3]

Here was a miracle fuel, and almost every nation came to rely on it. The remarkable economic progress of Japan rested on cheap oil carried in tankers from the Middle East, and oil provided seven tenths of her energy by the early 1970s. In western Europe in 1950 coal supplied 75 per cent of the energy but in 1972 only 23 per cent. The coal mine, which even more than the steelworks and the shipyards had been the secret of Europe's success, no longer seemed vital in the new oil era.

The Embargo of 1973

In 1972 and 1973 the tankers crowded outside the oil ports in the Persian Gulf, and at the throat of the pipelines in the Mediterranean. Record tonnages of oil were shipped because western Europe, the United States, and Japan were enjoying a boom. More oil was consumed each year than ever before, and its very cheapness was one cause of the prosperity and the fatter pay packets in a hundred western cities. But if the oil exporters so wished, they could impede the flow of oil: their bargaining position was so high that they were capable of demanding higher prices for their oil.

Late in 1973, trouble in the Middle East gave the Arab oil producers a political as well as an economic incentive to use their oil as a bludgeon. Why not refuse to supply that oil to the United States and any other nation which gave military aid to Israel? In the Six Days War of 1967 the Arab oil nations resolved to use oil as a weapon against Israel's backers but the quick ending of that war gave them no opportunity. As the Arabs lost that war, the temptation to use this strongest of all their weapons in any future war was increased. Moreover the long closure of the damaged Suez Canal after the war showed how the diverting of oil tankers to the long Cape route could disrupt international commerce. To go one step further and to refuse to load the tankers would be even more dislocating. Saudi Arabia, the largest of the Arab oil states, privately gave warnings that it might use oil as a weapon in the event of another clash between Israel and Egypt.

Other oil nations were quietly calling for action in 1973. The industrial world was booming and yet the oil which fuelled that world was absurdly cheap, and in real terms its price had fallen by about one third in the 1960s. The nations which gained most of their export income from oil were either poor or weak in nearly all other resources. As their precious deposits of oil could not last for many decades, they had to yield the maximum income while they lasted. The Organization of Petroleum Exporting Countries, known as OPEC, had been formed in 1960 to press these interests and seemed to achieve little until the early 1970s. In Vienna in September 1973, it began to demand higher oil prices, but it was not the master organiser in the subsequent chain of events. It was to be more a symbol, proclaiming that the petroleum exporters had to be taken seriously.

In the Middle East, meanwhile, political tension was high. On 6 October, Egypt and Israel began to fight a new war. One day after the war began, the government of Iraq nationalised the assets of two United States oil companies. The oil ministers of Middle East states assembled in Kuwait and planned stronger action. On 16 October, six oil nations in the Persian Gulf increased the price of their oil by two thirds, a startling leap, and began to reduce their production of oil. Three days later, Saudi Arabia and other Arab oil nations proclaimed an embargo on the export of oil to the United States of America. Four days later, an embargo was placed on the export of oil to the Netherlands, which was denounced as too supportive of Israel.

The oil-producing nations displayed unusual unity but the oil distributing companies were no longer united. There was little unity amongst the seven oil giants which controlled some 70 per cent of the oil market in the non-communist world. Moreover the smaller, newer US oil companies which had become prominent in the Middle East after Iran nationalised its oil industry depended largely on Middle East oil and, in this sudden crisis, urgently sought new sources. In October 1973, once the embargo was imposed, they were virtually deprived of oil. As their solvency was threatened, they turned elsewhere for oil, buying it at high prices. Their bidding did as much as the actions of the Middle East nations to boost the price of oil in the last months of 1973. Japanese trading houses were also bidding strenuously, for Japan's economy depended on imported oil. Soon the French government joined in the crazy bidding.[4]

The price of oil continued to soar, as the individual oil nations even more than OPEC took up the running. Late in October, the Shah of Iran grabbed the ball and ran. Between October 1973 and January 1974 the world's price of crude oil increased by almost 400 per cent. It even surpassed the rocketing wheat prices. Never, perhaps, in a period of general international peace, had the price of an essential commodity risen so quickly.

A Revolution in the Oil Lands

The leaping price of oil reflected another event quietly occurring in recent years: a transfer of economic and political power from the United States, Britain and a few rich nations to the Middle East and to North African nations which had recently been poor. In 1963 the big international oil companies controlled the supply of most of the world's oil, fixed the price of that oil, and received most of the profits. By 1973 their control and their share was much smaller and they no longer fixed the price. The old European colonies and protectorates, now independent, asserted their authority over the oil within their territories, either by demanding the largest share of the production profits or simply by nationalising foreign oil companies which had discovered the oil. Between 1969 and 1973, Algeria, Libya and Iraq nationalised foreign oil companies. The revolutionary Libyan, Colonel Ghadaffi, ruling a nation of a mere 2 million people, went further. He decided to charge more for his oil, being aided by Europe's environmental regulations that favoured oil such as Libya's which was low in sulphur. What Ghadaffi began in 1970, others completed in 1973. Here was an enormous shift in economic and political power, a shift that was perhaps as influential as the spectacular withdrawal of Britain, Holland, Belgium, Portugal and other empires from large areas of Africa and Asia. Without that revolution in political power the oil crisis could not have occurrred.

The United States had been the main loser in this shift of power and in 1973 it was again the main target of the Arab oil embargo, largely because it was the backer of Israel. It was also the largest consumer of oil, and in recent years had come to rely on heavy imports of Middle Eastern oil to supplement the oil flowing from its own wells. Accordingly it had the strongest incentive, by threat or negotiation, to break the embargo and also to reduce the price of oil.

The United States held at least two strong options, each of which would have removed the embargo. One option was to withdraw military support from Israel, but that was barely considered. The other was to apply military pressure against the Middle East's oil lands until the embargo was lifted. 'Only a few decades ago', wrote Professor Klaus Knorr, 'the great powers would have met such a challenge unhesitatingly with force'.[5] In the early 1970s, however, the United States was extremely reluctant to apply force in order to end the embargo, for the humbling lesson of the Vietnam war was vividly in mind. Any American military adventure in the Arab lands would also have alienated much support within the third world as well as in the western world. Moreover, if the strong American forces in the Mediterranean had pounced on the oil wells of the Middle East, the danger of Russian retaliation could have been high.

We grasp one reason why the price of oil soared if we acknowledge that the United States, as the world's leading military power, was so over-extended that it was exceptionally vulnerable to leverage from the small nations which produced most of the world's oil exports. It was over-extended in Vietnam. It was over-extended in the Middle East where its strong support for Israel jeopardised the flow of oil originating with Israel's bitter enemies. The United States, being over-extended, had to sacrifice either its ally Israel or its main source of overseas oil. As it was reluctant to apply direct force it could not win its incompatible goals of importing cheap oil from the Arab nations and exporting arms to Israel. Reluctant to sacrifice Israel it was forced to sacrifice a sure supply of oil. In 1979, when the price of oil jumped again, the United States was handcuffed even more by a timidity in using the threats which its military strength could sustain and by a clumsiness when trying to liberate the American citizens held as prisoners in Teheran. In supporting Israel in 1973–4 and in supporting the Shah before the Iran troubles of 1979–80, the United States jeopardised two vital sources of oil and triggered reactions which rocketed the price of oil. America's failure to impose her will, after provoking the oil-producing nations of the Middle East, was a key cause of the two leaps in the price of oil in the 1970s. The so-called energy crisis, which is usually seen as an economic crisis, was just as much a political crisis.

If this kind of situation had arisen in the 1890s, a major western nation would have used force. At that time the world's main economic powers were willing to use their military might in remote parts of the world. Thus when the world's main producer of gold, the Boer republic in the Transvaal, defied Britain in the 1890s, she was invaded and eventually defeated. Most of us might applaud the reluctance of the United States in the 1970s to use force, but the reluctance was in part a sign of a new attitude to military strength in the western world. A declining faith in technology, both military and peaceful, was to be a hallmark of the 1970s, and was possibly one of the causes of the economic recession beginning in that decade.

The astonishing side of the oil crisis was that every nation soon had as much oil as it needed but not as much as it wanted, for the wish to hoard oil was intense. Actually there was no grave scarcity of oil. The fear was not so much about oil supplies for the next month but about oil supplies in the longer term. The countries against which the embargo was directed did not see their own oil stocks run perilously low, and by February 1974 the high price quietened the demand for oil; at the new exorbitant price the world had a surplus and not a scarcity of crude oil. If there had been no fear for the future of oil, and if there had been faith in science as the problem solver, the price of oil would have increased but not sensationally. Amidst all the tension and fear, the frenzied bids, and the popular predictions that even the rich would soon have to shiver in winter through a shortage of oil, one fact was difficult to dispute. The crisis once it arose, was influenced almost as much by the mind as by the ground.

The Nature Movement and Its Quiet Influence

The United States could have avoided the worst effects of the oil embargo if it had realised well in advance that it was, year by year, becoming more vulnerable because of events which had quietly been happening at home. It had ceased to be self-reliant in oil, and had been forced to import more and more in the early 1970s. Its dependence on overseas sources of a strategic commodity made it what it had never been before – a potential target for its enemies. And in the creation of that target one crucial factor was the rise, within the United States, of a wave of feeling which was hostile to technology. Expressed in the simplest terms, the oil crisis of 1973 might have been serious rather than a crisis, if the United States had not been caught in a tug-of-war between its old business groups and its new conservation groups in the few years before and after the crisis.

The United States had slowly allowed itself to be at the mercy of the Middle East oil nations because it imported more and more of the energy which it could have produced at a higher cost in its own oil wells, coal mines and power stations. Coal was abundant in the USA but its production had sagged in the late 1950s and 1960s as oil became cheaper. Coal's output might have later revived but for the fact that coal was a target of environmental fears. The Clean Air Act of 1970 had increased the cost of burning coal in power stations. Conservationists had also protested against the open-cut or strip mining of coal – the cheapest method of extraction – because it devastated the landscape. In the early 1970s it was in America's strategic interest to subsidise the mining of more of its own coal but instead, in the interests of the environment, it imposed obstacles against the opening of new coal projects.

The oil tankers now reached American ports in a long procession from the Middle East, but the United States was capable of becoming far more self-sufficient in oil and gas. The new environmental movement, however, became vocal and began to affect economic decisions in the late 1960s. Controls were placed on the exhaust emission of motor vehicles, and that made the petrol less efficient and so indirectly increased its consumption. In 1969 a large spill of oil on beautiful Californian beaches led to such angry protests that the government, fearing further pollution of the coast, banned the exploration for oil on its own continental shelf – one of its promising oil areas. That ban increased the prospect of the United States remaining dependent on Middle Eastern oil. All these may seem minor effects of the crusades against technology and pollution, but together they helped to make the United States acutely vulnerable to pressure or blackmail from oil producers of the Arab lands and Persia.

In the strange chessboard of bargaining in 1973, Alaska was also vital. What happened in Alaska, or what failed to happen in Alaska, was as important as the discussions in the cities of the Middle East. A huge oilfield had recently been found in Alaska, and a pipeline planned to carry the oil across the frozen tundra and the mountains to refineries in the south was scheduled for completion in 1973. At a time of mounting concern for wildernesses, American conservation groups and nature scientists protested that a pipe-line would imperil the delicate web of plants, insects and animals. Their campaign delayed the pipeline. It was eventually begun in 1974, after the oil crisis had emphasised the danger facing America's security. If the Alaskan pipeline had been opened in the year originally planned, the United States would have been less damaged by an embargo on the Middle East oil consigned to her ports, and the price of oil on the international market would not have leaped so high and so quickly.[6]

The oil prices would have been raised less boldly in the last months of 1973 if alternative sources of energy had been at hand in the USA, Europe and Japan. Nuclear energy was an obvious alternative. In the 1960s nuclear power stations had been built in many lands but they did not supply as much of the power as their advocates had planned. Nuclear technology was not fully mastered; the safety of nuclear plants was not sufficient to satisfy well-informed critics; and ways of disposing of nuclear wastes were fiercely criticised. In addition the rising rates of interest deterred American investors who thought of building nuclear plants. All these difficulties were aggravated by the rise of the broad crusade against technology. The crusade sought stricter supervision of nuclear plants, and its success further deterred those who thought of investing in such plants, so that in 1973 the nuclear power stations were able to provide less than 5 per cent of the electricity consumed in the United States.

In the last resort some decisions made by oil-producers of the Middle East in 1973 were intuitive. They had to assess their own bargaining position before imposing an embargo on the shipping of oil to the United States, and before reducing their own total supply of oil and thus pushing up world prices, and in making these linked decisions they had placed some weight on the role of public opinion in the United States. They knew the predictions of a coming energy crisis in the world, and observed how the report from The Club of Rome had sent jitters through anxious minds in western lands in 1972. Therefore they predicted that many Americans would accept and even welcome a sharp increase in the price of oil, for dearer oil would emphasise The Club of Rome's warnings that the world must conserve its scarce natural resources. According to Edith Penrose, a distinguished observer of the behaviour of firms, the oil exporters had gained confidence from the widespread predictions made by the Doomsday school in America.[7] Warnings of a world-wide shortage of oil helped to reinforce 'the belief of the exporting countries that their long-run, as well as their short-run position was strong.'

'Seldom in human affairs do all of the influences on a complex problem become unfavourable simultaneously', wrote Professor James W. McKie of the University of Texas, an authority on sources of energy.[8] In 1973, it seemed, tornados came from nearly every point of the compass, and the relief parties expected in the wake of the tornados did not arrive. The price of oil rose dramatically because of the Israeli–Arab war, the recent boom in industrial life, the whole world's increasing dependence on oil, the bargaining sense and relative unity of the foreign oil producers, the disunity and panic of the oil importers, the vulnerability of the United States economy and the hesitation on the part of its government, the slowness of coal and uranium in serving as alternatives to oil, the delay in laying the pipeline across Alaska, and a variety of other factors. In this tangle of factors one weaved its way in and out, barely visible but powerful. This was the feeling that technology was dangerous and that nature was being looted greedily by man. This swing from technology towards nature did much to weaken the bargaining power of the United States, Europe and Japan, to increase the bargaining position of the Middle East and other oil producers, and to permeate events with a touch of doom and destiny. Without this change of mood, oil prices could not have risen so dramatically.

To point to the part played consciously and unconsciously by the Nature movement in increasing the price of oil is not to point a gun at that movement's ideals. In the long term it might well be acclaimed as one of the most meritorious movements of the twentieth century because of the attitudes which it challenged and the places of beauty which it preserved from destruction. When eventually the complex events and changes of our era are assessed, the soaring price of oil in the 1970s might well be adjudged as the most desirable of all the alternatives which could have happened.

Changes in the cultural mood of societies do have economic effects, both for good and bad. Changes in the values held by a society, or even minorities within a society, do affect economic life. It is hard to escape the conclusion that the world depresssion or recession of the late 1970s was foreshadowed by profound cultural changes. Those same cultural changes, moreover, were vital causes of the grain scarcity and oil panic of the early 1970s and their aftermath. Nothing was more deadening to confidence than the belief that oil could never again be cheap. And that belief was, in its origins, cultural as much as economic.

The industrial boom in the early 1970s had increased the demand for virtually all raw materials. Speculators, thinking the boom would persist, moved in and accentuated the whirl of rising prices. The increasing tension in the fixed exchange rates between international currencies, a system set up at Bretton Woods at the end of the war and now faltering, intensified the uncertainty about the economic future. The soaring price of wheat and petrol was an extreme form of what happened to other basic commodities. The price index of world commodities – mainly foods, fuels and other raw materials – showed these remarkable rises:[9]

1971	1% rise
1972	12% rise
1973	50% rise
1974	68% rise
1975	−9% fall

Meanwhile, commodity prices pushed up other prices, and wage demands added their pressure. The consumer price-index, while not reaching the levels of the commodity price-index, registered a rate of inflation seen in few countries since 1945 and seen in some countries in no year of the twentieth century. By 1974, of the major industrial countries in the west, only West Germany had an annual rate of inflation that was well below 10 per cent, while Italy passed 19 per cent and Japan 22 per cent. A year later the inflation rate in the United Kingdom was to reach 24 per cent, while Australia – once a country of stable prices – registered 15 per cent for the second successive year. Here was economic chaos.

The high and unpredicted leap in oil prices did incalculable harm. Business and the flow of trade were dislocated as much by the suddenness as the extent of that increase. Indeed part of that rise of 1973–74 was whittled away by the fact that in the following five years other goods increased more rapidly than oil. Accordingly, if the changes in oil prices between 1973 and 1978 had been spread evenly from year to year and had been to some extent predictable, there would have been a lesser blow to economic confidence. As it was, the oil leap in 1973 shook confidence everywhere. It impeded long-range planning in those industries where cheap fuel had been vital, and it bruised that vital industrial sector which centred on the motor vehicle, and its manufacture and use. Above all, it fostered a kind of nervous, jumping-jack inflation which spread quickly through the western world.

For many businessmen, 1973 appeared the turning point in the post-war world. It marked the end of at least two decades of very cheap oil, an era of cheap transport and cheap power and a steadily rising standard of living in all the richer nations. The same year also marked the beginning of what was at first called a recession but was later called a depression.

Flashback: A Forgotten Gold Crisis

When everything has been said about the oil crisis arising in 1973, one fact has to be restated. The jump in the price of oil and the fear of its continuing scarcity created economic bewilderment of a magnitude for which there was no precedent. In the earlier era of coal there could be no energy crisis and no parallel to the OPEC crisis of 1973, simply because the major industrial nations were the main producers of the energy which they burned and therefore could not be held to ransom by smaller nations which exported fuel.

Perhaps the nearest comparable shock in any other commodity in modern history stemmed from a perceived scarcity of supply of gold from the 1880s onwards, but that was more a slow fear than a sudden shock. It may also be argued that gold, being more an ornamental than a useful commodity, should in no way be compared to oil as a dynamo of economic activity. And yet gold in the nineteenth century was a kind of turbine of the monetary system, and it strongly affected economic activity and expectations of future activity. Gold was indispensable as a basis for credit in national and international finance, and to most financiers of that age, gold was as central as coal to the well-being of their world. An adequate, well managed stock of gold enabled governments and banks to operate credit and commerce in such a way that the production of wheat, coal, copper, wool, cotton and all the items of trade was more likely to meet the demand.

In the 1880s and 1890s the supply of gold was believed to be inadequate because of a dearth of new discoveries, and the shortage of gold was seen as a potential cause of a contraction of the money supply and a promoter of falling prices and of sluggish economic activity. An inadequacy of gold was the common explanation for the falling prices, a fall arousing such concern that from the 1880s onwards the period of deflation came to be called the Great Depression. In the 1890s the world output of gold, aided by major discoveries on the Rand and Western Australia field, grew rapidly, and the general rise in prices beginning about 1896 was seen as the result of plentiful gold; but that short-lived sense of plenty was followed by fears that the gold, though increasing, was still inadequate for big nations' special needs in the decade preceding the First World War. Europe's arms race and its scramble for gold were partners, in the view of one economic historian: 'As international security waned, monetary rearmament got under way: perhaps before, but certainly not later than, its military equivalent'.[10]

The world's output of gold grew between 1900 and 1907 before levelling out, but it was not sufficient to stock the vaults of competing nations. The shortage of gold was especially acute whenever there was a diplomatic crisis. Gold was almost worshipped by the prevailing economic theory as the quiet regulator of the supply of money, the disciplinarian of the banking system, the creator of stable exchange rates, the guarantee of stable prices in time of peace and vital for financing a war. We understand the importance placed on gold if we see how widespread were the predictions in 1914 that the First World War could not last long because no nation owned the gold needed to sustain a long war. A month after the war began, the London journal *United Empire* argued that the gold in the hands of the great powers 'is a matter of great importance, not only in determining the intensity with which operations may be carried on, but also the probable duration of the war.'[11] Some London financiers insisted it was financially impossible to carry on a war on the present scale for many months. The war was expected to end quickly, less through defeat on the battlefield than through a scarcity of gold which in turn would lead to runaway inflation, financial collapse and perhaps civil war in those nations which were stricken by inflation.[12] In fact a scarcity of gold was to exert little influence on the duration of the war, but in the decades before the war it helped to mould the mood.

Historians now believe that the late nineteenth century allowed itself to depend too much on gold, but possibly the late twentieth century will be deemed, in times to come, to have allowed itself to depend too much on oil. Such extreme dependence led to extreme vulnerability.

The Slaves Diminish

The oil crisis issued a wave of shocks and buffetings to the balance of payments, exchange rates, and budgets of those nations which were heavy importers of oil and suddenly found the oil too expensive. Even for new nations whose main source of foreign revenue was oil, the sudden deluge of riches was dislocating, and in handling that excess of wealth and in placing it on the world's money markets the new nations were bound to create uncertainty, no matter how skilfully they invested their funds.

The high standard of living won in the period from 1945 to 1970 had depended much on the cheapness of energy. It was as if the millions of people in the workplace, and all the machines they drove or tended, had been supplemented by millions of energetic but silent slaves who had been born millions of years ago. The family name of the slaves was Hydrocarbon. In the wake of the oil crisis, fewer of those now-expensive slaves were available for house-heating, urban transport, the growing of foods and the manufacturing of steel and cars and a medley of other activities.[13] With the withdrawal from the daily workforce of so many energetic slaves, it was not easy to maintain the standard of living of old.

In trying to explain the chaos, many international businessmen gave undue blame to the oil crisis and not enough to the dramatic increase in the world price of grain. The belief that oil was the culprit became itself a factor of importance. As oil was envisaged as remaining scarce in the future, and as it was vulnerable to the tensions of the Middle East and the commercial inexperience of new nations, could it be relied upon? This question received no reassuring answer during the remainder of the 1970s, and the revolution in Iran pushed up the price of oil again. Between 1971 and 1979 the price of oil had been multiplied by twelve – a mathematical formula for chaos, the miracle is that the chaos was curbed. In September 1979, at an Oxford seminar on world energy, importers and exporters of energy saw no hope of returning to the era of cheap oil, because any return would be brief. Ominously they also saw a tight 'nexus between the performance of the world economy and the energy problem'. A firm economic recovery required what was unlikely – cheaper energy.[14] To their surprise, relatively cheap oil was to return in 1986, at a time when the oil producers no longer possessed the bargaining position which they exploited in the previous decade.

Guilt and Gloom

The tilting of the seesaw from Technology towards Nature was a vital cause of the crisis that developed in the early 1970s. Moreover the concern for nature made it difficult to fight the rising levels of unemployment. New job-creating projects were delayed, even indefinitely, because the demands by conservationist lobbies and new government regulations made the investment too costly or risky. A chemical plant was not built because a neighbourhood group objected to the effluent passing, without adequate treatment, into a local river. A power-house was delayed because the particles escaping from the chimneys were a hazard or nuisance to neighbouring suburbs. A new mine was not opened because it endangered the landscape or the streams. In the United States the giant firm, General Electric, estimated that the gestation time of large industrial projects was increased by about five years, once the public campaign against pollution became strong. Some of the campaigns against pollution were appropriate, but they did exact an economic cost.

The distaste for technology was often accompanied by a sense of guilt: there was guilt that new technology was wasting too many of the world's scarce resources. It became common to denounce the United States, Western Europe and other rich lands as sinks down which oil and minerals from the rest of the world were drained. Some of the sense of guilt had been spread by the New Left. In the revived fascination with Marx in the 1960s, many members of the New Left interpreted the modern world as an international version of the old Marxist class struggle – the rich nations exploiting the poor nations while claiming to befriend them. The small nations provided an attentive ear to these arguments. The dramatic rise in oil prices in 1973 was in part a sign that Arab oil nations knew that the western guilt increased their bargaining position. They could raise the price of oil and simultaneously please many of those guilt-ridden citizens of those nations buying the dearer oil. Curiously the feeling of guilt among intellectuals was more common now than half a century previously when the master-servant relationship between west and east has probably provided more reason for a feeling of guilt. Oddly the guilt now was felt less by those who proclaimed the need for guilt than by those who were told that they should feel guilty. It was an emotional form of tear gas and was often fired at the public for purposes of quietening them.

The guilt was at a peak just when concern about the world's natural resources was reaching a peak. According to Christopher J. Hurn, a sociologist at the University of Massachusetts, the feeling of guilt that the west was milking the east and the north milking the south became more widespread in the early 1970s. 'It excites our moral passions', wrote Hurn, 'to believe that our wealth is the explanation for the poverty of the Third World'.[15]

As the west had been convicted of gluttony by the international preacher, the solution was to call for a new ascetic era in which economic development was no longer the west's road to heaven. Once 'economic growth' ceased to be such a widely-pursued goal, then the new values which challenged it or replaced it retarded economic recovery. Such was the economics of guilt.

A Luddite Revival

The recession of the 1970s was deepened by another facet of the revulsion against technology. Technology, hailed in the 1950s and 1960s as the creator of high prosperity and leisure, was now denounced as the destroyer of prosperity. The idea that new machines took away jobs was at least as old as the industrial revolution, and one man who in the 1780s expressed his fears by destroying the new industrial machines was Ned Ludd. He is said to have been a Leicestershire idiot but in his fears of what the new stocking frames might do, he was not idiotic. A generation later his surname became the nickname of the rebels who destroyed textile machines near Nottingham in 1811 and broke every lace-making machine in Loughborough in 1816. Called Luddites, they were probably busiest in years of heavy unemployment. At first operating in factory towns, they appeared on farmlands in the 1830s, and resented the threshing machines which at harvest time did work that once employed dozens of men in the days of the wooden flail. In the south of England in the 1830s many of the rural labourers protested at this job-devouring technology by breaking the machines or by burning haystacks. Several hundred convicts who had been found guilty of such offences were deported to Australia by the British government.[16]

Labour's opposition to new machinery was tending to decline during most decades of the twentieth century. In the world depression of the early 1930s, fear of the machine was surprisingly spasmodic – maybe because so few new industrial projects were even attempted. In the prosperous 1960s, observers of economic life were entitled to believe that Luddites largely belonged to the past, and yet the Luddites were resurrected in the 1970s.

One of their targets was micro-electronics and the microchip. Here, it was said, was a second industrial revolution. Just as the first industrial revolution of the textile industry and the steam engine had transformed the making and disseminating of goods, so the computer revolution was transforming the making and dissemination of information as well as goods. While secondary industry was the focus of the industrial revolution, tertiary industry was more the focus of the computer or digital revolution. This historical analogy made sense, and it warned also of the dislocation which the revolution might bring.

It was true that the new computers were abolishing jobs, and in the short term that was their purpose. They enabled fewer people to do more work and do it more efficiently. As a result, hundreds of thousands of existing jobs, or jobs that might otherwise have been created, were eliminated in banks, insurance companies, printing works, factories, petrol stations and supermarkets. It was unfortunate that the computer and microchip caught the imagination at the very time when fears of unemployment were rising. The microchip increased those fears, making technology seem the wrecker of a stable way of life.

There is a pervasive idea that new technology, because it eliminates many existing jobs, is essentially a creator of unemployment. And yet we have to be critical of that theory if we accept the widespread view that cheap energy, especially oil, was a major cause of the industrial boom in the western world in the quarter century after the Second World War. The cheap oil was an indirect example of how new technology – at first glance – abolished millions of jobs. Oil pouring from wells in the Middle East and other regions was so cheap and convenient that it enabled internal-combustion engines to eliminate the jobs of an army of coal miners in many lands, a regiment of coal shovellers and carriers and stokers at many ports, and swarms of wood-cutters in forests in every continent. It provided such cheap energy simply because the labour and capital involved in drilling for it, refining it, shipping and piping it were much less than that necessary in the era of wood, coal or steam; and yet – more important – its cheap energy boosted scores of other industries ranging from private automobiles to deep-sea transport and created millions of new jobs and raised the standard of living of all the advanced nations.

We take no notice of technology when it eliminates jobs in a boom era, but we pin undue blame on technology when it eliminates jobs in a depresssed era. If we were to accept the argument that technology, generally, is a destroyer of jobs we would have to explain the puzzle that technology is usually applied much more vigorously in times of full employment. If new technology essentially destroys jobs, how can there be full employment in those very years when new technology is introduced so vigorously? In contrast one characteristic of the decade 1975–85, in many industries in the western world, was the sluggishness with which new technology was applied. The crus-

ade against technology was both a sign of the economic troubles
and an accentuator of troubles.

No Rabbit in the Economist's Hat

Few economists, from 1973, actually knew why the economy
was ailing. Hitherto, economists had enjoyed a wonderful run
and were rightly seen as the members of the most advanced of
all the social sciences. They were said to possess so much understanding that they could make the economy obey. Now, in the
mid 1970s, these magicians could no longer produce a rabbit
from their hat, or if they did succeed in producing it their
audience was not confident that they could produce it a second
time.

   In the longer post-war boom, the profession of economics
had been on top of the world partly because the world was
more easily managed. From the end of the Second World War
to the late 1960s most advanced economies were running
smoothly, with neither inflation nor unemployment presenting
worries in the typical year. The United States, of all the advanced
nations, had the most difficulty in coping with unemployment;
and in the long period from 1948 to 1980 its unemployment fell
below 4 per cent only in the handful of years from 1951 to
1953 and 1966 to 1969, being years of the Korean and Vietnam
wars. Those special phases of low unemployment tended to be
the phases of high inflation. In the early 1970s, however, came
a new and bitter ailment in which serious unemployment was
mixed with high inflation and a stagnant economy. This dual
economic infection was called 'stagflation', and nearly every
country caught it early in the 1970s.

   In the textbooks on which most young economists had been
reared, there was no mention of such a disease. It defied the
previous canons of economics. Admittedly a New Zealander, A.
W. Phillips, teaching at the London School of Economics, had
warned in the late 1950s that low inflation and low unemployment could not be expected to be partners for long – Father
Christmas couldn't come every year, he warned – but he did
not foresee stagflation or that unhappy marriage of high unemployment and inflation. Twenty years of consensus amongst
economists came to end about 1969, when the economy was

beginning to misbehave.[17] Once economists – and the governments which listened to them – ceased to agree on how to
remedy economic problems, the problems were likely to be prolonged.

While economics as a profession became over-confident
towards the end of the long post-war boom, it had fair reasons
for its pride. A revolution in economic thought, led by John
Maynard Keynes in the 1930s and tested and found to be sound
by the economic policies adopted in most democratic nations
during the Second World War, had some part in achieving the
impressive economic results of the years from 1945 to 1970.
Keynes had diagnosed some of the main causes of unemployment and had prescribed remedies which were politically painless
for most politicians and their electors. Keynes simply said that
in lean times the government should spend, not save and scrimp.
Everyone loves a Father Christmas.

The employment theory of John Maynard Keynes, like almost
every brilliant theory in the social sciences, is primarily an
attempt – no matter how generalised – to explain a problem or
situation at a particular time. Keynes was trying to plumb the
causes of unemployment, as it existed in the depression of the
early 1930s. Forty years later Keynes was long dead and the
world he described had given way to a different economy and
structure of power, and to leaders whose economic experience,
hopes and anxieties were very different from his own. Even if
his diagnosis of the world of 1930 were correct and even if his
remedies for its gravest ills were ingenious, his message was less
relevant by 1970. And yet his very success made it all the more
difficult to prepare the way for a new prophet.

Economics Needs a New Home Ground

Many of the changes which ruffled economic life in the 1970s
and 1980s had stemmed in the first place from an area of experience and behaviour that was not normally studied by economists.
The swing from technology towards nature had strongly affected
the grain crisis, the 'energy' crisis, the acute inflation, the increasing sense of guilt, the revival of Luddite fears, a reluctance
to invest and to innovate, and a concern for the quality as
distinct from the quantity of life. These were only some of the

profound changes which made economic life in the 1970s
dramatically different from the 1960s.

Most economists do not yet see the significance of the swing
of the giant seesaw, and that in itself highlights one of the
reasons for the temporary decline of the prestige of economics.
The profession's own definition of the field of economics has
become too narrow. Culture and politics as well as economics
exert profound effects on economic life. The economy does not
exist in isolation, but economists – like members of nearly every
other discipline – have become specialists and have tended to
narrow down their field of study, both as individuals and as a
profession.

The strong and unexpected swing of the seesaw in the late
1960s and early 1970s came partly from a deepening consciousness of crisis, of a kind usually felt only during a great war.
Professor Fred Hoyle, the celebrated Cambridge astronomer,
insisted on the gravity of the crisis when he delivered his oration
'Science and Modern Civilisation' in 1969. He denounced the
'present age of the napalm bomb', the hysteria and other portents
of social collapse in the United States, the irresistible growth of
international organisations so strong that we as people 'do not
control our destiny', and an explosion of population so dramatic
'that it already amounts to a disintegration of society'. The
disintegration was unavoidable, and the advanced nations would
collapse first.[18] While he hoped that his audience was 'not too
shocked by these statements', similar invitations to be shocked
were frequent at that time. The common thread in these warnings
by scientists and social scientists, poets and articulate protestors,
was that the crisis had so permeated civilisation that it was
eroding the traditional solutions and answers. As technology
was such an essential part of the crisis – irrespective of whether
technology was seen as the guiding hand or simply an instrument
– it could offer no solution. For a civilisation which venerated
science and technology as its glass ball, this was indeed an
emergency. Many of the orations, books, tracts, songs and slogans
of this period carry haunting echoes of that urgency we find in
The Communist Manifesto of 1848, the belief that the world had
reached a crisis which the familiar old solution would not solve.

The richer, science-oriented nations of the western world in
1973 had to face an unusual problem in the Middle East. But
they were too ready to see it as a wider economic and biological

crisis and so they enhanced the bargaining position of the main oil producers, thus compounding their own problems. The state of the world was magnified in people's minds into a super-crisis. A temporary scarcity became an oil crisis which in turn was inflated into an energy crisis and then into a crisis affecting all new raw materials and nature itself.

The oil crisis, like the gold fears of an early generation, can be understood as a reflection of deep fears for the distant future rather than a realistic assessment of the economic situation existing at the time. That high watershed, the fierce inflation and the subsequent dislocation of the 1970s, is often viewed solely as an economic event and therefore explained essentially as the result of economic causes. But its causes went far deeper. It was more a cultural and political event, and it demonstrated how the seesaw of emotions and fears can flavour what we think are primarily rational activities.

This strong swing of the seesaw marked a loss of faith in technology and science more serious than any experienced since the rise of technology as the pilot and compass of western civil-isation. Technology has survived two world wars and remained the pilot. The faith in technology was not even shattered by the first terrifying nuclear weapons. Significantly Japan, the victim of the first atomic bombs, demonstrated a burning and even innocent faith in technology in the following thirty years.

Even today the recent swing of the great seesaw is not appre-ciated adequately. The swing created no high drama because for most of the time it was slow rather than jolting. It could not be dated and remembered vividly like 1914–1918. Even today it has not been labelled as an all-embracing event like the world depression of the 1930s. It was so wide ranging that it was diffi-cult to comprehend and so gradual that the impact did not startle. And yet it outweighed the two world wars in the force of its assault on the pilot of western civilisation.

Part Three

15 The Long Economic Waves

The prevailing cultural and intellectual mood is often said to be the result of the economic conditions. Prosperity, it is said, generates wide-ranging confidence, while the dour spirit of an economic depression finds its way into every cultural cranny. It is often pointed out that for much of the nineteenth century the economic fluctuations ran roughly parallel with the cultural fluctuations. This pattern is usually said to mean that economic conditions tend to flavour the cultural mood, and yet the pattern was reversed in the late 1960s and 1970s, and the reversal profoundly affected our world.

Fluctuations in the economic mood are inevitable. In simple societies where most people worked the soil, fine harvests promoted confidence just as poor harvests promoted despondency. Later, when economic life was centred more on cities, and manufacturing and commerce became the main employers of labour, a new fluctuation appeared. Called the trade cycle in England and the business cycle in the United States, is reflected the tendency in capitalism for boom to be followed by slump. Some economists thought the business cycle was essentially short in span, moving from slump to slump in the space of three to five years, while others paid more attention to a longer fluctuation called the Juglar Cycle which ran its full course from slump to slump about every nine or ten years. The existence of these cycles is now an axiom in economics, and the literature describing them is mountainous.

A Pattern in Economic Life

Some economic historians see these short-term cycles of boom and slump as part of a long economic fluctuation known as a long wave. These long waves, each occupying some forty to sixty years, appeared with the coming of the industrial revolution and the rise of a global economy in the late eighteenth century. The first wave is said to have run from about 1790 to the late

267

1840s, the second wave had completed its work by the end of the First World War or at the latest by the world depression of the 1930s, and the third wave is often said to be still with us. The present recession in the western world is presumed to be the ebb or downswing of the third long wave.

Not everybody agrees that these long waves in the international economy really exist. While it is easy to talk of the trade cycle or business cycle because dozens of them have occurred, it is not so easy to talk convincingly of the long waves because, by most calculations, only three have occurred in the last 200 years. The ultimate test of a hypothesis is its power to predict and it is hard to predict on the basis of only three past occurrences. Moreover the long waves, if they do exist, are complicated, and it not even easy to pin-point the year in which a long wave ends and a new wave begins.

Although the existence of the long waves is open to dispute, there is no doubt that in the nineteenth century the prices of international commodities did form a wave-like pattern of ebb and flow. In the wholesale prices of wheat, meat, sugar, copper, lead, tin, wool, cotton, tea and all the other major commodities of the world, there is an intriguing wave or pattern of rise and fall. Between 1790 and 1814, the time of the French Revolutionary and Napoleonic wars, there is a strong rise in the wholesale price index in the major countries of the western world. In turn that period of inflation was followed by one third of a century of deflation, a quarter of a century of inflation, a quarter of a century of deflation, and then a period of inflation. The contrast between each successive period stands out in this table of wholesale prices, compiled by Robert Triffin of Yale University:[1]

	UK %	Germany %	USA %	France %
1790–1814	Rise in prices in all countries			
1814–1849	−49	−45	−55	−27*
1849–1872	+39	+56	+66	+31
1872–1896	−39	−36	−50	−43
1896–1913	+32	+41	+49	+41

* Calculated for 1820–49.

At first sight those long-term movements in prices show dramatic fluctuations. But in the average year of each period from 1790 onwards, the annual rate of inflation or deflation was well under 2 per cent, and that must be designated a remarkably stable price level by the standards of our own time. It is possible that these alternating periods of slow inflation and slow deflation – stable as they seem to our eyes – also mark alternations in the tempo of economic activity and in the economic and political outlook. The high noon of faith in wide-ranging progress in the 1850s and 1860s does coincide with a period of rising prices. The subsequent period of falling prices was less optimistic in overall mood, and indeed it is possible to argue that the return to nature and the weakening faith in technology, which were conspicuous in the years between 1890 and about 1905, were the lagged effect of that period of falling prices.

Inflation, Gold and War

Any discussion of possible links between the economic conditions and the cultural mood must give a place to a brilliant young Russian bureaucrat and economist, Nikolai Kondratieff. He did not, to my knowledge, discuss this specific question but he raised the wider question of whether history repeated itself and the special role which economic fluctuations might play in creating such repetitions. Whereas many scholars before him had discussed several patterns, including the phases of war and peace in Europe and the phases of inflation and deflation, Kondratieff has come to dominate a corner of the literature because of the boldness of his approach, the role he assigned to economic events and his personal fate in Stalinist Russia.

In the 1920s, Kondratieff published several articles claiming that there were long waves in economic life and that the important inventions were partly the effect of these long waves. He argued rightly that international wars (and wrongly that revolutions) were part of these long waves and that they tended to come on the upswing. There was a remarkably bold and creative quality in Kondratieff's study of the past, so that even if his readers found some of his trends erroneous and many of his explanations puzzling, the reach of his mind still stood out. In essence he argued that economic activity, war and peace, and inventions belonged to a tightly enclosed system inherent in capitalism and that every forty or sixty years this system completed a full cycle and that certain trends could be predicted by those who understood the cycle. Kondratieff did not write at sufficient length on these complex events to allow us to understand fully his thinking, but one vital part of his system was a cycle of investment and another was a cycle of gold output, for he was describing largely the period between 1850 and 1913 when international and national finances were based largely on the gold standard, when gold was regularly transported to adjust debts between nations, and gold coins instead of paper money were the ultimate and legal form of payment within a country.[2] It was a hallmark of Kondratieff's thinking that such influential events as major wars, inventions and gold discoveries were not random but were primarily responses to a certain stage of the long economic waves or, as he called them, cycles.

He was far from the first economist to stress that the periods of the nineteenth century in which the world's gold supplies increased swiftly tended to be the periods of inflation. Even in the early 1850s, in the wake of the astonishing gold finds in California and eastern Australia, businessmen expected prices to rise because of the influx of gold, and our recent experience shows how expectations of inflation become in themselves a major cause of inflation. Likewise those who looked at the sheer volume of international trade generated by the purchasing power of the new goldfields in the early 1850s also saw the gold as inflationary. It is hardly surprising then that when new gold from San Francisco and Melbourne flooded Europe, there occurred the most rapid burst of inflation in the entire century between the end of the Napoleonic Wars and the outbreak of the First World War.

Kondratieff argued that the output of gold from new and old mines did not increase fast enough between 1815 and 1849 and so the commodity prices fell. In the following period, Sacramento and Ballarat and Bendigo yielded an astonishing quantity of gold, which spurred inflation of prices and vigorous economic activity and 'the increased tension of economic life', which in turn fostered wars. The period beginning in the early 1870s, however, mined inadequate gold for its financial needs and so prices fell, and economic and military activity shared in the mood of caution. Then came another flood of gold, this time from deeper company-owned mines in South Africa and Western Australia and other new goldfields. According to Kondratieff the gold helped to initiate an upswing which lasted from about 1896 until the First World War.[3]

In essence, Kondratieff argued that the output of gold from newly discovered and existing mines increased rapidly in certain periods, and the abundant gold fed the inflation and vigorous economic activity. The next period, however, mined inadequate gold, and so prices fell, and the economic and political tempo were quieter. He even argued that the gold discoveries themselves were not accidental but tended to come at about the end of each long wave, just when the international economy, declining in vigour, urgently required them. His gold argument, while challengable and indeed flawed, is not as eccentric as it seems. There are rhythms in mineral discovery, and they are influenced by the ebb and flow of economic activity.

In the Soviet Union in the 1920s, Kondratieff's theory was not smiled upon. Just when Trotsky, Stalin and other Soviet leaders were predicting the collapse of international capitalism and were seeing a favourable omen in the widespread unemployment in Europe, this high official was preaching the opposite message. Kondratieff insisted that capitalism was temporarily on the downward side of the wave, and that before long it would rise with the ascending wave. His message and his political activities were seen as treacherous. In 1930 he was sent to Siberia.

Those long waves in economic life are now given the title of the Kondratieff waves or cycles. The honour is appropriate but the brilliant Russian's theory left behind many more problems than it had solved. Furthermore, by 1930 the gold standard in western nations was being abandoned permanently, and gold mining ceased to affect the level of prices, and so there was uncertainty as to whether these long economic waves would continue. It was not even clear whether the periods of rising prices had always displayed a busier tempo and more prosperity than the periods of falling prices. A fine Belgian economic historian, Leon Dupriez, recently summed up Kondratieff's theory as 'too simplified, mechanistic and deterministic'.[4] The verdict, in my view, is fair. At the same time Kondratieff, to his credit, had an insight or instinct that some kind of loose, long-term pattern did exist and that events which were normally seen as unrelated were probably related. In short he posed a tantalising riddle rather than an answer.

The following table of companion events of the period 1790–1920 sets out my version of Kondratieff's riddle. He would disown this table as too much a sliced-down version of his ideas and contrary to several of his main ideas, and he would disown my explanations of the table, but in my view it represents all that can be safely salvaged from his theory. The table also includes a vital fourth line which is not part of his theory: a link between the economic and the cultural moods.

Long-Term Fluctuations of Commodity Prices, 1790–1920

	Price Upswing	Price Downswing
World's gold output:	quickly rising	slowly rising
International wars:	many	few
Economic mood:	confident	less confident
Mental and cultural mood:	confident	less confident

The table sets out tendencies. While it does not point to causes and effects, there is some evidence to suggest that each factor is both a cause and an effect, being part of a system of cross fertilisation. At the same time there is no inevitability in this pattern: it is loosely within the control of man.

Do Economic Events Shape the Cultural Mood?

We should not jump to the conclusion that rising prices promoted prosperity and a cheerful economic mood and that the mood simply permeated cultural and intellectual activities, thus helping to explain the movements of the seesaw. The periods of rising prices were not necessarily more prosperous than the period of falling prices which preceded or succeeded them. Between 1790 and 1920 the three periods of rising prices rather than the two periods of falling prices tend to convey the stronger feeling of economic energy and optimism, but the optimism sometimes seems stronger than the actual economic performance. That puzzle emerges if we compare one period of rising prices with the following period of falling prices. Thus the period of rising prices between 1849 and 1872 was viewed at the time as a kind of mid-Victorian boom, but for the average British breadwinner the real wages as distinct from money wages increased very little, and the increase was less in the inflationary 1850s than the more stable 1860s. Since an upswing tended to be a period of international wars, some of the economic output was wasted in preparations for war and in war itself, thus retarding a rise in the standard of living of the average citizen. On the other hand the downswing could seem more pessimistic than the facts warranted. In Britain much of the period 1872–96 was at the time called The Great Depression, because profits and wages and prices fell, and yet the evidence is clear that real wages for the average British working man were improved in those seemingly dour years.[5]

What is really happening in an economy can be less influential than that which people *think* is happening. A widely-held illusion, even though it is an illusion, will affect attitudes and events. Thus a decade of slowly rising prices, especially in peacetime, was generally viewed more confidently than a decade of slowly falling prices, even if the two decades happened to be equally prosperous.

On the other hand the years of rapid inflation, being usually a time of major war, can hardly be called exceptionally confident and healthy in economic terms. The last years of a major war might seem healthy according to the normal indicators – the levels of employment and output – but much of that employment and output is wasted and indeed is blown to bits. Likewise the fast inflation during the French Revolutionary and Napoleonic Wars was hardly cheerful for the breadwinners, for the price of bread increased more quickly than wages. Even in cultural affairs the war years and their buoyant economic indicators, while promoting a faith in one's nation and its culture, were hardly conducive to a faith in one's civilisation. In short, we should hesitate to see too close a relationship between rising or falling prices and the economic mood. The relationship is more revealing in times of peace or of minor wars. Even then the relationship is partly an optical illusion, believed at the time to hold validity and therefore to be of influence.

In years of peace the economic mood and the cultural mood tended to run in harmony. Until the puzzling appearance of stagflation in the early 1970s, a decade of rising rather than falling prices tended to be a time of cultural and intellectual optimism. It would be deceptively easy to come to the conclusion that the confident economic mood inspired a confident attitude to ideas and that the seesaw of ideas was really driven by a hidden economic engine, but I am wary of such a conclusion. For example in the late 1960s the cultural mood changed and the seesaw began to move before the economic downturn was itself visible: at that time the cultural change clearly preceded the economic just as in the 1870s and 1880s the economic had preceded the cultural change. There is another reason against simply accepting economic events as the prime engine. The neat pattern whereby a generation of inflation was followed by a generation of deflation was strongly influenced by the successive phases of war and peace, the wars being inflationary and the peace tending to be associated more with falling prices, though the pattern was scrambled after the Second World War. The special influence of wars also stands out if we examine the peaks of the long waves in prices. Thus the economic peak of 1814 marked the end of the Napoleonic Wars – only the isolated Waterloo campaign lay ahead; the next economic peak of 1872 came one year after the end of a chain of quick, deadly wars of which the Franco-Prussian was the last; and the next peak in 1920 came less than two years after the end of the First World War.

A Rocking-Chair of War and Peace

Between 1790 and 1920 the pattern of economic trends was the result of a variety of factors, of which wars exerted the sharpest effect. Thus the French Revolutionary and Napoleonic Wars of the years 1792–1815 encouraged steep inflation and the growth of each nation's debt, but once the wars were ended there grew a desire for economic stability and stable or even falling prices, and the subsequent thirty years were marked by a restraint in monetary policy and by falling prices. As major international wars were few, the peace helped to cement the financial restraint. Restraint, however, is never permanent.

A major war involving many nations is usually followed by a period of peace, especially if the war ends decisively. The end of a major war establishes a clear pecking order in international relations, and for many years it is easier to solve diplomatic disputes.[6] After a long period of peace the pecking order becomes blurred in international relations, and diplomacy becomes more difficult; and so the resort to war becomes the likely way of sorting out the hierarchy of power. Moreover, as the period of peace and normality becomes longer, the virtues of economic stability and stable prices are taken for granted, and so the old restraints on inflation become weaker. Significantly, there is evidence that in the long period 1850–1939 the specific years when prosperity was increasing and prices were rising were the years when most wars began.[7] International wars were more likely to begin in improving than in deteriorating economic conditions. Such a conclusion is more in keeping with the loose spirit than the facts of Kondratieff's theory: the conclusion points to a connection which he did not identify but which would have been palatable to his ideas.

After the Napoleonic Wars came a period of falling prices and international peace, followed by a period of renewed inflation and renewed fighting running from about 1849 to 1872, and at the end of that period Prussia's military victories re-established a pecking order, an effective threat system, in international relations. So followed a quarter of a century in which there were few international wars. Just as wars are inflationary, so the absence of war can be deflationary. The years 1872 to 1896, marked by falling prices, were followed by a new period of rising prices and a series of wars culminating in the First World War.

Many facets of the period between say 1790 and 1920 become more intelligible if we see a roughly spliced pattern of events. It cannot be called, as Kondratieff called it, a cycle because it is not really predictable; nor do the main trends affect each other in the way Kondratieff stated or hinted. Nonetheless the periods of major fighting gave way to long periods of peace; rising prices tended to go with the wars and falling prices with the peace; and the economic mood of most of the years of inflation were optimistic and were marked by a strong willingness to apply new technology. Indeed one could go further and suggest that the consciousness of an improving and malleable economy tended to make the outbreak of war more likely. The cultural mood did not defy this pattern nor did it conform neatly. The two moods, economic and cultural, marched side by side, with one and then the other stepping ahead. Thus the optimistic cultural and intellectual mood of the 1840s to the 1870s slightly preceded the buoyant economic mood, while the cautious mental mood emerging in the 1890s lagged a decade or more behind the cautious economic mood. As the economic mood of the first years of this century became more cheerful, the cultural and intellectual climate, though lagging, possibly became more positive until the outbreak of war in 1914 abruptly moulded a new frame of mind.

The Death and Resurrection of a Theory

The world depression of the early 1930s, the most serious dislocation recorded so far in the western world, focused interest on the Kondratieff riddle but the interest henceforth was overwhelmingly in the economic than in the vaguer political component of his long waves. The depression increased interest in him because it was a violent shock to a system which Kondratieff already diagnosed as fragile, a shock for which he offered an explanation. At the same time the world depression upset his theory for the simple reason that it showed an irregularity which he had not predicted: the downswing running from 1920 to 1932 was uncommonly short, being a mere dozen years. In the western world, however, some economists looked on Kondratieff's long waves with sympathy, and the brilliant J. A. Schumpeter[8] even revamped the theory in 1939, suggesting that major innovations in industry spurred each wave.* But as the economy recovered from the depression and as the upward spiral of prices and the post-war boom went on and on, it became difficult to take Kondratieff so seriously.

In the early 1970s, in the wake of the economic crisis and price explosion, Kondratieff was about to be resurrected but his theory faced at least three problems. Firstly it was vague in its explanations. Secondly, economists came to believe that they had now mastered the fluctuations in capitalism; and if they were correct then the long waves and the occasional violent shocks they had once administered could no longer occur. A

---

* For example, steam and steel in 1849–72 and chemicals, electricity and automobiles in 1896–1920.

third blow to Kondratieff was the sheer length of the latest upswing: by 1972 it had been continuing for some 40 years, following the post-First World War downswing that had lasted barely a dozen years. There was no real rhythm in such variable waves. These blows to the theory were not shattering but they were bruising. A further blow came in the early 1970s when the long upswing appeared to end but the prices not only kept on rising but rose rapidly. Traditionally, the Kondratieff theory in its leanest version had actually identified and labelled a downswing by its falling prices and an upswing by its rising prices, but the label was no longer appropriate.

Here was the irony. The economic events of the years from 1932 to 1973 had steadily eroded the theory, and yet such was the shock of the grain and oil inflation of the early 1970s, and such was the blow to an international economic system which had seemed to be manageable and even docile, that again a doctor was called for, and his name was Kondratieff. The economic but not the political aspects of his theory of long waves were revived. His riddle again was important.

The revival of interest was made easier by those few who had continued to study the Kondratieff riddle. The Belgian economist, Leon Dupriez, wrote a thoughtful book in 1947, and Ernest Mandel, who was fascinated by the waves when his fellow Marxists were not, boldly predicted in the cosy year of 1964 that troubles lay ahead for capitalism. In his German book of 1972, *Late Capitalism*, he suggested that the downswing in the long wave had already begun though in 1974 he changed his mind and designated the oil crisis of recent months as the beginning of the feared downswing. Other economists rushed to study this neglected theory. In 1979 a list of articles analysing the long waves in the recent issues of reputable journals ran to 43 pages. The long wave had become the centre of a research industry.[9]

Few doubted that in 1973 and 1974 the world's economic system was in a dramatic downturn or severe trough, and the theory of 'long waves' was one of the most attractive ways of trying to explain how the trough had been created. Significantly, in pessimistic years, theories based on cycles have the same intuitive attractiveness as ladder-shaped theories possess in optimistic periods. Unless we are alert we easily become captives of the mood of our time.

Able economists and economic historians were perplexed that the downswing of the 1970s was unlike any previous one: prices rose rapidly but the economy was stagnant or ailing. Stagflation did not fit into the traditional picture of the long wave. On the other hand it was possible to argue that the long waves stretching back at least two centuries were irregular and that each complete wave, being a composite of different variables, was not repetitive or predictable in the way certain older economists had hoped and imagined. This seems the more reasonable supposition.

One crucial facet of the long waves has perhaps not been noticed hitherto. The major turning points – the peak of the long wave and the beginning of the downturn – continue to be influenced more by political than economic events. Just as the economic peaks of the past came at the end of the major wars – the Napoleonic, Franco-Prussian and First World War – so the apparent turning point in the early 1970s seems to reflect a political rather than an economic event. The final phase of the in-fluential Vietnam War and the conspicuous facts that the world's strongest nation was over-extended overseas and suffering a loss of confidence at home were an essential cause of the leap in oil prices. The militarily-weak oil nations of the Middle East inflicted on the United States an economic version of what North Vietnam was inflicting militarily. Likewise the second jump in oil prices, during the Iran crisis of 1979–80, reflected the temporary weakness or loss of will of the United States, a mighty nation which was unable or unwilling to use those threats which great powers had traditionally used to impose their will on weak nations.

The theory of waves cannot be trusted as a predictor, partly because the waves are the result of a number of variables which in shifting combination can produce an outcome which is either similar to the past or surprisingly different. Human affairs on the global scale are too complex to lend themselves to clear-cut cyclical interpretations. It seems more realistic to see 'the long waves' as more like a choppy sea, untidy and unpredictable but the restless surface of that sea remains a vital mode of warning, particularly in periods of excessive optimism in the international economy.

The waves are more visible in economic than social life partly because the economy is the most measurable sector of our civilis-ation. With the aid of statistics on prices, interest rates, unemployment levels, investment and output we own a sensitive barometer of economic life but we have few precise measures of cultural and social life and not many of political life and tensions. A time will probably come when the seesaw is studied intently by mainstream economists. When they realise that a change in the cultural and intellectual mood can be a forerunner of a change in the economic mood, they will begin to make charts of the changing cultural mood, quantifying as best they can the changing sympathy for technology and nature by scanning opinion polls, newspapers, letters to the editor, titles of new books, themes of articles in intellectual and middlebrow magazines, and changes in fashion. It will not be easy to chart such oscillations because the cultural mood is not usually expressed in money whereas the economic mood is. Nonetheless even a rough chart of the cultural outlook in the late 1960s would have given warnings of what might soon be happening to the economic outlook, thus enabling some remedial steps.

I am not quite a follower of Kondratieff but I greatly respect him because of the riddle he raised rather than the answers he gave. He asked, as Marx and others had asked: what is the relation between political, cultural, economic and military events? Moreover, he asked it of a recent period of world history. In my own opinion, loose patterns are discernible in the history of the western world over the last two and a half centuries. One crucial pattern, which I set out in the book *The Causes of War*, is that a major many-nation or general war tends to be followed by a long period of peace but that ultimately the peace breaks down: victory or success is a *wasting asset* in military as well as in economic affairs, and cannot last indefinitely. The alternation of major wars and major periods of peace help to shape the long economic waves as well as the mental moods of the great seesaw. While the seesaw and long waves are very different phenomena, often they have been in accord. Sometimes a movement of the seesaw preceded a change in economic mood and sometimes the seesaw moved later.

To suggest that a powerful mental seesaw is at work is to attempt to answer a vital aspect of that vast and perplexing question which Marx, Kondratieff, Toynbee and many others have raised in different forms: the relation between the economic, political, military and cultural events, and the question of whether that relationship forms a pattern in modern history.

The seesaw is crucial not only because it has operated for so long but also because it is especially powerful during the long periods of relative peace in the western world. An understanding of the seesaw is vital during a period when global as well as national perspectives are influential. And in the future those global perspectives and the seesaw itself will probably increase in importance.

16 The Magic of New-Found Lands

A new-found land is an invention, like the steamship and the jet aircraft. Its discovery opens a new awareness and a range of possibilities. The fascination with primitive societies and with nature in the late eighteenth century relied on new-found lands – Tahiti, Mauritius, the east coast of Australia, the interior of North America. Without these new lands, the Noble Savage might not have been enthroned so easily.

The Coral Continent and Other Lands

In the era of faith in progress and its values, the new-found lands were also havens for the emotions. The inland plains of the United States, in the nineteenth century, were such a haven. So too were Canada, South Africa, the Argentine, Chile and southern Brazil, Australia and New Zealand. Whereas some of the new lands of the eighteenth century seemed to suggest that man was happiest when living primitively and close to nature, these newly-opened lands of the nineteenth century gave a different message. Their vast acreages yielded, under new methods of farming, harvests of which the native inhabitants had not dreamed. These new lands provided food, shelter, freedom and a sense of personal triumph to millions of white settlers. In California a plaque erected at the John Wayne Airport in Orange County sums up the bounty of these great spaces. The plaque proclaims that Wayne in his western movies showed the essence of the American West: 'a love of freedom, fundamental optimism, a search of the new frontiers, and a super strong patriotism.'

Those same spacious plains of the new world also gave food to millions who continued to live in Europe. Nothing did more to reinforce the most optimistic era of the nineteenth century than the new food sources. Earlier, Malthus, Mill and many other talented scholars had warned that food might be scarce, but the 1860s and 1870s came, and food was not scarce, even though Europe's population had multiplied. An age of optimism would have quickly turned to gloom if millions of the optimists suddenly glimpsed the prospect of themselves starving. Without the ploughing of the great plains of America, without the pampas of the Argentine, and without the grazing lands of Australia and New Zealand, the British Isles could not have fed themselves by 1880.

Each phase of extreme optimism and pessimism, or of extreme worship of technology or nature, seems to depend partly on discoveries of new territory. A mood depends more on new insights than on new territories but the insight is more powerful if it can be associated with a specific terrain. The new land catches the imagination and makes it glow. It is visual and can be pin-pointed on the map. More memorable than any abstract argument, it remains in the mind when other arguments have slipped from memory.

A crusade for nature must have its gardens of Eden. Likewise an era of rising faith in technology probably also needs – though less urgently – its garden of Eden, its place of abundance. The Edens of nature required large spaces but the Edens of the new technology thrived by their ability to concentrate intense energy in confined spaces. For Marx, Fourier and many of the optimists of the first half of the nineteenth century the new factory was potentially a paradise. Its steam engines, water wheels, textile machines and furnaces were capable of revolutionising Europe and lifting the standard of living of everybody. Thus Manchester, the mill town, was potentially a kind of Tahiti. To Marx and Engels, 'Factoryland' was a potential paradise if only the serpent of capitalism could be driven from the garden.

Those who were optimistic about the world's future sometimes had fantasies of new lands appearing above the seas. The writings of the well-known French geographer, Conrad Malte-Brun, gave hope that the coral insects in the tropical Pacific were making new coral reefs that in turn would become wide lands on which the human race could flourish. In the vast ocean between South America and Australia, wrote Sir Archibald Alison in 1840, 'the process of creation is going on with ceaseless activity; and myriads of insects, hardly visible to the human eye, are preparing beneath the glassy wave, a future continent of vast extent for the habitation of man.'[1] Alison estimated that the new coral continent would one day equal Asia in area and would provide abundant food for a population that would be five times larger than the population of the whole world in his day.

The gardens of Eden favoured by the disciples of nature on the one hand and the disciples of technology on the other hand were not the same. The lovers of nature liked their paradise to be far away: a remote and exotic paradise fired Europe's imagination. Those who enthroned technology saw their gardens of Eden as vast ranges of real estate which, with effort and ingenuity, could be converted into a paradise. The temperate zone was the most likely garden of Eden for the worshippers of technology because there the people of European stock, with the aid of hard work and new techniques, could transform nature. The shrinking of the untouched real estate in the temperate zone of the new world and the brief scramble to annex Africa played a part in the ebbing optimism of the 1880s and 1890s.

New-Found Lands, 1890–1914

By 1890 the explorers had been almost everywhere, the unfound places had largely been found, and the unoccupied had largely been occupied. Where could a new Tahiti be found in those seas now criss-crossed by steamship routes? Where could another Great Plains be found now that, in the Americas, the virgin lands seemed to be largely occupied.

The prospect of finding a new Tahiti was small, but when the respect for nature gathered pace, suitable new lands were found. They popped up mysteriously from ocean and plain. They had been there all the time, but their special qualities had not been noticed. Artists found new Tahitis on the west coast of Arica and the painter Gauguin found it in Tahiti itself. For those Europeans exulting in the strength and sensuality of the modern dance, the far away Russia of the steppes proved to be the new-found land. Nijinsky was another Colombus.

A wide range of scholars discovered primitive societies which others had seen but shunned – societies displaying qualities which the sophisticated cities of Europe had lost. Not long befoe the First World War, Freud, Durkheim and Malinowski turned to the 'primitive' Aboriginals of Australia and saw special qualities in them. These three scholars had not visited Australia, but it is possible to discover from afar.

Of those lands now displaying the new and exciting, not one was, strictly speaking, newly found. Exploration is not a single, once-and-for-all journey, at the end of which nothing remains unseen. Every land is explored again and again. What the first eyes fail to see will be seen later. Every generation has to redraw its maps, for no map is permanent.

If lands could be found and so stir the imagination, lands could be lost. Even the United States seemed lost when Frederick Jackson Turner made his famous but premature statement of 1893 that the frontier of virgin land had ended and that the magical era of the United States had passed. But the frontier was not finally closed, and in the imagination of Americans, the westward movement of pioneers and their covered wagons remained a symbol of what was still possible for the bold and enterprising. The 'new frontier' was one of President Kennedy's political neon lights, but at the end of the 1960s many American scholars said the spirit of the frontier had closed forever. Forever lasted only a few years. Likewise there were lost lands aplenty in the late 1960s, lost through pollution, through over-mining and over-farming. Just as Californian and Australian gold in the middle of the nineteenth century represented new-found lands, so the Middle East during the oil crisis of the 1970s symbolised, in the west's imagination, lands that once flowed with oil and now threatened to become barren. They were lost lands.

The Moonshot Age

A period of faith in material progress tends to find its own new-found lands even though, at the start of that period, the prospect of finding such lands seems sparse. In the 1950s and 1960s new lands emerged to spur the confidence of those who had faith in their own material civilisation. Mineral resources were found on a vast scale, often in regions which previously had produced no such minerals. Old agricultural lands produced far more than ever before, and new lands that had once seemed unfit for the plough were turned into cropland. To produce far more wealth from existing lands is as rewarding as to find completely new lands: sometimes it is more useful.

In the 1950s and 1960s at least one vast land was found. It embraced the southern and northern hemispheres and ran through the tropics and the arctic zone. It lay completely beneath the water, this old continental shelf, and yet a mere 20,000 years ago most of it had been inhabited by mankind. Dry until the last rising of the seas, these long strips of continental shelf formed submerged land that in total area was much larger than the present South America. Through the development of off-shore techniques of drilling, this drowned land began to produce only one commodity, but its oil boosted and extended the material optimism of the post-war era.

Another hidden land – outer space – spurred the optimism. For a time in the 1950s and 1960s there were hopes that the landing on the moon would provide a new source of wealth or even a new place of habitation. In fact it did provide a less visible but equally powerful asset: cheap and swift communications by satellite. The space probe, in quickening communications in the world, was far more influential than the digging of the Suez Canal had been in its era, and perhaps as influential as had been the first era of the international telegraph when cables, mostly laid between 1851 and 1872, linked England with every continent.

The periods of material optimism and faith in technology are nearly always periods in which new ideas are strenuously applied. The economic environment and the mental climate favour new technology. And by the law of averages, new lands – whether under the ocean or high in the sky – are more likely to be found and more likely to excite the imagination in buoyant periods than in cautious periods.

The Midget Bible and the Heroic Peasant

By the late 1960s the world was so closely mapped and so criss-crossed by travellers, that again all new lands seemed to have been found. But as the attractions of technology declined in favour, a new Garden of Eden was sought. Young nations emerging in Africa, Asia and the Pacific were now invested with a vague optimism. As imperialism had been seen as eco-nomic and cultural exploitation by socialists and many liberals, the end of imperialism might lead to a glorious blossoming in the born-again societies of the third world. Such were the hopes – sometimes genuine and sometimes feigned – expressed in Geneva and New York.

China caught the imagination for a time. It was both new and communist, and yet ancient and exotic. Its brief phase of isolation during the reign of The Gang of Four had made it all the more mysterious and enticing to people who lived far away. The little red book of sayings by Chairman Mao Tse-tung was now revered as a midget bible. The reports of tens of thousands of Chinese bureaucrats sent to the country to rehabilitate themselves by learning from peasants gave heart to all those who hated cities, bureaucracy, the modern era, and technology. China's new puritanism warmed the hearts of the cold-hearted. Its primitive socialism and its sheer austerity held for many European socialists the attraction which primitive Christianity sometimes has for many Christians. Moreover, China treated tourists as special people, and so the rigours and stern dogma of daily life in China were neither experienced nor imagined by most tourists who came with idealism and a willingness to listen. In scores of books written for the west, China was depicted as a new Utopia. Whereas the Chinese a century ago were regarded as almost unhuman, a race apart, many Europeans now saw 'the Chinese people as more than human, the very embodiment of perfection': so wrote Stephen FitzGerald, one of the most observant ambassadors living in Peking in the early 1970s.[2] What Tahiti had been in the imagination of certain radicals, China of the Red Guards and The Gang of Four now was, exactly two centuries later. Here was a place where mankind might be born again.

Of all the free nations of Europe, France was most attracted to China. The uprising in Paris in May 1968 was influenced by Chinese slogans and ways of thought. In the early 1970s a two week visit to China fulfilled for Parisian society 'the same function, and bestowed the same prestige, as the pilgrimage to Mecca in the Islamic world'.[3] Australians were also drawn to China, being second only to the Japanese as foreign tourists there. The French director of a Maoist weekly newspaper, later looking back on the French fascination with China, was forced to admit that the China he had admired in the time of the Red Guards, was partly fiction and partly fact. He realised that 'each epoch nourishes its own hopes of imaginary lands'.[4]

The glamour which western radicals saw in these poor nations in Africa and Asia was aided by the moral eclipse of Russia, especially after its invasion of Czechoslovakia in 1968. As the United States had disgraced herself in the eyes of radicals by her warfare in Vietnam, the two powerful nations of the world were in moral eclipse. As their power was seen as ugly, weaker nations gained prestige. A new morality was eagerly pinned to the Chinese, Cubans and the North Vietnamese. In those lands moral precepts were said to carry weight, and materialism and trickery, greed and personal ambition were said to be held in check. Moreover, as the movement towards nature gathered force, China and North Vietnam and Cuba were additionally extolled because they displayed a simple rural way of life. The peasant was now a hero: he used muscles instead of fossil fuels, he recycled his waste and used no chemicals in his farming. In fact – but it was not said aloud – he too loved chemical fertilisers and tractors but they were too expensive for him to buy.

For a decade, according to two French observers, the third world was 'the reservoir of theories, enthusiasms, and models'.[5] Africa bathed in this goodwill. Its independence movements were cheered. The early economic mistakes of its infant nations were, often with justification, attributed to the imperialist era and to the failure of Britain, France, Belgium, Italy and the other European masters to prepare Africans for independence or to assign them sensible national boundaries. Socialist experiments here and there in Africa were watched with special hope.

A wave of sympathy from white radicals, liberals, and from some conservatives washed Africa's shores. That wave of sympathy was driven by guilt, and the guilt was sometimes excessive Certain European writers now argued that racial prejudice was a hallmark of white man's society, and especially of capitalist societies. South Africa was singled out for denunciation with more fervour than its insensitive and archaic racial theories and practices would normally justify. In Europe and North America, enlightened opinion temporarily concluded that racial prejudice was the most sinister prejudice, and so black Africans earned sympathy because they had suffered from that prejudice and were said to possess no such prejudices themselves. During the first round of western smiles and handshakes, the evidence of strong racial prejudice in parts of black Africa was dismissed or, if seen, was excused as tribalism. This was condescension. In effect black

Africans were viewed as children, not answerable for their conduct by those Europeans who most loyally defended them.

The End of Faith in the Third World

Eventually this era of one-eyed tolerance waned a little. The rule of Idi Amin in Uganda and the tyranny within the Central African Republic were widely publicised. Asia offered similar warnings. The slaughter in Kampuchea, the rebellion in Iran, and a variety of other episodes changed the picture in the second half of the 1970s. Other real events, some of them interpreted unfairly, helped to lower that enthusiasm for the third world. The oil crisis of 1973–74 shocked most western nations: indeed it unduly angered some because here was the third world using threats against them and thus reversing the traditional roles in international behaviour. The Islamic revival in Iran in the late 1970s and the imprisoning of Americans as hostages in Teheran disillusioned a section of American opinion. As the ending of the war in Vietnam had moved the camera of accusation away from the USA, the camera of accusation might now turn to other regions before returning to the west.

It was no longer so easy to see in the third world such high hopes of racial harmony, nor to see a realisation of a new social order. Some of the glamour had evaporated from heroic peasant lands. The collapse of the Great Proletarian Cultural Revolution and the overthrow of The Gang of Four in China in 1976 ended one of the highest hopes. The revelations of acts and atrocities committed by The Gang of Four in the name of socialism and humanity, reduced the prestige of China in the eyes of Utopians, but western tourists still admired the simple peasant life they saw through their train windows. China by 1980 appealed to many tourists of radical or conservative political views – they liked the slow, stable rural life. China was now ceasing to be the mysterious land. Part of the Great Wall had fallen down, and western technologists were welcomed as they poured into China.

Mystery and wonder are vital ingredients of all Utopias, as well as most revolutionary movements and reforming crusades. In the post-war period Africa and Asia temporarily provided hope, wonder and mystery for many westerners, especially for socialists who admired technology and for those very different people who found hope in nature. What those nations had *not* become, attracted the nature disciples. What they might become, as societies, attracted the political radicals. But many of the expectations placed on the new nations of Africa and Asia had been unrealistically high and the enthusiasm too bubbly to last. As Rome was not built in a day, why should Lagos or Dacca be built in a day? Moreover some of the enthusiasm for the third world came not from a careful examination of its people and prospects but from feelings of guilt and shame for the past and present of European civilisation. Though the western world was more educated than ever before and more wary of superstition and blindness than ever before it still rode the seesaw of attitudes and emotions.

17 The Puzzle of The Seesaw

Why does one period of modern history feel optimistic and another period feel pessimistic? Why does a mood persist for decades and then change with surprising speed? Will for example the loss of confidence, visible in the western world since the late 1960s, continue into the 1990s?

Fluctuations and sharp extremes of mood have become more likely because the seesaw itself has been loosened in the last two centuries by a series of drastic changes in society. Most of these changes in themselves have not positively altered the angle of the seesaw, but they have oiled its axle, as it were, enabling it to respond more quickly to those outside pressures which, coming from major events and ideas of the real world, positively push the seesaw up or pull it down.

The Decline of Christian and Classical Views

In the last two centuries there has been a deep thaw in attitudes and ideologies in much of the western world. Previously, censorship prevented people's views from altering easily: the inertia of a relatively static way of life restrained alterations in ideas and moods. Moreover, so long as censorship had been imposed on the pulpit, printing press and public meeting, unorthodox views could not easily spread, but in the last two centuries in the western world there has been a marked decline of censorship. Sometimes the censorship has returned, becoming even stronger than in the past. Hitler succeeded in imposing on Germany his own view of the present, past and future, and in most of the communist nations the official view becomes everybody's view, and in most nations of the third world there are curbs on free speech. In such societies the intellectual mood changes much less frequently, though occasionally it can change drastically when a dictator is overthrown or a new policy is proclaimed.

Today most countries in the European liberal tradition offer to new ideas a freedom such as is unusual in the history of the world. Without this freedom the mood of a nation could not change so often and so unpredictably. The fluctuations between optimism and pessimism in the last two centuries partly reflect this freedom. The swing in mood has been most pronounced precisely in nations where the freedom is entrenched, and the classes or groups who have sensed the possibilities of this freedom have tended to initiate new ideas and new ways of interpreting the past and envisaging the future.

The decline of the all-powerful monarch was one cause of that thaw which liberated ideas, and the decline of Christian belief was part of the thaw. Most Christian sects, in viewing the future, concentrated on another world and discouraged Utopian solutions here on earth. The common Christian view was pessimistic about this world, and the pessimism was not easily altered, but it began to change in the nineteenth century. The official Christian churches in most European nations were losing their monopoly of truth, and in that more tolerant environment the new views of man's future were more easily disseminated.

The slow decline of Christianity prepared the way for new Utopias and doomsdays. Indeed some of the new views of the future contained many of the characteristics of a religion. Science and technology formed one new religion which promised to tell the future and reform the present. The new religion's high priests were the scientists, and their incense was coal-smoke and tar, they held their divine service at learned societies, and their missionaries were the railways and steamships, telegraphs and other scientific inventions which were reaching remote places. They had the unshakeable belief that reason and research would solve all problems.

For some of the wealthy the arts were becoming another religion. The great artists were acclaimed as major creators and minor gods. Their best art, of all the things on earth, had the best chance of immortality. Man, in this new ideology, was not immortal but great paintings and books were. Increasingly, talented artists were barometers of the changes in the cultural mood, and artists sensed and were often the first to express a new mood, and only later did the mood reach newspapers and political platforms. Marxism was yet another nineteenth century religion with its emphatic view of man's past, present and especially his future. In 1900 none of these new secular international religions – whether Technology or the Arts or Marxism – was yet able to gain in any western liberal nation the dominance which Christianity had once held, but their influence was spreading swiftly. The increasing fluctuation in mood in the western world partly reflected the decline of Christianity's official monopoly of wisdom and the rise of these rival creeds, battling for hearts and minds.

The diminishing study of classical Greek and Latin and the ancient Mediterranean civilisations has also paved the way for new views of the past and future. As late as the 1880s, most universities insisted that all students should be familiar with at least one ancient language, and the study of ancient Greece and Rome still exercised a profound influence on how educated people saw the future. Imbued in school and university with the idea that Athens and Rome were the most civilised cities in the history of the world, educated people tended – if they thought of an ideal state – to look backwards rather than forwards. Conscious that these great civilisations had declined and vanished, they were wary of extremely optimistic assumptions that their own triumphant European civilisation of the nineteenth century was imperishable. The long span of human history with which students of the classical civilisation were familiar also made them rather less vulnerable to sudden shouts – should they arise – that the western world now faced unprecedented dangers, for they knew that the world had faced many grave dangers in past centuries and that therefore any future dangers must be seen in perspective. They also were less likely, because they knew the glories of the ancient past, to be seduced by excessive pride in the present. And if they did take pride in the recent achievements of western Europe they were likely to see many of those achievements as the bonus dividends flowing from the triumphs of classical Greece and Rome. As Sir Henry Maine, the celebrated English jurist, claimed enthusiastically in 1875: 'except the blind forces of Nature, nothing moves in this world which is not Greek in its origin.'[1] The declining study of classics and the growing study of science paved the way for a different bias towards the past and the future.

We are All Canaries, Locked in Our Cages

In place of the more stable Christian and classical views of western society came quickly changing views. The scope for change has been widened by the increasing complexity and specialisation of work and the growth of cities. People reared in a city and possessing few or no links with rural life are more likely to hold extreme views about Nature and its powers, and more likely to idolise Nature and the everyday rural life or, at the other extreme, more likely to despise it. The benign attitude to Nature which was part of the counter-culture of the 1960s and 1970s was more widespread among people reared in relative comfort in the cities. Much of the support for the Nature movement came from the high proportion of the population whose main impression of living nature came from the family cat or dog, the canary cage and city park. Their second-hand city-centred impression of Nature also came from the tropical jungle, as arranged by skilled producers of programmes for colour television. The divorce from rural life helps to explain the speed and fervour with which many of the young adopted a new view of Nature which, irrespective of its merits, their rural grandparents could never have accepted.

While many people today are starved of experiences of Nature, others are starved of experience or knowledge of how a big city functions and indeed of how the world as a whole functions in this era of economic and technological complexity. Many scientists and technologists through no fault of their own are largely ignorant of the workings of the complex civilisation in which their discoveries take effect. Inevitably their role as specialists in one fragment of a very complex society means that they are often incapable of seeing the wide range of consequences which might flow from their own new theorems, machines and medicines. They exalt the benefits of science and technology, and forget to weigh the costs against the benefits.

Extreme positions are, through ignorance, easily adopted by many of those who enthrone Technology and by many of those who enthrone Nature. Through increased specialisation most of us are cut off from Nature and most of us are cut off from Technology. Even master technologists rarely understand the widening circle of ripples which their own new machines and processes generate, because the ripples soon flow far from sight. Even the admirers of nature do not seem to see the cage they will enter if they renounce too much of technology and return to nature. We have all become canaries, singing in very different cages.

The intense pride in Technology visible in the mid 1960s and the intense pride in Nature visible in the mid 1970s were simple attitudes. Our civilisation in its complexity tempts even its intelligent and informed citizens to adopt over-simple attitudes. Complexity calls for a specialist education and specialist occupations, but they in turn give rise to a specialist view of the world based on that fragment of knowledge which is our speciality. The city itself is a form of specialisation which divorces most of us from Nature, and the residential suburb is a form of specialisation which divorces most of us, especially in our learning years, from those facets of Technology that reside in industrial suburbs. Specialisation in learning seems to lead to a simplified view of our civilisation as a whole – a simplified knowledge of how the world actually works and a simplified knowledge of cause and effect.

I am not criticising the over-simplification and the polarisation of views which sometimes occur in well-informed debates where the competing sides find themselves, simply by the jostling and passions spurred by the debate itself, trapped in corners which they had not originally intended to occupy; we all find ourselves pushed into such corners. Rather I am writing about the way in which the sheer complexity of the facts makes it difficult for specialists to assess the issues, let alone to explain them persuasively. Many important issues are too complex to be outlined easily to an interested but ill-equipped audience. For the sake of clarity, an over-simplification of issues is often deemed essential among those who conduct the debate at the highest level, but it is even more essential for most of us who listen intently or half awake to lectures, television interviews, advertising jingles, and in conversation around the dinner table. In the process a complex many-sided viewpoint becomes a pictorial placard, and a book of 100,000 words is condensed into 200.

We would be less inclined to over-simplify issues if our education had been broader. If those who studied political science, sociology, anthropology and English also studied mathematics and one of the sciences at a high level, and if those who specialised in science knew more about classical civilisations and politics, a debate involving complex issues would not degenerate so quickly into half-truths. But freedom of choice has permeated education, especially in capitalist societies, and has fostered easy choices. While freedom of choice is the hallmark and strength of a democratic society, unduly it encourages specialisation which in turn fosters a simplified view of society as a whole. Freedom of choice, in one form or other, facilitates these fluctuations of mood in the western world.

As the world becomes more complex, extreme views about the world's future are likely – in certain conditions – to gain large followings in democratic societies, and Technology and Nature will continue to focus or represent those views at opposite ends of the seesaw. Whether the seesaw will move more quickly and reach the far extremes depends not only on those factors that encourage viewpoints to change with ease but on certain dynamic factors which tilt the seesaw in one direction rather than another.

Dynamic Pushers of the Seesaw

As we have seen in earlier chapters the visible events of the real world strongly influence the direction in which the seesaw moves. Major wars, famines, depressions, booms and armistices affect it. Long periods of peace aid a swing to nature. A succession of dramatic events has a compound effect, and the two world wars and the intervening world depression helped technology to control the seesaw from 1914 to 1945. Likewise the visible might of new technology and new prosperity helped to create the more confident angle of the seesaw in the 1950s.

These disasters and triumphs influence our view of the future, but it is easy to exaggerate their influence. Their effect depends on the experience and expectations of the spectators as well as on the events themselves. In essence, it is unwise to explain the ups and downs of confidence simply in terms of a chronicle of good or bad news. Sometimes the pessimism is visible before the arrival of the gloomy news which is said to have caused the pessimism, and likewise the optimism does not always come from a layer of cheerful news. In certain periods the cheerful and gloomy events arrive side by side, each appearing to pull in a different direction, and yet the mood of those periods will sometimes veer in one direction rather than another.

The second half of the nineteenth century illustrates the difficulty of finding simple explanations for the seesaw. In the 1850s and 1860s the mood in western civilisation was relatively optimistic, perhaps more so than at any later period, and yet those years saw an unpredicted revival of international war. The Crimean War (1853–56) was followed by a series of wars which included the Battle of Sadowa – the costliest battle the world had seen – and the American Civil War which produced a longer list of deaths than any previous war. These wars of the years 1853–1871 were not sufficient to sour the faith in progress while the freedom from serious international wars in western and northern Europe in the following twenty five years was paralleled by a weakened faith in progress.

The complexity becomes obvious if we face the fact that just as events affect people's view of their future, so their view of the future also affects events. The steep rise in oil prices in the early 1970s was clearly influenced by the preceding intellectual and social mood. Similarly, the outbreak of war is partly a consequence of economic, political and cultural attitudes as well as a definite influence on the mood that follows. Wars, depressions, revolutions, famines and other evidence from the 'real world' cannot be assessed accurately as guides to the future, no matter how skilled some minds may be assessing evidence. Our mind is not a precise computer. Moreover its warning sirens can be deceptively loud or misleadingly faint. It can cry 'wolf', warning us of a danger that does not exist or it can ignore the accumulating evidence of danger. Warnings that come from the 'real world' have to be measured against our own experience of past warnings and disasters, and our experience can be too limited or irrelevant to enable us to project evidence from the present into the future.

The mood of Europe and North America and their dependent nations in the era 1945–80 can be explained partly by oscillations of hope and fear. The Cold War, the fear of a nuclear war and the fear of a post-war depression coloured the mood of the late 1940s, but the fears were not fulfilled. As prosperity arrived and as the capitalist world avoided serious international wars, the hopes became high and remained high in the first half of the 1960s – except for the Cuban missile crisis. Indeed they were abnormally high, having swung slowly from the opposite extreme. Then in the United States, the dominant country of the western world, the unrealistic optimism began to retreat in the late 1960s. The failure of high technology to solve military problems in Vietnam, black urban unrest at home, and the acute divisions which the unwon war created helped to deflate the optimism.

Optimism which is too high is the more easily deflated, even by trivial or middling events.

In part our expectations respond to the visible evidence transmitted from the real world and in part they have a logic and rhythm of their own. In peacetime an economic mood of extreme optimism sows the seeds of its own ultimate destruction, for people become accustomed to the prosperity, taking it for granted and ceasing to value it so highly. Moreover they had initially believed that prosperity would solve the problems of their family as well as their nation, but this rarely happens: prosperity makes new problems just as adversity solved some of the old problems. And so the high expectations born in the first phase of prosperity begin to wilt even before the prosperity wilts.

In the twentieth century, much more than in earlier centuries, a phase of confidence in peacetime technology cannot sustain itself for too many years. If a phase of sympathy for new technology is accompanied by rapid economic development, the progress imposes increasing pressures on nature and on resources, enabling the defenders of nature to gather damning evidence and disciples too. Later, if the defenders of nature become powerful in politics and use the law or public opinion to restrain new economic projects and thus increase unemployment, they begin to lose public support. The seesaw pervades the whole sequence of events.

An extreme mood, being extreme, tends to be its own undoing. An extreme fear that a major war is coming can give way to relief when war actually breaks out, the reality being more acceptable than the anxiety that preceded it. Furthermore a war creates its own cushion of consolation, and people take comfort in their patriotism and even have a buoyancy so long as victory seems possible.

We do not know enough about mass expectations and the subtle and visible factors which promote or undermine them. Our expectations as a group probably have their own in-built oscillator. When our expectations become too high, and in time are not fulfilled, we sensibly set them at a much lower level. And if they prove to be too low, and are easily falsified by more cheerful trends, they will be set anew at a much higher level. As we know that in economic life the expectations rise and fall, thereby affecting economic events themselves, it would be understandable if those same expectations were influential in non-economic as well as economic fields.

Expectations are largely carried in our head and heart and not on paper and therefore are relatively simple and general rather than particular. In a favourable mood, people overlook many seeds of concern, and in an unfavourable mood they magnify those seeds. Several conditions that caused deep concern in the early 1970s were already present a decade or more earlier but were not a cause for alarm. The rapid increase in the use of energy, the industrial pollution, the globe's soaring population and the thinning of the world's remaining Nature wildernesses were all apparent in 1960 but these symptoms, potentially disturbing, aroused little anxiety until later years.

There is another reason why we misinterpret the present and therefore befuddle our vision of the future. As the future is a political prize and eagerly fought for, so every rival political, economic and intellectual interest – whether left or right – tries to predict the future in order to influence that future or prevent the coming of a future which they do not desire. Any interpretation of economic, social and political events today has implications for tomorrow. Thus, if I suggest that the present economic uncertainties of the western world are only temporary I am, whether I intend to or not, making a political statement. I am implying that we do not need a radical social order in order to remedy the weaknesses of the present. Likewise the *Manifesto of the Communist Party* of 1848 is a statement about the present designed to influence the future. It concludes with three sentences which are slogans for the future. 'The proletarians have nothing to lose but their chains. They have a world to win. WORKING MEN OF ALL COUNTRIES, UNITE!'[2]

A year later, Lord Macaulay's *History of England* analysed the past to point to the future. He explained that unless he deceived himself the history of his country in the last century and a half 'is eminently the history of physical, of moral, and of intellectual improvement'. The future of England, he wrote, was full of hope so long as the present institutions were not unduly tampered with and reshaped.[3] In essence the conditions of society which angered Marx gave hope to Macaulay. Here then is another reason why we cannot interpret the present and the near future with complete impartiality. Our political assumptions, whether conservative or radical, active or passive, constantly intrude. Sometimes the dominant political assumptions of scholars push the outlook of society into a new position.

Democratic, capitalist nations have another in-built mechanism which promotes changes of outlook. They offer high rewards for novelty – for new technology and for new designs in clothes, furnishings, motor cars and the gadgets of everyday life. The visual arts now welcome novelty and the media emphasises the new: the new *is* the news. Even in a bookshop, one of the most conservative of institutions, the newest books occupy the window and the front shelves. The live theatre, the variety show, the cinema and the television spectacular thrive on the new.

The hub of the world's automobile industry, Detroit, was in the 1950s a symbol of the public's eagerness for changes in style and decoration. Each year's model of a motor car had to appear with its fins, grill and bumper bars, colours and stream-lining in new guise. Even universities at the same time had come to resemble Detroits. Traditionally the home of the study of ancient Mediterranean cultures, and therefore venerating the old, their main claim for public funds today is that they are the pursuers of the new. Original research, a search for novelty, is enthroned in a way not imaginable in most universities in the 1850s, and often novelty receives the halo which should have been given to scholarship itself. A society which values the new and has the freedom to accept it is more likely to revise its attitude to the future.

The Gap in Generations

In assessing the influences which alter or accentuate a society's mood we should give some consideration to the different viewpoint of young people compared to that of the older generation. New ideas call for thousands of followers if they are to shake the world, and certain decades are more likely than others to produce followers who quickly fall behind the banners of new ideas. An Australian sociologist John Carroll argued that the young radicals in the United States in the years 1964 to 1968 tended to come from middle-class families with a strong mother and an ineffectual father. He argued that they resented their own parents and a permissive society which had 'failed to impose credible commands' on the young. Those student radicals of the 1960s were not the first rebels to come from such families, because an earlier group of rebels arising in the Russia of the czars of the nineteenth century are also said to have had parents who lacked authority. But it would be unfair to see too many of the educated young of the 1960s as primarily the offspring of new fashions in rearing children. Many held a grievance which, by any standard, was serious – namely they did not wish to die in a war which they thought was unjust and unnecessary.[4] The relations between many fathers and sons and between many of the old and young were certainly unusual in the 1960s, and the origins of those uneasy relationships deserve close study.

Certainly, the late-teenagers during the post-war prosperity had more money than before, continued as students for a longer period than previously and spent more time with their age group and less time with their family, and accordingly were more often within earshot of new ideas. Possessing more economic power than their age-group had ever possessed, subsidised generously by a rich economy to which they contributed little, this generation of students may be one key to explaining the extent of the change of mood in the late 1960s. At the same time the 'generation gap' is not new, and amongst wealthy families it probably was present even in the remote era of the males' powdered wig as well as the era of jeans. We should also be wary of putting too much trust in the view that nowadays each new generation opposes its parents In the United States during the Vietnam War most of the young people of military or near-military age did not necessarily oppose their parent's view of the war, and they hardly formed a united generation, because so many willingly went to Vietnam to fight. Amongst the young in the United States, an eagerness to serve in Vietnam was at least as characteristic as was the massive anti-war movement. If we count roughly thirty years as a generation, then the 'generation' which passed through youth from say 1950 to 1980 consisted of contrasting waves of people, different from their parents in some attitudes but not in others.[5]

To say that one generation is very different to another is often a loose way of saying that times change. A generation gap tends to be the effect of a mobile, fast-changing period and will be most visible when a nation itself is divided and perplexed by the changes. In the late 1960s, when China and the United States each experienced its own cultural revolution, the old and middle-aged and teenaged all shared in the tensions and divisive-ness, and so the generation gap was only one of several fissures that divide people. The middle-aged were probably as divided in their opinions as the young.

It is widely said that human nature does not change, and in the strict sense it cannot – nature is central and the very core of existence. But there have occurred strong changes in the way members of society see themselves and how they respond to outside pressures and to their own conscience and standards. One of those changes – identified by David Riesman in his book *The Lonely Crowd* – pin-points a new eagerness to respond to the latest ideas and to social and emotional pressures. Riesman suggested that in recent centuries, the social characteristics of European peoples have so altered that today they are unusually receptive to new ideas and pressures.[6] I think that Riesman's theory can be dovetailed into one facet of the seesaw's move-ment; it helps to explain why the post-war generation has been unusually receptive to new ways of thinking and feeling.

Riesman shrewdly observed that the character of western society differed between medieval times, the industrial revolution, and the years after the Second World War. In medieval times, most people were ruled by tradition and custom and by the vigilant, conformist, communal eye. Most people did not think their life would be different to that of their grandparents; they were fatalist and resigned to God's will; their strongest fear was to be humiliated and shamed by the judgement of the society and its censors. They respected the old because in an unchanging society the old were the founts of useful knowledge and experi-ence. In contrast, in an industrial society in the nineteenth century, social character was more inner-directed than tradition-directed. That rapidly changing society rewarded the innovator, and it no longer venerated tradition and the old who were the guardians of tradition. In Riesman's words: 'The greater choices this society gives – and the greater initiatives it demands in order to cope with its novel problems – are handled by character types who can manage to live socially without strict and self-evident tradition-direction.'[7] The moral compass; the sense of direction and purpose, of those inner-directed people was implanted in childhood by parents and teachers; and their special fear was to let themselves down, to deviate from their own inner standards and values. Their punishment was guilt. By the 1960s, however, that type of character was more to be found in the old than the young in commercial cities of the United States and parts of western Europe. The young, especially those of wealthy background, were in Riesman's eyes a new character type which he called 'other-directed'. Their behaviour was influenced less by tradition or by a firmly-set compass given to them when young: they were influenced more by their peer group, by the media, and a variety of signals to which they were alert. Belonging to the era of consumption rather than production, valuing leisure as much as work, they were the children of the first era of super-abundance. They were also the children of people who had lost some of their moral certainty, whose own inner compasses were oscillating, and so these 'other-directed' young people were more anxious about the future and their own future. Fearing less the shame and the guilt of earlier generations, for they had neither a strong sense of tradition nor strong moral convictions, they were more like a flag in the wind than a fixed compass. Understandably they were anxious, for they were prone to be buffeted, whether from the age they lived in or their own character. Riesman wrote his analysis of these three successive stages of social character in 1950, and the counter-culture of the 1960s gave weight to his diagnosis. In essence the seesaw can swing more easily for such a generation.

The Gap Between Nations

A national crisis, especially a crisis that at first is inexplicable as well as unexpected, produces not only followers for ideas but the ideas themselves. Scholars worried about the future of their nation and its values can easily magnify and project their worry into a wider fear for the future of the wider world. Equally the reverse can be true. European philosophers who, in the second half of the eighteenth century, believed in The Enlightenment, were possibly reflecting the sense of power of discovery of an era which science was asserting itself. Were those who, at the same time, disliked the changes to their civilisation, more inclined to see virtues in the noble faraway savage? Was the glorying in the idea of progress, a faith which was strongest in Britain and the United States towards the middle of the nineteenth century, really the projection onto the whole western world of an optimism born of the remarkable inventiveness and material success of those two nations? Were some of the pessimistic global ideas shaped in England in the 1890s the result of the fear that the British Empire had passed its prime? Was the vital role of Austria–Hungary as a seedbed of pessimistic ideas in the 1890s in part a sign of the deepening tensions in that multicultural society and of its declining military power? Certainly in the 1950s some of the American optimism about the world's future was a sign that all seemed well in America. Probably, fears that global problems were less manageable by the late 1960s reflected a new intuition that the United States's internal problems were less manageable. The soaring price of oil in 1973 was partly an effect of America's sense that her military power was no longer so effective.

In general, the attitude towards western civilisation was spurred less by fears and hopes about the civilisation than fears and hopes about the continued strength and vitality of one's own nation. After all, most of us, for most of the time, still regard our own nation rather than civilisation as the centre of our universe. It would not be surprising if hopes about the nation were unconsciously magnified into universal hopes.

Amnesia – A Disease of the Computer Era

Another facet of our times helps to explain these swings between optimism and pessimism. Our civilisation lacks a collective memory but requires one more than ever before. Whereas a Spaniard who ploughed the land in the tenth century did not need to know much about his past because it was much the same as his present, our present vanishes with bewildering speed, and its lessons are forgotten.

Pessimism and optimism have each been accompanied, knowingly or unknowingly, by a view of the past that is tightly linked to its view of the future. The excessive faith in progress in the first era of telegraphs, photography and railways was buttressed by a belief that primitive societies were abject. If, however, primitive societies had been seen as successful in their own way, then part of the evidence for human progress – for the superiority of present over past – would have automatically disappeared. Similarly the extreme pessimism about our technological society of the 1970s was accompanied by a belief that primitive societies displayed virtues which a high-technology society no longer possessed. To think that a simple tribe of the Kalahari Desert had a richly satisfying life, even though their kit of tools was feeble, challenged the idea that the 1970s were necessarily superior to the stone age simply by virtue of their sophisticated technology. If a horse runs a race against a rabbit, the horse by contrast seems astonishingly fast. We magnify the present and the near future by the contrast that we select from the past. The interpretation of optimism and pessimism is spotted with horses and rabbits and profoundly influenced by their presence or absence.

We cannot understand the rise of these unusual moods, whether of pessimism or confidence, without realising that they are linked to an interpretation of history. We feel a need to know the past: if we don't know it we unintentionally make it up. One hallmark of many of the radical movements of the late 1960s was their weak knowledge of history. Likewise some of the conservative movements of the 1980s shunned history and thought in the booming share market of 1987 that a repetition of the Wall Street crash of 1929 was virtually impossible.

Forces that Push the Seesaw

There can be little doubt that in the western world today the mood of society can change more quickly than it could in the nineteenth or eighteenth centuries. The factors which are capable of promoting oscillations in mood are more powerful and varied than ever before. The seesaw itself is more sensitive to slight pressures. These extreme swings of the seesaw come not only from war and peace, economic depressions and prosperity, the finding or depleting of new natural resources, inventions and pollution, but also from less tangible and more subjective factors operating in free societies. Of the subjective factors, the most influential are:

- The decline of Christianity and the declining influence of classical civilisations, thus paving the way for other competing views of the world and its future.
- An increasing narrowing of human experience, with the growth of cities, the cobwebbed complexity of western

civilisation, and the premium on novelty in so many facets of western life.

- A feeble or imperfect knowledge of the past and its relevance to the present.
- Political hopes and fears, including perceptions about the future of one's own nation, and a desire to shape that future.
- The cycle of expectations.
- Generation gaps, and especially the bargaining power and the social character of the young.

These factors do not all point in the same direction at the same time. All do not blow cold or hot together, but in aggregate they form a climate which, at times, can deepen the gloom caused by real events or brighten the hope inspired by real events. These factors are constantly interacting with events from the real world: they even create events in the real world.

Will the Seesaw Continue to Swing?

This seesaw of cultural and intellectual moods will probably continue to swing, so long as democracy persists. While we cannot predict with confidence when and where it will move, the history of the western world over the last 200 years suggests that any major prediction about national and international affairs cannot ignore the seesaw.

On the other hand, some critics would argue vehemently that the factors which ruled the past are dead, that the future will be unique and that past trends have no relevance to an understanding of the future. The seesaw, they would say, is outmoded. The argument that the present is absolutely unique is often a reflection of anxiety for the future. When a political scientist argues that 'the crucial problems of our time' – the dangers of nuclear weaponry and the population explosion, the pressures on the environment and the volatility of the international economy – are different in kind from the old questions that used to dominate the agenda of international relations, he is asserting that the world is entering an uncharted, hazardous era. Political science, sociology, anthropology and even history hold many exponents of this view that the study of history has become irrelevant. In one sense their argument is correct: each era has events, trends and achievements which no previous era experienced. But no modern era is as unique as we like to think it is. What is unique in the present is usually surrounded by continuity.

Many intelligent people in earlier eras made the mistake of thinking that they had little to learn from the past. Their sense of the uniqueness of the present was especially visible in those activities where the advance of technology made the present appear to be unprecedented and unique. Warfare was one such activity. After the Austro–Prussian War of 1866, and again on the eve of the First World War, many military observers believed they were in a completely new era. Henceforth, they said, all wars would be decisively cut short by the new military technology.[8] Their prediction was wrong. The first years of the nuclear era heard the same argument – that major wars would henceforth be shatteringly quick – but so far the wars have not been a dramatic break from the past. Admittedly the wars of the nuclear era are not yet nuclear, but even a 'nuclear war' in the future might consist mainly of conventional warfare and not be a short war.

There is little logic in the argument that the present has shaken itself free from the past. To say that the past has no relevance in interpreting the present is to make a profoundly historical statement and to claim an enormous knowledge of the past. And yet one observes that many who insist that the past is irrelevant are scientists or social scientists with a sparse knowledge of history. Some are 'practical men', with a deep sense of destiny but a shallow sense of history, men such as John Maynard Keynes depicted:

> Practical men, who believe themselves to be quite exempt from any intellectual influences, are usually the slaves of some defunct economist. Madmen in authority, who hear voices in the air, are distilling their frenzy from some academic scribbler of a few years back.[9]

If we disown history we are at its mercy. To have a reasonable knowledge of the past is to possess an anchor which is likely to prevent us from being swept towards false ideas about the present and future.

Some would argue that the seesaw is outmoded because technology, in the nuclear era, can never regain its former prestige. And yet technology has commanded high esteem even during the nuclear era, and one peak of the faith in technology was actually the vigorous nuclear decade, 1955 to 1965. Others would argue that the seesaw is permanently rigid because of a new and more enduring kind of crisis. I have before me a letter from an observant, respected American scholar who in 1983 suggested to me that we are 'entering a semi-permanent state of crisis' and that almost every aspect of that crisis has arisen from the dangers of technology and the vulnerability of nature, and that therefore technology can never again rise high on the seesaw and nature can never again fall low. No longer, he wrote, can my image of the seesaw be 'useful for predicting the future'. And yet his view is largely that of the doomsday thinking of the early 1970s, and since then the seesaw has moved in a direction which no member of the doomsday school predicted. With the aid of technology, the intense fears of famine so widespread in the early 1970s, now appear to be misplaced. The fears about the scarcity of nearly all resources, whether land or food or energy, have so far been emphatically disproved. Admittedly the warnings of famine possibly helped to push the seesaw away from that extreme position, for they stimulated food production. In the mid 1980s, ironically, a glut of food and minerals came at the very time for which a chronic scarcity was predicted.

The fears expressed in the early 1970s by the doomsday school were exaggerated, but this does not mean that the fears have permanently vanished: they will return at some time in the next half century. On the other hand the fears toward nuclear technology, not voiced strongly in the early 1970s, were revived a few years later at the very time when on most other fronts the fear towards technology was decreasing. The new anti-nuclear movement was strong amongst the young and especially vigorous in western Europe, and by the early 1980s it was more popular than ever before. Almost certainly the most intense crusade against any form of technology in the last two centuries, the anti-nuclear movement did not oppose all technology and possibly will retain its influence if it confines its opposition only to one branch of technology.

All in all, the last dozen years have produced signs of a slow, cautious swing of the seesaw back towards technology but many factors will determine whether that swing continues. The swing towards technology will be impeded in the next quarter of a century if new forms of pollution are identified, if nuclear reactors experience accidents which are more serious than those at Three Mile Island (1979) and Chernobyl (1986), if there are one or two years of poor global harvests, if a war involving nuclear weapons is fought, or if the world's climate should change through the effect of pollution of the atmosphere. The suspicion of technology will increase if, through political or economic causes, oil and phosphate and other strategic commodities jump in price and thereby accentuate fears of permanent scarcity. But these events of the real world, powerful as they are, will create the maximum fears only if the human eyes and minds which interpret them are also sympathetic. The ways in which the attitudes to nuclear weapons have waxed and waned shows the role of our emotions and ideologies in altering the messages that come from the real world.

A new topic is now a crucial part of the seesaw: the disease AIDS. Technology had led in the early 1960s to the invention of 'the pill', and the marketing and usage of the pill was aided by the liberating back-to-nature mood of the late 1960s, but the resultant sexual revolution hastened the spread of the disease AIDS after 1980. Thus a cycle of events which really began with a triumph of medical technology and was then accelerated by the reaction against civilisation and technology, has now turned full circle by seeking in medical technology a cure for this devastating disease. Curiously, in a subtle way, AIDS is now seen as a symbol of nature, of a corrupt Tahiti. This disease originating from central Africa disputes the picture that a simple society is a paradise of health and benevolence; Tahiti in the age of Captain Cook would similarly have ceased to be a paradise if it had been the source rather than the victim of venereal disease. Moreover, AIDS has been spread largely by homosexuals, and they had traditionally been seen as standing outside the main concourse of western civilisation until they made their public debut in the late 1960s as part of the counter-culture and the reaction against the mainstream values of western civilisation. If AIDS should become a devastating cause of death in the last decade of this century, it could dominate one end of the seesaw. Indeed in the short term it has more potential for terror than the fear which occupies the opposite end of the seesaw, the fear of nuclear war.

The seesaw does not have to move to an extreme angle in the next fifteen or fifty years. There is no innate reason why nature and technology cannot reconcile some of their differences. If technology were to cease to be the dynamo, and if the world entered a period of slow change in which change itself was no longer hailed as a virtue, then a half-stagnant world could reconcile some of the tension between nature and technology. If we were to enter a period in which new technology were restricted or enchained, then a powerful force behind the moving seesaw would wilt. Moreover technology and nature have not always been the magnets for opposing clusters of values and attitudes. During the two world wars they lived together harmoniously in the minds of most citizens. Technology was valued then because it provided the armour which defended one's country, while nature was valued because its soil, rocks, coast and landscape were the essence and symbol of the country being defended. In the face of a common enemy, a faith in technology and a faith in nature became allies: they could become allies again if crises in international politics become frequent.

The existence of the seesaw also depends on the continuation of a democratic western world. That cannot be guaranteed. Democracy is a freak condition in the world's history: civil liberties are not common liberties even today, and most people in the world have never possessed them. If the western world were to enter a state of emergency – and if through terrorism or civil wars or fear of an imminent nuclear war, civil liberties were to be permanently curtailed – then the weakening of freedom would slow down or virtually obliterate the seesaw of ideas. Likewise, a future war that caused as much destruction as say the Second World War might lead to a new political order in which a dominant nation or strong United Nations curbed not only freedom but a wide range of new technologies. A major war conceivably might give victory to communism, and that also would destroy the seesaw as we know it.

While the opposing forces of technology and nature have deeply affected the field of human affairs in the last two centuries, they are not beyond our control. The seesaw is not driven by a relentless, unalterable mechanism, nor does it always have to carry the same sets of opposing riders or attitudes at each end, for it is a result of human will and imagination, of human hopes and anxieties. The more we understand the seesaw, the more we are likely to prevent it from reaching positions so extreme and unrealistic that a rebound is almost inevitable.

Key Words and Definitions

To the following key words I give these meanings. For the most part they are orthodox definitions but every busy word acquires a variety of meanings and so some clarification may be useful.

The Enlightenment

A strong intellectual movement of the eighteenth century, it emphasised the need to break loose from traditional thinking and authorities and, instead, rely on independent reasoning, observing and experimenting. The Enlightenment was reformist, secular, humanitarian and optimistic. Most of its followers, while not atheists, rejected the official doctrines of the main churches and did not believe in miracles or other forms of divine intervention.

European Peoples

People of European birth or descent, whether in Europe or in North America, Australia, Argentina and other lands primarily settled by Europeans.

Man

It usually means man and woman. Mankind likewise includes woman. The words *man* and *mankind*, despite their disadvantages, are less clumsy and are clearer than their recent alternatives.

Nature

Ocean, sky, climate, the seasons, fresh water, land, natural resources, flora and fauna. Man is part of nature but has learned in part to regulate nature and harness natural resources through technology. Hence technology has enabled human beings to see themselves as separate from nature – more separate, at times, than is sensible.

Noble Savage

A term of praise, widely used since the eighteenth century, denoting people living in relatively simple societies, in an idyllic condition close to nature. Tahiti was the most famous of the paradises inhabited by the Noble Savage. John Dryden, the English poet, made popular this concept when he wrote: 'I am as free as nature first made man . . . When wild in woods the noble savage ran.' (See also *Savage*)

Opinions and Attitudes

This book looks mainly at the ideas of the articulate – whether scholars, artists, scientists, writers, teachers or politicians – who appraised the human condition and formed the audience for that appraisal. It deals therefore with only a small minority of the population but of course it is the influential minority whose opinions mirrored and shaped the mood of an age. It is too difficult to ascertain what the average man and woman thought on many of the issues discussed and traced in this book: even in our era of opinion polls it is not easy. Even in examining the ideas of the articulate it is not always easy to ascertain which is a minority and which a majority mood or viewpoint. Often the minority viewpoint amongst intellectuals gave flavour to the thought of a period and dictated the agenda of debate which made that period distinctive.

Optimism

A faith in one's civilisation and in its capacity to shape a satisfactory future, especially by using science and technology. Technology came to be esteemed as the main problem-solver and the main instrument of change, for it gave western man what he lacked in the past – a power to harness nature and its resources.

Pessimism

A lack of faith in one's civilisation and a fear that technology will not lead to man's triumph over nature but rather to his downfall or, at best, confusion and deterioration. A pessimist has more fears than hopes for the future. Distrusting the consequences of an idustrial and consumers' society, the pessimist often prefers a way of life that harmonises with nature rather than one that tries to tame nature. Simple societies where nature is not subdued are especially attractive to a pessimist.

Progress

Progress is a movement in a desired direction; the believers in progress – the optimists – think the world is improving and will continue to improve. I use the phrase *Heyday of Progress* to cover the period roughly from the 1840s to the 1870s when powerful thinkers in the western world believed that the pace of progress was unprecedented and that progress would go on and on.

Savage

A word widely used in the eighteenth and nineteenth centuries to describe people living in a society with a very simple technology. Their hardware and equipment were obviously simple but their skills, facets of their knowledge and their social relationships were not necessarily simple. Some were hunters and gatherers and some were gardeners and herd keepers. They were seen as close to nature because their technology was less able to control or harm nature. The word *savage* did not originally imply ferocity but rather freedom, and it is in the traditional sense that I use the word *savage* when discussing the perceptions held of such peoples in the eighteenth and nineteenth centuries. Occasionally, as an alternative, I use the phrase *primitive society*. These terms, loaded as they are, reflect the power of the seesaw in shaping our vocabulary and imagery.

Seesaw

The way in which the mood of a civilisation or nation oscillates between extremes of optimism and pessimism. The ideas and attitudes of intellectuals contribute to the motion of the seesaw and also reflect the state of the seesaw. Since 1750 there has been an increasing tendency for nature and technology to sit at opposing ends of the seesaw and act as magnets, competing for man's allegiance. As technology in the last two centuries has bcome the mainspring of our civilisation and the main instrument of change, those who have faith in our civilisation tend to admire technology but those who lack faith in our civilisation distrust technology and, at key times, turn to nature. A variety of other attitudes tend to cluster at each end of the seesaw, and move with it. As the seesaw of moods and ideas operates more freely where people are free to speak their mind, I do not see communist lands as part of the seesaw, though of course they influence it and are influenced by it. Nor do I see most nations of the third world, especially those in Africa, as belonging to the seesaw though they influence it and are influenced by it.

Technology

It covers all the man-made equipment, skills and processes of the material world, whether sailing ships and space shuttles, notions of how to run a farm or a school, techniques of the blacksmith and welder, the signalling flag and the telex. Every society, no matter how simple economically, has its technology, but the word is more frequently needed to describe a society whose ways of making, distributing and communicating are frequently changing.

Western Civilisation

The civilisation or society based on Europe and the lands settled primarily by Europeans, and strongly influenced by Christianity and by the classical values revived in the Renaissance. In the middle eighteenth century this civilisation saw itself as characterised primarily by civil order, moral character, manners and a system of obligations and courtesies based on people's station in society. Later, technology and science, a willingness to experiment and change, and a mounting body of knowledge and skills came to be seen, more than manners, as the hallmark of western civilisation. Soviet Russia is part of this Europe-based civilisation, and Japan, Singapore and several other quick-rising nations are coming close to it.

A Final Word on Bias

Most of the keywords used in this book are emotionally and politically charged, which is a pity but unavoidable. Keywords, despite the hopes of those who coin them or try to erase them, can never be neutral and germ-free. Once they become bland

and innocuous they cease to be keywords. I should add that I see many virtues as well as defects in the so-called savage, backward, primitive or simple societies and likewise in European civilisation. I prefer the latter but do not despise the former. At the same time one of the conclusions of this book is how difficult it is for each generation to assess its own society and past societies. The 'great seesaw' expresses that difficulty.

Acknowledgements

I worked on this book on and off for nine years, during which time I received help from many people. I was guided to sources of information or past arguments and theories by Chris Wallace-Crabbe, Marion Adams, Peter Chew, Inga Clendinnen, Greg Dening, Dinny O'Hearn, Claudio Veliz, Margaret Manion, Peter Jonson and Alan McBriar in Australia, by John Clive, Samuel McCulloch, Carleton Chapman, Stephen Graubard, Nur Yalman and Robin Brooks in the United States, and Sir Henry Phelps Brown in England. I thank the staff of the Baillieu Library at Melbourne University and the Harvard College Library, and also my successive secretaries, Liz Carey and Anna Constantinidis, who typed the manuscript. I record my special debt to Glenn Mulligan, Douglas Hocking, Margaret Rose and Anna Blainey who read all or many of the chapters and challenged arguments or pointed out inconsistencies; I am especially grateful to Glenn Mulligan for theoretical issues he raised.

I gained from the discussion which followed seminars or lectures I gave on aspects of this theme at Princeton University, the Anthropology Department at Harvard, the North American Conference on British Studies, the Friedrich-Ebert Stiftung in Bonn, the Australian and New Zealand Association for the Advancement of Science, the Adam Smith Society in Melbourne, the research department of the Reserve Bank of Australia, the New South Wales branch of the Economics Society, the Australian Academy of the Humanities, four New Zealand universities – Victoria, Otago, Auckland and Canterbury – as well as the University of Melbourne. I thank all who, by joining in these discussions, helped to clarify my ideas.

The topic covered by the chapters is vast and so the book must contain many imperfections, for which the responsibility is mine alone.

GEOFFREY BLAINEY
UNIVERSITY OF MELBOURNE

Notes

The following notes are selective. When in the narrative I cite the author and title of a book and discuss the book generally rather than for a specific point, I rarely list that book in further detail in these notes. I have also tended to use the narrative rather than these notes to express my debt to authors whose ideas have especially helped me. At the same time much of the evidence used in my argument comes from little-known sources, and they are documented in these notes. In some chapters are long sections of narrative for which I give no source, mainly because I am thinking aloud on the basis of evidence that can easily be found in encyclopedias or general history books.

1 The Seesaw: A First View

1. Thoreau derides the telegraph: Henry David Thoreau, *Walden*, (1854) Peebles Classic Library (New York) n.d., p. 44–5.

2 Happy Isle

1. Prophecy of Elias: Katharine R. Firth, *The Apocalyptic Tradition in Reformation Britain 1530–1645* (Oxford, 1979) p. 5–6.
2. Luther and end of world: Firth, p. 17.
3. E. S. de Beer, *The Literature of Travel in the Seventeenth Century*, pamphlet, Hakluyt Society (London, 1975) p. 5.
4. Origin of word 'optimism': Paul Hazard, *European Thought in the Eighteenth Century*, translation from French, Penguin paperback (London, 1965) p. 340.
5. Wesley's preface: John Passmore, *Dictionary of the History of Ideas*, 1974, vol. 3, p. 468.
6. Four-stages theory: 'Social Science and the Ignoble Savage', paper presented by R. L. Meek (University of Papua New Guinea) 6 August 1975.
7. Rousseau and Hottentots, E. H. McCormick, *Omai: Pacific Envoy*, Auckland, 1977, pp. 6–7.

8. Rousseau and Nigritia: cited by W. Stark, 'Literature and Thought', *New Cambridge Modern History*, vol. 8, p. 62.
9. Rousseau and killing: E. H. McCormick, *Omai: Pacific Envoy*, p. 151.
10. Beauty of American Indians: Benjamin Keen, *The Aztec Image in Western Thought* (Rutgers, 1971), p. 240.
11. Voltaire and fad for primitivism: J. A. Aldridge, *Voltaire and the Century of Light* (Princeton, 1975) p. 228.
12. Isselin and other scoffers at nature: Friedrich Meinecke, *Historism: The Rise of a New Historical Outlook* (London, 1972) p. 197.
13. Joy at seeing Tahiti: E. H. McCormick, *Omai: Pacific Envoy*, p. 16; John Dunmore, *French Explorers in the Pacific* (Oxford, 1965) vol. 1. pp. 110–112; Glyndwr Williams, 'Seamen and Philosophers in the South Seas in the Age of Cook', *The Mariner's Mirror*, vol. 65, Feb. 1979.
14. Kerguelen on the noble savage: Dunmore, vol. 1, p. 214.
15. Bougainville describes the girl with the sliding loincloth: Dunmore, vol. 1, p. 79.
16. Joseph Banks on Tahitian food: J. C. Beaglehole (ed.), *The Endeavour Journal of Joseph Banks 1768–1771* (Sydney, 1962) vol. 1, pp. 341, 347.
17. Tahitian abundance compared with France: this elementary point seems to be overlooked by historians of exploration but it can easily be inferred by glancing at such books as Fernand Braudel, *Capitalism and Material Life 1400–1800*, (Harper paperback New York, 1973) p. 39, and John Roberts, *Revolution and Improvement: The Western World 1775–1847* (Berkeley, 1976), p. 12.
18. Banks on Aboriginals: Beaglehole (ed.), vol. 2, pp. 125, 130.
19. Cook on Aboriginals: J. C. Beaglehole (ed.), *The Journals of Captain James Cook* (Cambridge, 1968), vol. 1, p. 399.
20. Cook and Shelvocke's book: Glyndwr Williams, "'Far more happier than we Europeans': reactions to the Australian Aborigines on Cook's voyage" *Historical Studies*, (Melbourne, October 1981) no. 77, p. 507.
21. Botany Bay's climate and soil: G. Blainey, *A Land Half Won* (Melbourne, 1980) pp. 10–13, 23.
22. John Dryden, *The Conquest of Granada by the Spaniards*, part 1, written in 1670.

23. Chief Justice Pedder of Tasmania on savage freedom: *Van Diemen's Land: Copies of all Correspondence . . . on the Subject of the Military Operations* (Hobart, 1971) p. 82.

24. Noble savage not in New Zealand: cannibalism was another reason why the Maoris were not idolised. See J. C. Beaglehole, *The Life of Captain James Cook* (London, 1974) pp. 212–3.

25. 'In the Jeffersonian era': Bernard W. Sheehan, 'Paradise and the Noble Savage in Jeffersonian Thought', *William and Mary Quarterly*, 1969, vol. 26, p. 327.

26. J. G. Herder, *Outlines of a Philosophy of the History of Man*, tr. from German (London, 1800) p. 168.

27. Crévecoeur, cited by B. W. Sheehan, p. 347.

28. Black Africa: William B. Cohen, *The French Encounter with Africans* (Bloomington, Indiana, 1980) pp. 64–5, 72, 95.

29. Andanson in Senegal, cited in Cohen, p. 70.

30. *Encyclopaedia Britannica*, first edn (Edinburgh, 1771) vol. 3, p. 253.

31. Saint-Pierre on birds and butterflies: Henry Hunter's translation, *Annual Register . . . 1796* (London, 1800) pp. 394–5.

32. J. H. Bernardin de St. Pierre, *Paul and Virginia: An Indian Tale*, translated from the French (Hartford, 1834).

33. Peron's dynamometer: M. F. Peron, *A Voyage of Discovery to the Southern Hemisphere*, tr. from French (London, 1809), pp. 312–4; F. C. T. Moore in his translation of Joseph-Marie Degerando, *The Observation of Savage Peoples* (London, 1969) p. 38.

34. French officers chasing Tasmanians: Peron, p. 200.

35. Romanticism in Europe: Anthony Thorlby, *The Romantic Movement* (London, 1966); Lilian R. Furst, *Romanticism*, (London, 1969); Mario Praz, *The Hero in Eclipse in Victorian Fiction* (Oxford, 1969) esp. pp. 37–65.

36. P. van Tieghem, *La Preromantisme*, 5 vols., 1924–47, cited in Thorlby, p. 22.

3 The Best Is Yet To Be

1. The optimistic predictions: Jerome H. Buckley, *The Triumph of Time* (Harvard, 1966) pp. 35–52; Walter E. Houghton, *The Victorian Frame of Mind, 1830–1870* (Yale, 1957) ch. 2.

2. Gatling's invention: John Ellis, *The Social History of the Machine Gun* (London, 1975) p. 27.

3. Oliver Wendell Holmes, *The Autocrat of the Breakfast Table*, being vol. 1 of the 14 vol. edition of *The Writings of Oliver Wendell Holmes*, Boston, Riverside edn, c. 1890, vol. 1 pp. vi, ix.

4. Darwin on elephants: Philip Appleman, (ed.), *Darwin: A Norton Critical Edition*, New York, 1970 (being an anthology of Darwin's writings); pp. 87, 117; 'Nature may be compared', ibid., p. 84.

5. 'We behold the face of nature': ibid., p. 116.

6. Stephen Gould, lecture at Harvard University, October 1982.

7. Darwin on Aboriginals and Negroes: Charles Darwin, *The Descent of Man* (London, 1882 edn), pp. 156, 191–2, 619.

8. Spencer's career: F. C. S. Schiller on 'Spencer' in *Encyclopaedia Britannica*, 11th edn (Cambridge, 1911) vol. 25, p. 635.

9. Spencer's views: Appleman (ed.), *Darwin*, p. 489 for the 'most powerful intellect'; p. 496 for 'like a vast human caricature', both of which came from Chapter 2 of Richard Hofstadter's *Social Darwinism in American Thought* (Boston, 1955).

10. The 'gigantic means of production': Lewis S. Feuer (ed.), *Karl Marx and Friedrich Engels: Basic Writings* (Fontana paperback, 1969) p. 54.

11. Cotton textiles dominate British exports: Eric Hobsbawm, *Industry and Empire: An Economic History of Britain since 1750* (London, 1968) p. 51.

12. *Critique of the Gotha Programme*, L. S. Feuer (ed.), p. 160.

13. Similarities of Darwin and Marx: Jacques Barzun, *Darwin, Marx, Wagner* (New York, 1958 revised edn), esp. pp. 169–70.

14. Gothic: Kenneth Clark, *The Gothic Revival* (Penguin paperback, 1964) Walter Scott, p. 58, rise of Oxford Movement and other aids to Gothic, pp. 93, 137–8; Gothic as common as haystacks, p. xxi.

15. For the suggestion that there is a link beween the birth of skyscrapers and zenith of gothic spires I can offer only my intuition.

16. The Anglo-American success in commercial architecture:

Henry-Russell Hitchcock, *Architecture: Nineteenth and Twentieth Centuries* (Penguin, 1968 edn) p. 250.

17. Skyscraper's aura: Hitchcock, p. 252.

18. Modern architecture's faith in mechanical progress: Lewis Mumford, *The Highway and the City* (Mentor paperback, 1964 edn) pp. 173–5.

19. Archibald Alison, *The Principles of Population* (Edinburgh, 1840) vol. 1, p. 79.

20. Malthus the man: J. M. Keynes, *Essays in Biography* (London, 1933) p. 132 for speech defect; p. 116 for dispute with father.

21. Malthus on bending the bow: *Encyclopaedia Britannica* (Cambridge, 1911) vol. 17, p. 516 n.

22. Malthus modifies his theory in later editions: a theme of G. Himmelfarb and W. Petersen, it is discussed in Robert Nisbet, *History of the Idea of Progress* (New York, 1980), Basic paperback, pp. 216–20.

23. Famines in 1840s: John Roberts, *Revolution and Improvement: The Western World 1775–1847* (Berkeley, 1976) p. 143.

24. Economics and scarcity: Oleg Zinam, 'The Myth of Absolute Abundance', *American Journal of Economics and Sociology*, January 1982, vol. 41, pp. 61–2.

25. Decline of Malthusian fears by mid-century: Jonathan Hughes, *Industrialization and Economic History* (New York, 1970) p. 198; J. Roberts, *Revolution and Improvement*, pp. 143, 146–50.

26. Hearn and biological evolution: J. A. La Nauze, *Political Economy in Australia: Historical Studies* (Melbourne, 1949) p. 61.

27. Hearn on Rousseau and Ricardo: W. E. Hearn, *Plutology: Or the Theory of the Efforts to Satisfy Human Wants* (Melbourne, 1863) p. 474.

28. Jevons on Hearn: La Nauze, p. 50.

29. Carey and Hearn on the fertility of distant regions: Hearn, *Plutology*, pp. 110–14.

30. Galton on the potential of eugenics: a valuable summary is in Derek Freeman, *The Making and Unmaking of an Anthropological Myth* (Harvard, 1983) esp. pp. 7–11.

31. Lifting standards by one notch: Ethel M. Elderton on Galton in *Chambers' Encyclopaedia*, 1924, vol. 4, p. 475.

32. Explanations of Europe's post-1815 peace: G. Blainey, *The Causes of War* (London, 1973) pp. 18–22.
33. J. S. Mill on peace: cited by J. Hughes, *Industrialization and Economic History*, p. 7., Henry T. Buckle, *The History of Civilization in England* (London, 1885 edn) vol. 1, p. 223.
34. *North American Review*, No. 57, cited in J. R. McCulloch, *A Dictionary of Commerce* (London, 1854 new edn) p. 384.
35. The Crimean War: Buckle, vol. 1, p. 195.
36. J. E. Cairnes, 'International Law', *Fortnightly Review* (Nov. 1865) p. 123.
37. Belief that wars would henceforth be short: G. Blainey, *The Causes of War* (London, 1973) pp. 119–21, 206–7.

4 A Pocket Watch For Progress

1. A. R. Wallace, 'On the Progress of Civilization in Northern Celebes', *Transactions of the Ethnological Society of London*, 1866, vol. 4, esp. p. 66.
2. *'Man only in Australasia'*: cited in Bernard Smith, *European Vision and the South Pacific 1768–1850* (London, 1960) p. 203.
3. Leichhardt's observations: M. Aurousseau (ed.), *The Letters of Ludwig Leichhardt* (Cambridge, 1968) vol. 2, pp. 675, 757.
4. *The Journals of John McDouall Stuart* (London, 1865) p. 166.
5. An Australian geography book: Alexander Sutherland, *A New Geography for Australian Pupils* (Melbourne, 1885) p. 8.
6. McLennan's view: cited in Fred W. Voget, *A History of Ethnology* (New York, 1975) p. 256.
7. Melville and South Seas: Lee C. Mitchell, *Witnesses to a Vanishing America: The Nineteenth-Century Response* (Princeton, 1981) pp. 194, 196, 202.
8. Tylor: cited in Fred W. Voget, *A History of Ethnology*, p. 181; D. J. Mulvaney, 'Discovering Man's Place in Nature',

The Australian Academy of Humanities: Proceedings 1971 (Sydney, 1971) pp. 50–1.

9. The Russian zoologist: E. M. Webster, *The Moon Man: A Biography of Nikolai Miklouho-Mackay* (Melbourne, 1984) see p. 340 for Darwin, and p. viii for return to Russia.

10. *Beeton's Dictionary of Universal Information* (London, 1861) vol. 1, pp. 1–3.

11. Cuvier's theory: John C. Greene, *The Death of Adam* (Iowa, 1959) esp. pp. 128–9, 235.

12. Peter Marris, *Loss and Change* (London, 1974) p. 6.

13. Primitive men like wild animals: John Lubbock, *Pre-Historic Times* (London, 1865) pp. 484–5.

14. Lubbock's other views: savages neither 'free nor noble', p. 484; crime and illiteracy, pp. 488–9; on the happy future, p. 492; Utopia now possible, p. 491.

15. Ages and stages of man: T. K. Penniman, *A Hundred Years of Anthropology*, London, 1952, pp. 69, 222; David Whitehouse in Andrew Sherratt ed., *The Cambridge Encyclopedia of Archaeology* (New York, 1980) pp. 18–19.

16. Morgan's views: Whitehouse, p. 18; Lee C. Mitchell, *Witnesses to a Vanishing America*, 182; C. M. Hinsley Jr., *Savages and Scientists* (Washington, 1981) p. 135–6.

17. Engels misunderstands Morgan: Marvin Harris, *The Rise of Anthropological Theory* (New York, 1968) p. 246.

18. Marx and Engels on primitive society: Alfred G. Meyer, *Marxism: The Unity of Theory and Practice* (Harvard, 1970), pp. 55–7; Lewis S. Feuer, (ed.), *Karl Marx and Friedrich Engels: Basic Writings* (London, 1969) esp. p. 49 n.

19. Lubbock on Fuegians, *Pre-Historic Times*, p. 432.

20. *A Universal Gazetteer*, (ed.) G. Landmann (London, 1840) see Terra del Fuego (sic).

21. European glass: J. C. Beaglehole (ed.), *The Endeavour Journal of Joseph Banks 1768–71* (Sydney, 1961) vol. 1, p. 228.

22. Smith, *European Vision*, p. 22.

23. Engraving depicts shapely furs: Sydney Parkinson, *A Journal of a Voyage to the South Seas* (London, 1773) opp. p. 7. While I see this engraving as highly romanticised, it is interpreted as realistic and a stark comment on the savage by R. Joppien and B. Smith (eds), *The Art of Captain*

Cook's Voyages (Yale, 1985) vol. 1, pp. 16–17. The engraver was Thomas Chambers of London.

24. Scenes from Nativity: see plates, 22 to 25, B. Smith, *European Vision and the South Pacific*.

25. Hawkesworth's pliant pen: *European Vision*, p. 22.

26. Glyndwr Williams, in *Historical Studies* (Melbourne, No. 77, October 1981) p. 510.

27. Lazy Portuguese in Brazil: Banks, *Journal*, vol. 1, p. 205.

28. Contented Fuegians: Banks, *Journal*, vol. 1, p. 224.

29. Height of Fuegians: Banks, vol. 1, p. 227; Fitzroy, cited by Lubbock, p. 433.

30. Charles Darwin, *The Descent of Man*, London. The quotations come from the 21st Chapter of the 1874 or revised edition, and are found in the final two paragraphs.

31. Survey of living anthropologists on warfare: Moni Nag, 'Anthropology and Population', *Population Studies*, 1973, vol. 27, p. 61.

32. Edward Gibbon, *Decline and Fall of the Roman Empire*, quotations come from ch. 3 and ch. 71.

33. Macaulay and classics: G. O. Trevelyan, *The Life and Letters of Lord Macaulay* (Oxford, 1932) vol. 1, p. 396–7, vol. 2, p. 139.

34. Macaulay's 160 years of progress: *Macaulay's History of England* (Everyman edn, 1957) vol. 1, p. 2.

35. 'Some traveller' from New Zealand: Macaulay's *Essays*, being his review of Ranke's *History of the Popes*, 1840, paragraph 3.

36. *Illiad* locomotives: Richard Jenkyns, *The Victorians and Ancient Greece* (Oxford, 1980) p. 194.

37. Australian bishop: H. H. Heaton, *Australian Dictionary of Dates* (Sydney, 1879) p. 102.

38. Paris and punishment: Owen Chadwick, *The Secularization of the European Mind in the Nineteenth Century* (Cambridge, 1975) p. 259.

39. Strauss on Jesus: Albert Schweitzer, *The Quest of the Historical Jesus: A Critical Study* (London, 1911) ch. 7, 8.

40. Stanley's sermon: Arthur P. Stanley, *The Persian King: A Sermon Preached in Westminster Abbey . . . Sunday, June 22nd, 1873*, pamphlet (London, 1873) p. 3.

41. Mill: quoted in F. L. Baumer, *Modern European Thought*, p. 323.

42. Malthus's influence: Arthur Koestler, *The Act of Creation* (London, 1966) pp. 140–3.

5 Will The West Decline?

1. Pearson in Russia and USA: John Tregenza, *Professor of Democracy: The Life of Charles Henry Pearson* (Melbourne, 1968) pp. 29–30, 50–1.
2. Australian career of Pearson: William Stebbing (ed.), *Charles Henry Pearson* (London, 1900) esp. ch. 10–18.
3. 'If we were certain': C. H. Pearson, 'The Causes of Pessimism', *The Fortnightly Review* (London, October 1893) esp. ch. 10–18.
4. Pearson's predictions: C. H. Pearson, *National Life and Character: A Forecast*, London, 1893: 'We are blind instruments of fate', p. 83; 'the preponderance of China', p. 130; on weakness of cities, p. 155 ff. On a nation's failure to realize its vulnerability, see his essays in *Fortnightly Review*, 1893, vol. 60, pp. 151, 450.
5. Review of Pearson's book: Tregenza, pp. 231–3.
6. Theodore Roosevelt, *American Ideals and Other Essays, Social and Political* (New York, 1912) in which ch. 13 is a reprint of his *Sewanee Review* article of 1894 on Pearson.
7. Yellow Peril: From 1904, the famous British geographer, Sir Halford Mackinder, with his emphasis on the Eurasian heartland as a pivot of world's history, stood in this tradition.
8. Solovyev's fears: Egbert Munzer, Solovyev: *Prophet of Russian-Western Unity* (London, 1956) esp. pp. 63, 75–7, 103–4; *Great Soviet Encyclopedia* (New York, 1976 edn), vol. 24, p. 307.
9. The frontier as a line of 'effective Americanization': Ray A. Billington (ed.), *Frontier and Section: Selected Essays of Frederick Jackson Turner* (Spectrum Book, 1961) p. 39.
10. 'The Western wilds': *The Atlantic Monthly* essay is reprinted in Billington; see esp. p. 91.
11. Flood of food and fibres to Europe: Sidney Pollard, *Peaceful Conquest: The Industrialization of Europe 1760–1970* (Oxford, 1981) pp. 264–70.
12. Uranium prediction: 'Address by Sir William Crookes', *Report of the British Association for the Advancement of*

Science (London, 1898) p. 27.

13. Crookes' argument: '*Address*', 'My chief subject', on p. 4; danger to wheat imports, pp. 7–8; scarcity of nitrates, pp. 16–17; 'the great Caucasian race', p. 18; wheat as 'munitions', p. 5.

14. Jevons on coal: W. S. Jevons, *The Coal Question* (London, 1865).

15. Wheat prices falling until 1890s: S. B. Saul, *The Myth of the Great Depression, 1873–1896* (London, 1969) pp. 14, 34–5.

16. Wadham's conversion: G. Blainey (ed.), *Sir Samuel Wadham: Selected Addresses* (Melbourne, 1956) pp. 1, 24–5.

17. Shaler on minerals: *The Autobiography of Nathaniel Southgate Shaler* (Boston, 1909) p. 429.

6 Temple Of The Wild

1. The new anti-science mood was visible in some fields in the 1880s.

2. The return of emotion: W. J. Turner on Swinburne, *The Great Victorians* (Pelican paperback, 1938) vol. 2, p. 476; Noel Annan, *Leslie Stephen* (London, 1984) p. 159 n.

3. Nikolaus Pevsner, 'Art and Architecture', in *New Cambridge Modern History*, vol. 10, p. 147.

4. Price of a Monet: Pevsner, *New Cambridge Modern History* vol. 11, p. 157.

5. Gauguin and van Gogh: Pevsner, vol. 11, pp. 167–8; Philippe Roberts-Jones, *Beyond Time and Place: Non-Realist Painting in the Nineteenth Century* (Oxford, 1978) esp. pp. 100–1, 112–14, 133.

6. 'It always strikes me': I'm ashamed to say I can't find where I gathered this quotation, and I had virtually deleted it when the *Faber Book of Aphorisms* (London, 1970) p. 86 revealed that at least it does exist, though where exactly is not disclosed.

7. Proust on Picasso: G. D. Painter, *Marcel Proust* (London, 1977) vol. 2, p. 333 n.

8. Stravinsky: O. J. Hale, *The Great Illusion 1900–1914* (New York, 1971) pp. 161, 163.

9. Hermann Hesse, *Autobiographical Writings* (New York, 1972) pp. xiv, 71. The translation from German to English gains if, near the end of the passage, the comma becomes a colon.

10. Klee and Chinese acrobats: Margaret Plant, *Paul Klee: Figures and Faces* (London, 1978) p. 67. For Stravinsky, see p. 55.

11. New Thinkers: H. Stuart Hughes, *Consciousness and Society* (London, 1958). Richard Pipes, *Modern Europe*, Homewood, 1981, esp. pp. 105–117; F. L. Baumer, *Modern European Thought*, pp. 387–9.

12. Durkheim's views: Malcolm Biddiss, *Age of the Masses*, p. 112; Simon Clarke, *The Foundations of Structuralism* (Brighton, 1981) pp. 9–12.

13. Freud denounced: Ernest Jones, *Sigmund Freud: Life and Work* (London, 1958) vol. 2, pp. 122, 138.

14. Freud's private letter, to Lou Andreas-Salome, 25 November 1914: *Sigmund Freud: His Life in Pictures and Words* (University of Queensland Press, 1978) p. 207.

15. J. A. Froude on the Germans: John Clubbe (ed.), *Froude's Life of Carlyle* (London, 1979) p. 560.

16. Delayed translation of German pessimistic works: W. Caldwell, 'Pessimism', *Chambers' Encyclopaedia*, 1924, vol. 8, p. 52. See dates in bibliographical note.

17. Nietzsche's later influence: on Sarajevo assassin, see James Joll, *Europe Since 1870*, London, 1976, p. 166; on Oswald Spengler, *The Decline of the West*, Modern Library, New York, 1962, p. xix of a revised preface written in December 1922; on T. Mann, see Robert Nisbet, *History of the Idea of Progress* (New York, 1980) p. 285.

18. Novelists: Lionel Trilling, *Beyond Culture* (London, 1966) pp. 19–28; Thomas Munro in *Journal of Aesthetics and Art Criticism* (December 1958) p. 146, for Henry James.

19. Raymond Williams, *The Country and the City* (Paladin paperback, 1975) p. 379.

20. Breuer's hiking credo: cited in Henry C. Meyer, *The Long Generation* (New York, 1973) p. 29.

21. Scout movement: R. Nash, *Wilderness and the American Mind*, pp. 147–9; English *Dictionary of National Biography 1912–21*, for C. A. Pearson and *1941–50* for Robert Baden-Powell; Michael Rosenthal, *The Character Factory:*

Baden-Powell and the Origin of the Boy Scout Movement
(London, 1986) for attitudes to race and eugenics.

22. Saving Niagara: N. F. Dreisziger, 'The Campaign to Save
Niagara', *New York History*, vol. 55, October 1974.

23. Hetch Hetchy: Roderick Nash, *Wilderness and the American
Mind* (New Haven, 1973) rev. edn., ch. 10.

24. John Muir, *The Yosemite* (New York, 1912) pp. 8, 262.

25. Jack London and Upton Sinclair: R. Nash, *Wilderness and
the American Mind*, p. 156; Andrew Sinclair, *The Savage:
A History of Misunderstanding* (London, 1977) pp. 112–14.

26. Kathy Laster, survey of 19th century utopian literature:
'*Utopian Literature and Intellectual Mood*', M.A. thesis
(University of Melbourne, 1980).

27. The flesh of fashion: C. W. and P. Cunnington, *Handbook
of English Costume in the Nineteenth Century* (London, 1970)
3rd edn, pp. 511–37; Iris Brooke, *A History of English
Costume* (London, 1949) 3rd edn, inc. p. 213, for sleeveless
evening gown; Francois Boucher, *20,000 Years of Fashion*
New York, n.d., pp. 376 ff; Stella M. Newton, *Health, Art
& Reason: Dress Reformers of the Nineteenth Century* (London,
1974).

28. Hardware and skills in primitive societies: G. Blainey,
Triumph of the Nomads: A History of Ancient Australia
(Melbourne, 1975) pp. 125, 130.

29. Lionel Trilling, *Beyond Culture* (London, 1966) p. 15 ff.

30. Boas's background: lectures by Professor N. Yalman at
Harvard University in 1982; John J. Honigmann,
The Development of Anthropological Ideas (Homewood,
Illinois, 1976) p. 195.

31. 'Boas's account of the potlatch': Marvin Harris, *The Rise of
Anthropological Theory* (New York, 1968) p. 307.

32. Boas's German mentors: Derek Freeman, *Margaret Mead
and Samoa* (Harvard, 1983) pp. 5–12, 24–8.

33. 'Treadmill of oscillation', F. W. Voget, *A History of Ethnology*
(New York, 1975) p. 802.

34. Baldwin Spencer and movie: D. J. Mulvaney and J. H.
Calaby, '*So Much That Is New*': *Baldwin Spencer 1860–1920*
(Melbourne, 1985) p. 217.

35. Spencer on Aboriginals' personal qualities: Baldwin Spencer,
Native Tribes of the Northern Territory of Australia (London,
1914) pp. 38–41.

36. Unless you have the concept of a seesaw in mind you are likely to miss the evidence for a softening of the attitude to primitive societies around the 1890s. Recognition of the softening can scarcely be found in V. G. Kiernan, *The Lords of Human Kind: European Attitudes to the Outside World in the Imperial Age* (London, 1972) p. 336. Interestingly his important survey does not mention such key witnesses for the 'softening' as Pearson and Crookes.
37. John Passmore, *The Perfectibility of Man* (New York, 1970) p. 189.
38. Wallace on inventions: cited by Arthur Koestler, *The Act of Creation* (London, 1966) p. 695.
39. Spencer on 'white savages': David Duncan (ed.), *Life and Letters of Herbert Spencer* (New York, 1908) vol. 2, p. 121.
40. *The Cambridge Modern History*, 'The Latest Age' (Cambridge, 1910) vol. 12, p. 15, chapter by Stanley Leathes.

7 Cold and White: The Role of Climate and Race

1. Charles Montesquieu, *The Spirit of Laws* (New York, Colonial Press edn, 1899) vol. 1, p. 221 ff.
2. Alison's theory of the cold north: Sir Archibald Alison, *The Principles of Population* (Edinburgh, 1840) vol. 1, esp. p. 266.
3. Henry T. Buckle, *History of Civilization in England* (London, 1885 edn), p. 44.
4. Galton and Marshall: Alfred Marshall, *Principles of Economics* (London, 1890) vol. 1, pp. 12 n., 16–17, 262.
5. H. A. L. Fisher, *A History of Europe* (London, 1946 edn), pp. v, 9, 1219.
6. Origin of topi: *Shorter Oxford English Dictionary*, 1956, edn, vol. 2, assigns the first use of word to 1826.
7. Peter Fleming recalls: 'Goodbye to the Bombay Bowler', *Points of View*, Brian Inglis (ed.) (London, 1962) p. 120–1.
8. *Sydney Morning Herald*, cited by W. F. Mandle, 'Cricket

and Australian Nationalism in the Nineteenth Century', *Journal of Royal Australian Historical Society*, vol. 59, (December 1973) pp. 234.

9. Cleanliness imported from India: C. Northcote Parkinson, *East and West* (Mentor paperback, 1965) pp. 192–3.

10. Soap: John Burnet, *A History of the Cost of Living* (Penguin paperback, 1969) pp. 139, 175; Daniel J. Boorstin, *The Americans: The Democratic Experience* (Vintage paperback, 1974) p. 145.

11. Soap in slang: Eric Partridge, *A Dictionary of Slang* (Adelaide, 1982) pp. 797, 799.

12. European globe-trotters: Frederick G. Burnaby, *On Horseback Through Asia Minor* (London, 1877); D. W. Carnegie, *Spinifex and Sand* (London, 1898); R. L. Jack, *The Back Blocks of China* (London, 1904).

13. New Hebrides people: *Journal of Commodore Goodenough*, (ed. by his widow) (London, 1876) p. 278.

14. Voltaire and The Enlightenment: Robert Nisbet, *History of the Idea of Progress* (Basic paperback, 1980) pp. 287–8.

15. Gobineau: see especially T. K. Penniman, *A Hundred Years of Anthropology* (London, 1952) rev. edn, p. 84 ff.

16. Anglo-Saxon cult: Reginald Horsman, 'Racial Anglo-Saxonism before 1850', *Journal of History of Ideas*, July 1976, esp. pp. 387–88. For an Edwardian example, see C. E. W. Bean, *Flagships Three* (London, 1913) pp. 11–18, 338–9.

17. Commodore M. C. Perry, cited by Geoffrey S. Smith, 'The Navy before Darwinism', *American Quarterly*, vol. 28, 1976, pp. 50–1.

18. Sir Charles Dilke, *Greater Britain* (London, 1869), 3rd edn, p. vii; Sir Charles Dilke, *Problems of Greater Britain* (London, 1890), pp. 2–4.

19. God's mission for Teutons: Oscar Handlin, *The Uprooted* (New York, 1951) p. 277.

20. Australia and Pacific Islands' women: *Historical Records of Australia* (Melbourne, 1914) Series 1, vol. 1, p. 14.

21. Gobineau on French empire: W. B. Cohen, *The French Encounter with Africans* (Bloomington, Indiana, 1980) p. 260.

22. Pearson's higher and lower races: C. H. Pearson, *National Life and Character* (London, 1893) pp. 30, 69 n., 85.

23. Asians and Africans will 'throng the English turf': Pearson, p. 85.
24. Anti-semitism wanes and revives: Fritz Stern, *The Failure of Illiberalism* (Chicago, 1975) p. 46.
25. Jewish role in city professions: Peter Phillips, *The Tragedy of Nazi Germany* (London, 1969) p. 108.
26. Attacks on Jews as symbols of the modern: Fritz Stern, *The Politics of Cultural Despair* (New York, 1965) pp. 93–5, 170–171.
27. Conor Cruise O'Brien, London *Observer*, review section, 8 September 1985. Analysing Poliakov's new *History of Anti-Semitism*, O'Brien went far beyond the book itself.

8 The Great War and Other Half-Shocks

1. Esperanto, Olympic Games and other peaceful portents: G. Blainey, *The Causes of War* (London, 1973) p. 23.
2. G. P. Gooch, *History of Our Time, 1885–1913* (London, 1914 edn), pp. 248–9. See also H. Butterfield on G. P. Gooch, in *Dictionary of National Biography, 1961–1970* (Oxford, 1981) p. 439.
3. Cannibal and Herbert Spencer: Norman Angell, *The Great Illusion: A Study of the Relation of Military Power to National Advantage* (London, 1914 edn), p. 202.
4. Gilbert Murray on death toll: cited in H. A. L. Fisher, *The History of Europe* (London, 1946 edn), p. 1156 n.
5. Socialists' expectation of short war: Sir Llewellyn Woodward, *Prelude to Modern Europe 1865–1914* (London, 1972) pp. 263–4.
6. Hopes of a short war in 1914: G. Blainey, *The Causes of War* (London 1973) ch. 3; R. A. Preston, S. F. Wise, and H. O. Werner, *Men in Arms: A History of Warfare* (London, 1962) p. 260.
7. War expenditure compared to national product: J. J. Spengler, 'Population and Potential Power', *Studies in Economics and Economic History*, M. Kooy, (ed.), (London, 1972) p. 138.

8. W. Trotter, *Instincts of the Herd in Peace and War* (London, 1916) p. 256.

9. President Wilson, cited by H. G. Nicholas, *The American Union* (Penguin edn, 1950) p. 246.

10. The arms race perceived as cause of World War 1: G. Blainey, *The Causes of War* (London, 1973) pp 135–141.

11. Stanley Kauffmann, "*U.S. and World Film: A Two-Way Exchange*", Dialogue, 1977, vol. 10, p. 101.

12. Stalin's Scientists: Roy Medvedev, *Let History Judge: The Origins and Consequences of Stalinism* (London, 1971) pp. 227–8. For Stalin on eucalypts, see p. 523 n.

13. Five-Year and Other Long-Term Plans: Asa Briggs, in *New Cambridge Modern History*, vol. 12, pp. 522–3.

14. Tom Wright, *A Trade Unionist in Russia* (Sydney, 1928) esp. pp. 95–99.

15. Bertrand Russell, *The Autobiography of Bertrand Russell* (Boston, 1968) vol. 2, p. 143.

16. J. M. Keynes and *The Economic Consequences of the Peace*: see Robert Skidelsky, *John Maynard Keynes*, London, 1983, vol. 1, p. 394, for the book's translations.

17. Forecasts of famine: J. Overbeek, *History of Population Theories* (Rotterdam, 1974) esp. pp. 91–2, 112–17, 136; E. M. East, *Mankind at the Crossroads* (New York, 1923) p. 347.

18. Australian scholar-official: W. D. Forsyth, *The Myth of Open Spaces* (Melbourne, 1942) p. 202.

19. The crisis of underpopulation: W. B. Reddaway, *The Economics of a Declining Population* (London, 1939) J. J. Spengler, *France Faces Depopulation* (Durham, North Carolina, 1938).

20. Birth of the bomb: Banesh Hoffmann, *Albert Einstein* (Paladin paperback, London, 1975) ch. 10: Henri Michel, *The Second World War* (London, 1975) pp. 765–70.

21. Jacob Bronowski on physics: *The Ascent of Man* (London, 1973) pp. 330, 349.

9 The Beckoning Moon

1. Orwell on survival of civilisation (1946): Raymond Williams, *Orwell* (London, 1971) p. 66.

2. Existentialism: Michael D. Biddiss, *The Age of the Masses: Ideas and Society In Europe since 1870* (New York, 1977) pp. 246, 322–3.

3. 'In humble spirit': Arnold Toynbee, *A Study of History*, D. C. Somervell abridgement (London, 1946) p. 534.

4. Toynbee's American influence: W. H. McNeill 'Toynbee', in *International Encyclopaedia of Social Science* (New York, 1979) vol. 18, pp. 775–9.

5. Medical advances: Caroline F. Ware, K. M. Panikkar and J. M. Romein, *History of Mankind* (New York, 1966) vol. 6, pp. 473–81.

6. Frogs for schools: *Wall Street Journal*, 7 December 1982, p. 1.

7. Jonathan Benthall, *The Body Electric: Patterns of Western Industrial Culture* (London, 1977) p. 60.

8. Keynes's 1936 warning: J. M. Keynes, *General Theory of Employment Interest and Money* (London, 1964 edn), p. 381.

9. Brendan Bracken on Keynes and inflation: private letter to W. S. Robinson, 28 July 1953 (University of Melbourne Archives).

10. Colin Clark, *Conditions of Economic Progress* (London, 1940?)

11. *Economist*, December 1959: cited by Christopher Booker, *Spectator* (London, 22 December 1979) p. 16.

12. Jim F. Heath, *Decade of Disillusionment* (Bloomington, 1976) p. 13. He cites Eric Goldman on p. 5.

13. Stephen E. Ambrose in *Reviews in American History*, September 1984, p. 442.

14. Two catch-phrases of prosperity were the titles of books: Donald Horne, *The Lucky Country* (Melbourne, 1965) and J. Kenneth Galbraith, *The Affluent Society* (London, 1958).

15. Sense of a new era: there is an excellent survey in Krishan Kumar, *Prophecy and Progress: The Sociology of Industrial and Post Industrial Society* (London, 1978) esp. pp. 189–193.

16. 'The Great Society': Jim F. Heath, *The Decade of Disillusionment*, p. 193.

17. Barbara Ward, *The Home of Man* (London, 1976) pp. 185–6, 260.

18. Rapid economic growth 1945–70: Jonathan Hughes, *Industrialization and Economic History: Theses and Conjectures* (New York, 1970) p. 269.

19. Boom in jet travel: John Newhouse, *The Sporty Game* (New York, 1983) pp. 110–11, 227.
20. Kenneth Boulding's grades: K. E. Boulding, 'Economics for Good or Evil', *Technology Review* (Boston, 1976).
21. C. P. FitzGerald, 'China', *New Cambridge Modern History*, vol. 11, pp. 439, 442.
22. Mao's optimism: Nigel Harris, *The Mandate of Heaven: Marx and Mao in Modern China* (London, 1978) pp. 48–9.
23. Historians' comment on declining hunger in India: *New Cambridge Modern History*, vol. 11, p. 22 (F. H. Hinsley) and p. 428 (Percival Spear).
24. *Everyman's Dictionary of Economics*, Arthur Seldon and F. G. Pennance (ed.), (London, 1975) pp. 344–5.
25. Asian hopes: Cranley Onslow (ed.), *Asian Economic Development* (London, 1965) V. K. R. V. Rao on India, ch. 3; G. Corea on Ceylon, ch. 2; J. F. Kennedy is cited on p. 224.
26. The rise of Japan: *Britannica Book of the Year, 1967*, pp. 44, 431; Masanori Moritani, *Japanese Technology* (Tokyo, 1982) pp. 29–30, 47.

10 The King Is Dying

1. Robin Clarke, (ed.), *Notes for the Future: An Alternative History of the Past Decade* (London, 1975) p. 63.
2. Mumford, Dubos and other new critics of technology: summarised by Samuel C. Florman, *Dialogue*, 1977, no. 1, p. 71 ff.
3. Leopold's views: Roderick Nash, *Wilderness and the American Mind* (New Haven, revised edn, 1973) esp. p. 182 ff.
4. Thomas Merton's views: Paul Wilkes (ed.), *Merton By Those Who Knew Him Best* (San Francisco, 1984).
5. Pollution low in Gallup Polls: Godfrey Hodgson, *America in our Time* (New York, 1976) p. 402.
6. Barry Commoner, *The Closing Circle: Nature, Man and Technology* (New York, 1971) esp. ch. 9.
7. Hothouse effect: William W. Kellogg and Robert Schware, 'Society, Science and Climate Change', *Foreign Affairs*, Summer 1982, esp. pp. 1081–2.

8. Environmental crusade: Hodgson, *America in our Time*, pp. 403–8.

9. E. F. Schumacher, 'The economics of permanence', 1970, in Robin Clarke (ed.), *Notes for the Future*, esp. p. 81.

10. Michael J. Arlen, *Living-Room War* (New York, 1969) pp. 6–8, 81–3.

11. Nuclear fears in late 1970s: Nigel J. Henham, 'The European Peace Movement: Its Effect on United States Arms Control Policy 1981–82'. Political Science Department thesis (University of Melbourne, 1983).

12. Vincent Buckley, 'Poetry and Pollution', *Quadrant* magazine (Sydney, 1971).

13. Garret Hardin, 'The tragedy of the commons', in *Notes for the Future*, p. 69. The article originally appeared in *Science* in December 1968.

14. 'River towns are winged towns': Odell Shepard (ed.), *The Heart of Thoreau's Journals* (New York, 1961) p. 196. Journal entry of 2 July 1858.

15. 'Thoreau's Vietnam': Edward Hepburn, foreword to *Walden*, Peebles Classics Library, New York, n.d., 7th paragraph.

16. Seyyed Hossein Nasr, *Man and Nature: The Spiritual Crisis of Modern Man* (London, 1976) ch. 3.

17. The English Fabians: A. M. McBriar, *Fabian Socialism and English Politics 1884–1918* (Cambridge, 1966) pp. 114–5.

18. John Passmore, *The Perfectibility of Man* (New York, 1970) p. 193.

19. Robert Nisbet, *History of the Idea of Progress* (Basic paperback, New York 1980) p. 177. Neither Passmore nor Nisbet realised that in the 19th century, during the powerful alliance of free trade and liberalism, large numbers of intellectuals were very sympathetic to business.

11 Rise Of The Counter-Culture

1. The natural look: Angela Carter, *The Sunday Times* (London, 14 November 1982) p. 36.

2. James Morris on the Beatles: reprinted in Richard C. Lukas (ed.), *From Metternich to the Beatles: Readings in Modern European History* (Mentor paperback, 1973) p. 220.

3. The Beatles: Jonathan Eisen (ed.), *The Age of Rock: Sounds of the American Cultural Revolution* (New York, 1969) vol. 1, pp. 126–60.

4. Paul McCartney tells Alan Aldridge: ibid., p. 140.

5. Hare Krishna and Transcendental Meditation: Kenneth Leech, *Youthquake* (London, 1973) esp. pp. 73–80.

6. New left students: Jim F. Heath, *Decade of Disillusionment: The Kennedy-Johnson Years* (Bloomington, 1976) pp. 240–7.

7. Marcuse the seer: Frank E. and Fritzie P. Manuel, *Utopian Thought in the Western World* (Harvard, 1979) p. 800.

8. Robin Clarke on the counter-culture: Robin Clarke (ed.), *Notes for the Future: An Alternative History of the Past Decade* (London, 1975) p. 11.

9. Gary Snyder, 'Passage to more than India', in *Notes for the Future*, p. 210.

10. Hallucinations: Morrow and Suzanne Wilson (ed.), *Drugs in American Life* (New York, 1975) Helen H. Nowlis, *Drugs on the College Campus* (Anchor paperback, 1969) Godfrey Hodgson, *America in Our Time* (New York, 1976) pp. 328–31.

11. Eartha Kitt at White House: J. F. Heath, *Decade of Disillusionment*, p. 262.

12. Passmore on Marx and LSD: John Passmore, *The Perfectibility of Man* (New York, 1970) p. 315 n.

13. Lionel Trilling on art: *Beyond Culture: Essays on Literature and Learning* (London, 1966) p. xvii.

14. Robert Graves on technology versus crafts: R. Graves, 'Science, Technology and Poetry', *Notes for the Future*, p. 138.

15. Bob Dylan's music: *The Age of Rock*, vol. 1, pp. 200–07, vol. 2, pp. 49, 71; G. Hodgson, *America in Our Time*, pp. 334–8.

16. Rock music born of revolt: Jonathan Eisen in *The Age of Rock*, vol. 1, p. xv.

17. Gary Snyder on the 1967 Be-In: Snyder in *Notes for the Future*, p. 207.

18. Woodstock festival: Barbara G. Myerhoff, 'Organization and Ecstasy', in Sally F. Moore and Barbara G. Myerhoff,

Symbol and Politics in Communial Ideology (Cornell, 1975), pp. 36–7, 45–8.

19. Altamont concert: G. Hodgson, *America in Our Time*, p. 338.

20. Darwin's 'face of nature': Charles Darwin, *On the Origin of Species*, 6th or 1872 edn, ch. 3.

21. Finland's famine in 1690s: Fernand Braudel, *Capitalism and Material Life 1400–1800* (Harper paperback, 1974) pp. 41–2.

22. Russian travel books: *Encyclopaedia Britannica* (Cambridge 1911) vol. 10, p. 168.

23. Earthquakes and floods: Eric Jones, *The European Miracle* (Cambridge, 1981) esp. pp. 22–37; Angus Martin, *The Last Generation* (Fontana paperback, 1975) pp. 119–20. It is significant that Sidney Pollard's history of Europe 1760–1970, *Peaceful Conquest* (Oxford, 1981) has only one reference to famine in its index: the Russian famine of 1933.

24. Eric Jones, *The European Miracle*, pp. 38–9, 226–7.

25. The prophet Cayce: William I. Thompson, *At the Edge of History* (Harper paperback, New York) 1972, pp. 171–4, 181.

26. Bermuda Triangle: G. O. Abel and B. Singer, (ed.), *Science and the Paranormal: Probing the Existence of the Supernatural* (New York, 1981) esp. pp. 298–308.

27. Gallup polls on flying saucers: G. H. Gallup, *The International Gallup Polls, Public Opinion, 1978* (Wilmington, 1980) pp. 329–30.

28. Paul Kurtz, foreword to Abel and Singer, *Science and the Paranormal*, p. vii.

12 The Return of The Noble Savage

1. Kroeber and Boas on 'primitive' cultures: Derek Freeman, *Margaret Mead and Samoa* (Harvard, 1983) pp. 39–49, 57.

2. Boas on Africa: Franz Boas, *The Mind of Primitive Man* (New York, revised edn, 1938) esp. pp. 253 ff.
3. Margaret Mead, *Coming of Age in Samoa* (London, 1929).
4. Evans-Pritchard in Africa: E. E. Evans-Pritchard, *Social Anthropology* (London, 1951) pp. 98–9.
5. Harold Macmillan's 'Winds of Change' speech was made in Capetown on 3 February 1960: Neville Williams, (ed.), *Chronology of the Modern World* (London, 1966) p. 672.
6. Arthur Miller on Africa; Alfred Kazin (ed.), *Writers At Work*, 3rd Series (New York,1976) p. 226.
7. Violence in American cities 1964–67: Godfrey Hudgson, *America in Our Time* (New York, 1976); Jim F. Heath, *Decade of Disillusionment*, p. 254, for Rap Brown.
8. The 'original affluent society': see R. B. Lee and I. De Vore, *Man the Hunter* (Chicago, 1968).
9. Anthropologists on tribal warfare: Moni Nag, 'Anthropology and Population', *Population Studies*, 1973, vol. 27, p. 61.
10. Cannibals: W. Arens, *The Man-eating Myth* (New York, 1979) The argument was challenged by Derek Denton, *The Hunger for Salt: An Anthropological, Physiological and Medical Analysis* (Berlin, 1982) esp. pp. 101–13.
11. Australian prime minister: speech to House of Representatives, Canberra, 26 October 1971.
12. Trader Martin: Ashley Montagu, 'Lewis Henry Morgan and Charles Martin on the American Indian', in *Frontiers of Anthropology* (New York, 1974) p. 277. Montagu's own comment is on p. 272.
13. Aboriginals as destroyers: G. Blainey, *Triumph of the Nomads: A History of Ancient Australia* (Melbourne, 1982 edn) pp. 51–66, 82.
14. The Kung Bushmen: Edward O. Wilson, *On Human Nature* (Harvard, 1978) pp. 82, 100.
15. H. A. L. Fisher, *A History of Europe* (London, 1946 edn) p. 1219.
16. Stephen Graubard, *Daedalus: Journal of the American Academy of Arts and Sciences*, special issue on Australia, vol. 114, no. 1, 1985, p. vii.
17. Geographer's view of environmental determinism: Daniel B. Luten, 'Ecological Optimism in the Social Sciences', *American Behavioral Scientist*, 1980, vol. 24, p. 134.

13 Descent to the 'Ocean Of Misery'

1. Population predictions in 1950s: William Page in H. S. D. Cole *et al.*, *Thinking about the Future* (London, 1973) pp. 172–3.
2. Colin Clark elaborated on his views in *The Myth of Over-population* (Melbourne, 1973).
3. Paul Ehrlich on Britain in 2000: address in London on 25–6 September 1969, reprinted in Robin Clarke (ed.), *Notes for the Future* (London, 1975) esp. p. 52.
4. Pearson report: William Page in *Thinking about the Future*, p. 173.
5. The new stone age: Harrison Brown, 'Resource Needs and Demands', reprinted in *Notes for the Future*, esp. pp. 32–3.
6. Increase in world's grain per capita in 1950s and 1960s: Lester R. Brown, 'Soils and Civilisation: the decline in food security', *Third World Quarterly* (January 1983) p. 104.
7. Third World as food importer: Edwin M. Martin, 'Rapid Population Growth Hampers Development', *Economic Impact*, 1982, no. 4, p. 84.
8. Agriculture, 1945–70: *American Journal of Agricultural Economics*, 1981, vol. 63: Dale E. Hathaway, 'Agriculture and Government Revisited', pp. 779 ff; Wayne D. Rasmussen and Jane M. Porter, 'Strategies for Dealing with World Hunger', pp. 810 ff; Walter P. Falcon, 'Reflections on the Presidential Commission on World Hunger', pp. 819 ff.
9. Change of climate in wheatlands: John R. Tarrant, *Food Policies* (Chichester, 1980) pp. 42–3.
10. Variations in yield per hectare in 1950s, 1960s: Lester R. Brown, 'Global Economic Ills', *The Futurist* (Washington, June 1978).
11. Georg Borgstrom, *Too Many: A Study of the Earth's Biological Limitations* (New York, 1969).
12. Borgstrom's contradiction on extent of poverty can be seen in Robin Clarke (ed.), in *Notes for the Future*, p. 35.
13. The 'ocean of misery': Borgstrom, *Too Many*, p. xii.
14. 'Deserting the globe': Borgstrom, *Too Many*, p. 337.

15. The 'biggest famine in history': *Too Many*, p. 317.
16. World population's rate of growth declines after 1965: *The Economist* (London, 28 August, 1983) p. 30.
17. Coal statistics and Club of Rome: Daniel Luten, 'Ecological Optimism in the Social Sciences', *American Behavioral Scientist*, October 1980, vol. 24, p. 148 n.
18. Failure of Russian harvest in 1972: *Foreign Agriculture* (Washington, 20 March 1972) p. 3; (8 January 1973) p. 9; John R. Tarrant, *Food Policies*, pp. 287–8.
19. *Foreign Agriculture* on China: 26 February 1973, p. 5.
20. Climate of 1972 near to normal: John R. Tarrant, *Food Policies*, p. 282.
21. Peruvian fishing industry: Georg Borgstrom, *Too Many*, p. 236; Myrl C. Hendershott, 'Oceanography', *Britannica Book of the Year, 1974*, p. 529.
22. Soy beans instead of fishmeal: Tarrant, *Food Policies*, pp. 281–3.
23. Soy bean boom inflates Brazilian coffee: Lester R. Brown, 'Global Economic Ills', *The Futurist* (June 1978) graph on p. 166.
24. Prices rises from 1971 to July 1973: *Britannica Book of the Year, 1974*, p. 198.

14 The Oil Crisis: A Turning Point

1. Forests and charcoal: Melvin Kranzberg and Carroll W. Pursell Jr., *Technology in Western Civilization* (New York, 1967) vol. 1., pp. 155, 223.
2. Coal famine in 1873: W. W. Rostow, *British Economy of the Nineteenth Century* (Oxford, 1948) pp. 74, 212.
3. Size of sea trade: T. M. Rybczynski, *The Economics of the Oil Crisis* (London, 1976) p. 3.

4. The background to the OPEC crisis: 'The Oil Crisis: In Perspective', *Daedalus*, Fall 1975, vol. 104, no. 4, esp. chapters by Klaus Knorr, James W. McKie, and Raymond Vernon. See also Amin Saikhal, *The Rise and fall of the Shah 1941–1979* (London, 1980) pp. 109–13.

5. Klaus Knorr on 'force': *Daedalus*, Fall 1975, p. 236.

6. Environment problems in US and Alaska: James W. McKie, *Daedalus*, Fall 1975, pp. 75–6; 'Alaska Highlights Energy Crisis', *Petroleum Press Service*, May 1972, pp. 159–61, and November 1973, p. 408.

7. Edith Penrose, *Daedalus*, Fall 1975, p. 54.

8. 'Seldom in human affairs': James W. McKie, *Daedalus*, Fall 1975, p. 75.

9. Index of World Prices 1971–5: Victor Argy, *The Postwar International Money Crisis: An Analysis* (London, 1981) p. 165.

10. Arms race and scramble for gold: Marcello de Cecco, *Money and Empire: The International Gold Standard, 1890–1914* (Oxford, 1974) p. 124.

11. *United Empire: The Royal Colonial Institute Journal* (London, 1914) vol. 5, p. 692.

12. Gold and 1914 war: G. Blainey, *The Causes of War* (London, 1973) pp. 214–6.

13. Importance of cheap oil: Barbara Ward, *The Home of Man* (Penguin, 1976) pp. 7–9, 260.

14. Oxford seminar on energy, September 1979: Robert Mabro (ed.), *World Energy Issues and Policies* (Oxford, 1980) p. 363.

15. Christopher J. Hurn, 'The New Pessimism', *Dialogue*, 1978 no. 2, p. 32.

16. Rural Luddites of 1830s: George Rudé, *Protest and Punishment: The Story of the Social and Political Protesters Transported to Australia 1788–1868* (Oxford, 1978) pp. 103–23.

17. Consensus amongst economists in 1950s and 1960s: James W. Dean, 'Why Economists Disagree', *Wilson Quarterly*, Autumn 1982, vol. 6, no. 4, p. 87.

18. Fred Hoyle, *The Melbourne Oration; Science and Modern Civilisation*, pamphlet (Melbourne University, 1969), esp. p. 10–11.

15 The Long Economic Waves

1. Triffin on price swings: Robert Triffin, *Our International Monetary System: Yesterday, Today, and Tomorrow* (New York, 1968) p. 18.
2. N. D. Kondratieff, 'The Long Waves in Economic Life', *Readings in Business Cycle Theory*, American Economic Association, 1950, pp. 20–42.
3. Kondratieff argues that gold discoveries not accidental: G. Blainey, 'A Theory of Mineral Discovery: Australia in the Nineteenth Century' (*Economic History Review*, 1970) no. 2, pp. 298–9.
4. Leon H. Dupriez, '1974, A Downturn of the Long Wave?', Banca Nazionale del Lavoro, *Quarterly Review* (Sept. 1978) p. 199.
5. Prices and real wages in England, 1849–76: W. W. Rostow, *British Economy of the Nineteenth Century* (Oxford, 1948) esp. p. 91.
6. A major war creates a pecking order in international relations: G. Blainey, *The Causes of War* (London, 1973) pp. 118–20.
7. Wars tend to break out when prices rise and prosperity increases: A. L. Macfie, 'The Outbreak of War and the Trade Cycle', *Economic History*, a supplement to *The Economic Journal*, February 1938.
8. J. A. Schumpeter, *Business Cycles* (New York, 1939).
9. Discussions on Kondratieff: Ernest Mandel, *Late Capitalism*, London, 1975; W. W. Rostow, *The World Economy: History and Prospect* (Austin Texas, 1978). I also acknowledge the help through personal letters on this subject from Colin Clark, 3 September 1981; from W. S. Etheridge of Renison Goldfields Consolidated, 2 June 1982: and draft paper from W. Rosenberg, Department of Economics, University of Canterbury, New Zealand, January 1979.

16 The Magic of New Found Lands

1. Insects making a new coral continent: Archibald Alison, *The Principles of Population* (Edinburgh, 1840), vol. 2, p. 497.
2. Stephen FitzGerald, *China and the World*, Canberra, 1977, p. 5. FitzGerald was Australia's first ambassador to communist China, 1973–6.
3. French tourists to China: Albert Bressand and T. de Montbrial, 'The Ups and Downs of Mutual Relevance', *Daedalus* (Spring 1979) p. 113.
4. French Maoist newspaper: Jean-Pierre le Dantec, cited *Daedalus* (Spring 1979) p. 113.
5. Third world as a reservoir of theories: Bressand and de Montbrial, p. 115.

17 The Puzzle of The Seesaw

1. Sir Henry Maine, Rede Lecture, in *Village Communities in the East and the West* (London, 3rd edn, 1876).
2. K. Marx and F. Engels, *Manifesto of the Communist Party*, in Lewis S. Feuer, *Marx and Engels* (Fontana paperback, 1969) p. 82.
3. T. B. Macaulay, *History of England* (Everyman edn, 1957) vol. 1, p. 2.
4. John Carroll, *Puritan, Paranoid, Remissive: A Sociology of Modern Culture* (London, 1977) ch. 5.
5. The generation gap: Annie Kriegel, *'Generational Difference: The History of an Idea'*, *Daedalus* (Fall 1978) esp. pp. 29–31; Joseph Adelson, *What Generation Gap? Dialogue* (1976) vol 9, pp. 24–32.

6. David Riesman, *The Lonely Crowd* (New York, 1950) esp. ch. 1.
7. The 'greater choices this society gives': Riesman, p. 15.
8. Belief in the period 1860–1914 that wars would be short: G. Blainey, *The Causes of War* (London, 1973) pp. 206–17.
9. John Maynard Keynes, *General Theory of Employment Interest and Money* (London, 1936) p. 384.

Index